Subversive Silences

Subversive Silences

Nonverbal Expression and
Implicit Narrative Strategies in the
Works of Latin American Women Writers

Helene Carol Weldt-Basson

Madison • Teaneck
Fairleigh Dickinson University Press

©2009 by Rosemont Publishing & Printing Corp.

All rights reserved. Authorization to photocopy items for internal or personal use, or the internal or personal use of specific clients, is granted by the copyright owner, provided that a base fee of $10.00, plus eight cents per page, per copy is paid directly to the Copyright Clearance Center, 222 Rosewood Drive, Danvers, Massachusetts 01923. [978-0-8386-4172-9/09 $10.00 + 8¢ pp, pc.]

Associated University Presses
2010 Eastpark Boulevard
Cranbury, NJ 08512

The paper used in this publication meets the requirements of the American National Standard for Permanence of Paper for Printed Library Materials Z39.48–1984.

Library of Congress Cataloging-in-Publication Data

Weldt-Basson, Helene Carol, 1958-
 Subversive silences : nonverbal expression and implicit narrative strategies in the works of Latin American women writers / Helene Carol Weldt-Basson.
   p. cm.
 Includes bibliographical references and index.
 ISBN 978-0-8386-4172-9 (alk. paper)
 1. Spanish American fiction—Women authors—History and criticism. 2. Spanish American fiction—20th century—History and criticism. 3. Nonverbal communication in literature. I. Title.
 PQ7081.5.W45 2009
 863'.64099287—dc22
                                                              2008037923

PRINTED IN THE UNITED STATES OF AMERICA

For Marc, Rebecca and Marshall

Contents

Preface
From Feminism to Gender Theory   9

Acknowledgments   13

1. Language and Silence:
A Theoretical Overview   17

2. Paradoxical Silence, Part I:
"Overreading" the Works of Marta Brunet   36

3. Paradoxical Silence, Part II:
Silence/Narrative Voice in the Works
of María Luisa Bombal   60

4. The Encoded Silence of Rosario Castellanos:
Coding, Paradox, and Parentheses   80

5. Hyperbolic Silence:
Agon and Irony in the Works of Isabel Allende   104

6. Symbolic Silence:
Rosario Ferré's Equation of Women and Puerto Rico   138

7. Parodic Silence:
Ritual and Genre in Laura Esquivel   170

8. Cultural Silence:
Naive Narrators, Inverted Icons, and
Bilingual Gaps in the Works of Sandra Cisneros   194

9. Conclusions:
Toward a Feminist Poetics of Silence   226

Notes   233

References   249

Index   269

Preface
From Feminism to Gender Theory

During the ten years over which I have worked on this book, feminist studies have undergone many significant changes that intersect with my approach in this text. Perhaps not the least significant of these innovations is the movement away from the term "feminism" and toward a focus on the notion of "gender." To the poststructuralist critic, "feminism" implies a recognition of fixed dichotomous categories, such as women/men and femininity/masculinity. Twenty-first century criticism tends to view such divisions as simplistic and questions their apparent normative reinforcement of other unduly reductive categories, such as that of heterosexuality (Krolokke and Sorensen 2006, 15). Poststructuralism urges a shift in focus toward the changing position of each subject in power relations and agency acquisition. Contemporary feminists challenge the concept of universal womanhood as essentialist and emphasize how gender concerns differ according to sexuality, race, class, and other varying elements (Ahmed 2000; Baxter 2003; Butler 1999; Haraway 1991; Lloyd 2005; Rakow and Wackwitz 2004). Some critics situate this new critical discourse within "third-wave feminism," a movement with its origins in the mid-1990s and ongoing in the present.[1]

Such contemporary shifts and concerns suggest the need to adumbrate the title of this book and its approach. With its focus on silence as a pervasive and subversive element among Hispanic women writers, the title suggests a certain commonality among women that may be erroneously equated with the outmoded concept of the uniformity of all women. The idea of a "feminist perception" set forth in this book derives from Sara Mills's work on the notion of feminist affiliation (Mills, 1995a), which appeared on the cusp of the transition from feminist to gender analysis. For some, this concept may similarly evoke notions of a universal female identification that may appear to be at odds with contemporary, postmodern thought on the necessary difference between women of distinct social and economic classes, as well as ethnic backgrounds. Although some view Mills's paradigm as fundamentally a structuralist communication model of the text (text as message and reader as receiver) (Krolokke and Sorensen 2006, 101), Mills goes beyond the classic model by emphasizing the importance of such contextual parameters as the genre and medium of the message, the particular backgrounds of the writer (speaker) and reader (listener), and other variable circumstances of the communicative event. Mills's work is thus consistent with twenty-first century innovations that emphasize the positioning of different speakers in discourse and their relative agency based on distinct contextual elements and categories, such as class, race, and age.

Many contemporary critics still acknowledge the functionality of the notion of feminism, through their continued application of the term to communication theory and through their designation of an ongoing current of third-wave feminism (Freedman 2001; Krolokke and Sorensen 2006; Rakow and Wackwitz 2004).[2] Thus, the concept of feminism has not vanished, but rather feminism in the singular form has been replaced by a multiplicity of feminist approximations that make the unity implied by the term "feminism" an impossibility. We must now speak of a diversity of approaches, sometimes even antithetical in nature, to issues surrounding the works of women writers, their publication, and the image of women in general in literature or other disciplines. Within this plurality of feminist approximations, poststructural gender analysis, through its deconstruction of traditional categories, is one of many possible methods that yield information pertinent to gender construction and affinities.

Despite the poststructuralist shift away from the term "feminism," Rita Felski acknowledges that feminist critics can still examine commonalities among women writers without lapsing into hopeless essentialism. Felski states:

> Critics . . . are often interested in the bigger picture; moving beyond the author's explanations and intentions, they look for patterns, conventions and clusters of themes that span multiple works and can tell us something revealing about a certain sensibility, worldview or historical moment. There is nothing wrong with reading in this way or with searching for signs of commonality in writing by women. Yet scholars must also be willing to admit the limits of their sample, the partiality of their explanations, the power of the counterexample, the texts that disprove the rule. (Felski 2003, 93)

The reader should take into account Felski's words with regard to this study. This book asserts that many twentieth century Latin American and Latina women writers employ thematic and stylistic silences in their narratives and that the embedding of these themes and structures within their texts frequently situates the reader within a feminist perspective. The specific nature of this feminist perspective will obviously vary according to the individual background of each real reader. The general identification with women's equality and agency in the texts (the creation of a general implicit reader), will be experienced differently by black, white, lesbian, heterosexual, middle-class and working-class women and men, as well as other groups (the real readers of the text), and hopefully this study will open up the way for further examination of such differences. In other words, I suggest that the idea of the creation of a general feminist perspective through textual structures can be a useful concept for understanding Latin American and Latina women's literature. I neither claim that all women authors write using silence nor wish to suggest that male writers do not employ the silent narrative strategies studied here. However, texts written by men rarely suggest feminist insights through the use of such structures. I argue that silence is a signifier that traditionally connotes male domination and female passivity, but has been appropriated by the texts in question precisely to subvert silence's patriarchal meaning and invest it with a combative dimension. Frequently the employment of parody, irony, and other indirect strategies achieves this reversal of the notion of patriarchal silencing. Such use of irony and parody within texts ranging from the 1980s to the early twenty-first century prefigures the so-called performance turn of third-wave feminism where "mimicry, irony and parody now serve to open up spaces of feminist empowerment . . . in which women can subvert dominant culture and open up to other ways of acting and thinking" (Krolokke and Sorensen 2006, 157). The application of Mills's textual model emphasizes a space of overlap between various possible methodologies (structuralist and poststructuralist) and illustrates the continuing validity of such notions as feminism and feminist perspective. These concepts need not imply a conflation of all women, who continue to exhibit both common and distinct concerns based on their individual experiences and backgrounds. Indeed, as this book hopes to illustrate, the silence portrayed by women writers will vary according to many factors, including their own age, economic class, and ethnicity, as well as those of their characters and their audiences. This postmodern emphasis will culminate in the analysis of the works of Sandra Cisneros, who brings her working-class, Chicana perspective to bear on her thematic and narrative use of silence. Cisneros contrasts with the bourgeois writers who are studied in the earlier chapters of this book, and shows how the specificity of her ethnic and working-class environment influenced her unique use of silence in her texts.

Acknowledgments

There are many people I would like to thank for their help in the publication of this book. First, untold thanks go to Mirella Servodidio and Arnaldo Cruz-Malavé, for their excellent suggestions regarding early drafts of the book. I would also like to thank my colleague Charles Stivale, who offered invaluable advice about my project proposal. In addition, much appreciation goes to my copyeditor, Wyatt Benner, who carefully edited the manuscript, as well as Dr. Harry Keyishian, Director of Farleigh Dickinson University Press, who believed in the value and importance of this book. As always, I wish to acknowledge the constant inspiration and support of my mother, Lucille Weldt, and my father, the late Bernard Weldt, who passed away a month after this book was accepted for publication, but whose spirit will always be behind each and every one of my academic endeavors. Above all, I would like to thank my husband, Marc, who has been an indispensable sounding board for ideas and strong supporter of my career, as well as my children, Rebecca and Marshall, who patiently understood why I couldn't always volunteer at school with the other moms because I was working on a book. One might say that over the course of the past ten years, my family suffered the ups and downs of the writing of this book in silence, and for this I owe them many thanks.

An earlier version of part of chapter 2 appeared in *Alba de América* 25.47–48 (2006): 273–84, and earlier versions of sections of chapters 5 and 8 appeared respectively, in *Revista de Estudios Hispánicos* (Puerto Rico) 21.1 (2004): 183–98 and *Cuadernos de Aldeeu* 16.1 (2003): 201–9. I thank these journals for allowing me to use this material.

Finally, I gratefully acknowledge the permission of the following publishers to reprint material from their books:

CARAMELO. Copyright © 2002 by Sandra Cisneros. Published by Vintage Books in paperback in 2003 and originally in hardcover by Alfred A. Knopf, Inc. Reprinted by permission of Susan Bergholz Literary Services, New York, NY and Lamy, NM. All rights reserved.

THE HOUSE ON MANGO STREET. Copyright © 1984 by Sandra Cisneros. Published by Vintage Books, a division of Random House, Inc. and in hardcover by Alfred A. Knopf in 1994. Reprinted by permission of Susan Bergholz Literary Services, New York, NY and Lamy, NM. All rights reserved.

LIKE WATER FOR CHOCOLATE by Laura Esquivel, copyright Translation © 1992 by Doubleday, a division of Random House, Inc. Used by permission of Doubleday, a division of Random House, Inc.

OF LOVE AND SHADOWS by Isabel Allende, translated by Margaret Peden, translation copyright © 1987 by Alfred A. Knopf, Inc. Used by permission of Alfred A. Knopf, a division of Random House, Inc.

WOMAN HOLLERING CREEK. Copyright © 1991 by Sandra Cisneros. Published by Vintage Books, a division of Random House, Inc. and originally in hardcover by Random House, Inc. Reprinted by permission of Susan Bergholz Literary Services, New York, NY and Lamy, NM. All rights reserved.

THE YOUNGEST DOLL by Rosario Ferré, translated by Jean Franco, translation copyright © 1991 by University of Nebraska Press.

Subversive Silences

1
Language and Silence: A Theoretical Overview

Women's Problematic Relationship to Language

SILENCE AND ITS IMPLICIT COUNTERPART, LANGUAGE, ARE TWO ELEMENTS that reappear in feminist studies across such varied disciplines as sociolinguistics, social anthropology, and literary criticism. An examination of the development of feminist thought regarding both language and silence is a prerequisite to the analysis of literary silences, especially when they are viewed as positioning the reader within a feminist perspective. Discussions about women and silence (whether as a behavior imposed upon women by patriarchal society or as a strategy deployed by women in response to patriarchal ideology) as well as women's relationship to language dominate much of the feminist criticism that has been written over the last four decades. This chapter will trace the evolution of feminist thought with regard to these two elements in order to show how they have become inextricably intertwined. What follows is a general overview of the main currents of feminist approximations to the topics of language and silence and is not intended as an in-depth analysis of each theory.

Muted-Group Theory

One of the earliest and most influential works about women's relationship to language is Shirley Ardener's *Perceiving Women* (1975). In that volume, Ardener unites several articles in the field of social anthropology that focus on the role of women in various societies. The volume includes two articles by Edwin Ardener that present what has come to be known as "muted-group theory": "Belief and the Problem of Women" (1972), and "The Problem Revisited" (1975). They suggest that since women throughout history have been excluded from the public sphere, public discourse has evolved as a male-dominated instrument. Language thus reflects the needs and concerns of men and inadequately expresses uniquely female zones of experience. Shirley Ardener summarizes this argument thus in her introduction:

> It is possible to speculate further and wonder whether, because of the absence of a suitable code and because of a necessary indirectness rather than spontaneity of expression, women, more often than may be the case with men, might sometimes lack the faculty to raise to a conscious level their unconscious thoughts. Edwin Ardener suggested that women's ideas or models of the world around them might nevertheless find a way of expression in forms other than direct expository speech, possibly through symbolism in art, myth, ritual, special speech registers and the like. (S. Ardener 1975, viii–ix)

The Ardeners' work inspired a series of feminist studies by others who agree that women speak and write differently from men. These pieces attempt to define gender differences in language. Over the past thirty years, many other critics have disputed the validity of a separate or differing language for women.

French Feminism

Two feminist nuclei support the basic ideas of muted-group theory. These are the French feminists of the 1970s who postulate une écriture féminine (a feminine writing) and the sociolinguists of the past thirty years who find evidence to support a modified version of women possessing a "different" language than men.

The most important proponents of *écriture féminine* are Julia Kristeva, Hélène Cixous, and Luce Irigaray, although some significant differences exist among them. These theorists combatively rewrite the male-centered psychoanalytical theories of Freud and Lacan that base the development of women's language purely on women's relationship to the father and male sexuality. Since the French feminists view Western culture as having systematically repressed women's unique sexuality, they see this sexuality as the key to their expression. For Kristeva, language has two aspects: the semiotic, which comes from the maternal body and is more closely identified with nature and the unconscious, and the symbolic, which comes from the father's and is generally equated with culture and conscious behavior (Kristeva 1984, 21–56). The semiotic aspect of language makes itself heard through "rhythm, intonations, gaps, meaninglessness and other forms of cultural, syntactical and textual disruption" (Roman 1994, 13). For Cixous, women must learn to exploit this semiotic aspect of language in order to "write their bodies" as a form of combat against phallologocentric culture. Cixous, like Kristeva, posits that a feminine writing is capable of reconnecting to the presymbolic rhythms of the mother's body, consequently breaking with the binary logic that limits both language and culture (Cixous 1974, 28; Sellers 1994, xxix).

Irigaray criticizes Freud's failure to impute sexual difference to the logic of discourse. She specifically links bodily pleasure to the suppressed female unconscious and sees linguistic eroticism as the only way to overcome such repression (Jones 1997, 372–74; and Roman 1994, 15). However, exactly how women can translate into writing their reexperiencing of preoedipal sexual pleasure, or *jouissance*, is highly problematic. Irigaray notes that women cannot express their sexual pleasure in language, because it is forbidden, and hence must cross "back through the mirror that subtends all speculation" (Irigaray 1985, 7). According to Lacan, the mirror phase is when the subject learns to know itself as a reflection of the mother. This stage precedes separation from the mother/body and incorporation into the male symbolic order (the father/language). Although Irigaray does not specify here how women can achieve this crossing back in time, she speaks specifically about employing silences and women's need to mimic masculine discourse in order to undermine it (Irigaray 1985, 75–76). Despite the postulates of the French feminists, attempts to define the characteristics of a discretely female writing have been largely unsuccessful. Nina Baym quotes Christiane Makward's definition of the traits of a feminine writing based on the ideas of the French feminists: "open, nonlinear, unfinished, fluid, exploded, fragmented, polysemic, attempting to speak the body i.e., the unconscious, involving silence, incorporating the simultaneity of life as opposed to or clearly different from pre-conceived, oriented, masterly or 'didactic' languages" (Baym 1997, 282).

Baym points out that there is no evidence that women have actually written in this manner; this is, rather, a prescription for how women should write in the future. However, many feminists feel this definition is essentialist and that such writing would only perpetuate traditional female stereotypes that portray women as irrational and disorganized

(Baym 283). Ann Rosalind Jones adds that *écriture féminine* has also been attacked for being "theoretically fuzzy and fatal to constructive political action" (Jones 1997, 374). Indeed, concepts such as "unfinished" and "exploded" are vague, while men's language can also be "polysemic" or "nonlinear." Elaine Showalter concurs with the deficiencies of the notion of *écriture féminine* and its lack of support by scholarship (Showalter 1997, 225).

Sociolinguistic Theory

The second nucleus of thought supportive either directly or indirectly of muted-group theory originates in feminist sociolinguistic theory. Representative sociolinguists in this area include Cheris Kramarae, Dale Spender, Robin Lakoff, Deborah Tannen, Pamela Fishman, and Deborah Cameron.

Cheris Kramarae's *Women and Men Speaking* (1981) proposes four different models of sociolinguistic research, of which the muted-group theory is one. Kramarae states that the three fundamental conclusions to be drawn from muted-group theory are : (1) females have more difficulty than males in expressing themselves within public modes of discourse; (2) males have more problems than females in understanding what members of the other gender mean (because females are forced to function within the dominant male culture and adopt their modes of expression, while the reverse is not true); and (3) females are likely to find ways to express themselves outside dominant public modes of expression (both in verbal and nonverbal behaviors) (Kramarae 1981, 1–32).

Dale Spender's *Man Made Language* (1980) is perhaps the most famous study based on the premises of muted-group theory. Spender is not actually a linguist, but rather a radical feminist who claims that the English language has been literally man-made and is primarily under male control. She analyzes sexism in English vocabulary, pointing out such voids in the English language as the existence of "potent" and "virile" to describe a healthy sexuality in men, but the lack of equivalent terms for women, who are deemed either "frigid" or "nymphomaniac" (Spender 1980a, 201). Although Spender's work was enormously popular, it has also been criticized for glossing over important issues in the sociolinguistic study of language.

While Kramarae and Spender focus on the ways that women have been left out of the constructive process of male-dominated language, Robin Lakoff, Pamela Fishman, and Deborah Tannen examine concrete speech differences between men and women. Lakoff claims that there are gender differences in the "choice and frequency of lexical items; in the situations in which certain syntactic rules are performed; [and] in intonational and other supersegmental patterns" (Lakoff 1975, 8). Lakoff suggests that there are certain adjectives that are only used by women, such as "adorable," "divine," "charming," "sweet," and "mauve" and that these and other traits reflect the process of female socialization in childhood (12). Fishman dissents with Lakoff's interpretation that these differences are due to early gender socialization. She attributes certain speech differences, such as the more frequent use of questions by women, as a strategy that they employ to introduce conversational topics that would otherwise be ignored by men, who generally do not view these topics as important. Thus, speech characteristics relate to conversational problems that are situational, and in the long run reflect women's inferior social position (Fishman 1988, 253–58).

Similarly, Deborah Tannen in her studies *Talking Voices* (1989) and *Gender and Discourse* (1994) states that certain speech patterns, such as tag questions, indirectedness, lack of adversariness, and topic raising are more frequent in women's speech than in men's. Tannen argues that these characteristics should not be seen as better or worse than men's, but simply as different, reflecting alternative conversational goals (Tannen 1989, 1994). Deborah Cameron places these three theories in historical perspective. She sees Lakoff's view of female language deficiency as predominant in the 1970s, when the woman's movement was in its incipient stage; Fishman's idea of female language reflecting male dominance as most popular in the 1980s, during the most aggressive stage of the feminist movement; and Tannen's idea of neutral difference as reigning in the 1990s, when the movement was tempered a bit by its successes (Cameron 1995, 31–44). Cameron criticizes Tannen's oversimplification of gender differences in language, pointing out that although there is nothing inherently preferable about certain "gender specializations" (such as women seeking intimacy and men seeking social status through language), their functions are indeed political and lead to inequalities in the social structure, because women are thus trained for the "abdication of autonomy" while men are trained to "exercise power" (Cameron 1995, 40–41). Cameron further indicates that these political functions of different genderized language styles should be the focus of the next decade.[1]

Muriel Saville-Troike links language to silence by viewing both as communicative strategies. Saville-Troike's study argues that both silence and language (vocal or nonvocal) are communicative in nature, and each has its own complex dimensions and structures. The author identifies three basic types of silence: (1) silence that carries propositional content and is dependent upon adjacent vocalizations for interpretation (denotative); (2) silence such as pauses and hesitations that may also carry meaning of a nonpropositional nature (connotative and symbolic); and (3) silence that structures communication but is not a communicative act in its own right, such as silence that accompanies certain ritual acts. The author offers a taxonomy of silences, grouped as follows: institutionally determined (locational, ritual, membership, hierarchical, taboo), group-determined (situational, normative, symbolic), or individually determined (sociocontextual, linguistic, or psychological silences, which can be either interactive or noninteractive) (Saville-Troike 1995, 3–18). Saville-Troike's work is independent of gender considerations and focuses purely on the semantic implications of silence.

Saville-Troike's study provides an important bridge between the topics of language and silence in feminist criticism by emphasizing the communicative value of silence. The concept of silence as a manifestation of female oppression has been associated with feminist studies from their inception, since women writers have long been silenced, forbidden to publish, forced to write under male pseudonyms, and generally omitted from the literary canon. However, over the years, the concept of silence has undergone a major transformation in feminist studies, evolving into a form of feminist resistance. Feminist critics who speak of the role of silence include Amy Kaminsky, Sara Castro-Klarén, Marjorie Agosín, Josefina Ludmer, Lucía Guerra-Cunningham, Elaine Showalter, and Debra Castillo, just to name a few.

Silence: Passive or Empowered Strategy?

Amy Kaminsky in *Reading the Body Politic: Feminist Criticism and Latin American Women Writers* views silence as an extension of the concept of absence. Since the traditional role of women in history has been that of absence or silence, the task of a feminist poetics should be that of establishing a presence "in the face of erasure and silence" (Kaminsky 1993, 25). Kaminsky's discussion of silence is somewhat traditional, because it associates silence with repression. This is also true of the way in which Castro-Klarén interprets silence, for she alludes to the silencing of women writers as a form of perpetuation of their subservient role.[2] In contrast, another group of critics views silence as a potentially subversive tool. Both Marjorie Agosín and Josefina Ludmer discuss silence in this manner with regard to Sor Juana Inés de la Cruz's famous *Carta Atenagórica* [Letter Worthy of Athena]. Agosín suggests that "mutism and silence can also be ways of evading authority, ways of taking refuge in the interiority of imagination in order to say only in this space what one wants to say" (Agosín 1993, 16). Agosín does not offer any comprehensive theory of silence as a communicative strategy, but extends its relevance to such writers as María Luisa Bombal, Marta Brunet, and Isabel Allende.

In her landmark article "Tretas del débil" [Tricks of the Weak] which appeared in the feminist collection *La sartén por el mango: Encuentro de escritoras latinoamericanas* [The Frying Pan by the Handle: Encounter of Latin American Women Writers] (1985), Josefina Ludmer analyzes silence as a space of resistance in the writings of Sor Juana Inés de la Cruz. Ludmer shows how Sor Juana separates knowledge from saying and reorganizes it as not saying, or silence, in order to empower herself and respond to religious authorities from her position of subordination and marginality. Ludmer, like Agosín, suggests that silence is not necessarily a passive strategy (Ludmer 1985, 47–54).

Both Lucía Guerra-Cunningham and Elaine Showalter see silence as a potentially subversive element that should be understood in terms of women's fundamental diglossia or need to express themselves through a male-dominated discourse, which perforce becomes dialogic or double-voiced in the Bakhtinian sense.[3] Both critics found their assumptions on the aforementioned muted-group and sociolinguistic theories. They claim that for every explicit theme or level of a text written by a woman writer, there is also an implicit or "silent" theme that is not directly expressed (Guerra-Cunningham 1990, 129–64; and Showalter 1985, 243–70).[4] Showalter is particularly concerned with comprehending the cultural context of language as a way of talking about the specificity and difference of women's writing. The women-culture model proposed by Showalter has the advantage of taking into account the influences of both the female (as a positive source of solidarity and a negative source of powerlessness) and male traditions (Showalter 1985, 265). Showalter, appropriating Bakhtinian concepts and terminology, states:

> The concept of a woman's text in the wild zone is a playful abstraction: in the reality to which we must address ourselves as critics, women's writing is a "double-voiced discourse" that always embodies the social, literary, and cultural heritages of both the muted and the dominant.

> Women writing are not, then, *inside* and *outside* of the male tradition, they are inside two traditions simultaneously....
>
> How can a cultural model of women's writing help us to read a woman's text? One implication of this model is that women's fiction can be read as a double-voiced discourse, containing a "dominant" and a "muted" story, which Gilbert and Gubar call a "palimpsest." (Showalter 1985, 263–66)

Showalter suggests that women writers, who are forced to write simultaneously within a male and female tradition, always present a "silent" plot (the female tradition) behind the dominant story (the male tradition) in their fiction. This idea is grounded in Bakhtin's theoretical principle that different "languages" or "voices" can be heard within a single discourse uttered by a sole speaker, as long as they represent differing viewpoints or specific linguistic styles associated with such viewpoints (Bakhtin 1984, 184). Showalter expounds on this basic concept by emphasizing the possibility that the discourses that compose a plot can simultaneously tell two stories to the reader.

Debra Castillo in *Talking Back: Toward a Latin American Feminist Criticism* (1992) speaks at length of the role of silence in feminist studies. Acknowledging the traditional silencing or repression of women in the past, Castillo states:

> The revolutionary response to silencing is resemanticization: to use silence as a weapon ... Under old traditional codes, the woman ... remained silent and withdrawn. In the counterhegemonic response to this official silencing, she executes a dizzying dance of negativity, appropriating silence as a tactic neither for saying nor for unsaying, but for concealing a coded speech between the lines of the said and the unsaid. (D. Castillo 1992, 38–41)

Castillo's "coded speech between the lines of the said and the unsaid" refers to "silent" techniques of indirection, such as irony, metaphor, and the like.

Silence and the Reader-Reception and Narratological Models

Two theorists whose work is key for comprehending how silence can transcend its traditional passive connotation and become a subversive feminist tool in women's writing are Nelly Furman and Sara Mills. Furman suggests that the issue involved in understanding language is not so much whether it is inherently sexist or male-dominated, but rather, how the language is read (Furman 1985, 66).

Sara Mills addresses this question of how a text lends itself to be read from a feminist position in *Feminist Stylistics* (1995). Mills indicates that she is concerned with "the way readers form interpretations which are related to their gender—where the process of interpretation rests on cues in the text which have a different significance, or are significant to a different extent, depending on the reader's gender-identity."[5] Mills proposes a feminist reader-reception model of the literary text that takes into account both the context of the text's production (implied and real authors) and reception (implied and real readers). In other words, Mills argues that all texts incorporate response-inviting structures whose meaning can be actualized in a variety of potential ways according to the specific reader.[6] Mills's principal hypothesis is that some texts are written in ways that do not lend themselves to being read within a feminist perspective, while others include textual cues that can potentially (depending upon the specific reader) be interpreted in a way that concretizes the text's "feminist affiliation." These cues include a variety of stylistic (grammatical, lexical, and transitivity choices) and thematic options (Mills 1995a, 31–34). One major allure of Mills's approach, as noted in the preface, is that it allows for the taking into account of differences in class and race, both on the production (author) and reception (reader) sides of the text. Moreover, although Mills herself is British and examines British texts, her theory is easily transcultural, because it allows for the interpretation of textual cues according to the specific environment in which a text was produced, as well as the variety of environments in which it might be read. This fact counters the criticism that a theory based on the literature of one country should not be applied to another, because of the necessary contextual differences. Thus, from the outset, Mills's theory avoids the two major pitfalls that have been described in feminist Latin American studies.

Despite the attractiveness of these aspects of Mills's approach, it is necessary to refine her terminology. Her notion of "affiliation" suggests that both writers and readers of texts must always identify with feminist ideology in order to respectively posit and actualize specific textual meanings. Although I generally agree—and, indeed, argue—that this may frequently be the case, one can certainly envision how certain authors might be able to incorporate such meanings or readers position themselves to receive or become aware of such feminist messages without necessarily "affiliating" with feminist causes. Moreover, with regard to literature, Mills focuses mainly on verbal strategies that suggest feminist affiliation, whereas in this book, as we shall see, I am specifically focusing on the relationship between silence/indirect strategies and the formation of feminist meaning. Consequently, it may be more appropriate to speak of "feminist perception" and "feminist nonverbal perceptions," which imply both a degree of comprehension or responsiveness to feminist cues, as well as a direct relationship to the topic of silence, rather than "affiliation," which suggests the necessary subscribing to a specific worldview. I like the term "perception" because it simultaneously connotes both the notion of a particular observation, insight, or idea (which is what the implied author is communicating to us with regard to feminism) and the notion of awareness or consciousness, which is the ability of the implied reader to understand these cues. Moreover, "perception" directly relates to the primary issue regarding silent cues: their lesser degree of potential perceptibility when compared to verbal strategies. "Perception" emphasizes the process of cognizance rather than association and is therefore more appropriate to a study of indirect narrative strategies. In a similar vein, I would like to suggest the use of the term "feminist-oriented" reader to replace Mills's "feminist-affiliated" reader, because the term "orientation," from which it derives, focuses on the concept of positioning, the process of adapting to or familiarizing oneself with something (in this case, with a certain ideology), as opposed to "affiliated," which once again emphasizes the obligatory adoption of a specific viewpoint.

The employment of indirect narrative techniques to create textual cues that structure a position of feminist perception for the reader suggests an important connection between reader-reception theory, feminism, and narratology that defines the approach toward Latin American women writers used in this book. The possible connections between feminism and narratology were first adumbrated by Susan Lanser in her landmark article "Toward a Feminist Narratology" (1986). Lanser suggests the void (which has since begun to be filled by her studies and those of others) of gender-based research in the field of narratology and posits questions whose answers lie in the overlapping of these two formerly separate fields of inquiry: "one might ask for example, what kinds of illocutionary acts the narrator undertakes and whether she undertakes them in a discourse of 'presence' or 'absence'; if we take absence to encompass such practices as 'irony, ellipsis, euphemism, litotes, periphrasis, reticence, pretermission, digression, and so forth.' These questions in turn might lead to a much needed theory that would define and describe tone in narrative" (Lanser 1997, 681). Lanser alludes to the creation of a feminist discourse based on narrative "absence," which is the approach I adopt here. This book posits a feminist/narratological analysis of textual cues of silence that in turn signal a feminist perspective to the reader.

SILENCE AND PREVIOUS LITERARY ANALYSIS

The use of silence and/or forms of indirect discourse (narrative absence) as a feminist strategy has been examined in some American, Asian American, and British writers. The first of the existing books on silence in women writers of other nationalities, Janis Stout's *Strategies of Reticence: Silence and Meaning in the Works of Jane Austen, Willa Cather, Katherine Anne Porter, and Joan Didion* (1990), focuses on how these writers use a paucity of speech by their characters as well as a deliberate lack of narrative commentary as a form of criticism of social norms that limit the rights and freedom of women. Stout adeptly shows how these writers attribute a positive connotation to the failure to speak or a conciseness of speech, whereas excessive speech is associated in their novels with falseness and stupidity. What is not said, or the failure to say, creates lacunae in the text that must be filled in by the reader and is thus a strategy designed to invoke reader participation. Moreover, authors like Joan Didion also use "textual voice," or the blank space to create both a moral and feminist commentary.[7] Stout's emphasis on the role of reader participation in the creation of potentially feminist meanings meshes with the approach to Latin American women writers suggested here, although Stout concentrates mainly on the concept of reticence, defined as a character's reluctance to speak, as opposed to characters who are mute or muted, or self-impose silence as a coping strategy or subversive weapon. The second book is Patricia Ondek Laurence's *The Reading of Silence: Virginia Woolf in the English Tradition* (1991), where she examines what she terms Woolf's "narrativity of silence" as a manifestation of the ineffability of life.

King-Kok Cheung, in *Articulate Silences: Hisaye Yamamoto, Maxine Hong Kingston, Joy Kogawa* (1993), offers a brilliant study of types of silences in Asian American women writers. Cheung emphasizes the cultural valuation or devaluation of silence. She points out that, in contrast to American culture, where silence is seen as negative, Asian culture has traditionally accorded a positive connotation to silence, since Asian culture values reserve and Asian writers tend to favor the implicit. Cheung defines three types of silence in her book: rhetorical silence, provocative silence, and attentive silence. Rhetorical silence refers to silence as both theme (the societal repression of both men and women) and method (the form of "muted plots" that manifest themselves through devices such as ellipses, irony, and unreliable narration). Provocative silence refers to the paradox "whereby parental and historical silence spurs creativity.... The absence of information is used as a pretext for artistic license allowing the author to give voice to the voiceless and to subvert patriarchal and historical orthodoxy" (Cheung 1993, 24–25). Cheung's "attentive silence" focuses on the different gradations of silence and illustrates how silences can be used to communicate positive emotions such as love and forgiveness. The author shows how the traditional interpretation of silence as either oppressively imposed or stoically adopted is reductive and culturally biased (Cheung 1993, 25–26). Cheung's approach, like my own, emphasizes the role of indirect discourse in such forms as irony and "double-voiced discourse" to create a "muted plot" behind the novel's principal one. However, the employment of these implicit techniques differs from their use in the fiction of Latin American women writers because they do not serve a subversive purpose in the fiction of Asian American women writers, nor do they correspond to the evolution of the feminist movement.

Male versus Female Writers

Although, as we have seen, several important critics of Latin American literature suggest the subversive potential of silence and techniques of indirection in Latin American women writers, to date no comprehensive study of this phenomenon exists.[8]

As recently as the year 2000, an issue of the journal *Monographic Review / Revista Monográfica* was dedicated to the topic of silence in Hispanic literature, suggesting the ongoing importance of this topic in the twenty-first century.[9] The volume presents a series of articles that discuss the role of silence in specific Peninsular and Latin American writers, both male and female. However, no global theory of the employment of silence is achieved through this collection. Nonetheless, a survey of the articles presented does indeed suggest that silence is used differently by men and women writers. The critics who focus on twentieth-century male prose writers indicate that silence is used as a manifestation of political victimization leading to death and annihilation in the Spanish writer Ramón Sender (Vásquez 2000); as a strategy for facilitating deceit in the work of Raúl Guerra Garrido (Higuero 2000); as a sign of resignation when confronted with war and violence in the works of Juan Rulfo (Ortega 2000; Guerrero 2000); and as a symbol of abused life in the form of scarred bodies in the works of Augusto Roa Bastos (Viera 2000). In contrast, the critics who analyze twentieth-century female writers discuss silence as a form of empowerment in the essays of the Spanish writer Soledad Puértolas (Merithew 2000); with regard to Latin American literature, as a rhetoric of opposition in the memoirs of the writers Margo Glantz and Marjorie Agosín (Goldberg 2000); as a strategy with communicative power to express the inexpressible in the works of Elena Garro (Melgar 2000); and as a weapon in the struggle for identity in the works of Diamela Eltit (García-Corales 2000). In other words, although many male writers employ similar silent themes and narrative strategies, these techniques create different messages and position the reader in distinct ways than they do in the works of female writers.[10] The fact that many of the female writers, especially those from Latin America, were shown to use silence combatively implies the need to study this phenomenon further in order to achieve a better understanding of the employment of silence in the narrative by Latin American women writers. The intersection between feminism and silence is hinted at but not fully developed in many of the pieces on Latin American women writers from *Monographic Review / Revista Monográfica*. Consequently, this book proposes to examine how silence is constructed in the works of several representative women writers as a cue signaling their texts' feminist perspective. "Silence" will refer not only to the absence of words, but also to the use of nonverbal strategies (ritual, symbol, illustrations, and the like) as well as indirect narrative techniques.

Toward a New Theory of Silences

As this overview suggests, the idea of silence with combative overtones is not entirely new to feminist theory. However, the study of how silence is manifested through a number of indirect strategies, especially in the specific women writers studied here, has not been previously examined in twentieth-century Latin American literature. Strategies vary according to each writer and her time period, suggesting a possible relationship between narrative form and the reader-reception context, a relationship that has never been thoroughly explored.

This book proposes and examines six types of silence in Latin American women's writing: paradoxical, encoded, hyperbolic, symbolic, parodic, and cultural silences. Paradoxical silence refers to the simultaneous employment within a text (or series of texts by a writer) of silence as a sign of female passivity and feminist rebellion. This use of silence is found in texts by women writers in the 1930s and 1940s, notably Marta Brunet and María Luisa Bombal. Encoded silence refers to the use of indirect textual strategies that mitigate or partially conceal feminist protest. This type of silence can be found in many Latin American texts that immediately precede the emergence of the feminist movement in the late 1960s and 1970s, such as the works by Rosario Castellanos. Hyperbolic silence is the exaggerated use or presence of silence in a text, usually to provoke the reader's doubt concerning its credibility. The reader is led to reject the passive connotation of silence through the linkage established between hyperbole and a context of situational irony. Consequently, the notion of passive silence characterizing women itself becomes ironic. Such is the case of silence in the works of Isabel Allende. Symbolic silence derives from encoded silence, because it relates to the use of techniques of indirection such as metaphor. However, symbolic silence more concretely refers to the use of syntagmatic textual associations and paradigmatic cultural elements to create indirect and hence symbolic meanings in a text. The silent strategy of association creates ambiguous, polysemic discourse for the reader, such as in the works of Rosario Ferré. The fifth silence, parodic silence, refers to implicit connections between a text and conventions of genre. Silence is employed to accentuate a genre-based parody and hence may itself be referred to as parodic. The works of Laura Esquivel illustrate this use of silence through her mimicry of both romance and science fiction novels. Finally, cultural silence designates silences that are inextricably related to specific racial, ethnic, and class differences. Such silence is found in Sandra Cisneros's use of Mexican cultural icons and bilingualism in her texts.

The selection of these particular women writers is not arbitrary. Bombal and Brunet are two of the first "feminist" Latin American authors, whose works serve as a necessary precursor to understanding the fiction of contemporary Latin American women writers. Rosario Castellanos is Latin America's first self-proclaimed feminist. Allende and Esquivel are among the few Latin American women writers whose works have attained the status of international best-sellers, a category that gives them an important and unique role with regard to both a male and female readership. Ferré's fiction is representative of the parallel between women and other marginalized groups, notably the Puerto Rican anticolonial population, whose culture is subservient to that of the United States.[11] Finally, Cisneros is a Latina writer whose work presents an alternative perspective to that of mainstream, bourgeois society (largely represented by the other writers of this volume) in its emphasis on working-class, ethnic, and racial differences. I also selected these writers because they epitomize different employments of silence as a communicative strategy, although all seven ultimately use silence as a textual cue to signal the text's feminist perception to the reader. As the following theoretical outline suggests, each writer's texts blend stylistic and thematic silences to construct a feminist perspective for the reader that directly relates to the development of the feminist movement in Latin America.

A Synopsis of Theoretical Applications

What follows is a brief overview of the various theoretical methodologies employed in the present book to elucidate the role of silence in each of the selected writers. Each chapter relies on a different theoretical perspective, chosen on the basis of the distinct narrative strategies of the authors.

In chapter 2, "Paradoxical Silence, Part 1: 'Overreading' the Works of Marta Brunet," I use Nancy K. Miller's theory of "overreading" to discuss the works of this early twentieth-century Chilean writer. "Overreading" a text refers to the process of deciphering a veiled feminist poetics within a work. As an example, Miller retells and reinterprets the Greek myth of Arachne, who enters into a weaving contest against the goddess Athena. According to Miller, both Arachne and Athena weave "mininarratives": Athena's tapestry depicts the punishment of humans who challenge the gods, while Arachne's tapestry depicts the protest of women who were victims of divine desire. Hence, each weaving of a tapestry symbolizes a particular message, and Arachne's is one of feminist rebellion. Miller employs weaving as a metaphor for women's writing and suggests that prefeminist narratives should be read from the particular critical positioning of overreading (N.K. Miller 1988, 83). Overreading in turn implies reading a text from a specifically feminist perspective that endeavors to interpret it both as symbolic of a uniquely feminine subjectivity and of a feminist poetics that, for reasons of feared negative reader-reception, the text could not openly state. I show how silence can be simultaneously overread as a feminist weapon and indicator of female passivity in Brunet's narratives, consequently constructing what I call a paradoxical silence for the reader. I also show how many of Brunet's stories metaphorically suggest mininarratives through nonverbal activities similar to weaving.

In chapter 3, "Paradoxical Silence, Part II: Silence / Narrative Voice in the Works of María Luisa Bombal," I both adopt and adapt Susan Lanser's theory of authorial voice and personal voice and their relationship to free indirect style. Lanser examines the role of overt commentary on the part of the textual narrator in novelistic discourse, which she sees as an exercise of authority or power on the narrator's part. This commentary or "voice" can take three forms: authorial (third-person narration), personal (first-person narration), or communal (group narration). Sometimes authorial and personal narrations fuse in the form of free indirect style, where a narrator reports a character's discourse indirectly and the boundaries between the two are confused (Lanser 1992, 3–41). This chapter shows how the narrative absence of such overt commentary in Bombal's *La última niebla* [The Final Mist] can also be seen as a feminist statement as well as how the boundary blurring of free indirect discourse signals a muted yet active feminist protest to the reader in the novel *La amortajada* [*The Shrouded Woman*]. This posits the presence of certain "silent" narratological structures (free indirect discourse that "silences" or negates the notion of a specific voice) as well as the absence of others (overt narrator commentary that manifests itself as an absence in the text) in Bombal's works. These silent strategies signal a feminist perception to the reader and their ambiguity also constructs a paradoxical silence similar to Brunet's.

Chapter 4, "The Encoded Silence of Rosario Castellanos: Coding, Paradox, and Parentheses," illustrates how the silent narratological coding strategies described by Joan Radner and Susan Lanser are deployed in Castellanos's texts to express a feminist message to the reader. According to the two critics, there are six coding techniques that women writers use to simultaneously express and disguise feminist content: (1) appropriation (use of materials normally associated with male culture, but situated within a context that suggests a feminist interpretation); (2) juxtaposition (the strategic placement of two or more voices/paragraphs or other elements to suggest an ironic connotation); (3) distraction (the creation of a textual "noise" or interference that obscures the intended message); (4) indirection (the use of inexplicit narrative techniques such as metaphor, ellipsis, and hedging); (5) trivialization (the employment of a mode or genre considered inferior by the dominant culture); and (6) incompetence (the suggestion of feminist rebellion through insistence upon incompetence at activities traditionally or stereotypically associated with women) (Radner and Lanser 1987, 414–22). This chapter illustrates how Castellanos metaphorically and symbolically employs parentheses to criticize women's marginal status and the inadequacy of patriarchal language. I theorize that Castellanos's heavy reliance on narrative coding techniques constitutes an encoded silence whose effect is to subtly manifest the text's feminist perception to the reader and thus make its message more acceptable to the audience than an explicit commentary.

Chapter 5, "Hyperbolic Silence: Agon and Irony in the Works of Isabel Allende," studies Allende's novels *La casa de los espíritus* [*The House of the Spirits*] and *De amor y de sombra* [*Of Love and Shadows*] as enactments of Wolfgang Iser's reader-reception theory of textual agon or play (Iser 1989, 325–39). Iser interprets textual construction as a fight between conflicting norms or values that cannot ultimately be resolved by the reader until the text's conclusion. In both of Allende's texts, a feminist-oriented position enters into conflict with the traditional, patriarchal viewpoint. Within these passages of conflicting norms, women's hyperbolic silence is used to construct the feminist discourses and is portrayed as both positive and subversive.

In addition, this chapter analyzes Allende's *Cuentos de Eva Luna* [*The Stories of Eva Luna*] from a perspective of narrative irony. Allende's irony is subtly constructed through its inversion of three ideological techniques: stereotyping, compensation, and collusion. These are three ideological devices employed by men in fiction to perpetuate the traditional image of women in society. By portraying women according to a traditional model (stereotyping), exaggerating feminine morality (compensation), and insisting upon women's role in their own subordination (collusion), male writers promulgate a passive, traditional female image that suits male-dominated society (Greene and Kahn 1985, 22). Allende appropriates these same devices in her fiction but then ironically subverts them through hyperbole. The hyperbolic depiction of women's silence and passivity leads the reader to question their validity and interpret such portrayals as ironic. The reader comes to reject the passive connotation of silence through the linkage established between hyperbole and a context of situational irony. Consequently, the notion of passive silence characterizing women itself becomes ironic.

Chapter 6, "Symbolic Silence: Rosario Ferré's Equation of Women and Puerto Rico," employs Tzvetan Todorov's theory of symbolic or indirect discourse to describe the ways in which the Puerto Rican writer constructs her texts *Papeles de Pandora* [Pandora's Papers], *Maldito Amor* [*Sweet Diamond Dust*], and *La casa de la laguna* [*The House on the Lagoon*]. This chapter illustrates how these texts can be understood through both paradigmatic associations (the interpretation of a lexical item based on the shared knowledge of a community) and syntagmatic associations (the contradiction or repetition of varied assertions belonging to the same context) (Todorov 1982, 30–38). These two types of associations create ambiguous discourse in Ferré's texts, as do other indirect or silent techniques, such as gender naturalization and textual voice. This last element, which refers to any textual element that signals a meaning visually, through differences in print (Ross 1979, 300–310), particularly pertains to the novel *The House on the Lagoon*. Ferré's use of highly indirect discourse is a symbolic technique that results in what I term "symbolic silence." Symbolic silence derives from encoded silence, because it relates to the use of techniques of indirection such as metaphor. However, symbolic silence more concretely refers to the use of syntagmatic textual associations and paradigmatic cultural elements to create indirect and hence symbolic meanings in a text. The silent strategy of association creates ambiguous, polysemic discourse for the reader.

Chapter 7, "Parodic Silence: Ritual and Genre in Laura Esquivel," shows how Esquivel's texts *Como agua para chocolate* [*Like Water for Chocolate*] and *La ley de amor* [*The Law of Love*] exemplify Gérard Genette's concept of parody, resulting in the conveyance of a feminist message to the reader. By examining how *Like Water for Chocolate* mimics romantic serial novels (using Andrés Amorós's study of the *novela rosa* and Janice Radway's analysis of romantic fiction) and how *The Law of Love* imitates both romance and science fiction novels, the chapter illustrates how parody functions as a silent narrative technique that can communicate a subversive message to the reader. This chapter also applies Muriel Saville-Troike's theory of silent communication to show exactly how thematic silence is used by Esquivel to help construct the parody of traditional romantic serial novels. Finally, I show how Esquivel parodies and inverts traditional gender roles in her third novel, *Tan veloz como el deseo* [*Swift as Desire*]. Esquivel's silence is viewed as parodic, because it refers to implicit connections between a text and conventions of genre. Moreover, thematic silence is employed to accentuate a genre-based parody.

Chapter 8, "Cultural Silence: Naive Narrators, Inverted Icons, and Bilingual Gaps in the Works of Sandra Cisneros," illustrates how ethnicity and class differences are reflected in the use of silence in Sandra

Cisneros's texts. This chapter demonstrates that age (childhood and adolescence) affects narrative perspective, resulting in implicit evaluation of events that must be extracted from the narrative and constructed by the reader. Esperanza Cordero's silent narrative evaluation in Cisneros's *The House on Mango Street* is illustrated through the application of the linguistic theories of Dell Hymes and William Labov, who show how child narration frequently lacks explicit evaluation. In addition, the chapter also focuses on the silences created for the non-Mexican or non-Chicano reader by Cisneros's feminist use and inversion of stereotyped Mexican cultural icons, such as La Malinche or the Virgin of Guadalupe, in her short story collection, *Woman Hollering Creek*. Finally, the chapter explores the linguistic gaps created by Cisneros's bilingualism, drawing upon the observations made about the intranslatabilty of linguistic emotional content by such theorists as Mary Besemeres, Robert Shrauf, Ramón Durazo-Arvizu, and Doris Sommer. I demonstrate that the simultaneous use of Spanish and English creates silences that help articulate a feminist message linked to Chicana ethnicity and the plight of the working class in Cisneros's latest novel, *Caramelo*.

Chapter 9: "Conclusions: Toward a Feminist Poetics of Silence," extends my observations and paradigms of silence established throughout the book to other Latin American and Latina writers, with suggestions for future study.

Each chapter combines an analysis of narratological techniques, such as irony, parody, hyperbole, symbolism, and the like, with reader-reception theories and strategies, such as overreading and textual agon, to illuminate how the reader can be led to construct a feminist message or perception from the text. My analysis of the functioning of silence within Latin American women's writing leads to the construction of a theory of distinct silences that vary according to the writer, country, and era in which each text was written.

2
Paradoxical Silence, Part I: "Overreading" the Works of Marta Brunet

TWO EARLY TWENTIETH-CENTURY WRITERS, MARTA BRUNET AND MARÍA Luisa Bombal, foreshadowed the contemporary feminist use of silence as a subversive weapon. The first of these writers, Marta Brunet (1897–1967), was born to a wealthy family in the small town of Victoria, Chile, and was educated at home, on her family estate. Her cultural formation benefited from a three-year trip to Europe, after which she began her career as a writer publishing poetry in a local newspaper. She published her first novel, *Montaña adentro* [Within the Mountain], in 1923. This work established Brunet as an important literary figure, as did the attention her novel and later texts received from the Chilean critic Alone (Peña 1999, 139). She moved to Santiago in 1925 and worked for various newspapers including *La Nación* [The Nation] and *La Hora* [The Hour]. Brunet was appointed consul to Buenos Aires in 1939. Her diplomatic career lasted until 1952, when the government of Carlos Ibáñez del Campo asked her to resign. She taught literature at the University of Chile for about ten years. In 1962, she resumed her diplomatic career as cultural attaché to the Chilean embassy in Río de Janeiro. She died of a cerebral hemorrhage in 1967 (Jehenson 1995, 30). Brunet's works can be divided into two groups: a regionalist phase that includes *Montaña adentro* (1923), *Bestia dañina* [Treacherous Beast] (1925), *María Rosa, flor del quillén* [María Rosa, Flower of the Quillén] (1927), and *Aguas abajo* [Downstream] (1943); and a second, urban phase that includes *Humo hacia el sur* [Smoke toward the South] (1946), *La mámpara* [The Outer Door] (1946), *María Nadie* [María Nobody] (1957), and *Amasijo* [Lump of Dough] (1962) [Jehenson, 1995, 29–30]. These are all novels, with the exception of *Aguas abajo*, which is a collection of short stories. Brunet's other short story collections are *Reloj del sol* [Sundial] (1930), *Raíz del sueño* [Dream's Root] (1949), and *Solita sola* [Solita Alone].

In both rural and urban scenarios, Brunet's principal concentration is on female protagonists in a patriarchal society. According to Linda Koski, Brunet's *criollista* settings serve as a "distraction" from her feminist themes; which made her works more acceptable for the time period in which they were written, but also obscured the feminist content of Brunet's fiction from critics (Koski 1989, 48–52).[1] Lucía Guerra indicates that Brunet's work received more critical acclaim when she adopted the *criollista* format than when she subsequently wrote on more overtly feminist topics, such as in the novel *María Nadie* (Guerra-Cunningham 1987a, 26). This observation supports the idea that Brunet's social circumstances forced the author to disguise her feminist themes in order to make her literature more palatable for the reader of her time.

The Concept of Overreading

Brunet's work invites reading her texts according to Nancy K. Miller's theory of "overreading" developed in "Arachnologies: The Woman, the Text, and the Critic." Such a reading elucidates the previously undetected feminism of Brunet's fiction. As we discussed in the first chapter, Miller suggests that certain texts by women writers published before the feminist movement arose might contain feminist messages that went unperceived by readers during the prefeminist era. Consequently, Miller argues, contemporary readers should actively seek out such messages and the corresponding theory of feminine writing embedded in this discourse (their veiled feminist poetics) (N.K. Miller 1988, 77). Miller bases her theory of overreading on an analogy with the Greek myth of Arachne. Her main point is to "discover the embodiment in writing of a gendered subjectivity; to recover within representation the emblems of its construction" (80–83). For Miller, a crucial element of the technique of overreading is the uncovering of a poetics of writing on the part of the female artist. Her ideas are very similar to those of Sara Mills concerning the reading of texts from a feminist perspective based on certain cues. The main difference is that Miller emphasizes the application of this technique in prefeminist texts and also stresses how these texts embody a female poetics of writing.

This chapter accordingly proposes to overread Brunet's thematization of silence in her short stories and in the novel *María Nadie* (1957), using Miller's approach. Overreading will demonstrate how Brunet uses silence both in a traditional sense (as a sign of female oppression) and in a more contemporary sense, as a weapon against male domination and a metaphor for women's (nonverbal) "writing" or expression. Since Brunet vacillates between a traditional, passive silence and a combative, subversive silence, we may think of her employment of silence as paradoxical.

Silence as a Sign of Oppression

Many stories belonging to different stages of Brunet's writing depict silence as a sign of female oppression. Such silence may be interpreted as a manifestation of Miller's notion of "gendered subjectivity" in the sense that it reflects the unique position of women at that time in patriarchal society. This traditional silence is the central motif that embodies an exclusively female perspective of society in at least three of Brunet's stories.

"Aguas abajo" [Downstream] from the collection of the same title (*Aguas abajo*, 1943) presents the anguished situation of a mother whose daughter supplants her as head of the household, becoming the new "woman" of her stepfather (the mother's second husband). The mother is told that she must endure this situation in silence or leave the premises. Thus, the mother desperately attempts to suppress her weeping: "the woman convulsively plastered her apron against her mouth to extinguish it [a sob] without any noise at all. Because they had told her that 'they didn't want to hear her'" (Brunet 1962, 105).[2] It is particularly interesting that the mother chooses to stay with the family at the story's conclusion, seizing upon the hope that her daughter will end up being only the lover and that this will leave room for her to continue as the mistress of the house (106).

It is likely that in the 1940s, this story was read as a love triangle between the stepfather, mother, and daughter, with strong *criollista* overtones in the regional dialect of the speakers. However, overreading this text in search of gendered subjectivity and a feminist poetics demonstrates that Brunet conveys a second layer of meaning and a metaphor for the female writing process in her story. The contemporary feminist reader perceives a different tale behind the love triangle: the power struggle between men and women in society. Brunet defines two possible societal roles for women (both in relation to men) that confer a measure of power: sexual mate and head of the household. The "power" wielded in both instances is clearly of the private (versus public) order and is bestowed by the patriarchal authority (the stepfather/husband) that also supersedes it. In other words, the status of sexual mate also carries with it the "power" of running the household, unless the man of the house decides otherwise and reestablishes the mother in her former position because of the daughter's inferior capabilities in this regard. The mother has no voice in the determination of her role in the family, which is here a symbol or microcosm of society in general. Silence is a sign of woman's impotence before the male-dominated social order. If the mother were to leave the family, there would be no possible societal role for her to occupy, and hence she opts to remain in the house as displaced victim. The fact that the characters have no names, but are simply referred to as "the man" and "the woman" (suggesting their universality) reinforces the emblematic nature of the household and the woman's passive silence.

Brunet provides a metaphor for her presentation of a "muted" story (the tale of women's societal condition) within a dominant one (the more immediate story of the love triangle) in the first paragraph of the text, in which the narrator describes the structure of the characters' house: "The house was at first made of reeds and adobe with a whitewash of clay. But, with the passing of time, the man began to bring up slabs of stone from the river and made other stone walls around the already existing ones. It was like a house placed inside another house" (100).[3] We can think of this description as an example of the embedding of a feminist poetics within the text; women must write a muted or symbolic second plot within a text's obvious one to protest their role in society.

Brunet's story "Gabriela" from *Reloj del sol* can also be overread as a symbol of society. "Gabriela" shows the societal silencing of women through the wresting of authority from their public discourse. During a social gathering, the topic of fatal accidents arises, inspiring the relation of various stories on this theme. A young woman named Gabriela reveals that one day, death followed her in the form of something cold and horrible. She lost consciousness and entered into a feverish state from which she slowly recovered. Despite Gabriela's use of language to tell this story, she is otherwise described as silent and mute. Gabriela breaks her typical silence to relate an important experience in her life. The other women at the gathering believe her tale, which causes them to shake with fear. The men, however, react with disbelief and label her a talented "hysteric" (37). It is especially important that the man who calls her hysterical at the story's end is a doctor. This fact lends particular authority to his discourse (since doctors are such respected members of society) and renders his terminology factual rather than judgmental. Like "Aguas abajo," "Gabriela" can thus be read on two levels. On the surface, "Gabriela" presents the recounting of what appears to be a fantastic tale of an encounter with death. However, when "overread" in search of gendered subjectivity, the tale becomes a commentary on women's voice (or lack thereof) in the public arena. Female experience communicated through male-dominated language is discounted and discredited as neurotic or pathological. Hence, women are relegated to a passive silence.

The third story, "Raíz del sueño" [Dream's Root], from the collection of the same title can also be overread as symbolic of patriarchal society. The story's silent protagonist, Elena, is prone to horrible nightmares. Her silence and dreams are a reaction to the patriarchal authority that represses her desires for friendship and self-determination. In this instance, patriarchal authority is represented through an authoritarian female figure, Elena's mother. We are told that the widowed mother was extremely jealous of her daughter, who was her only reason for living (Brunet 1962, 124). When Elena refuses piano lessons, her mother tells her that she will have to take them because she wants her to do so. When Elena asks to be allowed to play with a friend, her mother refuses and insists that she is allowed to hit her just because she is her mother. The absolute authority of the parental role becomes a symbol of the patriarchal order that forces Elena into a world of silence and nightmares because it will not allow her to become who she wants to be. That is why we are repeatedly told: "Her voice was within her, lost" (122).[4] Silence epitomizes the passive role women must adopt before patriarchal society. This transference of patriarchal authority to the figure of the mother must be overread in the text; it is only apparent when the reader searches for gendered subjectivity within it. A clue to this idea of transference is found in the narrator's comment that Elena's mother was "transferring her love of the father to her daughter" (124).[5] This comment suggests that we can also transfer the representation of patriarchal authority from the father figure to the mother. Otherwise, the text simply reads as a story about a domineering mother who suppresses her daughter's voice. This same transference of patriarchal authority to the mother is also perceptible in Laura Esquivel's *Like Water for Chocolate*.

In the three stories just analyzed, silence is clearly oppressive, rather than paradoxical. However, the silence in these stories dialogues with the subversive silence of other Brunet tales to create an overall paradoxical vision of silence within Brunet's oeuvre as a whole. In all three stories, having the protagonist's situation act as a symbol for women in society must be overread in the text; it is not immediately apparent to the reader unless he or she specifically positions himself or herself within a feminist perspective.

Paradoxical Silences

In the next four stories, silence is at once submissive and subversive and thus clearly paradoxical. The first of these, "El espejo" [The Mirror], presents the self-analysis achieved by an aging and obese woman confronted with her image in a mirror. Silence is superimposed upon the object of the mirror as a motif whose changing signfieds parallel the different stages of the woman's life. When the protagonist first examines herself in the mirror, silence allows her to contemplate her evolution over the years. She continues looking at herself, but now listens to *the dense silence of her blood within her.* Surrounded by cold, immobile. Is that her? She herself?" (Brunet 1962, 299, my emphasis).[6]

In the protagonist's youth, silence offers a welcomed refuge in which she can quietly occupy herself with household chores (299). Later, she marries without ever questioning why, because as a woman she has no other choices. Her life "cannot be anything other than what it is. She lives it intensely, profoundly, with the specific knowledge of her female condition" (300).[7] However, the protagonist's initial acceptance of her married role is undermined by the silence of routine and lack of authentic communication that come to characterize the relationship between her and her husband, who are constantly repeating the same dialogue, which thus ends up being "a form of being silent aloud" (301).[8]

The emptiness of the woman's life is underscored by the loss of youth and beauty that previously defined her existence and that leads to her eventual introspection through the mirror. This loss is brutally emphasized by her husband's advice that she should buy a new dress and take better care of her appearance. The protagonist's rebellion against the role prescribed for her by patriarchal society, the role of beautiful wife in a loveless marriage, is symbolized through her smashing of her silver tray into the mirror. Brunet employs cultural objects that reflect gendered roles in patriarchal society: the silver tray signifies traditional female domesticity, while the mirror refers to woman's role as sexual object. Brunet develops the symbolism between these two objects and the life of the female protagonist, by emphasizing the objects' loneliness and sudden realization of their condition. We are told that the tray and the mirror appeared "infinitely unprotected in their respective solitudes" (298) and that with the sudden entering of light it seemed as if they awoke from "a painful interior insomnia" (298).[9] This personification of the two objects exactly parallels the feelings and process of introspection of the story's protagonist.

Brunet further emphasizes the connection between the mirror and her protagonist through the latter's discovery of a flaw in the mirror's quicksilver, a flaw that is described as a sign of the "faded yellowish leper of time" (298).[10] Thus, just as the mirror ages, so does the woman, and it is this aging process that leads to her realization of the artificial way in which she has led her life.

Brunet presents the specific conflicts and silent protest of a bourgeois, aging woman. The silver tray, at the same time that it symbolizes domesticity, is also a sign of wealth and social status that underscores the portrayal of a woman from a certain socioeconomic group. Obviously, as we shall see in some of Brunet's stories that focus on working-class women, poor females do not possess high-value objects like the silver tray, and thus their silent protest must take a different shape than that of privileged women.

In this story, two types of silences collide. On the one hand, silence represents the futility of the woman's life as predetermined by the roles prescribed by the patriarchal order. The silence that exists between her and her husband testifies to the emptiness of their marriage. On the other hand, the silent shattering of the mirror through the tray may be seen as a rebellious act signaling the evolution to subversive silence. In this sense, we may interpret "El espejo" as enacting a paradoxical use of silence, because the elderly woman finally rebels against her oppressive silence and empty life by the silent protest of smashing the two culturally gendered objects.

"Ruth Werner" (also from *Reloj del sol*) epitomizes Brunet's paradoxical use of silence. It is a strange story in which the very strong and independent woman of the title eventually appears to submerge herself into the role of silent, submissive lover. Ruth Werner initially defies all traditional gender stereotypes. In a powerful reversal of typical gender roles, we are told that Ruth "possessed a husband" (Brunet 1962, 42)[11] who served her as a mere decorative object. The narrator indicates that she is brilliant, wealthy, and capable of doing whatever she wants, but incapable of subordinating herself to any task, because she does "not admit any servitude" (42).[12]

One day Ruth goes for a walk through the seamier part of the city and ends up in a café where she smiles at a man whom she believes to be an acquaintance of hers. The man signals to her, and when she joins him, we learn that he is a stranger who thinks she is a prostitute. When the man urges her to enter his car, she attempts to explain to him his mistake, but he refuses to believe her. Ruth enters the vehicle to avoid a public scandal, and there undergoes an incredible transformation. She was initially described as "stubborn and mute," but now she reencounters her former self, the primitive woman of the past, a "female submissive to the male, in a violent kidnapping" (46).[13] The story ends by informing the reader that Ruth becomes the "passionate and submissive lover" of the man, who is named Gonzalo Prieto.

On the surface, it appears that Brunet overturns her original role reversal and casts Ruth Werner in the stereotyped role of silent, subservient female. However, it is also possible to read Ruth's passivity and submissiveness as ironic. After all, in Paris of the 1930s, the married Ruth Werner subverts the traditional role of dutiful wife and engages in a passionate extramarital affair. It is hard to view her as "submissive." Perhaps the fear of social scandal that overtly leads her to silently enter Prieto's car is actually a feminist act in which Ruth Werner defies societal norms and freely enacts her own sexuality. As Cecilia Rubio aptly points out, Ruth converts her passive role of prostitute (for which she is originally mistaken) into the active role of lover (as she is referred to at the end of the story) (C. Rubio 1995, 102). Hence, silence is at once both passive and subversive.

The story provides several clues that allude to Ruth's ambiguous nature. First, at the onset of the narrative, she is described as simultaneously masculine and feminine in her appearance. She wears a very short skirt, but has a boyish haircut and she is likened to "an ambiguous figure, like those that Chana Orloff stylized" (Brunet 1962, 42).[14] Ruth's physical ambiguity prefigures her ambiguous, paradoxical silence at the end of the story, when the reader is unsure whether she is passively accepting the predetermined fate of women or consciously enacting a passionate, socially prohibited feeling (acting more like a man than a woman).

A second clue to the story's conclusion can be found in the intertextual reference in which the narrator of "Ruth Werner" compares the protagonist to a heroine in Rachilde's work (42). Rachilde was a late nineteenth-century / early twentieth-century French novelist, whose work is considered to be antirealist and decadent in its aesthetics. According to Diana Holmes, the decadents despised the romantic fiction genre, and Rachilde viewed love as a purely "cerebral emotion" (Holmes 2003, 19). Nonetheless, Holmes claims that Rachilde reproduces many characteristics of the romance genre, although often in a "spirit of parody" (Holmes 2003, 19). These comments suggest an interesting analogy between "Ruth Werner" and Rachilde's work. Ruth, like Rachilde, treats love as a cerebral emotion: "Love, as long as it was a platonic manifestation, entered in her cerebral life, in which only the perfume of its liquor was necessary to create intoxication" (Brunet 1962, 43).[15] Ruth views love intellectually until she meets Prieto and succumbs to true passion. However, just as Rachilde parodies romantic fiction, the reader is left to question Ruth's brusque change at the story's end and wonder whether Brunet's imitation of woman's enslavement to passion through submissive silence is not in fact a mocking parody of the inordinately passionate denouements of traditional romantic fiction, a parody similar in spirit to Rachilde's.

Once again, as in "El espejo," Brunet chooses to focus on the situation of a wealthy, upper-class woman, who comes from a milieu similar to Brunet's own upbringing. Initially Ruth's privileged socioeconomic status allows her some freedom to rebel against traditional female stereotypes, and thus "possess" her husband and dress as she pleases.

Nonetheless, the sterility (lack of passion) of her life coincides with her privileged environment. It is thus perhaps significant that Ruth's transformation occurs when she ventures out of her elegant neighborhood and wanders into a poor section of town. Her extraction from her familiar surroundings provides the necessary context of difference and ambiguity for her to participate in extraordinary actions, such as entering Prieto's car and becoming his lover. Her silent acceptance of this new role, which, as we have seen, may ultimately connote a social protest, can only occur when Ruth finds herself outside her normal social context. Consequently, there may be an implicit commentary on social difference (the upper-class woman would not dare to exceed marital bounds, but placed in a lower-class environment, she succumbs to passion) embedded in the discourse of "Ruth Werner."

A third paradoxical use of silence is found in the story "Soledad de la sangre" [Loneliness of the Blood], which is perhaps the most commented-upon story written by Brunet. Both Cecilia Rubio and Gabriela Mora view silence as an internalization of oppression in "Soledad de la sangre" (C. Rubio 1995, 102; Mora 1984, 83). However, if we examine the story closely, we see that silence is also used with subversive intent.

The protagonist of "Soledad de la sangre" is a wife who earns her own money through knitting children's clothing. She ends up receiving large sums of money for her work, which enables her to buy many household items. In this sense, weaving/knitting can be thought of as symbolic of power, since it grants the woman the ability to make purchases that would otherwise be impossible and affords her a measure of independence. The only thing she buys purely for her own enjoyment is a record player and two records. Although her husband disapproves of this purchase and will not allow her to buy any more records, he does permit her to listen to the photograph once he is asleep, largely because the woman astutely purchases a leather jacket for him as a gift, which softens his attitude toward her phonograph as a "waste of time" (Brunet 1962, 111).

The playing of the phonograph becomes a nightly ritual. After her husband goes to bed, the woman takes out the device and plays her two records, a waltz and a march. This music without lyrics is vocal but nonverbal. As she listens to the phonograph, the woman recalls her happy youth in the North and the boy she once loved who disappeared, a key event in her life that signaled the road to her present loveless marriage. The phonograph's music thus becomes a nonverbal (wordless) means of communication of the dreams and thoughts of the woman, who is simultaneously associated with silence: "That [phonograph] was her luxury. . . . She had to keep her memory, take care of her daydream, and only in a country of silence could she do so" (Brunet 1962, 110–13).[16] Hence, the phonograph and knitting/weaving (through its association with the phonograph as its means of purchase) are nonverbal expressive forms that substitute for writing as a form of communication and symbolize the woman's desires and power.

One day, when the husband is attempting to close a business deal with another man during dinner, the guest spies the phonograph and asks the woman to play it. The woman reacts with a silent, resentful refusal, attempting to distract the guest from his request by plying him with liquor. Her silent thoughts not only reflect the subversive power of silence, but also an internal rebellion on the point of explosion: "The woman looked at them, quietly. They must not approach her phonograph again, it was hers, her inner life resided there, her evasion from the colorless days" (Brunet 1962, 116–17).[17] The woman incubates a silent rebellion against the attempts of the men to possess her unique form of self-expression: the phonograph. Hence, when the guest finally touches the apparatus, the woman bites him, performing a silent, aggressive act. Thus, both silence and the nonverbal serve as weapons used by women to combat the patriarchal order. However, the phonograph is broken in the scuffle that ensues. Thus, the men representative of the patriarchal order destroy the only authentic form of expression that made bearable the woman's routine and loveless existence.

The destruction of the protagonist's phonograph seems to imply the failure of silence as a subversive tool against patriarchy, yet the story's ending suggests the contrary. Although the wounded protagonist at first flees the house, desiring death, she ultimately chooses to embrace life. This decision is based on her connection to her silent memories (of which the phonograph was only a catalyst), which serve as her weapon against her tedious, loveless marriage.

Other Brunet stories present silence as an effective weapon against patriarchy, as do more contemporary narratives. For example, "Piedra callada" [Silent Stone] (from the collection *Aguas abajo*) pits the silent mother-in-law, Eufrasia, against her barbaric son-in-law, Bernabé. Eufrasia disapproves of her daughter Esperanza's marriage. We are told that both Eufrasia and Bernabé endured the courtship period in silence and that once the marriage took place, Eufrasia "Never mentioned her daughter" (Brunet 1962, 87).[18] When Esperanza moves far away with Bernabé, Eufrasia only receives news of her through the majordomo's wife, Cantalicia. However, upon hearing such news, Eufrasia refuses to comment (88). Silence is clearly the mother's form of rebellion/punishment when faced with her daughter's disobedience.

When Esperanza is hospitalized, the head of the hacienda orders Eufrasia to visit her daughter's family and help take care of her children. Eufrasia stoically endures the rough trip through the mountains in silence (90), thus converting silence into a sign of her strength and endurance. Similarly, when Eufrasia learned of Esperanza's impending operation, "the old woman tightened her lips . . . and didn't say anything" (90).[19]

Bernabé is unhappy with the presence of his mother-in-law in his household, while Eufrasia is equally dissatisfied with her son-in-law's physically abusive behavior, of which she becomes aware upon her arrival. Their battle of wills is initially portrayed as one of silences; they mutually refuse to speak to one another (91).

After Esperanza's death, Eufrasia hatches a plan to rid herself of Bernabé and gain custody of her grandchildren. She suggests to Bernabé that he remarry and offers to relieve him of the burden of child care.

This enrages Bernabé, who orders everyone to bed without finishing his or her maté. However, once he is sound asleep, Eufrasia disobeys him by silently serving the children their tea (Brunet 1962, 95–96). This rebellion occurs on a larger scale when Eufrasia plans Bernabé's murder. Eufrasia's role in Bernabé's death is never explicitly stated in the text. Nonetheless, the reader is led to deduce her agency through her silent activities: Eufrasia "made secretive trips along the path until she confronted the bridge over the ravine. . . . . The man put his foot on the bridge. . . . He suddenly hesitated, wounded in the forehead by a stone; he vacillated, oscillated, and disappeared between the walls of the ravine, submerged in the dampness. . . . Now I won . . . and forever . . . Ha!—She said it, thought she said it, *but from her closed mouth, as if the lower lip were barred, she didn't move a muscle nor did a sound come out*" (99–100, my emphasis).[20]

If we return now to the story's title, "Piedra callada," we see how the silent stone that murders Bernabé is Eufrasia's form of silent expression. The throwing of the stone is a silent act of retribution for Bernabe's physical abuse of his wife and children. Eufrasia does not need words to emerge victorious from her contest of wills with Bernabé, the story's representative of patriarchal authority.

The stories "Piedra callada" and "Soledad de la sangre" (as well as "Aguas abajo" from the previous section) contrast with "El espejo" and "Ruth Werner," because they portray working-class women as opposed to wealthy ones. The author portrays differences between these two groups of women in her stories. Although subversive silence is present in all of these tales, the protagonist Esperanza of "Piedra callada" and the wife in "Soledad de la sangre" exhibit less freedom and more oppressive silence than their rich counterparts in "El espejo" and "Ruth Werner." In "Piedra callada," Esperanza is beaten by her husband and does not herself employ subversive silence. Only her mother, Eufrasia, is able to use silence as a weapon, in large part because she is financially independent (having an excellent and well-established working situation) and does not rely on her son-in-law, Bernabé, for subsistence. This helps her to oppose him with silent weapons. Similarly, in "Soledad de la sangre" the husband and wife are not rich. However, the wife is able to find her silent outlet through her music, precisely because she establishes her own knitting business, and can purchase her records and thus some freedom and independence from her husband. Brunet shows how lack of economic independence for working-class women fosters passivity and inability to engage in behaviors of protest.

The paradoxical silence of these four stories bears a direct relationship to their marriage plot structure. "El espejo" and "Soledad de la sangre" enact what Annis Pratt refers to as the plot of domestic enclosure, in which marriage is presented as an institution that dulls female initiative and maturation (Pratt 1981, 41). In each of these stories, the female protagonist is personally unfulfilled by her relationship with her husband and, as we have seen, rebels against this reality through some type of silent activity (the symbolic shattering of the silver tray in the first; the silent dreaming through listening to nonverbal music in the second) at the same time that silence reflects her subordinate status to her husband. Similarly, Ruth Werner's marriage lacks passion and is merely a social convenience against which she ultimately rebels by silently entering Gonzalo Prieto's car and becoming his lover. Ruth's silence, when faced with Prieto's misconception that she is a prostitute, ambiguously suggests both a passive acceptance of rape and a rejection of her loveless marriage. In all three of these texts, the paradoxical silence employed to characterize the protagonists also corresponds to the simultaneous complicity and rebellion against gender norms that is often manifested in the paradigm of the marriage plot (Pratt 1981, 41).

The story "Piedra callada" takes these ideas one step further, injecting the presence of the mother figure into this type of plot. After her daughter's death, Eufrasia's presence in her son-in-law's household not only reveals her daughter Esperanza's silent suffering faced with her husband Bernabé's physical abuse, but also counters this oppressive silence with a subversive one in which she challenges Bernabé's authority and ultimately murders him. Although Esperanza accepted her subservient role, Eufrasia subsequently rebels against it on her behalf. The two women together epitomize the conflicted or paradoxical stance of women within the marriage plot.

The story "Aguas abajo" represents a variation on the archetype of patriarchal enclosure. Since the tale's protagonist is rejected by her husband and supplanted by her own daughter, she does not exhibit the usual vacillation between acceptance and rejection of patriarchal norms. Her conflict revolves around her imposed loss of functional role within the nuclear family. Consequently, the silence represented is purely oppressive, rather than paradoxical, because there is no role for her to rebel against anymore. Nonetheless, "Aguas abajo" shares the representation of marriage as a suffocating, stifling force. In all these stories, the nature of each silence springs out of the narrative plot development.

Metaphors for a Feminist Poetics

In some of Brunet's stories, silence or silent rituals become an alternate feminine language that can be overread in the text in much the same way as Miller overreads Arachne's tapestry. As we have seen, overreading involves a focus on the act of writing as represented in the text. I propose that nonverbal forms of expression/rituals are used by Brunet as metaphors for writing/reading. Such is the case in three important Brunet stories: "La nariz," [The Nose], "Misia Marianita" [Miss Marianita], and "La Machi de Hualqui" [The Healer from Hualqui].

The first of these, "La nariz," is a fascinating tale of a little girl who "reads" noses. As she gets older, Margarita interprets noses as if they were texts reflecting the true feelings of their authors (Brunet 1962, 265–67). Margarita is misunderstood, as are many avant-garde writers/artists. The adults fail to comprehend her concept of noses as a form of textuality. Her mother and her nanny view her as strange, as if she came from "another world, surrounded by silence" (265).[21] This is also the case of the other children at school, who laugh at her and think her odd because of "the nose thing" (269).[22] Margarita becomes progressively sadder and more silent as she tries to suppress her interest in noses. Only her father seems to understand her and provide her with a measure of sympathy. When Margarita finally confides in him, her father decides to take her with him to his properties near the mountains on a business trip. There Margarita is allowed to enjoy her solitude and silence: "She thought: 'this is what I wanted, yes, this. To be alone, *to not speak*'" (265, my emphasis).[23]

Finally, Margarita, with the help of a puppy who befriends her, discovers her true talent as a "writer" of texts with the language of "noses." One day, the puppy digs up a root in which Margarita discovers the image of a nose. The dog then helps her to uncover bits of tree trunk, stones, and other natural elements with which Margarita can "write" her "text" and finally express herself:

> They looked all that day, all the next: stalks, pieces of curled up roots . . . stones, enclosed in their muteness of centuries, which were necessary to pound, handle, so that they would acquire meaning and say something. . . . the authoritative hands handled and conquered the tenacious opposition of the long vine of a wire, attaching one branch to another, a root to a stone. Upon suddenly seeing her father, she triumphantly showed her work.
>
> "Wouldn't you say that it is your portrait . . . ?"

"Now I know why I like noses."

Her father also knew it. It was as if symbols without meaning were spelled. That Margarita learned to read them. To read them without difficulty. And to write in that language. (272–73)[24]

Margarita's silent expression through sculpture with her peculiar language of noses parallels the idea of inscribing in the text a feminist poetics that differs from traditional male-dominated language. This form of "writing" is misunderstood by those around her, and it only finds an outlet when patriarchal authority (in this case represented by Margarita's father) allows Margarita to realize her sculptures. The father's nurturing stance, although superficially incompatible with the notion of oppressive patriarchal authority, parallels patriarchal control of the mechanisms of production and publication. Only when Margarita's father permits her to express herself and provides her with the conditions necessary to do so does Margarita finally achieve self-expression through her nose sculptures. She is finally allowed to "publish" her work. In the story, patriarchy is synonymous with adult authority figures, both male and female. Hence, in addition to Margarita's father, her mother, grandmother, Aunt Elena, and nanny are all responsible for suppressing her creativity.

"Misia Marianita" from the collection *Reloj del sol* presents a similar analogy between elements of quotidian life and textuality. Misia Marianita is an old lady whose entire life has been spent in her treasured neighborhood, which is like an old friend. On her daily walks, she studies every detail of the buildings with keen interest. Marianita never alters her path until one day she suddenly decides to walk up the hill. This variation of her daily stroll represents a scandalously daring behavior on her part. She climbs the hill until she arrives at a spot with a bench from which she can observe her entire neighborhood "from a new angle" (Brunet 1962, 70)[25] and discovers that "each rooftop was a problem to be solved" (70).[26] By climbing the hill, Misia Marianita can now "read" the "text" of the buildings of her town from a new perspective; the rooftops are a nonverbal language that she seeks to interpret. Each day she climbs a little farther up the hill in order to "to encompass more horizon" (70).[27] Although the ascent tires her, the fresh perspectives provided by each climb afford renewed meaning to her life. She tells the girl seated next to her on the bench that familiar things and factual knowledge can become tiresome, while viewing things from a distance (such as the buildings in her town), has forced her to make new connections and become aware of the truth, creating an inordinate passion for life.

This is the strategy that Miller suggests for reading feminist texts. Misia Marianita is the silent, sheltered female protagonist who finally finds meaning in her life through rereading (and hence rewriting, since reading and writing are opposite faces of the same coin) her town. The buildings of the town become elements of a silent, symbolic feminist language through which Marianita can finally express herself. Shortly after her revelation of the importance of her new interpretive strategy to the girl on the bench, Marianita dies, presumably taxed by the effort that climbing the hill meant for her aged body. However, the young girl who waits for Marianita to reappear now possesses the key to future feminist expression.

"La Machi de Hualqui" is a story that mixes silent ritual with feminist revenge on patriarchal society. The Machi is a witchlike figure associated with silence and ritual (Brunet 1962, 258). When the young girl enters the Machi's house, the Machi orders her to sketch the man who abandoned her, and she does so with astounding accuracy because she is a painter (260).

This nonverbal act is followed by another silent ritual in which the Machi sews shut the mouth of a frog and asks the girl to think of the man who abandoned her. Eventually the frog dies, and the Machi tells the girl that she is now avenged. We learn that the Machi's daughter committed suicide because she was abandoned by a man. The next day the girl reads in the newspaper about her lover's death from a sudden heart attack, and she goes mad. At the story's end, she is described as a "poor crazy woman" (263)[28] who hums a monotonous song, croaks along with the frogs, and never speaks.

Silent ritual becomes another "language" through which feminist rebellion against patriarchal dominance in society is manifested. This rebellion is clearly seen in the figure of the Machi, who accepts that she will be condemned to hell for exercising black magic, but considers it well worth it in order to avenge the mistreatment of young, innocent women such as her daughter and the story's protagonist. The rebellion of the nameless protagonist, however, is not as clear as the Machi's, since her participation in the rituals is only halfhearted, and she subsequently goes insane upon learning of her lover's death. Though little is known of the man killed by the Machi's magic, we are told that his portrait in the newspaper showed him "with a sensual and hard mouth and a chin squared out of willfulness" (Brunet 1962, 263).[29] In these few words, Brunet manages to convey a negative image of the man as someone who mistreated the young girl. The Machi's rites are a silent or nonverbal "writing" that can be overread as containing a message of feminist rebellion against such patriarchal abuse.

Two of the three stories that specifically concentrate on a feminist poetics—"Misia Marianita" and "La Machi de Hualqui"—deal with single women rather than married ones. Pratt calls such pieces "odd-women fiction," because they focus on women who do not fulfill traditional female roles within the nuclear family (Pratt 1981, 123). In other words, single women intrinsically rebel against societal rules by not conforming to the expected norm of marriage. Consequently, the plot structure of these narratives lacks the vacillation between complicity and rejection of patriarchal norms observed in the marriage plot and associated with a truly paradoxical silence (understood as passive silence versus subversive silence). Instead, these works focus on women's attempts to find a space of personal development and satisfaction for themselves (127).

Although Brunet's work taken as a whole swings back and forth between an oppressive silence and a subversive one that makes it paradoxical, those pieces that center on the single women tend to concentrate specifically on either the expressive (or nonexpressive) dimension of silence. Expressive silence is akin to subversive silence, because they share a positive/active connotation, whereas the nonexpressive dimension of silence relates to oppressive silence, because they share the negative/passive view of the term. The plot structure of these narratives gives rise to expressive silence, because the single woman by nature is solitary (both because she has no husband and because she is often shunned by society) and hence frequently finds herself alone and thus relegated to expression through silent discourses or actions.

"Misia Marianita" fits the stereotype of the "old maid," typical of the single woman plot, yet the protagonist also manages to achieve a delayed fulfillment at the end of her life, in the form of her observation/analysis of the rooftops of her town. The story plot differs from the standard single-woman plot development, because it does not present the protagonist's shunning by society. The text develops the expressive role of silence through Misia Marianita's use of the town architecture as a metaphor for reading women's texts. Nonverbal elements (the town buildings) are converted into expressive tools (a symbol for feminist reading strategies) that Marianita passes on to the young girl who accompanies her on the hill.

We have already observed how the magical rites of the Machi in "La Machi de Hualqui" were used to communicate a subversive revenge. At the same time that silence is combative in this story, it also serves as an expressive strategy at the tale's end, when the spurned female protagonist goes mad precisely because of the death of her former lover achieved through the Machi's magical rites. The fact that the protagonist becomes mute and makes nothing more than occasional croaking sounds suggests to the reader her descent into insanity, and also effectively expresses her remorse and inner conflict. In addition, "La Machi de Hualqui" plays with the archetype of the single woman associated with witchcraft. Normally, witchcraft is an unfounded accusation leveled at single women who dare to enjoy their unwed status (Pratt 1981, 122–23), whereas in this tale, actual witchcraft is employed as a silent form of revenge that backfires on the protagonist and leads to her total alienation. Brunet attempts to invert an element of patriarchal ideology (the witchcraft association) by using it as an instrument of feminist revenge, yet only partially achieves a reversion of the concept, since witchcraft ultimately leads to female punishment in the form of insanity.

"Raíz del sueño," studied under the rubric of oppressive silence, is the counterpoint to the two aforementioned narratives that employ silence as a form of expression, because here silence is developed strictly as an inexpressive element. In this story, the unmarried protagonist finds herself in a constant state of anxiety because of the nightmares she always suffers. These nightmares revolve around her lack of personal fulfillment as a single, friendless woman. As in other narratives of this type, her state of singleness, which derives from her mother's restrictive authority, is punished both through Elena's silence and the nightly torture of her nightmares. The focus on expressive or inexpressive silence in all these tales organically springs from the protagonists' solitary status.

Brunet and the Women's Movement

The majority of the stories analyzed here were written by Brunet in the 1930s and 1940s, and consequently their paradoxical silence reflects the ambiguous status of women in that era. In *Latin American Women and the Search for Social Justice*, Francesca Miller informs us that in the early twentieth century

> [t]he development of a feminist critique of the traditional social order was most vocal in the Southern Cone nations of Uruguay, Argentina, and Chile, where the combination of relatively advanced public education systems open to both the sexes and the influx of European im-

migrants seeking better lives combined to produce a new class of educated, articulate women whose reformist ideals intersected with those of their male counterparts on issues of health care, social welfare, and general political reform, but diverged on issues of equal female rights in marriage, to jobs, to higher education and political power. (F. Miller 1991, 68)

According to Lisa Baldez, who focuses on Chilean feminism in *Why Women Protest*, the women's movement, centered on the suffrage issue, emerged in Chile during the 1930s as party politics began to divide along issues of class rather than religion. The shift in focus from religious to class issues led to greater female mobilization and a general leftward movement of the electorate through the formation of the Popular Front (uniting the Socialist, Communist, and Radical parties). In turn, this political shift led to the granting of more importance to women's issues in the political arena. In 1935, the group called Movement of the Emancipation of Chilean Women (MEMCH) was formed; it "joined middle-class and working-class women in a broad, cross-partisan coalition" (Baldez 2002, 24). Brunet was a member of MEMCH and was frequently vocal about her political stances, including her support of women's suffrage and her stand against fascism during the Spanish Civil War (Oyarzún 2000, 253–54). The contradiction between the emerging voice of women for health care and other social reforms supported by male counterparts and the patriarchal lack of support for equal rights in other arenas, such as education and especially the family, is suggested by Brunet's paradoxical employment of silence in her stories. As we have seen, many of these stories focus on the unequal rights of married women ("Aguas abajo," "El espejo," "Soledad de la sangre," "Piedra callada"), whereas others concern themselves with the general lack of authority granted to women, both married and single ("Gabriela," "Raíz del sueño," "La nariz"). Brunet's *criollista* stories elucidate the plight of peasant women, whereas stories like "Ruth Werner," "El espejo," "Gabriela," and "La nariz" analyze the role of upper-class women. Brunet's focus on women's inferior social position can be understood in light of the status of the women's movement in Chile in the era in which she wrote. Changes in the legal code were slow to evolve, and women did not receive the vote in Chile until 1949. Thus, it is impossible not to read Brunet's texts within the context of the evolution of the Chilean feminist movement. Indeed, her employment of paradoxical silence reflects the dichotomy between women's inferior status and their emerging political voice in the 1930s and 1940s.

Overreading the Novel *María Nadie*

María Nadie (1957), Brunet's second-to-last novel, presents the life of María López, a supposedly ordinary woman, so average she is referred to as María Nobody. María López is actually a very independent woman for the era in which she lives. She works as a telephone operator in a small town to which she has recently moved. We later learn that this relocation was motivated by earlier events in her life. She fell in love with a rich and insensitive man, Gabriel, who entered into a carefree sexual affair with María, visiting her whenever he pleased and totally controlling the relationship. Finally, when María became pregnant, he wanted her to get an abortion. She refused, but hemorrhaged after they had violent sex. When María recuperated from the miscarriage, she finally terminated her relationship with Gabriel.

María Nadie is a novel whose gendered subjectivity is highlighted if we read it through Miller's process of overreading. The political power structures of gender are revealed through María's affair with Gabriel, which reflects the unequal status granted women in relationships in the past (the novel takes place in the 1950s). María had to sit and wait passively for Gabriel to decide to see her, and the only way in which she could exercise any control in the relationship was to finally end it. Moreover, her sexual involvement with Gabriel exposes a double standard implicitly criticized in the narrative. After their first sexual encounter, Gabriel expresses surprise at María's virginity, and then almost disgust at her need to wash up after their encounter (Brunet 1997, 124). Although the text implies that casual relationships of this nature are frequent for Gabriel (he has numerous keys on his key chain), he suggests that María should be punished for her behavior, as if their sexual contact were somehow her fault. He tells her that she is "sick in the head," that she deceived him, and that she "deserves a good beating" (124).[30] Thus, the love story between Gabriel and María contains traces of gender politics and a sexual double standard that can be deconstructed through overreading the text from a feminist perspective.

When María moves to a new town to distance herself from Gabriel, she is suspiciously viewed by her neighbors as a strange, unfriendly, and problematic individual because she is a single, independent, quiet woman. Their hostile reception of María eventually leads to her decision to move to yet another town at the end of the novel.

María's role as social rebel is expressed through her silence and other nonverbal signifiers. For example, the townspeople criticize

María for being "indecent" (54) because she chooses to wear pants instead of skirts and hence does not dress like the other women of the town. In the 1950s, pants were still a gendered symbol of masculinity.

María's silent rebellion began in her unhappy childhood. Her mother was calculating and her father was weak. The family frequently changed residences owing to the father's position as a public employee. María sought refuge from her family in her silence. In each new house she "created her environment: a corner for her bed, her clothes, her books. A corner, the most propitious for silence, to read and dream" (107–8).[31]

This same silence characterizes María in adulthood. We see this in the novel's narrative situation, in which María recounts her past to the townspeople through a nonverbalized dialogue with herself directed at her neighbors. Here she indicates her propensity to speak to people purely in her imagination. She reflects, "After these monologues directed at this or that person, I am convinced that I have said it and my surprise is to come across the reality of my silence" (129).[32]

María's silence represents an attempt at communication with the townspeople that ultimately fails. It can be interpreted positively, as having expressive value, but also negatively, because the townspeople never really hear her words or understand her. Despite this ambiguity, in other contexts within the novel *María Nadie* silence is positively connoted as a sign of María's strength, rebellion, and superior character.

Since María, by her own admission, is unable to communicate her feelings through patriarchal language, she turns to other forms of expression in the novel. In addition to her silent narration of her past, which serves to inform the reader of important events (but not her supposed interlocutors, the townspeople), María turns to ritual. She enters into a game of make-believe with two little boys, Cacho and Concho, who accept her presence without questions and pretend she is a princess. Their game is a silent, secret ritual about which no one else is to be told:

> [I]mmediately they added her to the game. . . .
> One must not tell it to anyone. What happens in the cove is the secret of three. Now we are three for a secret. Three: Three. Three—and they solemnly extended their hands sealing the pact over and over again. . . .
> Cacho and Conejo were my adorable companions in a storylike precinct. They accepted me as if I came out of a magician's hat, without a past, without a future and for that reason they were my parcel of happiness (65–66, 130).[33]

This secret game is a vehicle of self-expression for María, who is allowed to be herself and is unconditionally accepted by the boys, in contrast to the way in which her presence is constantly questioned by society.

Despite María's lack of acceptance and comprehension by her fellow townspeople, the novel ends on a positive note, stressing María's freedom (she decides to start over again in a new town) and the possibility of regaining her identity: "I will leave. María Nobody will also have an open door before her. I will be María López again. A door open before me. It might be toward a radiant life. It might be toward *inexpressible* sorrows. But it will be life" (Brunet 1962, 138, my emphasis).[34] Once again, Brunet emphasizes the silent, incommunicable aspect of María's life through her use of the word "inexpressible" in these final lines of the novel (Brunet 1997, 138).

Brunet also suggests an implicit symbolic analogy between the trapped bird that is freed by Cacho, and María, who pursues her freedom at the novel's conclusion. At the beginning of the text, Cacho captures a mockingbird as a gift for María. When Cacho and Conejo discover that María has given the violets they bestowed upon her to Cacho's father, Reinaldo, Cacho angrily frees the imprisoned bird (70). The silent, symbolic connection between María and the bird is underscored by the fact that the townspeople call María "evil bird" when they discover her relationship with the two boys and impute ill intentions to it (101). On the novel's final page, María herself states, "I will leave at the hour in which an evil bird should return to its nest" (138).[35] The parallel freedom attained by the bird and María as representative of women in general can also be seen as a feminist message that the reader must over-read in the text.

Compared to Brunet's stories of the 1930s and 1940s, *María Nadie* reflects a different and less vocal moment in the women's movement. Many scholars who have studied the feminist movement in Latin America, such as Patricia Chuchryk, indicate that the movement withdrew from the political front in Chile (as well as other countries) after the attainment of women's suffrage in 1949 (Chuchryk 1994, 66). Julieta Kirkwood identifies five principal phases of the women's movement: (1) 1900–1930, the initial rise in women's mobilization; (2) 1930–50, the era of the suffrage movement and incorporation of women into political life; (3) 1964–70, women's increased participation in organizational and working environments; (4) 1970–73, period of subordination of the women's rights movement to national political consolidation; and (5) 1973–89, the era of the resurgence of the feminist movement linked to the fight for democracy (Kirkwood 1986, 40–41; Oyarzún 2000, 251). Marjorie Agosín identifies three major feminist phases: the formative stage (which coincided with the initiation of the movement and the fight for women's suffrage), a period of isolated struggles (which corresponded to the 1950s and early 1960s, the period omitted from Kirkwood's schema because it represents a lull in feminist activity between first-wave and second-wave feminism), and the stage of coordinated action (which refers to the feminist/political oppositions of the 1970s and 1980s) (Agosín 1987, 21). The use of silence in *María Nadie*, published in 1957, reflects the 1950–64 stage of the temporary lull in the Chilean women's movement. Although *María Nadie* shares a paradoxical use of silence with Brunet's other stories, as well as a concern for women's issues (i.e., single motherhood versus abortion; the presentation of an independent, self-supporting single woman with opportunities within the workforce), the character of María López and the nature of her silence lack the combative dimension developed by the author in her earlier works. There is no longer an oppressive silence versus a combative one, but rather a fluctuation between an inexpressive silence and expressive silence. María's silent, playful ritual with Concho and Cacho or her silent dialogue with the townspeople does not convey the same force as the symbolic fight over the phonograph in "Soledad de la sangre," Eufrasia's murder of Bernabé using the "silent stone" in "Piedra Callada," or the magical rituals that induce death of the abusive males in "La Machi de Hualqui."

María Nadie, like the stories "Raíz del sueño," "Misia Marianita," and "La Machi de Hualqui," has a single-woman plot, although it is perhaps more standard in its presentation of the shunning of the single woman in society. María's attempts to employ silence as a form of communication produce variable results. As we already observed, María was largely unsuccessful in the instances in which she attempted to speak to the townspeople through an unvoiced monologue in which she explained her previous background and current motivations. However, her silent rituals, such as her enactment of a princesslike role among the trees and flowers, playing with Cacho and Concho, manage to express her sweetness and kindness, at least to the little boys, and afford her a self-expressive outlet. This latter example can be thought of as an exemplification of the "green-world archetype" (Pratt 1981, 16–17) in which women manifest an extraordinary love of nature. These and other silent discourses are the forms of communication available to the single woman who is scorned by society for being different.

In sum, Brunet's thematic use of silence as both a sign of oppression and a subversive weapon leads to the construction of a paradoxical silence that varies in its connotations depending upon whether the work focuses on the single woman or married woman in its plot. Her presentation of a potentially subversive silence, as well as her inscription of the process of feminist production through a nonverbal "writing," make her a precursor to silence in several more contemporary twentieth-century writers.

3
Paradoxical Silence, Part II: Silence/Narrative Voice in the Works of María Luisa Bombal

MARÍA LUISA BOMBAL WAS BORN IN VIÑA DEL MAR, CHILE, TO A wealthy family. When her father died in 1920, the family moved to Paris, where Bombal was educated. She returned to Chile in 1931. In 1933 she moved to Buenos Aires, where she married the Argentine painter Jorge Larco. In Argentina, Bombal established friendships with important literary figures, such as Neruda, Borges, Guillermo de la Torre, and Pedro Henríquez Ureña, just to name a few. These intellectuals published in the vanguard journal *Sur* [South] under the direction of Victoria Ocampo (Guerra-Cunningham 1980, 19). Both Bombal's first novel, *La última niebla* [The Final Mist] (1935),[1] and her second, *La amortajada* [*The Shrouded Woman*] (1938), initially appeared in *Sur* and reflect its influence. Ocampo viewed the life of women as one of impossible self-realization due to the socioeconomic reality of that time and encouraged women to express their problems (Guerra-Cunningham 1980, 21–22). This literary environment clearly shaped Bombal's opinions on the plight of women in society as expressed in her fiction. Bombal's most famous short stories are "El árbol" [The Tree], "Trenzas" [Braids], "Lo secreto" [The Secret Thing], "Las islas nuevas" [The New Islands], and "La historia de María Griselda" [The Story of María Griselda]. Following her husband's death, she moved to New York. She eventually remarried and had a daughter with Count Raphael de Saint-Phalle. After the death of her second husband in 1970, Bombal returned to Chile, where she died in 1980 (Smith 1997, 132).[2] Bombal is known as one of the first Latin American women writers to depict female eroticism in her prose, and her work marks the transition from a realistic regionalism to the poetic representation of reality.

The role of silence in Bombal's works has been the subject of some controversy among contemporary critics of Latin American literature. We can divide these critics into two camps: those who feel that Bombal treats silence in a traditional manner, as a sign of female oppression (alienation and escapism),[3] and those who assert that Bombal's use of silence is combative vis-à-vis the patriarchal order.[4] The reason for this debate clearly stems from the fact that Bombal, just like Brunet, employs a paradoxical silence in her texts. Bombal's incorporation of thematic, stylistic, and narrative silences in her novels *La última niebla*, and *The Shrouded Woman*, and in her short story "El árbol" simultaneously communicates a passive intent and a subversive intent to the reader.

IMPLICIT VERSUS EXPLICIT NARRATIVE AUTHORITY

Bombal's use of silence can be framed within the context of the feminist discussion of narrative authority by Susan Lanser in her book *Fictions of Authority: Women Writers and Narrative Voice* (1992). Lanser suggests important unexplored relationships between feminism and narratology, asserting that narrative technique is ideological in nature (Lanser 1992, 5). As we discussed in the first chapter, Lanser discusses the overt authoriality, or extratextual commentary (reflections, judgments, and generalizations about the world "beyond" the fiction), of three narrative voices (authorial, personal, and communal) (16–17). According to Lanser, such overt commentary is an exercise of power or authority on the narrator's part, although she points out that "non-hegemonic writers and narrators may need to strike a delicate balance in accommodating and subverting dominant rhetorical practices" (6). In other words, often texts, under the constraints of social and literary conventions, must reproduce the same structures they oppose. Despite Lanser's omission of such forms as interior monologue because they are not directly capable of narrative self-reference, interior monologue is pertinent to a discussion of textual power or authority.

Consequently, a simultaneous analysis of silent or implicit narrative commentary as well as explicit narrative commentary in Bombal's novelistic narrative techniques proves important. The implicit author of *La última niebla* and *The Shrouded Woman* succeeds in making statements about the female condition through a variety of silent or implicit narrative strategies, notably blank spaces, interior monologues, and free indirect discourse (which, following Lanser, I view as a muting technique that can nonetheless exert authority, as analyzed below with regard to *The Shrouded Woman*). Hence, we can think of Bombal's choice of interior monologue as a silent subversive strategy used to implicitly denounce the relegation of women to nonauthoritative, private discourses.[5] Bombal's reliance on interior monologue is subversive in three ways: first, because it represents a radical departure from the authorial narratives of *criollismo* (naturalism and positivism) that are focused outward toward the relationship between man and nature (environment); second, because the excessive (almost exclusive) use of interior monologue replicates and thus implicitly denounces the lack of public voice for women in the era in which she wrote; and third, because interior monologue is the authentic vehicle of self-expression and meaningful existence that combats the protagonist's loveless marriage and helps her to survive.

Silence in *La última niebla*

Bombal's short novel *La última niebla*, published in 1935, broke with the *criollista* tradition then in vogue, by focusing on the psychological portrayal of its unnamed protagonist through a narration almost exclusively composed of interior monologues. The novel's narrator/protagonist marries her cousin Daniel, who is still in love with his deceased first wife. One night, when the couple is visiting the city, the protagonist is unable to sleep and goes for a walk. She meets a stranger and they make love. For years after the encounter, she dreams of her lover, and these fantasies sustain her through her loveless marriage. However, at the end of the novel, she comes to believe that her encounter was simply a fantasy. *La última niebla* incorporates silence through a variety of strategies that include silence as theme, blank spaces, silent ritual, and implicit symbolic constructions. These four silences are used to construct a fifth silence in the novel: the silent, possibly fantastic adventures of the narrator expressed through interior monologues are textually counterpoised to "reality" embodied in the explicit voice of the narrator's husband, Daniel, to create a silent, subversive, dialogic battle between female desires and patriarchal tradition. The novel opposes textual indices suggesting the encounter was real to those suggesting it was imagined. The ones suggesting it was imagined are associated with Daniel's negative, destructive comments designed to eliminate any trace of his wife's autonomy and self-realization. Thus, an implicit dialogue is constructed on the topic of feminine roles in which the patriarchal view of women can be questioned. This dialogue serves as a cue that suggests a possible reading of the text from a feminist perspective. Such a reading is one of many potential interpretations of the text.

Thematic Silence

Let us begin by examining the use of silence as explicit theme in *La última niebla*. During the first twenty pages of the novel, prior to the protagonist's encounter with the stranger, innumerable passages speak of the silent atmosphere enveloping her. These passages portray silence negatively as a site of repression and lack of communication. For example, the protagonist feels as though the omnipresent silence is strangling her: "Silence, a great silence, a silence of years, of centuries, a terrifying silence that begins to grow in the room and within my head" . . . (Bombal 1988, 12, my translation).[6]

Textual Voice

Thematic silence is immediately followed by a second silence, what Stephen Ross calls "textual voice" (anything in the printed disposition of a text that signifies without semantic content), in the form of blank spaces (Ross 1979, 306–10). According to María Luisa Bastos, the strategic placement of blank spaces in the novel suggests implied meanings or connections between certain novelistic passages. For example, the novel's initial narration of the protagonist's marriage to Daniel is immediately followed by a blank space or narrative silence, which in turn is followed by the narration of the death of a young girl. Bastos asserts that the juxtaposition of the initial scene in which Daniel rejects the protagonist with the second scene of the dead girl suggests that an unloved woman is equivalent to a dead one. Bastos thus affirms the communicative importance of narrative silence within the text (Bastos 1985, 558). In this particular case, the blank space aids in the articulation of a traditional, imposed, oppressive silence that envelops the lives of women.

There are many as yet unexamined instances of a communicative narrative silence through the blank space in *La última niebla*. Another example can be found after the section about the narrator's tenth wedding anniversary. The passage ends with her observation: "Daniel's unpleasant glance crosses mine" (25).[7] After a blank space, the narrator affirms: "Today I have seen my lover" (Bombal 1988, 25).[8] It is not a coincidence that the protagonist insists upon the physical presence of her lover right after her husband's aloof treatment on their anniversary. The blank space implies both the connection between the narrator's need to evoke her lover and the disagreeable reality of her marriage, as well as the contrast between her spouse's cool behavior and the passionate relationship with the stranger. It may also lend support to the interpretation of her lover as a fantasy, since he "magically" appears when she is faced with an unpleasant marital event.

Similarly, the narrator juxtaposes her sudden sexual reencounter with Daniel to the gradual fading of her lover's image (29). In between these two episodes, a blank space underscores the ephemeral and possibly imaginary nature of her encounter with her lover by implying that the physical strengthening of her relationship with Daniel weakens her memory of her lover.

The blank space between the section in which the narrator attempts to minimize the importance of her sexual relationship with Daniel (she insists upon the fact that she has not betrayed her lover) and that in which all the autumn leaves of the garden are burned suggests a symbolic connection between the leaves and the narrator's dreams of the stranger (31). Earlier in the text, the protagonist manifests her nostalgia for abandoned gardens and desire that Daniel not have the fallen leaves swept away. The nostalgia for the autumn leaves parallels the protagonist's nostalgia for her lover, especially since their encounter allegedly took place in a house with just such an abandoned garden (Bombal 1988, 19). The blank space that separates the rekindling of a sexual relationship with Daniel from the destruction of the leaves suggests that Daniel will be responsible for annihilating the reality and combative value of her lover. Indeed, just as Daniel orders the leaves swept away or burned, he destroys the narrator's subversive use of silent fantasy by suggesting the unreality of her lover in this very section of the novel.

If we examine these three narrative instances sequentially as a unit, we can observe how the blank spaces function to signal a progression within the plot: as the narrator's physical relationship with her husband becomes stronger and acquires a certain reality, her memory of her supposed lover gradually decreases to the point of total destruction. The blank spaces intercalated throughout the text reinforce the articulation of this narrative development.

3 / PARADOXICAL SILENCE, PART II

Subversive Silence through Ritual and Dreams

A third form of silence can be found in Bombal's use of silent ritual as a vehicle of female expression. Later on, we shall see how many contemporary female writers, notably Ferré and Esquivel, use ritual as a more authentic form of expression for woman than language. Marjorie Agosín examines *La última niebla* as an enactment of a female version of the rites of passage of primitive societies. Using the theory of Joseph Campbell, Agosín asserts that Bombal's protagonist undergoes the three basic stages of the hero's voyage: departure (her trip to the city in search of a purposeful existence), initiation (her sexual encounter with her lover through which she completes her search and validates her existence), and return (to the countryside). Other traditional rites include the heroine's period of separation from the world during her adventure in the mist and her ceremonial bathing in the pond, which mimics the rite of baptism or purification (Agosín 1983, 30–41). For us, the importance of the heroine's participation in ritual is its value as a nonverbal form of communication. The protagonist's search for her own authentic feminine identity is achieved through silent ritual, rather than through use of patriarchal language. This equation between ritual and both self-expression and self-awareness leads us to the second, positive dimension of silence in the novel.

As the novel evolves, silence is slowly converted into a combative weapon against patriarchy. The transformation of thematic silence occurs when the narrator/protagonist has her initial encounter with the stranger. Whether dream or reality, the protagonist uses this rendezvous, narrated through interior monologues, to express her desires and rejection of her role as dutiful wife in an unhappy marriage. She subsumes silence as a language of self-expression and converts it into a positive force: the fantasies and daydreams constructed around her lover contest her dull and passive reality with her husband. The description of this initial encounter (Bombal 1988, 18–21) is crucial to the novel's ultimate comprehension, because it contains all the seeds for the debate concerning the reality of the narrator/protagonist's relationship with a stranger. The "supernatural" aspect of the lover's face described by the narrator/protagonist, the incredible nature of the meeting, and the fact that at the end of this segment the protagonist finds herself in bed next to her husband, Daniel (suggesting that the sexual encounter took place between her and her husband, not a stranger), have all been cited as facts that serve as clues that the encounter is merely a fantasy.

The site of the sexual encounter also has symbolic value that points toward its imaginary nature: because the stranger's house is located on a narrow, sloping street with a gated, abandoned garden. The stranger is described as having difficulty untying the rusty chain that encloses the home and the yard. According to Cirlot, precincts or enclosed spaces, such as the town square where the protagonist meets her lover and the house with the gated garden where they make love, represent the notion of inner life of thoughts and self-protection, since they derive from tactical formations used in the military and elsewhere against adversaries (Cirlot 1971, 263).

A final element that points to the fictitious nature of the encounter is found at the novel's conclusion. After the protagonist reveals the meeting to Daniel and he insists it was all a dream, she comes across the house in the city that she believes to be her lover's, only to learn that the man who owned the house was blind and died fifteen years ago.

All of the above elements initially suggest that the relationship only exists in the protagonist's imagination. If we return to the original description of the entrance into her lover's house, however, the fact that she and her lover did not "bump into any furniture" and that her lover guided her every step without having to turn the lights on suggests the familiarity of a blind person with every inch of space in his own home, precisely so that he can successfully navigate that space without help. It is also possible that the man became blind after the encounter. Moreover, the episode was described with specific details, such as the lover's eye color, his odor, and his wearing of a medallion (Bombal 1988, 21). The novel provides at least two other clues suggesting the possibility that the relationship is reality-based: the first is the disappearance of the narrator's straw hat, which she claims to have worn that night. The hat is proof to the narrator that her now fading memory was of something real and that she left the hat in her lover's house (24). The other shred of reality is associated with the hired hand, Andrés, who appears to confirm the protagonist's perceptions on several occasions. For example, when she is bathing in the pond, Andrés is witness to the arrival of a carriage whose passenger the protagonist believes to be her lover (Bombal 1988, 28). In another instance, the protagonist's belief that she has heard her lover's footsteps by her window is confirmed by that fact that Andrés tells her that one day he saw a carriage leave the grounds at full speed (28).

The relationship of the varied details is complicated and at times contradictory. Very few temporal markers are provided, although these would be crucial in determining the validity of the protagonist's story. For example, as we saw earlier, we are told that the protagonist celebrates her tenth wedding anniversary. This passage is followed by a blank space in which an incalculable time period has passed, and then the protagonist informs us that she has seen her lover once again (25). At the end of the novel, we are told that if the blind man were her lover, he has been dead for fifteen years. Does this mean that the encounter had to have been imaginary, because this man was already dead? Or does it mean that more than fifteen years have passed since this second encounter? Or perhaps the protagonist is mistaken and the man in the carriage is not her lover at all? The novel never explicitly resolves the matter.

The important point to be made here is that throughout the text, the protagonist takes the initially negative silence surrounding her and constructs a positive world in which to survive, whether it is a memory of erotic fulfillment or a dream of the same. This world is constructed through unspoken interior monologues that ostensibly lack narrative authority, since there is no explicit narrator commentary. Nonetheless, such interior monologues prove the salvation of the protagonist, because they provide a purpose for her life and assert her identity. As she says in one instance: "My only desire is to be alone to be able to dream, dream freely" (23).[9] This faded memory or tenuous dream survives and sustains the protagonist for years, until one night she makes the mistake of discussing it with her husband. He informs her that she never went out at night, that she must have imagined it because they had been drinking and slept heavily, and that had she really encountered a stranger, she would have remembered his voice, which she is incapable of doing: "He didn't speak to you? You see, he was a phantom . . . This doubt that my husband has infiltrated in me; this so great and absurd doubt!" (31–32).[10]

Thus, with a few cutting words, Daniel manages to destroy the protagonist's faith in her silent encounter, which symbolizes her autonomy and desirability. Whether or not Daniel is right is immaterial; the point is that the verbalization of the protagonist's silent, private world leads to its destruction. Up until this point, silence and interior monologue were effective tools for combating a bleak patriarchal reality. However, from this point on in the narrative, the protagonist doubts the reality of her lover and the power of her own silence, and thus she loses the purpose of her existence to the authority granted to patriarchal discourse.[11] Hence, Bombal's use of interior monologue is a means through which the narrator/protagonist can assert her own authority, and not merely a passive strategy.

This vacillation between silence as alienation and silence as a combative response to patriarchy constructs a paradoxical silence that nonetheless may serve as a cue of feminist perception for the reader. Whether the silence is oppressive or combative, Bombal situates the reader within the specifically female viewpoint and experience of her protagonist in *La última niebla*. Consequently, as Mills has shown, the reader perceives that he or she is being placed within a perspective that deviates from agreement with the validity of traditional gender roles. One has to admit that in the era in which Bombal wrote, even an imaginary lover, as tenuous as it may seem, was a form of rebellion against the role of dutiful wife and mother ascribed to women by patriarchal society.

Silence/Narrative Authority in *The Shrouded Woman*

María Luisa Bombal's second novel, *The Shrouded Woman* (1938), is also largely predicated on silent structures and techniques. *The Shrouded Woman* fundamentally employs the same types of silences as *La última niebla*: silence as theme, and blank spaces and silent ritual as forms of subversion and communication. In addition, *The Shrouded Woman* employs techniques of silence or indirection through its narrative situation. In contrast to *La última niebla*, which was narrated exclusively in the first person (and largely through interior monologues), *The Shrouded Woman* employs a third-person omniscient narrator, in addition to the interior monologues of the dead protagonist. This third-person narrator closely identifies with the protagonist through the technique of free indirect style, which, as we shall see, has important implications concerning the novel's creation of narrative authority.

Thematic Silence

Just as in *La última niebla*, silence evolves in the novel from a space of oppression and negativity to a space of peace and reflection from which the protagonist, in death, can finally express herself. The simultaneous presence of oppressive and combative silence (and silences that are at once both) constructs the same paradoxical silence we observed in Bombal's previous novel. The protagonist of *The Shrouded Woman*, Ana María, has led an unhappy life. Her first love, Ricardo, abandons her without explanation, and she subsequently loses their child in a miscarriage. When she cannot have Ricardo, she agrees to marry Antonio, all the while desiring her first love. Antonio starts out as a good husband, and they share a passionate relationship. However, Ana María cannot come to terms with her life (the loss of Ricardo) and asks Antonio to let her return to her father's home. This separation effects a radical change in both characters. Ana María discovers that she now desires and loves Antonio, but during their separation Antonio's feelings for Ana María have cooled. Although Antonio takes her back, they never recapture their initial passion. Antonio becomes a womanizer, and Ana María's inability to recover his love makes her unhappy throughout her entire life. She later sustains a scornful relationship with another man, Fernando, whose love for Ana María only inspires in her a deep disdain.

At the outset of the novel, the silence Ana María experiences in her life is seen in a negative light. When she marries Antonio, we are told that the silence of the night "seemed to presage catastrophe to her" (Bombal 1988, 136).[12] Later on, silence proves an ineffectual means of regaining Antonio's love: "In vain she had used up all the unconscious methods of passion to reconquer Antonio; tenderness, violence, reproaches, *mutism*, amorous assault" (142–43, my emphasis).[13] However, as the novel progresses, silence begins to take on a positive, powerful cast. When her love for Antonio turns to hate, it is described as "a *silent* hate that instead of consuming her, fortified her" (145).[14] The strengthening power of silence culminates in death, when Ana María's silence provides her with a space of peace and reflection (97).

While Ana María communicates her feelings after death through silent interior monologues similar to those in *La última niebla*, in life the protagonist replaces words with another form of nonverbal communication: knitting/weaving ("tejer"):

> [H]e used to sink himself into the contemplation of that silent girl who knitted while stretched out on a long straw rocking chair.... If only you had pulled on the thread of my wool, if you had undone my fabric, mesh by mesh ... entangled in each one was a temptuous thought and a name I will not forget. (133, my emphasis)[15]

Ana María's knitting is equated with thought and communication. It contains a message that her husband, Antonio, is never able to interpret (her love for Ricardo).

Mayela A. Vallejos-Ramírez studies the subversive and communicative role of weaving and knitting in Latin American fiction. Vallejos-Ramírez, citing the ideas of Ana Rueda, indicates that women have channeled their expertise in the domestic arts into the creation of alternative texts expressive of their own voice (Vallejos-Ramírez 1997, 2–4). These ideas coincide with Miller's concept of overreading, or examining how certain supposedly prefeminist texts embed a feminist discourse through images of weaving and other similar metaphors for writing. Ana María's true feelings are expressed through her knitting, which communicates her failure to passively accept her socially dictated marriage to Antonio. This inversion of a sign traditionally associated with female domesticity serves as a cue that demonstrates how the text may be read from a feminist perspective.

Silence and Narrative Technique

In death, Ana María expresses her thoughts and feelings to the other characters through interior monologues, although her words are never actually voiced or heard. Consequently, her communication is inherently silent. Nonetheless, this silent discourse allows Ana María to finally comprehend her life and to come to terms with it. The novel's narrative situation is somewhat complex. In addition to the protagonist's interior monologues, the narration primarily consists of a third-person, anonymous narrator, who appears to be independent from Ana María, but often fuses with the character. This technique, known as free indirect discourse, has important implications for the question of narrative authority. According to Lanser, free indirect discourse blurs narrative responsibility, creating a complicity between narrator and character, without deauthorizing the former (Lanser 1992, 74). In other words, it constructs an ambiguous narrative voice, a cross between what Lanser calls "authorial narrative voice" and "personal narrative voice" (terms that refer to the overt authoriality of the third-person narrator and the narrator/protagonist, respectively) (Lanser 1992, 77).[16]

On a continuum, we may think of free indirect style as a "muting" technique that tones down, but does not eliminate, the authoritative value of the narrator's voice in the novel. Thus, like irony, which states things indirectly, we can view free indirect discourse as a technique of silence or indirection that acts implicitly and sometimes subversively within the narrative.

A good example of this fusion between narrator and character is found in the segment that narrates the presence of Ana María's son Alberto during her wake. The third-person narrator clearly adopts the character's perspective, and the words of the discourse oscillate between granting narrative responsibility to the narrator and granting it to the protagonist. In the opening lines, the narrator himself or herself suggests this very identification:

> Now María Griselda's husband alone remains near her.
> How is it possible that she too calls her son: María Griselda's husband!
> Why? Because he is jealously watchful of his beautiful wife! Because he keeps her isolated and far away at the southern estate! . . .
> Suddenly those lowered eyelids begin to look at her fixedly, with the unfathomable constancy with which the eyes of a demented man look.
> Oh, open your eyes, Alberto! . . .
> Now he presses María Griselda's picture to the flame of one of the candles and dedicates himself to burning it. . . .
> Doesn't she perhaps give up a little bit of her beauty in each portrait?
> Yes, but now the fire stripped the last one. There remains only one María Griselda; the one he maintains sequestered in a far away southern estate.
> Oh, Alberto, my poor son! (Bombal 1988, 117–18)[17]

Although the narrator states in third-person narration that "María Griselda's husband" is near "her" (Ana María) at the wake, the narrator then questions how the protagonist can call her own son "María Griselda's husband," thus suggesting that the perspective of the initial reference should not be attributed to the narrator at all, but rather to the character. The rest of the segment is narrated in the third person, but with exclamations that clearly reflect Ana María's feelings ("Oh open your eyes Alberto!"). Finally, the section ends with a switch to clear first-person narration ("my poor son"). It is significant that this oscillation in the narration occurs with regard to the subject Alberto, since Alberto's behavior toward his wife, María Griselda, is a classic example of patriarchal authority superimposed on women. Due to excessive jealousy, Alberto refuses to allow María Griselda to leave the house. This attitude is condemned by the discourse that reveals it; however, we are not sure whether to attribute this condemnation to the narrator or the protagonist. This ambiguity can be thought of as a form of indirect or silent expression, since we cannot effectively attribute the words to a specific party and hence confer "voice" upon a specific entity. Nonetheless, this ambiguous voice potentially acts as a textual cue to the reader to adopt a feminist perspective. Although this narrative passage does not exhibit true "authorial voice" in Lanser's sense (because there is no specific extratextual commentary), the possible association of feminist ideas with the third-person omniscient narrator through free indirect style in some ways also serves to authorize the speaker, because usually greater objectivity and credibility are granted to third-person (versus first-person) narrations, since they are considered more "objective."

This overt oscillation suggests the possibility of a similar technique in other somewhat ambiguous passages. For example, after narrating Ana María's recognition of the fact that Antonio had affairs with other women, the narrator reveals the effects of her relationship with her husband on Ana María:

> Years passed. Years in which she withdrew and became day by day meaner and more limited.
>
> Why, why must the nature of woman be such that a man always has to be the axis of her life?
>
> Men, they succeeded in putting their passion in other things. But the destiny of women is to stir up the pain of love in an ordered house, in front of an unfinished tapestry. (Bombal 1988, 143)[18]

The words that follow those of the first paragraph may be a continuation of the third-person narration or may belong to Ana María herself, representing a personal reflection about gender roles and their effect on her own life. In either case, the comments carry an implicit criticism of societal roles for men and women and exemplify overt authoriality. Men are allowed to have other occupations, but women are relegated to the role of wives. Although the passage refers to "woman's nature" (which some have interpreted as an essentialist commentary on women), the reader can infer that rather than an inborn trait, the fact that man is the "axis of woman's life" has been socially determined, made to be woman's "destiny," and is therefore being implicitly criticized either by the third-person narrator or by the character who questions this precept. Once again, the ambiguity of voices contributes to the "muting" of the voice without eliminating its narrative authority.

Several other passages of the texts convey an implicit criticism of patriarchal authority, although in these cases the narrative voice is clear. For example, in the beginning of the novel, when the third-person narrator describes the presence of Ana María's children at her wake, she states that her sons "seemed not to wish to recognize any right for her to live anymore" (96).[19] It is interesting that the narrator makes this comment with regard to Ana María's sons and not her daughter. This narrative comment once again suggests the tyranny of patriarchal authority in women's lives. Ana María's sons were ashamed of her whims and youthful behavior, and only ascribed to her the role of mother, granting her no rights to an existence independent of her family.

Similarly, when Ana María seeks a divorce from Antonio due to his infidelity, the attorney in whom she confides paternalistically betrays her by calling Antonio to their meeting in an attempt to salvage the marriage. The narrator comments that the lawyer "had betrayed her with his plans, so kindly and awkwardly as her own father would have done!" (144).[20] The attorney discourages Ana María by evoking social norms: "Consider that there are measures that a lady cannot take without lowering herself" (144),[21] he tells her before Antonio's calculated entrance. Thus, Ana María's attempts to establish a different type of life are thwarted in part by a paternalistic authority determined to enforce accepted social conventions. Although the narrator appears to tolerate such a condescending, paternalistic attitude on the attorney's part, the passage serves as a cue that, depending upon the reader's background, might signal a feminist perspective to him or her through an ironically interpreted narrative voice.

In sum, the use of silence in *The Shrouded Woman* once again vacillates between silence as sign of oppression and silence as weapon, and is thus paradoxical. Its fusion of narrative voices achieves an antipatriarchal commentary that may situate certain readers within a feminist perspective.

Silent Expression through Symbolism in "El Árbol"

Bombal's story "El árbol" (1939) is my final example of how paradoxical silence may signal a feminist perspective to the reader. Bombal employs three uses of silence in "El árbol": silence as theme, music as a form of nonverbal expression, and silence through nonverbal symbolism. The story's protagonist, Brígida, was married to a much older man, Luis, whom she subsequently divorced. The story begins with Brígida's reflections during a concert about her marriage and its eventual termination. Brígida's intuitive understanding of the music serves as a vehicle of "communication" for her self-analysis. We are told that Brígida heard the concert music unfold "clearly, narrowly, and judiciously capricious," while she simultaneously recalled episodes from her youth. (45–46).[22] Music, not words, allows Brígida to analyze her past. As we saw in the previous chapter with regard to Brunet's story "Soledad de la sangre," instrumental music, unaccompanied by lyrics (such as the works by Bach, Beethoven, and Chopin that Brígida listens to at the concert), is a nonverbal (albeit vocal) form of expression. It is this nonverbal aspect that makes the music akin to silence as a form of expression. Daniel Cárdenas underscores the importance of the words "clearly, narrowly and judiciously capricious" for describing the music Brígida hears. For Cárdenas, each adjective corresponds to one of the three musical pieces Brígida listens to while recalling different periods of her life—namely, those of Mozart, Beethoven, and Chopin (Cardenas 1980, 56). However, if one closely examines the relationship between Brígida's memories and the music, one sees that these words are rather descriptive of the three stages of development of Brígida's mental processes, only in inverse order. The first segment, in which Brígida listens to Mozart, establishes a connection between the music and Brígida's youth. The music contests her father's label of Brígida as "retarded" and instead suggests that at this stage she was simply "judiciously capricious." We see her whimsical nature in her doll playing and failed music lessons. However, we also see that Brígida was not slow or stupid, but rather capable of appreciating the worthwhile things in life, such as music and love. In the second section, it is Beethoven's music that makes Brígida recall her marriage to Luis (Bombal 1988, 47). This section relates to the "poverty" ("estrecha" means narrow or strict) of Brígida's marital relationship with Luis, in which he was incapable of satisfying her physical and emotional needs (Cárdenas 1980, 56). Finally, when Brígida listens to Chopin, everything becomes "clear" to her about her marriage. "Clear" is not really a reference to Chopin's music, but rather to the clarification of Brígida's perspective on life achieved through the felling of the tree:

> She has remained a prisoner of the webs of her past, she cannot leave her dressing room. Her dressing room invaded by a terrifying white light. . . .
> They had taken her privacy, her secret away from her; she found herself naked in the middle of the street, naked next to an old husband who turned his back on her to sleep. (Bombal 1988, 55)[23]

The second level of silence is thematic. Brígida explicitly uses silence as a weapon against her husband's indifference in the story. When Luis fails to comply with his promise to take Brígida to Europe, she reacts with a passive silence (50) that quickly evolves into a conscious, subversive strategy. Luis's lunchtime phone call is met with Brígida's refusal to come to the telephone, "angrily brandishing that weapon that she had encountered without thinking about it: silence" (51).[24]

Bombal's third use of silence prefigures the use of indirect, symbolic discourse that will be studied in detail in chapter 6 with regard to the work of Rosario Ferré. In *Symbolism and Interpretation*, Tzvetan Todorov elaborates a theory of symbolism that suggests that although all discourse is predicated on both direct and indirect meanings, some discourses lend themselves more readily than others to indirect or implicit associations (Todorov 1982, 27). Bombal's discourse in "El árbol" employs both "paradigmatic associations" (those related to the collective memory) and "syntagmatic associations" (indirect meaning established through the relationship between various textual segments) in the construction of the symbolic value of the tree (Todorov 1982, 30–31). Symbolic discourse, such as having a tree connote meanings other than the physical plant, is an indirect strategy of expression. Such indirect techniques, as discussed in the first chapter, are akin to silence, because they distinguish themselves by their lack of reliance on words or direct verbal statements to communicate an idea. Within the text, the tree lends shade to Brígida's dressing room, turning it into a place of refuge and tranquility for the protagonist. When the tree is cut down, Brígida is finally able to see that her resignation to a loveless and childless marriage with Luis was a lie, and that is why she decided to divorce him. According to Cirlot, in the Christian religion and Roman art the tree symbolizes an "axis between two worlds" (heaven and earth), as well as human nature (Cirlot 1978, 78). Consequently, within the context of the story, the tree represents Brígida's situation as a woman caught between the world of social conventions and that of her own desires of personal fulfillment. Bourgeois values of marriage, propriety, and so on, are pitted against individual values of love and passion. Moreover, human nature, as symbolized by the tree, is inherently dependent on social norms. Thus, the inauthenticity of the world of social convention "shades" or "blocks" the reality of Luis's coldness and Brígida's general unhappiness with her life, just as a tree shades us from the sun. However, when the tree is knocked down, Brígida is capable of seeing Luis as he truly is and realizing the validity of her own desires. When he asks her why she is now leaving and why she had previously stayed, Brígida simply responds by stating that they have cut down the rowan tree.[25] The narrator of Bombal's story refers to the tree as "un gomero." One of the many possible meanings of *gomero* is a tree from the moraceous, or berry-giving, family (*Pequeño Larousse ilustrado* 2005, 492). Barbara Walker's *Woman's Dictionary of Symbols and Sacred Objects* offers an interesting symbolic interpretation of the rowan tree, which, according to *Webster's*, is also a tree yielding a small red berry. Walker says the rowan tree "represented the second letter of the druidic tree alphabet, luis (L). The tree stood for magic and was sacred to the Goddess Brigit. It was thought efficacious in breaking evil enchantments" (Walker 1988, 470). It seems highly unlikely that the connection between the legend behind the rowan tree and the names of the two protagonists of the story "El árbol," Luis and Brígida (Brigit in English), is purely fortuitous. Thus, the potential association between the tree and magic enchantments indicates the possibility that Brígida's acceptance of her mediocre marriage is an evil spell that is broken only when the tree is cut down. This association between the tree in "El árbol" and the rowan tree also lends some support to Mercedes Valdivieso's identification of the tree with the figures of both Brígida's husband (Luis) and her father (Valdivieso 1976, 71).[26] Other dictionaries of symbols, notably Chevalier and Gheerbrant's, list many other possible symbolic associations for trees, including the death/rebirth cycle (Chevalier and Gheerbrant 1994, 1026). They also note that Eliade signals at least seven different lines of possible interpretations for tree symbolism (Chevalier and Gheerbrant 1994, 1026–27). The reader will obviously select the associations that appear most relevant within the context of the story.

Brígida's fundamental dilemma is that of all of Bombal's protagonists. However, in "El árbol," in contrast with *La última niebla* and *The Shrouded Woman*, the protagonist is able to take concrete action within the social reality that oppresses her and combats it by a divorce, instead of through dreams or a silent, posthumous discourse.

La última niebla, The Shrouded Woman, and "El árbol" chronologically coincide with the first stage of Brunet's short stories. Like Brunet's work, the paradoxical nature of Bombal's use of silence fundamentally reflects the contradictory first stage of the women's movement in Chile, when men accepted some of women's concerns for social reform, but refused to validate equality for women within marriage, education, jobs, and politics. The tentative nature of the early Chilean feminism of Brunet and Bombal clearly echoes a moment in which women were yet to attain suffrage and any semblance of equal rights with men, but nonetheless were beginning to vocalize their specific concerns as women. The incorporation of themes/structures of paradoxical silence in their works illustrates how gender issues intersected with social factors of the time period in which these works were written. In other words, paradoxical elements in these texts were specifically directed toward the implicit readership of the time, which was not ready to receive overt, radical, feminist messages but rather was foregrounded in the emerging feminist debates of the era. Such readers were capable of actualizing a limited feminist message based on their experiences and social conditioning. Although a more militant feminist faction was slowly emerging in parts of Latin America, women's literature of that era became the voice of the less explicit and dogmatic feminist branch of the time (Guerra-Cunningham 1980, 22).

Silence, Plot, and Characterization in Bombal's Works

Bombal's employment of paradoxical silence also relates to her choice of the marriage plot in all three of the texts analyzed here. As we saw in our discussion of Marta Brunet's works, the focus on marriage almost always invites a natural oscillation between complicity and rejection of patriarchal values. This vacillation on the part of the women within the plot structure manifests itself within a simultaneous expression of passive silence and subversive silence. Bombal's first novel is an excellent example of this. On the one hand, the novel's unnamed protagonist accepts patriarchal norms through a number of her actions: she agrees to a loveless marriage with her cousin Daniel, even though she is aware of his fixation with his deceased first wife, because this is the socially appropriate role for women. She defers to her husband's wishes on a number of occasions, including his sporadic sexual desires (Bombal 1988, 28–29), and many have interpreted the lover she describes as a mere fantasy, maintaining that she actually remains physically faithful to her husband. Moreover, the protagonist never discusses her discontent with Daniel, nor does she seek a divorce. On the other hand, the protagonist rebels against her marriage through her silent interior monologues, in which she expresses her lack of conformity with a passionless, loveless union and speaks of a lover whom the reader can never classify as either real or imaginary with any certitude. She combats Daniel's coldness both by affirming her sensuality through her ceremonial bathing in the pond (Bombal 1988, 14) and by her attempts to locate her lover and disprove Daniel's words at the end of the novel. The protagonist also tries to commit suicide as a form of protest against her stifling, unhappy marriage. In sum, her silence is at once a sign of her marital oppression and her rebellion against the role she is forced to occupy.

The reader can also observe the parallel between paradoxical silence and Bombal's narrative plot in *The Shrouded Woman*. On several occasions Ana María attempts to rebel against patriarchal norms. First, the protagonist engages in a premarital sexual relationship with Ricardo. Then she tries to abandon her husband, Antonio, twice: once, when they first marry and then again, when she discovers Antonio's infidelities. Despite these attempts, Ana María ultimately complies with patriarchal norms, allowing Antonio to convince her that divorce would be socially unacceptable. She remains faithful to Antonio throughout their marriage, and allows his emotional abandonment to embitter her life. This oscillation between the passive and subversive within the plot of *The Shrouded Woman* leads to a concomitant swing between oppressive silence and combative silence within the novel.

Perhaps the most interesting of the three texts in this regard is Bombal's short story "El árbol." In this tale, the protagonist Brígida's actions suggest complicity with patriarchal norms, because she accepts societal labels that deem her stupid and acquiesces in marriage to a much older man, her father's friend, Luis. Moreover, Brígida tolerates Luis's cold, passionless, condescending behavior for the greater part of the story. Nonetheless, she finally manifests discontent with Luis after he reneges on a promised summer vacation in Europe, responding to him with a subversive silence. Her decision to divorce Luis when the symbolic tree is felled also constitutes a rebellion against patriarchal norms. The acts of suffering in silence and using silence as a weapon naturally spring from the contradictory actions and sentiments within the plot. The important distinction between this piece and Bombal's earlier texts is that ultimately rebellion wins out over complicity with societal norms.

Bombal's protagonists, like herself, are all wealthy women who find themselves trapped in unhappy marriages. These are not women struggling for economic subsistence, but rather characters who exclusively focus on societal expectations that limit their freedom. Bombal exposes the dilemma of the upper-class woman who must succumb to societal pressures. Such class rules about social propriety are brought to bear on the unnamed protagonist of *La última niebla*, who agrees to marry her cousin Daniel, even though she does not love him, because it would clearly be worse for her to remain single. Similarly, Ana María in *The*

Shrouded Woman retracts her divorce proceedings because her husband and lawyer convince her that this would be a form of social suicide. Only Brígida from "El árbol" is able to resist upper-class societal imperatives and finally divorce her unloving husband, perhaps because she is portrayed as nonconformist and naturally rebellious at the outset of the story, and is thus internally less subject to exterior social dictates.

4
The Encoded Silence of Rosario Castellanos: Coding, Paradox, and Parentheses

ROSARIO CASTELLANOS WAS BORN IN MEXICO CITY IN 1925 BUT LIVED in Comitán in the province of Chiapas, Mexico, until 1941. Her family members were wealthy landowners there until the implementation of land reform in Mexico under the government of Lázaro Cárdenas. Due to the loss of their estate, Castellanos's family relocated to Mexico City, where Rosario attended the Universidad Nacional Autónoma de México (UNAM) from 1944 to 1950, obtaining a master's degree in philosophy. Her master's thesis, "On Feminine Culture", was the first piece she wrote on the role of women in society. Her graduation was followed by a scholarship to the University of Madrid and a period of European travel (Ahern 1988, 3). Upon her return, Castellanos became the director of Chiapas cultural programs from 1951 to 1953. In 1958, she married Ricardo Guerra and had a son. The two were later divorced. In addition to her work as a journalist, Castellanos was a professor of comparative literature at UNAM from 1967 to 1971 and a visiting professor of Latin American literature at various universities in the United States in 1967. She became the Mexican ambassador to Israel in 1971. She died in Israel in 1974, officially as the result of an electric shock (Smith 1997, 182). Despite this reported cause of death, there has been much speculation that Castellanos was either murdered or committed suicide owing to some mysterious letters to her ex-husband and son that were posthumously published. Some critics have noted that she suffered from bouts of depression throughout her life, and that her son's return to Mexico to live with his father may have provoked a final depression and suicide (Steele 1996, 96).[1] Castellanos's works include ten collections of poetry, seven collections of essays, and one play. Her fictional prose works are her short story collections *Ciudad real* [*City of Kings*] (1960), *Los convidados de agosto* [The August Guests] (1964), and *Álbum de familia* [Family Album] (1971), and the novels *Balún Canán* [*The Nine Guardians*] (1957), *Oficio de tinieblas* [*The Book of Lamentations*] (1962), and *Rito de iniciación* [Initiation Rite] (1996). The last of these novels, published posthumously, was originally written in the 1960s. Castellanos decided to destroy the novel, but a copy was discovered about twenty years after Castellanos's death by Eduardo Mejía.[2] Castellanos was one of the first Latin American writers to address issues of female inequality in her essays and fictional prose. Consequently, her work suffered a significant degree of censorship. When she was the ambassador to Israel and thus occupied a public position, the Mexican president had persuaded her to postpone the publication of her most openly feminist work, the play *El eterno femenino* [The Eternal Feminine] which did not see print until 1975. Moreover, upon her death, a representative of the Mexican embassy allegedly came to her house and destroyed all her papers, which possibly included new literary works (Steele 1996, 72–74).

The two most fundamental aspects of Castellanos's fiction are *indigenismo* (presentation of the viewpoint and inferior social status of the Mexican indigenous population) and her representation of feminist concerns. The former aspect is largely expressed in her novels *The Nine Guardians*, *The Book of Lamentations*, and the book of short stories *City of Kings*. The latter aspect is primarily manifested through *Los convidados de agosto*, *Álbum de familia*, and *Rito de iniciación*.

Coding Techniques in Castellanos's Short Stories

In "The Feminist Voice: Coding in Women's Folklore and Literature" Joan Radner and Susan Lanser discuss various techniques that women writers use to covertly express their ideas. The authors list the six coding techniques discussed in the first chapter: appropriation, juxtaposition, distraction, indirection, trivialization, and incompetence (Radner and Lanser 1987, 412–25). These strategies can be understood as a form of textual silence, since they do not explicitly state ideas but rather rely on the reader's ability to construct a message encoded between the lines of the text. Rosario Castellanos employs many of these techniques in her short stories to "silently" express a feminist message.

Radner and Lanser's concept of coding through juxtaposition helps to read the story "Los convidados de agosto" from the collection with the same title. This story presents the plight of Emelina, a thirty-five-year-old unmarried woman, who every year looks forward to the August fair as a potential opportunity to meet a spouse. At the fair, Emelina meets a man who takes her to a bar and plies her with liquor. After getting thoroughly drunk on wine, Emelina is about to go off in a taxi with the stranger, when her brother Mateo and his friend Enrique arrive on the scene and whisk Emelina away. Eduardo disparages Emelina for ruining her family's honor. Emelina defends her conduct in the following manner:

> Enrique's breathing was swollen with anger. He shook Emelina with scorn. 'You have dishonored your name! And with a nobody! An opportunistic foreigner!'
> Emelina denied it vehemently. . . .
> Enrique began to walk without destination through the desolate streets. From far away he heard the echo of the marimbas, the rockets, the fair. It didn't even stop when Enrique knocked on the door of the brothel with the convenient loud knocks of the door knockers. (Castellanos 1964, 95, my translation).[3]

This conclusion to Castellanos's story contains an ironic juxtaposition. The author counterpoises Emelina's thwarted desire for a sexual encounter (which is deemed dishonorable) to Enrique's casual entrance into the brothel. Castellanos implicitly criticizes the existence of a sexual double standard for men and women. However, no explicit commentary is voiced in the text. The message is silently but effectively conveyed to the reader. Indeed, Castellanos's placement of this ironic juxtaposition at the very end of the story may lead many readers to ignore its importance as the narrative's major theme, and focus on the other events of the story that lead up to it: the customs of the August fair and Emelina's frustrated desires for marriage and family. However, the feminist-oriented reader, who is more likely to be receptive to the silent feminist cue of ironic juxtaposition than the nonfeminist-oriented reader, will perceive that the details of the narration culminate in the story's conclusion in a manner that emphasizes the issue of the sexual double standard as major theme.

Two other stories in *Los convidados de agosto* thematically deal with silence. The first, "Las amistades efímeras" [Fleeting Friendships] is the story of the relationship between the narrator, a writer, and Gertrudis.

The two friends are characterized as complete opposites: the narrator is incessantly talkative, while Gertrudis is perpetually silent (Castellanos 1988b, 144). The narrator proceeds to tell Gertrudis's life story: One day Gertrudis runs off with a stranger who stops at her father's store. They go to a hotel, they make love, and then they are forced into a shotgun marriage the next day by Gertrudis's father. The abductor/husband, Juan Bautista, is subsequently whisked away to jail for stealing and cutting telegraph wires. When Juan is finally released from prison, he tells his wife that he wants to leave her to marry his high school sweetheart. Gertrudis sets off to work as a maid where her old friend, the narrator, lives. The two are forbidden to associate by the narrator's parents. Finally, one day, Gertrudis and the narrator go to the movies. The narrator is upset by her friend's facility to forget the past (one minute she is sad because she learns of Juan's death; the next she is happily munching on candy at the movies). The narrator permanently abandons Gertrudis and returns home to write: "I tried to write, but I couldn't. What for? It was so hard! Maybe, I repeated to myself, my head in my hands, maybe it's simpler just to live" (154).

The story clearly contrasts two completely opposite lifestyles: the narrator's (living through words and analysis) versus Gertrudis's (silently living through actions and experiences). Gertrudis lives each moment, transgressing social norms in the process, without fear of the consequences. Hence, silence is equated with action and social subversion. The talkative narrator feels compelled to end her friendship with Gertrudis because of the realization that she functions on a totally different plane (that of thoughts and discourse). The transient nature of Gertrudis's memories disturbs the narrator, who searches for permanence in the written word. This opposition between the ephemeral and the eternal is hinted at in the story's title.

The second piece, "El viudo Román" [The Widower Román] is a tale of revenge.[4] Carlos Román is a widower who has spent years as a recluse mourning the death of his wife, Estela. Slowly Román begins to resume social contact by making friends with the local priest. He then goes on to show interest in remarrying a young woman named Romelia. After their wedding night, he returns Romelia to her family, claiming that she was not a virgin, although Romelia contradicts him, offering to show her family the bloody sheets. The reader then discovers through Román's confession to the priest that his marriage to Romelia was a calculated act of revenge. He reveals that on his wedding night to his first wife, Estela, letters that Estela had written to a former unnamed lover were anonymously delivered to Román. When he confronted Estela, she refused to name her lover. Despite Román's offer to forget the past, Estela only wanted to return to her first boyfriend. After this night she fell ill and never recovered. Román suspects that Romelia's brother Rafael was his wife's anonymous lover. He marries Romelia both to confirm this suspicion (by seeing her brother's handwriting on a piece of paper kept in a locket she always wears) and to destroy the family's honor through denying her virginity. Hanna Geldrich-Leffman points out that Romelia's relationship with Román is characterized by the submissive silence traditionally associated with women: "Using the only language available to her, that of her body, she offers irrefutable proof of her innocence: the blood stain on the sheet. But her language is not accepted, her text is not even looked at. Only the male discourse is heard" (Geldrich-Leffman 1992, 31). Ironically, Romelia is characterized as the honorable and obedient daughter par excellence. Hence, her silence functions in the same submissive manner.

In contrast to Romelia, the story's other main female character, Estela, is characterized by subversion of the traditional woman's role. Estela transgresses acceptable social behavior for a woman, becoming Rafael's lover. Although she follows social norms by marrying Carlos Román once Rafael spurns her, she refuses to acquiesce to Román's demand that she reveal her lover's identity. Her silence is inherently subversive and is implicitly counterpoised to Romelia's:

> She tried to dash out into the street to find him, perhaps to thank him for the vile deed he had just committed—who knows? The fact is I didn't let her go. I stopped her forcibly, and we spent the entire night fighting. I talked like a madman; I swore, I pled, I promised. She didn't stop crying; she shivered from cold, from fever, and cowered before my blows, yet she would not utter his name, that name which she never wrote and which I was subsequently never to get out of her because from that moment on she was never again able to talk. (Castellanos 1988d, 203)

Estela's silence, in consonance with her personality, is a subversive response to the demands of patriarchy. Note that Román's actions are all verbal (speaking, cursing, begging, promising), while Estela's are all nonverbal (crying, shaking, bending when struck). Transgressive silence is counterpoised to patriarchal discourse.

Silence in "The Widower Román" once again reverts to the paradoxical silence seen in Brunet and Bombal. The two characters, Romelia and Estela, represent respectively the traditional and subversive dimensions of silence.

Silence in the form of indirect techniques of expression resurfaces in Castellanos's collection *Álbum de familia*. The first and most overtly feminist of the stories is entitled "Lección de cocina" [Cooking Lesson]. The story presents the thoughts of a newly married woman while she prepares a piece of beef for dinner. Much of her contemplation centers upon her loss of identity through marriage and the silly, hypocritical norms according to which married women are expected to behave. The first of these norms is the ability to cook, which the narrator of "Cooking Lesson" clearly does not have. During the course of the story she burns the meat, and then ponders what excuse she should use for not having dinner prepared when her husband gets home. This is a good example of literary "incompetence," which is the assertion of incapability with regard to activities considered typically female, in order to express resistance to patriarchal expectations (Radner and Lanser 1987, 420). The act of burning the meat (as well as all the narrator's meditations on her inability to understand the cookbook she is reading) is an indirect cue to her rebellious stance.

A second technique of indirection that Castellanos employs in "Cooking Lesson" is that of hedging, defined as a "range of strategies . . . for . . . weakening a message: ellipses, litotes, passive constructions, euphemisms, qualifiers" (Radner and Lanser 1987, 420). There are at least eight examples of ellipsis in "Cooking Lesson," of which I will examine the most significant.

When the narrator is asserting her independent existence from her husband, she states: "I, too, am a consciousness that can close itself off, abandon someone and expose him to annihilation. I . . . The meat, under the sprinkling of salt, has toned down some of its offensive redness and now it seems more tolerable, more familiar to me. It's that piece I saw a thousand times without realizing it, when I used to pop in to tell the cook that . . ." (Castellanos 1988a, 209). In this passage, there are two cases of textual ellipses. The first is used to interrupt (and thus perhaps weaken) the narrator's declaration of her own identity, while the second ellipsis cuts off the narrator's contrast between cooking as a wifely duty and cooking as a servant's duty. Nonetheless, the message remains that it is inappropriate to expect cooking to be the sole responsibility of the woman in a marriage, thus equating the wife with a maid.

Ellipsis clearly serves as an attenuator when the narrator is ironically giving thanks for the benefits of marriage: "Thanks for letting me out of the cage of one sterile routine only to lock me into the cage of another, a routine which according to all purposes and possibilities must be fruitful. Thanks for giving me the chance to show off a long gown with a train, for helping me walk up the aisle of the church, carried away by the organ music. Thanks for . . . "(Castellanos 1988a, 210). This passage is a good example of Bakhtin's double-voiced discourse, because within the narrator's ironic words we also hear the voice of society (Bakhtin 1984, 195). The fact that the narrator refers to her postmarital routine as a cage suggests that she does not believe it will be as "fruitful" as people have suggested to her. The notion of the fruitfulness of married life is clearly a discourse appropriated from the voice of society. Consequently, in one sentence we hear two voices, each with a clearly different opinion. The terminal ellipsis serves to temper the passage's irony, which is another indirect or silent means of protest in the story.

The narrative ends with an ellipsis that is perhaps the best example of hedging: "I accepted that when I got married and I was even ready to accept sacrifice for the sake of marital harmony. But I counted on the fact that the sacrifice, the complete renunciation of what I am, would only be demanded of me on The Sublime Occasion, at The Time of Heroic Solutions, at The Moment of Definitive Decision. Not in exchange for what I stumbled on today, which is something very insignificant and very ridiculous. And yet . . . "(Castellanos 1988a, 215). The narrator contemplates the sacrifice she is making if she lies about the burnt dinner. She is disturbed by what she initially views as the insignificance of the event for which she is relinquishing her identity (how she would normally behave in such circumstances). By terminating the paragraph with an ellipsis, the narrator leaves to the reader's imagination the completion of her thoughts. Although Radner and Lanser suggest that this technique usually weakens the message by rendering it silent or implicit, thus forcing the reader to fill in the blanks, Castellanos, to some degree, manages to simultaneously reduce and highlight the subversive message of her story. The reader infers that although the cooking issue is fundamentally unimportant, it is nonetheless symbolic and indicative of the hypocrisy the narrator will be forced to adopt on a larger scale. Consequently, ellipsis, through silence, simultaneously weakens a message (by making it less explicit) and underscores it (by engaging the reader's participation in its construction). The open-endedness constructed through ellipses allows for the possibility that a feminist reader might construe an even stronger meaning, whereas a nonfeminist reader can accept the subversive message as less threatening in its truncated and hence attenuated form.

In addition to the explicitly marked textual ellipses, Evelyn Fishburn points out the presence of elliptical phrases in the story that characterize the narrator's discourse when she is subverting her expected societal role. In contrast, when the narrator appears to conform to this role, her sentences are nonelliptical (perfectly formed) (Fishburn 1995, 105). Once again, the encoded silence implied by textual ellipses serves as a subversive weapon and cue of the text's feminist perspective.

Another mode of indirection, metaphor (Radner and Lanser 1987, 420), is also frequently employed by Castellanos. In metaphors, one object symbolically represents another based on an implicit similarity. Since this relationship is implicit, it can be seen as another nonverbal or silent form of discourse.

In "Cooking Lesson," Castellanos uses the image of cooking meat metaphorically. Fishburn, parting from Lévi-Strauss's notion of the raw and the cooked, suggests that cooking is a means by which nature is transformed into culture, and hence it parallels the new bride's socialization into her domestic role as wife (Fishburn 1995, 98). I would like to take Fishburn's interpretation one step further by suggesting that the meat's identification with the story's protagonist also serves as a symbol of feminist rebellion. A number of similarities between the meat and the protagonist set up the initial metaphor, such as their red color: "Red, as if it were just about to start bleeding. Our backs were that same color, my husband and I, after our orgiastic sunbathing on the beaches of Acapulco" (Castellanos 1988a, 208). This description is immediately followed by a description of a painful sexual encounter owing to their sunburns. The meat about to bleed also suggests the self-admitted prior virginity of the protagonist. Similarly, parallels are drawn between the two when the narrator compares sex with her husband to having a gravestone cover her (211), while simultaneously referring to the meat as in a "deceased state" (212). The narrator is also described, like a piece of meat, as bearing "the owner's brand" (211). These similarities accumulate throughout the text and lead to a judgment concerning the narrator's ultimate irreducibility to patriarchal society (which can be thought to be represented by the recipe that attempts to "tame" the meat/woman) (Furnival 1990, 63): "This meat has a toughness and consistency that is not like beef. It must be mammoth" (Castellanos 1988a, 211). In other words, the meat is not easily rendered edible through cooking, just as the protagonist is not easily amenable to her conversion into a homemaker. At the end of the story, the meat does not end up deliciously cooked and served on the kitchen table for dinner, but burnt at the bottom of the garbage can. Although the protagonist projects that the burnt meat will stand as a sign of her inutility ("it doesn't smell of human flesh here, but of useless woman") (213), in reality the meat stands as a sign of refusal to accept its socially relegated place: "This piece of meat's mother never told it that it was meat and ought to act like it" (213). Thus, the meat indirectly conveys the text's feminist message through what may be viewed as an encoded silence.

There are a few instances in which the text explicitly speaks of the protagonist's silence. In these passages, the main character appears to adopt the traditional, passive, female silence of the past. For example, she does not complain to her husband during painful sex, and later, when referring to her domestic duties, she states that she will "ruminate my resentment in silence" (211). Nonetheless, this self-proclaimed, nonsubversive silence is contradicted by the transgressive nature of the other silent or indirect techniques employed in the story, including a generally ironic tone when referring to societal expectations for women.

"Cabecita Blanca" [Little Blank Head] is a story whose message is completely based on ironic juxtaposition. Although the protagonist, Justina, is the traditional, silent, submissive wife who never utters a word against her husband, after his death she is clearly conscious of the improvement of her life as widow instead of wife ("The appropriate place for a husband was the one in which her deceased Juan Carlos was now resting") (Castellanos 1971, 49, my translation).[5] Throughout her marriage, Justina displays a nonsubversive silence to her husband, which is the reason he married her in the first place (52). Before marriage, when Justina's mother encouraged her to be prudent, we were told that Justina "understood for prudence silence, agreement, submission" (53, my translation).[6]

Despite her overall submissiveness, Justina does exhibit some nonverbal, subversive behavior. When her husband is shouting at their son Luis, Justina pulls the tablecloth out from underneath the dishes on the dinner table, causing them to crash to the floor. This silent act provokes her husband's angry exit (55).

Justina's naive judgments about the excellent qualities of her husband are juxtaposed to the reality of his narrated actions. Although the reader is never explicitly told that Juan Carlos is having an affair with his secretary, he or she is given ample clues. The fact that he was working long hours, that Justina receives an anonymous letter about the affair, and that the secretary's house is conveniently only a few blocks from theirs is enough to suggest to the reader that Juan Carlos has been unfaithful. Thus, when the narrator adopts Justina's perspective and states such thoughts as "Few had señora Justina's luck in finding such a good and responsible man" (62, my translation),[7] we know that these words are ironic and that the ultimate assessment of Juan Carlos is far from positive. A feminist criticism is silently encoded within the text through ironic juxtaposition.

We can comprehend Castellanos's choice of coding techniques as a logical offshoot of the plot structures of her short stories. Although her stories span various plot archetypes (marriage, the novel of Eros, etc.), all the stories share an unexpected plot twist at the end of the narrative. Such plot twists usually express ideas that run counter to societal norms. Consequently, the plot twists lead to coding techniques that mitigate the strength of the subversive message and make it more acceptable to the reader. The stories "The August Guests," "Fleeting Friendships," "Cooking Lesson," and "Little Blank Head" all illustrate this correspondence. For example, earlier in this chapter, we observed the ironic conclusion to the tale "Los convidados de agosto." The story's plot, centering on the marital and sexual ambitions of Emelina, concludes with her "rescue" from a stranger by her brother and his friend. The reader expects the story to end with Emelina's return home. He or she might also expect Emelina to accept or rebel against this denouement. However, the reader surely does not anticipate that the story will conclude with the scene in which Eduardo, the brother's friend, knocks on the brothel door immediately after chiding Emelina for her dishonor. I examined how this concluding scene constitutes an ironic juxtaposition between Emelina's sexual behavior and Eduardo's that unmasks and criticizes the double sexual standard for men and women. Hence, the ironic plot twist (Eduardo's behavior) invites the use of silent coding techniques (ironic juxtaposition).

Similarly, "Fleeting Friendships" ironically juxtaposes two types of women with disparate attitudes toward silence. The plot centers on the close friendship between Gertrudis, who is characterized by her silence and impulsive actions, and the narrator, who is known for her verbosity and careful contemplation of things through writing. No narrative clues suggest the surprise denouement in which the narrator permanently abandons Gertrudis in a movie theater and returns home to write, albeit unsuccessfully. The development of the relationship between the two women, despite their differences, never hints at the possibility of an eventual rupture. The narrative's initial conformity with the Eros plot structure (of which friendship between two women is a variant) (Pratt 1981, 95) is undermined by the story's surprise ending. The narrator's final, wistful comment ("maybe it's simpler just to live") (Castellanos 1988b, 154), is both straightforward and ironic. On the one hand, the narrator does indeed struggle with writing, and as we saw, Gertrudis's silence is shown to be more active and subversive than the narrator's words. On the other hand, when the reader contemplates Gertrudis's life, he or she understands that by no means has it been "simple," or desirable. Consequently, the juxtaposition of the attitudes of Gertrudis and the narrator has ironic overtones, and once again, the coding technique helps to execute the unexpected plot twist.

The ironic twist in "Cabecita blanca" occurs during the course of the story's development rather than in its denouement. Throughout the narrative there is a simultaneous juxtaposition of Justina's invocations of "your poor father" (Castellanos 1971, 47), when faced with her disobedient children, with narrative comments that suggest Justina's contentment with the death of her husband ("Fortunately her poor father was dead and buried in a perpetual tomb in the French Pantheon" [48]; and "The appropriate place for a husband was where her dead Juan Carlos was now resting" [49].[8] These comments shock and surprise the reader, who does not expect them in light of the rest of the characterization of doña Justina as a submissive, naive wife. In this instance, coding techniques (indirection, irony, juxtaposition) are motivated by the complexity of the characterization of the protagonist more than by plot structure. In other words, Castellanos does not merely present the story of a passive woman who loses her husband, but rather presents a woman who simultaneously accepts and rejects patriarchal control in a complicated interplay of emotions. The formerly submissive Justina develops a consciousness of her previous subjugation once her husband is dead, and consequently undergoes a surprising evolution as a person in the course of the story.

The plot twist in "Cooking Lesson" is largely perceived through its employment of narrative hedging, or ellipsis. As we saw earlier in this chapter, this coding technique reflects the desire to both express and conceal a feminist message. The story initially appears to be a comic rendering of the lack of expertise in the kitchen of a recently married woman, which also serves as a springboard for the protagonist to recall the events leading up to her marriage and honeymoon. Despite some initial complaints proffered regarding her husband's lovemaking and her lack of cooking experience, the reader does not suspect the depth of the narrator's discontentment until the story's elliptic conclusion, in which she states that although she is perfectly willing to sacrifice her identity for something important, she never counted on doing so regarding something so insignificant as cooking a meal. Her final words are: "And yet . . ." (Castellanos 1988a, 22), a phrase that elliptically trails off, suggesting that perhaps the episode of the cooking lesson is not as trivial and comical as we were initially led to believe. Through silent narrative coding in the form of ellipsis, the text suggests how the insignificant narrative events ironically reflect significant conflicts, and how the plot evolves from one type of events to the other.

It is interesting to note that although the plots of many of these stories follow the same archetypes as Brunet and Bombal's fiction (the marriage or single-woman plots), they form a different variation of these plot structures through their use of ironic character/plot twists, which result in the employment of a different kind of silence (encoded versus paradoxical silence). Perhaps the single exception to this rule among the stories by Castellanos studied here is "The Widower Román," which centers on the marriage plot and relies more on paradoxical silence than on encoded silence. This story, in some sense, is also a variation on the standard conflicts of the marriage plot, because it presents two marriages that involve the same man (Romelia's and Estela's marriages to Román), instead of focusing on a single relationship. The two women each enact a separate aspect of the marriage plot: Romelia represents complicity with patriarchal norms and hence uses oppressive silence, while Estela represents rebellion against patriarchal norms and hence employs a subversive silence. Once again, the paradoxical silence naturally springs out of this narrative plot division.

SILENCE IN *RITO DE INICIACIÓN*

Rosario Castellanos also encodes a feminist message in her novel *Rito de iniciación* (1996). As Eduardo Mejía indicates in the epilogue to *Rito de iniciación*, the novel is unlike anything Castellanos had previously written (Castellanos 1996, 372). Following a *nouveau roman* style, the work focuses on the psychological evolution of a young girl from the provinces in the 1950s, named Cecilia Rojas, who decides to move to Mexico City and attend the university there. Cecilia's story is one of self-discovery. The protagonist evolves from a sheltered girl imbued with the provincial goals of marriage and family to a budding writer who comes to terms with her own sexuality and finds happiness within herself. Early seeds of the novel can be found in Castellanos's essay "La imagen de la mujer" [The Image of Women], where she speaks of a woman's first sexual encounter as an "initiation rite" and the importance of such "liminal" experiences in the process of female self-discovery and comprehension (Castellanos 1995a, 16–21). Castellanos theorizes here about the very process her protagonist undergoes in *Rito de iniciación*. In the novel, Cecilia enters into a sexual relationship with her classmate Ramón Mariscal as a means of self-knowledge. When Mariscal is offered a European scholarship and the two part ways, the separation becomes Cecilia's "liminal" experience, which converts her into "who she is," reaffirms her goal as a writer, and reveals her own inner strength. Today's audience would not view this theme as particularly revolutionary; however, it certainly was just that for the 1960s public for which it was originally intended.

As we have seen, Castellanos uses many techniques of indirection in her collections of short stories, *Los convidados de agosto* and *Álbum de familia*, a strategy I refer to as encoded silence. In *Rito de iniciación*, Castellanos uses both thematic and stylistic silence to situate the reader within a feminist perspective in at least three different ways: (1) Castellanos explicitly problematizes woman's relationship to words and silence, (2) the female look is presented as a silent form of feminist knowledge and expression,[9] and (3) parentheses are employed as a paralinguistic sign of both the insufficiency of patriarchal language for female expression and women's marginal condition. This chapter will systematically examine these three variants of silence as a cue to the reader of the text's feminist perception.

Castellanos was very aware of the relationship between language and patriarchy, and discussed the use of language as an instrument of domination of both Indians and women in a number of her essays (MacDonald 1980, 41–64). In "Notas al margen: El lenguaje como instrumento de dominio" [Notes on the Margin: Language as an Instrument of Domination] Castellanos posits in the following terms the very linguistic dilemma much discussed, as we have seen, by contemporary feminists:

> The usufructors of language perverted it over the course of three or four centuries; they sacked it. It is not worth the trouble to appeal to the local court because the treasure, that treasure, is irrecoverable.

We have to create another language, we have to find another starting point, search for the pearl within each shell, the pit beneath the peel, because the shell holds still another treasure, the peel another substance. Word is the incarnation of the truth, because language has meaning. (Castellanos 1988c, 252)

This paradox of language is reflected in *Rito de iniciación* through the text's constant vacillation between the positive and negative values of both words and silence. The novel's characters are frequently portrayed in terms of their muteness or loquacity. Sometimes silence is seen in its traditional sense as a sign of female oppression or stereotyped gender roles, while other times silence is accorded a positive, combative, or expressive dimension. The same is true of words that are sometimes seen as a means to authenticity, and other times as devoid of powers of expression. This fluctuation mirrors Castellanos's previously expressed conception of the paradoxical nature of language as a force of both domination and liberation and relates her work to the paradoxical silence seen in chapters 2 and 3.

The fluid values of speech and silence in the novel can best be traced through the novel's protagonist, Cecilia. At the beginning of the novel, silence is clearly portrayed in a negative fashion as the traditional role of women in a patriarchal society. Cecilia's mother is described as silent, while her father is talkative (Castellanos 1996, 18). Cecilia herself is characterized by a verbosity that is viewed as totally inappropriate by society and leads to her ostracism: "little by little the approbatory smiles were freezing into a gesture of antipathy because of her loquacity" (18).[10]

Cecilia might as well be mute, like her mother, since her speech is completely ignored by her boyfriend, Enrique (20–21). Furthermore, when Cecilia tries to explain herself to Enrique by offering him her diary to read, this leads to his flight from the relationship and final abandonment. Prior to Enrique's disappearance, Cecilia only used silence as a refuge when faced with his sexual advances. This silence was misinterpreted by Enrique as a form of coquettishness on Cecilia's part. Once Enrique is gone, however, Cecilia becomes silent due to her abandonment by Enrique but allows her mother to verbally condemn his behavior instead. This silence on Cecilia's part is a manifestation of false modesty, since she views it as inappropriate to voice such thoughts of Enrique's betrayal, but secretly agrees with her mother.

After Cecilia's breakup with Enrique, she decides to attend college in Mexico City, despite her mother's disapproval of the plan. Clara, Cecilia's mother, writes to a distant cousin who lives in Mexico City and inquires about appropriate living arrangements for her daughter. Clara's letter to her cousin Beatriz is a good example of the expressive values of silence and techniques of indirection, since she elicits an invitation for Cecilia to live with Beatriz by simply inquiring in her letter about the most convenient way to settle her daughter in Mexico City. She never directly asks her cousin to take Cecilia into her house (Castellanos 1996, 28–29). It is through this subtle hint that Cecilia ends up living with her unmarried cousin in Mexico City.

In "La participación de la mujer mexicana en la educación formal" [The Participation of the Mexican Woman in Formal Education], Castellanos points out the negative charge of the phrase "se queda una soltera" [one remains single]: "Because one doesn't choose to be single as a form of life, but rather, as experience already tells us, one remains single, that is, passively accepts a destiny that others impose upon us. . . . And why is it that the necessities of the others are real and those of the single person are barely whims? Because what she needs, she needs for herself and no one else, and that, in a woman, is not permissible. She must share, give. She only justifies her existence through other people" (Castellanos 1995c, 32, my translation).[11]

Beatriz is portrayed as an unmarried woman through choice, not lack of opportunity, and her home is described as one filled with decorative elements that affirm her right to spend money on herself and fully live her own life: "She bought solid furniture, she unpacked antique tableware, she hung curtains and pictures. Her relatives . . . didn't fail to express their disapproval. But they couldn't prevent Beatriz from ending up having a cozy house" (Castellanos 1996, 34).[12]

Beatriz belies the traditional notion of *la soltera* (the old maid) and leads a perfectly happy and independent life. Beatriz is also associated with silence, but her silence is an instrument of her freedom, rather than a passive acceptance of male-dominated society. For example, when she is first contemplating buying the house she now lives in, she does not argue with her friends and relatives who try to dissuade her. Instead, she respectfully listens to their arguments without answering, but in the end does what she wants by purchasing the home (33–34). Thus, silence acquires a combative dimension.

Silence briefly swings back to its negative connotations when Cecilia describes her relationship with her parents (their lack of communication) in terms of silence, indicating that any attempt to speak to them is a waste of time. Silence is also associated with Cecilia's initial moments of alienation when she first arrives in Mexico City: "She closed her eyes so that she would not be seen and her lips so that no one would invoke her. Blind, mute, invisible, and deaf. One more step sufficed and in the same spot where Cecilia Rojas was before, now there was no one" (51).[13] However, this conversion into "nobody" in reality is a necessary prelude to Cecilia's eventual transformation into a happy and independent woman. It serves as what Mircea Eliade terms a "scenario of initiatory death," which paves the way for later rebirth and characterizes many puberty rites (Eliade 1958, 30–31).

When Cecilia meets her first friend in the city, Sergio, while waiting in line to register for courses at the university, she initially ignores his attempts to introduce himself. He then poses the question: "This silence, is it knowledge or lack of femininity?" (Castellanos 1996, 73).[14] This question introduces the two fundamental poles around which silence revolves in the novel: silence as a form of wisdom versus stereotyped conceptions concerning female loquacity and/or silence. The novel acknowledges that silences can be used in different ways for different purposes. Cecilia observed how her family members used silence as a combative language when she lived with them in the provinces (91). Cecilia's father refuses to acknowledge her decision to study literature instead of history, believing "that a fact is nullified by not mentioning it" (106).[15]

Cecilia's friendship with Sergio and incorporation into his circle of friends at the university is a turning point in the novel's depiction of silence. From this point on, silence begins to acquire expressive and creative dimensions linked to women. In the chapter "Erótica" [Erotics], silence is presented both as a form of wisdom and a form of communication. When Cecilia immerses herself in her readings, silent meditation becomes a desired state. The reader is told that her silence was no longer a sign of timidity, but rather one of plentitude. Nonetheless, Cecilia continues to question the pros and cons of silence with regard to speaking to Lorenzo about the obscene drawing in his notebook, fearing equally her silence and her loquacity (135).

Silence as wisdom implies a natural counterpart: the folly of or difficulty with expression through words. Cecilia's new stance makes her painfully conscious of the limitations of language, especially in its written form: "Her problem was words.... In that mansion [of writing], the only inhabitant now was silence" (189–90).[16]

Silence also characterizes the sexual relationship between Cecilia and Ramón Mariscal. Cecilia's reasons for entering into this relationship are described by the narrator as a rite of passage toward self-discovery:

> [W]hat was going to be decided or confirmed in the sexual act was something much more important than that which her vanity legislated over or her prudishness: it was her existence itself. . . .
> This sector of her relationship had been declared a zone of silence. Because to refer to her Mariscal did not dispose of more than the common terminology that Cecilia refused to listen to. She pretended that those same words with which her mother would have termed her a prostitute would hurt her delicacy, although, in truth, she was in disagreement not only with their condemnatory nuance but also with their merely descriptive meaning. (233–34)[17]

For Cecilia, sex is not just a pleasurable act, but also an important ritual that communicates her search for self-knowledge. Language would mar the authenticity of her physical relationship with Mariscal, because it is saturated by the negative connotations that society of that era had accorded to premarital sex. The concept of negatively charged language regarding female sexuality recalls Dale Spender's ideas on man-made language. Silence is thus converted into a more authentic space of expression than words.

The novel concludes with a discussion between Sergio and another member of the group, Villela, about Cecilia's silence (or lack thereof). Their conversation pits one female stereotype against the other (the silent submissive female versus the chatterbox). Villela insists that Cecilia speaks too much and therefore she must be a virgin, while Sergio maintains that Cecilia is actually shy, silent, and intelligent.

Once again, intelligence and silence are equated. Villela incorrectly interprets Cecilia as loquacious, while Sergio suggests the contrary. Women are forced to fit into one male stereotype or the other. However, at the end of the novel, Cecilia silently walks the streets of the city alone with her thoughts and defies all female stereotypes. She has discovered herself and is happy with the revelation: "She felt distant, surprised, and totally happy" (368).[18]

Rito de iniciación is an example of what Annis Pratt terms the archetype of the novel of development (Pratt 1981, 13). According to Pratt, the goal of such novels is usually to groom the heroine for marriage. Consequently, Castellanos's version of the bildungsroman is certainly a subversive twist on the normal plot development, since her protagonist, Cecilia Rojas, is groomed away from this marital goal and toward an independent existence and career as a writer through her social and educational experiences in Mexico City. In this novel, paradoxical silence does not stem from antithetical tendencies toward patriarchy on the part of the female protagonist, but rather from the language-versus-silence debate that permeates both characterization and novelistic development. As we previously observed, both speech and silence have fluid connotations within the text, which moves back and forth between the expressive and uncommunicative dimensions of each. The shifting values placed on both language and silence by the protagonist, Cecilia, directly relate to her attempts to develop a writing career and the frustrations she experiences therewith, as well as her social interactions with her boyfriend, Mariscal, and the other members of her college group. This collision of varied connotations combined with Cecilia's professional and personal ups and downs culminates in the novel's conclusion, in which she establishes her own identity and is happy with her nontraditional fate (the previously outlined abandonment by her boyfriend and relegation to solitude). In this sense, paradoxical silence, characterization, and the bildungsroman plot twist all become inextricably linked.[19]

The Function of "the Look" in *Rito de iniciación*

Rito de iniciación also employs "the look" as a nonverbal form of communication. Many critics discuss the importance of both the male and female look or gaze in fiction. Robyn Warhol studies this phenomenon in Jane Austen's *Persuasion*, where looks come to function for Austen's last heroine as an alternative language, a means of communication without recourse to words (Warhol 1996, 23). According to Warhol, the look is an intradiegetic phenomenon that occurs between characters, whereas "the gaze" refers to the text's extradiegetic focalization (the reader or viewer's adoption of the viewpoint of a specific character). Warhol suggests that in *Persuasion* the looks of male and female characters serve different purposes: women's looks are a source of knowledge while men's looks function on the level of appearance and serve to objectify what they look at (104–5).

In *Rito de iniciación*, the protagonist Cecilia Rojas is characterized largely through her powers of observation and the philosophical meditation that such observation elicits. Just as in Warhol's analysis of *Persua-*

sion, the female look functions as a source of knowledge confirming the accuracy of feminine perceptions and serves as another nonverbal language for women.

The theme of the look begins to evolve in the novel as a consequence of Cecilia's discovery of an obscene drawing in Lorenzo's notebook. This discovery invests new power in the act of looking. Cecilia meditates on this power in the following passage: "That light that exposed defenseless objects to a look that would never again manage to be diverted. The naked object before the fixed gaze. Between the two antagonists no obstacle would impede the observation without attenuators of the most minimal edge of a reality" (Castellanos 1996, 138).[20] The look is a source of knowledge capable of revealing the true reality of an object: "An incident that Cecilia interpreted (in order to explain it, to justify it, to excuse it) as the obvious revelation before a foreign gaze, a gaze that was even disinterested in her femininity to a certain degree" (138).[21] Moreover, the look functions both ways, and hence serves a communicative purpose, as Cecilia concedes when she states, "I want the other to look at me, as the Hindus say, with a favorable look" (177).[22] In other words, looks contain judgments, messages to be interpreted, as when Cecilia's mother used to look at her disapprovingly during her childhood: "One of those looks that give each action the weight of a judgment" (149).[23]

Similarly, when the two student activists (ironically termed "he of the voice" and "the mute ox") arrive to talk to the group, we see them through Cecilia's powers of observation (150–51). Looks are also actions that, according to the poet Manuel Solís, can either destroy or paralyze their object (Castellanos 1996, 219).Even during her sexual encounters with Mariscal, Cecia functions as an observer acquiring information about her object: "Cecilia applied herself, furiously; to learning the art of pleasing. . . . She divined his fantasies and took care to comply with them. This application, in addition to its immediate utility, helped her to maintain herself on the margins, like an attentive observer, not like an alienated participant" (233–34).[24]

Finally, Cecilia summarizes the communicative/informative power of her "look" when, toward the end of the novel, she completes her voyage of self-discovery: "I want to be me, obscure, quiet, anonymous. In order to only *look*, to understand something, as small as it might be, to tell myself in secret that which I have understood" (322, my emphasis).[25] Silence and the look merge to create a feminine space of self-revelation and identity. "The look," just like Radner and Lanser's techniques of indirection, constitutes a form of encoded feminist silence within the text.

Parentheses in *Rito de iniciación*

The third and final manifestation of the silence-versus-language debate is found in Castellanos's use of parentheses. Parentheses are a paralinguistic element that often appears in Castellanos's work, but whose frequent presence in *Rito de iniciación* grabs the reader's attention as an important stylistic marker. It is interesting that both Denise Delorey and Gabrielle Parker view parentheses as having important metaphorical value in women's fiction (Delorey 1996, 103–98; Parker 1990, 116–17). In her study of Virginia Woolf, Delorey explores how Woolf puts her real subject in parentheses; in other words, she constructs her novels on the basis of "moments of being" seen as parenthetical to the real world and not on the great events associated with patriarchal narratives (Delorey 1996, 94). Delorey sees the analogy between narration and parentheses as "a feminist narrative principle" that opens up "gaps" in a text that "allow the subjectivity of language to move beyond form to truths which are perhaps unpresentable" (105).

Castellanos's *Rito de iniciación* is similar in this regard, because the novel's action is minimal, consisting largely of Cecilia's thoughts and observations, as well as a number of intellectual discussions among the members of the group (and in one section, among several writers). Thus, Castellanos, like Woolf, presents us with the "moments of being" excluded from the male narrative.

This analogy to parentheses, however, does not explain the actual use of parentheses itself. For this we must turn to Parker's study of the French writer Michèle Perrein. According to Parker, Perrein's use of parentheses is metaphorical, reflecting the marginal situation of her heroines in society. Parker also sees parentheses as "an invisible wall which imprisons women and cuts them off from the normal process of communication" (relegating them to silence) (Parker 1990, 116–17). Parker's idea of the symbolic value of parentheses is also applicable to the marginalized status of women in *Rito de iniciación*. The symbolic, as we shall see in chapter 6 on Rosario Ferré, functions as a form of indirect and thus "silent" signification in the text. In addition to this symbolic function, however, I would like to suggest that parentheses operate in another manner in the novel. Parentheses, as a qualifying or amplifying phrase, have been frequently devalued as a rhetorical figure of digression. Robert Grant Williams shows the importance of the presence of parentheses in discourse, indicating that use of parentheses changes the relationship between the words in the "properly grammatical" syntactic space and the parenthetical phrase. This connection between the two spaces can function in a variety of ways, which include antagonistic or complementary, interruptive or continuous, and imitative or innovative relationships (Williams 1993, 66). Williams's description of parentheses brings to mind Bakhtin's concept of dialogic discourse. Parentheses can establish different relationships with the text into which they are interpolated, ranging from confirmation to negation. Depending upon such relationships, parentheses can help to create different but always integral meanings in a text.

Upon examining Castellanos's use of parentheses in *Rito de iniciación*, we see that in the majority of the cases, parentheses are used to further explain statements made in the main body of the text. Castellanos's constant use of parentheses reflects a need for clarification that underscores the inadequacy of patriarchal language for female expression.[26] If we return to Castellanos's observations on language cited earlier in this chapter, we see that the persistent employment of parentheses may reflect the need to create a new language, one that can express the experiences of the oppressed as well as of the oppressors. Thus, parentheses, in addition to their role as a nonverbal marker of marginalization, allude to the so-called other side of the coin of silence: feminist attempts to revitalize and reappropriate language to reflect their own concerns and voice the experiences that patriarchal language has rendered "silent." This is the task the novel's protagonist, Cecilia, faces in her chosen career as a writer. In this manner, *Rito de iniciación* reflects on both the subversive and nonsubversive values of silence as well as language.

The use of parentheses in Castellanos can be seen as either a form of encoded silence or a form of symbolic silence (to be discussed in chapter 6), depending upon one's perspective. As we saw earlier in this chapter, Radner and Lanser list metaphor as a coding technique. Since metaphor bases itself on a similarity between an object and the thing that stands for it, we can think of parentheses as a marginal linguistic form that encodes women's marginal status. Hence, parentheses would be another form of encoded silence. If, however, we understand parentheses as a clarification technique that exposes the limits of man-made language for women, the connection between parentheses and what they stand for is no longer based on a concrete similarity between parentheses and the object. Hence, the connection becomes more symbolic than metaphoric.

In this case, Castellanos's employment of parentheses can be seen as a precursor to Rosario Ferré's symbolic silence, which I discuss in chapter 6.

Castellanos and the Mexican Feminist Movement

Castellanos's encoded silence corresponds to a moment of hiatus between the first and second waves of Mexican feminism. Miller documents the general decline of the women's movement in Latin America during the 1950s: "But by the late 1950s the fiery zeal of the early feminists was no longer apparent: the first wave of feminism in Latin America was at ebb tide. The older generations of feminists were dying or dead; the causes around which they rallied were no longer in the political foreground" (F. Miller 1991, 143).

Carmen Ramos Escandón confirms this decline in the women's movement specifically with respect to Mexico. She claims that after Mexican women obtained the right to vote in 1953, the feminist movement in Mexico began to lose its effectiveness. Escandón attributes this decline to the movement's "somewhat elitist character, narrow urban base and fragmentation over class issues. Efforts to counter the ingrained sexual stereotyping made little headway and were repeatedly frustrated at critical times by the activism of Catholic and conservative groups.... By the late 1960s, the movement was practically nonexistent as an autonomous movement" (Escandón 1994, 45).

This lull in the feminist movement during the 1950s and 1960s was already documented with regard to Chile and the later works of Marta Brunet in chapter 2. Despite many differences in the political development of Chile and Mexico (Chile had a long democratic tradition, while Mexico underwent a major social and political revolution in 1910), all the Latin American countries appear to have suffered a decline in feminist activism after suffrage was obtained. In Chile, the women's movement collapsed shortly after the election of Carlos Ibáñez del Campo. Ibáñez attempted to marshal women's support for him by arranging a meeting between Argentine congresswomen representative of the Argentine Women's Party, headed by Eva Perón, and seven leaders of Chilean women's groups. The Argentine congresswomen secretly offered the Chilean women a check in exchange for relinquishing their independence and formally joining forces with Ibáñez. Although some of the Chilean women's leaders, such as Felicitas Klimpel, refused the bribe, news of the episode leaked to the press, which severely discredited Chilean women's groups and led to their eventual demise (Baldez 2002, 29–30). Although the Mexican women's movement continued to have isolated groups that made some political gains in the 1950s, the fundamental status of women remained unchanged, and the movement did not regain significant momentum until the 1970s (F. Miller 1991, 139).

It is interesting to note the differing responses of Brunet and Castellanos to the decline in feminism of the postsuffragist years prior to the second-wave feminism of the 1970s. As we saw in chapter 2, Brunet's later texts (notably *María Nadie*) seemed to parallel this attenuation by a less-vehement tone, less-extreme circumstances in the lives of her protagonists, and a less-militant silence (compared to the extremely combative silence of the suffragist era found in her earlier stories). Castellanos's work appears to respond to similar events by encoding subversive feminist silence to make it less obvious and more acceptable to patriarchal society. Nonetheless, this encoding in no way represents a diminution of feminist thought. On the contrary, Castellanos reacts to the feminist lull by consistently exposing women's inferior societal status in her texts. Encoding techniques reflect the reality of a society not yet primed for more overt feminist strategies.

Although Castellanos does focus on subaltern, indigenous characters in many of her works, the stories discussed here that exhibit feminist silence, as well as her *Rito de iniciación*, largely present bourgeois women (similar in background to her own) and their specific problems. It is interesting to note that two of Castellanos's protagonists are writers (which in Latin America is a career that usually signifies a comfortable economic status). In both "Fleeting Friendships" and the novel *Rito de iniciación*, the narrators are aspiring writers who come to appreciate the feminist value of silence as they struggle with their identity as authors. The narrator of "Fleeting Friendships," just like Cecilia Rojas in *Rito de iniciación*, is initially presented as a loquacious woman. It is only after contact with Gertrudis, her silent, working-class friend, that the narrator of "Fleeting Friendships" comes to understand the power of silence. Similarly, Cecilia's initial loquacity is gradually transformed into a contemplative, feminist silence as she matures through the process of the female bildungsroman. Such career and identity problems are far removed from the concerns of the working-class Gertrudis of "Fleeting Friendships," whose silent functioning reflects the situation of a woman who comprehends the importance of action versus words, and who must toil in order to subsist. Similarly, the well-educated protagonist of "Cooking Lesson" can afford to burn dinner as a form of silent protest, whereas working-class women characters, like Gertrudis, find a more pragmatic way to symbolize their anger. Castellanos's silences may all be codified in some manner, but her female protagonists execute their protests in ways that reflect their particular socioeconomic status.

5
Hyperbolic Silence: Agon and Irony in the Works of Isabel Allende

ISABEL ALLENDE WAS BORN IN LIMA, PERU, IN 1942, TO CHILEAN parents. Her father, Tomás Allende, a Chilean diplomat, was a cousin of the Chilean president, Salvador Allende, Isabel's godfather. Allende's parents divorced in 1945. Owing to the diplomatic career of her stepfather, Ramón Huidobro, Allende was educated abroad in a variety of European countries as well as Lebanon. She returned to Chile in 1958 to complete her education because of Lebanon's political unrest. In 1962 she married Miguel Frías. Her daughter, Paula, was born in 1963 and her son, Nicolás, in 1966. Allende worked as a journalist for the magazine *Paula* (1967–74) and also as a television interviewer (1970–75). After the Pinochet military coup in 1973, Allende lost her position with *Paula* on political grounds. She published her first novel, *The House of the Spirits*, in 1982 and her second, *Of Love and Shadows*, in 1985. During this period, Allende lectured in various colleges in the United States, including Montclair State University, the University of Virginia, and Barnard College. She divorced her first husband in 1987 and married William Gordon, a California attorney, in 1988. Allende currently resides in the United States. Her daughter, Paula, died of a rare disease known as porphyria in 1992 (Rodden 1999, xv–xviii).

Allende is the most popular contemporary Latin American novelist. In addition to her first two novels mentioned above, her list of works include the novels *Eva Luna* (1987), *El plan infinito* [*The Infinite Plan*] (1991), *Paula* (1994), *Hija de la fortuna* [*Daughter of Fortune*] (1999), *Retrato en sepia* [*Portrait in Sepia*] (2001), *La ciudad de las bestias* [*The City of Beasts*] (2002), *El reino del dragón de oro* [*The Kingdom of the Golden Dragon*]

(2003), *El bosque de los pigmeos* [The Forest of the Pygmies] (2004), *Zorro* (2005), and *Inés del alma mía* [Inés of My Soul] (2006). The trilogy of novels published between 2002 and 2004 were specifically written for teenagers. She also has two collections of short stories, *The Stories of Eva Luna* (1989) and *Afrodita* (1997).

Isabel Allende's status as a best-selling author has nourished the emergence of a considerable bibliography on the writer. These studies focus on a variety of topics, notably her use of magical realism, her fiction's relationship to Chilean history, and both male and female characterization within her texts. Silence, although sometimes mentioned, is not the focus of the current literary criticism.[1] This chapter examines hyperbolic silence as theme and narrative technique in three of Allende's most famous works: *The House of the Spirits* (1982), *Of Love and Shadows* (1985), and her collection of short stories, *The Stories of Eva Luna* (1989). I will show how Allende's texts, largely through the use of irony and hyperbole, both thematically and stylistically underscore the active, subversive value of silence and use this inversion of traditional silence as a signal to the reader to view the text from a feminist perspective.[2]

The House of the Spirits and *Of Love and Shadows* within the Context of Chilean Feminism

One of the reasons that the reader may choose to interpret hyperbolic silence as a subversive strategy in Allende's novels is that it appears within the context of a plot that traces historical Chilean feminism. According to Lisa Baldez, Chilean feminism emerged and developed during moments of political reorganization in Chile because women perceived the "climate of conflict as an opportune moment to press for gender-specific demands" (Baldez 2002, 24). Thus, the moments of formation of opposition to the Allende (1971–73) and Pinochet (1973–90) governments, respectively, provided the environment necessary for women to mobilize and protest along gender lines within a specific political context. This correspondence between the formation of new political alliances and feminist activism also applies to the early development of first-wave feminism in Chile. Women's mobilization through the group MEMCH (The Movement for the Emancipation of Chilean Women) peaked in 1935, the same year that the Popular Front (a coalition of Socialists, Communists, and the Reformist Radical Party) was formed (Baldez 2002, 24).

This early period of Chilean feminism was focused on the question of women's suffrage, which, once obtained in 1949, led to the disintegration of the movement. This period is captured in *The House of the Spirits* through the character Nívea, the family matriarch, who is a leader of the women's suffrage movement. During the first few pages of the novel, the reader is told that Nívea fostered her husband's political ambitions largely because she was hoping that if he won political office, he would then be able to help gain the right to vote for women.

The years prior to the Allende government (the period from 1949 until the early 1970s) were characterized only by isolated feminist struggles (Agosín 1987, 20–23), whereas the Allende and Pinochet regimes constituted periods of coordinated action on the part of women in opposition to each of these governments. The famous Chilean sociologist Julieta Kirkwood confirms that the postsuffrage period was characterized by an overwhelming passivity on the part of women, especially those who belonged to progressive political parties, and that this inaction was only somewhat broken by the resurgence of the Christian Democratic Party (1964–70). The Christian Democratic Party provided women with "a revised secularized religious ideology that permitted them to maintain conservatism but this time with a progressive language" (Kirkwood 1986, 58–60).[3] Isabel Allende continues her tracing of this development of the Chilean feminist movement through Clara, whose adult life corresponds to the aforementioned lull in feminist activism (during the 1950s and 1960s). Clara verbalizes the elitist nature of the first-wave feminism she experienced in her childhood and the need to unite feminism to class concerns. In addition, she transmits her mother's social-feminist message to the workers at *Las Tres Marías*, thus keeping alive the family's feminist tradition (Allende 1986, 81). When Clara returns to the city, she also becomes an expert in helping the poor acquire social services through the state and the church. Nonetheless, her actions do not correspond to any coordinated efforts to achieve feminist goals, as do the subsequent feminist mobilizations during the Allende and Pinochet governments. Indeed, Clara's efforts to help the poor illustrate the dilution of the feminist movement into charity and public assistance during the time period prior to the Allende government (Kirkwood 1986, 84).

During the democratically elected socialist government of Salvador Allende (1971–73), conservative women mobilized to protest widespread food shortages. On December 1, 1971, middle-class women led a demonstration known as the March of the Empty Pots. Thousands of women banged on empty pots as they marched toward the presidential palace. When a pro-governmental group attacked the women, the police intervened and the march was terminated. After the march, its organizers formed a new group called Fem Power who considered themselves "the Chilean version of Women's Liberation" (Baldez 2002, 87). The empty pots became an important symbol of female mobilization in Chile. After the Pinochet coup, this symbolic meaning of the pots ironically became "inverted when people began to bang on them to voice their opposition to the military dictatorship" (82). Allende recounts this now famous march in *The House of the Spirits*: "The women of the opposition, paraded in the streets pounding their empty pans in protest against the shortages in the stores" (Allende 1986, 362).

Although Salvador Allende did initiate some programs and legislation to help women, he still emphasized traditional female roles, such as that of mother, in his speeches. Many leftists continued to hold patriarchal attitudes toward women, preferring their wives to stay out of politics and in the home. Hence, although women gained certain rights (longer maternity leave, day care, etc.) under Allende, which helped integrate them into the workforce, the fundamental social structures remained unchanged. Nonetheless, some contend that although women under Allende's government were engaged in traditional female activities, such as teaching and learning domestic skills like knitting, the fact that women were being trained to enter the workforce was an act that challenged traditional gender roles (Shayne 2004, 110). Allende extended the Centros de madre (Mother's Centers), established for middle- and upper-class women under the Christian Democrats, to working-class women, and these became locations for establishing feminist/political alliances (Shayne 2004, 81).

The House of the Spirits reenacts female mobilization under the Allende government through Blanca's activities as a sculptor. The reader is told that Blanca "began to teach ceramics in the shantytowns, where the women had organized to learn new trades; and for the first time, she took an active role in the political and social life of the country (Allende 1986, 347).

Blanca also picks up the development of the feminist movement in two significant ways. First, she leaves her husband, Jean de Satigny. Even after Satigny's death, she refuses to marry her lifelong lover, Pedro Tercero, preferring to live a single and independent life. Blanca clearly performs what was considered an unacceptable role for women: "Blanca preferred those furtive hotel rendezvous with her lover to the routine of everyday life, the weariness of marriage" (Allende 1986, 311). Despite the fact that Blanca's lover is a leftist senator under the Allende government, he espouses patriarchal ideology when he abandons Blanca because she refuses to marry him and adopt the traditional role of dutiful wife.

After Augusto Pinochet's 1973 military coup, women were the first group to mobilize to protest the dictatorship, largely owing to their "public invisibility," which allowed them to meet inconspicuously and initiate networks of resistance (Shayne 2004, 95). Ironically, some of the women who initially supported Pinochet's coup later became his opponents upon discovering the magnitude of his human rights abuses.

The first opposition group to the Pinochet dictatorship, formed under the auspices of the Chilean Vicariate, was the Association of the Families of the Detained and Disappeared. It was primarily composed of women in search of their husbands, sons, and brothers. Many of these women were to become *arpilleristas*, a term referring to the crafters of Chilean burlap tapestries that depict the atrocities of the dictatorship and were illegally exported from Chile and sold around the world to both sustain the poor women and to manifest their political protest. The *arpilleristas* also displayed their political protest through appearing in the streets and plazas and waving white handkerchiefs (Agosín 1987, 10–17). This form of political protest suggests a possible interpretation of the symbolism Allende constructs on the basis of the color white through the names of her protagonists (Nívea, Clara, Blanca, Alba) in *The House of the Spirits*. These names may be understood (among many other potential associations) as a symbol of protest akin to the white handkerchiefs used by the *arpilleristas*.[4]

The Chilean feminist movement experienced a true resurgence in 1983 under the umbrella organization known as MEMCH '83. As we discussed earlier, this group was originally formed in the 1930s. The purpose of its reconstitution was to call for a public forum to organize women against the pervasive male domination of Chilean society (Agosín 1987, 23). Pinochet's dictatorship was seen by some Chilean women to parallel the patriarchy they suffered at home. Shayne notes: "The motto 'democracy in the country and in the home' spoke to patriarchy in both macro- and microstructures of society, leftist parties included" (Shayne 2004, 113). Baldez adds that "Chilean feminists . . . linked the transfer of gender roles with an end to military rule, comparing the authoritarian system of political rule to the dominant pattern of behavior within Chilean families" (Baldez 2002, 161–62). Women were instrumental in bringing about Pinochet's downfall in the plebiscite that ended his dictatorship in 1989.[5] In *The House of the Spirits*, Alba's (Clara's granddaughter) life corresponds to the period of the Pinochet dictatorship. The fusion of feminist consciousness and opposition to Pinochet is projected through this character. During Allende's government, Alba participates in the student movements and her boyfriend, Miguel, belongs to a radical faction. After the coup, Alba helps those in danger of being "disappeared" escape from Chile. She is eventually captured by the government, tortured, and raped. Alba's resistance parallels the public activism of women in the wake of dictatorship. The connection between Alba's political activity and women's unity can be seen in the relationship established between Alba and the other female political prisoners. Ana Díaz, a former university companion, helps Alba endure harsh prison life, and the women experience a sense of solidarity singing and resisting together. Once Alba is freed, she fondly recalls her sense of community with the other female prisoners. It is possible to interpret this solidarity as a prelude to the feminist activity that arose after the Pinochet coup among women previously involved in left-wing politics, although some critics view Alba's attitude as a glib glossing-over of the era's violence (A.A. Nelson 2002, 202). In 1978 a group of professional Chilean women formed ASUMA (the Association for the Unity of Women), which later joined with the Academy of Christian Humanism to achieve human rights gains under Pinochet. ASUMA was one of the groups that formed the basis for creating a feminist movement in Chile in the 1980s (Baldez 2002, 135–36).

Of Love and Shadows also traces the development of the feminist movement under the Pinochet dictatorship. The novel reenacts the coalition established between professional and working-class women over human rights issues to achieve a feminist movement. This can be seen through the figures of Irene Beltrán and Digna Ranquileo, who unite to help Digna's daughter, Evangelina Ranquileo. Evangelina's disappearance sparks an alliance between the two women in which Irene uses her position as a journalist to help Digna discover the whereabouts of her daughter: "Francisco started to come with them, but Irene motioned him to stay behind, certain that if she was alone with Digna they could establish a solid female complicity. . . . Digna knew that in spite of the apparent abyss separating them, she could tell Irene the truth, because in essence they were sisters—as finally, all women are" (Allende 1988, 111–12).[6]

This solidarity parallels the emerging solidarity between upper-class women and lower-class women during the late 1970s and 1980s. According to Francesca Miller, by the end of the 1970s "a cross-fertilization occurred: women of diverse cultures and ethnicities and social and economic strata became aware of the urgency and immediacy of one another's concerns" (F. Miller 1991, 201). Indeed, the entire novel may be seen as the chronicle of the development of political consciousness in Irene, representative of the Chilean bourgeoisie. Irene, through her contact with Digna and Evangelina, evolves from a spoiled, ignorant, upper-class woman into an individual aware of the abuses of the dictatorship and the linkage between authoritarian governments, the economic plight of the working class, and discrimination against women.

Other female figures, such as Hilda Leal, also capture the specific character of the women's movement in Chile under Pinochet. Severe repression in the early 1970s, made it difficult for people to meet in groups and organize in any systematic way. Nonetheless, women began to organize as early as three weeks after the coup when the Association of Democratic Women was formed. Baldez states: "In the beginning they used traditional female activities to camouflage their meetings. Tea parties and group knitting sessions enabled them to get together to organize their activities" (Baldez 2002, 71). Women obtained permission to assemble by disguising the political nature of their groups. Hilda Leal's activities clearly mimic this tendency. Her religious group meetings actually have political content if only in the form of prayer vigils against Pinochet (Allende 1988, 98). The important point is that Hilda's actions are in no way apolitical. Similarly, the manner in which Hilda disguises the nature of her meetings to her family—namely, by pretending that she is engaging in sporting activities, recreates the way in which women under the Pinochet dictatorship disguised the true nature of their organizations.

Allende also brings feminist issues to light through the problems of some of her female protagonists. Digna's husband beats her, while her daughter, Evangelina is a rape victim. Irene, as a journalist, reveals the perils of prostitution. The plight of unmarried pregnant women is brought to the fore through the narration of Irene's nanny giving birth to a dead baby while alone in the house. Irene's relationship with Gustavo Morante, a military captain, reflects the traditional ideas about women held in Chile, particularly by the conservative Right, which considered the women's liberation movement a threat to society. Despite the less-direct historical link between the Chilean feminist movement and *Of Love and Shadows*, the reader can still perceive specific connections to the movement as it evolved in Chile in the 1970s and 1980s, and this feminist theme, viewed in conjunction with the text's use of silence, helps the reader to arrive at a feminist-oriented interpretation of the text.

There is an interesting link between Allende's use of irony and hyperbole in her fiction and the development of Chilean feminism as an offshoot of Chilean politics during the Allende and Pinochet governments. We have seen how the Chilean women's movement arose in conjunction with anti-Allende and anti-Pinochet protests in Chile. This political era was specifically characterized by the exaggeration of the problems of the Allende government by anti-Allende factions, which was what ultimately led to Allende's downfall: "The conservative media engaged in an aggressive campaign to discredit every government program and hyperbolize every problem in order to convey a climate of increasing social disorder and economic chaos" (Baldez 2002, 72). Moreover, the entire Chilean political situation suffered an ironic bent: many of the same people who initially supported Pinochet's coup later became his opponents because of his human rights abuses. Similarly, symbols that were used against the Allende government, particularly by women, were later ironically turned against Pinochet himself, such as the banging on the empty pots. Finally, some political analysts have noted the irony of the fact that the political opportunity that led to the creation of the 1980s Chilean feminist movement was the highly patriarchal dictatorship of Pinochet (Shayne 2004, 111). Consequently, Isabel Allende's overwhelming use of irony and hyperbole, even in nonhistorical texts such as *The Stories of Eva Luna*, mirrors the feminist movement in Chile as linked to the major factions in Chilean politics. The Chilean audience who experienced the events of the 1970s and 1980s was both well aware and extremely perceptive of strategies of irony and hyperbole, since they characterized Chile's ongoing political reality. Allende's use of hyperbolic silence addresses the Chilean public through very familiar and hence highly comprehensible techniques.[7]

Silence and the Construction of Agon in *The House of the Spirits*

Now that we have an understanding of how Allende's novels interface with their historical context (which provides a foreground for a feminist perspective), we can approach silence in Allende's novels through the textual structure of play suggested by Wolfgang Iser. Iser counterpoises play to representation as a foundation for literary interpretation, indicating that play has two major advantages: it does not need to concern itself with meaning, and it allows for the conception of a work as a "dynamic interplay that moves toward a final result" (Iser 1989, 327–29).

Iser defines four diverse strategies, each of which permits a different type of game. The first and most pertinent of these strategies, "agon," is defined as a "fight or contest" when a text centers on conflicting norms or values. The reader must decide between these opposing positions (Iser 1989, 333).[8] Iser's textual play based on agon is a helpful tool for conceptualizing how Allende structures her novelistic discourse using the theme of silence. Allende structures her novels as a fight between traditional patriarchal norms and the emerging feminist views of her female protagonists. The reader must decide which viewpoint is the "meaning" of the novel, hence halting the text's play of positions.

Iser's theory aids in my articulation of the role of silence in Allende's novels *The House of the Spirits* and *Of Love and Shadows*. Allende does not employ silence in the negatively charged patriarchal sense—as a manifestation of oppression—but rather in a largely positive sense, as an affirmation of female strength and equal rights. Wherever positions of patriarchal authority appear in the text, they collide with textual cues of silence. These cues subvert the traditional passive value of silence, thus inherently suggesting the invalidity of patriarchal positions that clash with the attempts of the female protagonists to assert their own independence and identity.

The House of the Spirits opposes Esteban Trueba's narration and perspective to the worldviews of the female characters with whom he interacts in the novel, especially the narration by his granddaughter, Alba. Susan Frenk notes that Trueba embodies authoritarian patriarchy through a number of strategies, including demeaning discourses, censorship, and violence (Frenk 1996, 72). Trueba is associated with traditional patriarchal practices and viewpoints from the onset of the novel. For example, the novel's first chapter focuses on Esteban's fiancée, Rosa del Valle, who suffers an untimely death, having consumed a poisoned drink destined for her politician-father, Severo del Valle. Rosa's death proves devastating for the entire Valle family, but especially for her younger sister, Clara. Clara, in direct defiance of societal norms, attends Rosa's funeral, although Esteban clearly indicates the impropriety of such behavior: "It was the custom then for women and children not to attend funerals, which were considered a male province, but at the last minute Clara managed to slip into the cortege . . . She stayed by my side all along the way, a small, silent shadow . . . At that moment I hadn't been told that she hadn't spoken in two days; and three more were to pass before the family became alarmed by her silence" (Allende 1986, 34).

Esteban, despite his sympathy toward Clara, espouses the patriarchal viewpoint that funerals are a man's domain. Nonetheless, Clara silently challenges the patriarchal norm through her attendance at Rosa's burial, a presence directly associated with Clara's silence ("silent shadow"; "she hadn't said a word in two days"). These two perspectives enter into agon or play, but it is too early in the novel for the reader to determine which stance is the text's (the implied author's viewpoint): Esteban's (society's) or Clara's.

The decision to become mute for nine years is Clara's hyperbolic reaction to her sister's death and the trauma of witnessing Rosa's autopsy. Rosa's autopsy turns into a double violation: on one level, Rosa's beauty is destroyed by the need to cut open her body to determine the cause of her death. On another level, Rosa's body is violated by the doctor's assistant, who is sexually aroused by it during the autopsy:

> She stayed until the young man she had never seen before kissed Rosa on the lips, . . . and between the legs. . . . She stayed until the assistant took her in his arms with the same tenderness with which he would have picked her up and carried her across the threshold of his house if she had been his bride. She could not move until the first lights of dawn appeared. Only then did she slide back into her bed, feeling within her the silence of the entire world. Silence filled her utterly. She did not speak again until nine years later (39)

The narrative voice conveys the medical assistant's behavior in quasi-positive terms. Although he treats the corpse in a sexual manner, his tenderness is underscored, which mitigates the impropriety of the assistant's actions. Patriarchal discourse would have us accept or condone the "rape" of Rosa's cadaver because of the assistant's tender feelings and/or the provocation of Rosa's extraordinary beauty, described earlier in the chapter. However, Clara's adoption of a long-term, hyperbolic silence after witnessing this scene enters into play or agon with such ideology, suggesting the rebellion against the sexual abuse of women.

Another instance in which Clara uses silence as a rebellion against physical abuse occurs after Esteban discovers that their daughter Blanca is having an affair with Pedro Tercero García. Esteban's angry reaction encapsulates a patriarchal attitude toward women's right to sexual freedom and underscores the inordinate role attributed to women in childrearing. Esteban blames Clara for Blanca's behavior and then physically beats her when Clara defends their daughter, stating that Esteban was guilty of having similar relationships without the mitigating factor of love. Clara's reaction to such abuse is the adoption of a conscious, permanent silence toward her husband: "Clara never spoke to her husband again. She stopped using her married name and removed the fine gold wedding ring that he had placed on her finger twenty years before" (201).

The way in which Clara fights back against Esteban's physical and verbal abuse is through an exaggerated silence, which no longer signifies traditional passive submission in patriarchal society but rather becomes an active weapon of retaliation in Allende's text. Once again, an agon is created between a traditional, male perspective (a sexual double standard, conventional ideas about relationships governed by social class, and the female burden of responsibility in moral development, all expressed in Esteban's discourse) and new feminist ideas of female equality (elimination of the sexual double standard), which Allende couples with social equality (acceptability of a union between people of different social classes).

Blanca's relationship with her husband, Jean de Satigny, parallels to some degree Clara's relationship with Esteban. Blanca marries Satigny for respectability because she is pregnant with Pedro Tercero's child. Allende implicitly criticizes patriarchal values here through irony, since Satigny proves himself to be anything but respectable. When Blanca discovers his sadistic homosexual involvement with the Indian servants of the household, she abandons Satigny. We are told that "she never spoke of him again, nor did she offer any explanation for her flight from the conjugal abode. Clara, who had spent nine years without speaking, knew the advantages of silence and asked her daughter nothing, joining in her efforts to erase all memory of Jean de Satigny" (265).

It is not a coincidence that each female member of the Valle family is associated with some type of nonverbal ritual or expression. Caroline Bennett notes this tendency and associates it with "muted-group" or "wild-zone" theory. Whereas Bennett sees these magical and nonverbal behaviors as passive and antithetical to political action (Bennett 1998, 359–60), I believe that these activities are associated with sociopolitical changes that challenge societal norms and the reigning political order represented in the novel. This creates an agon between traditional male politics and rebellious female social consciousness, which collide throughout *The House of the Spirits*. Female efforts to effect social or political change are manifested through or accompanied by nonverbal forms of expression or silent ritualistic actions that substitute for the words of patriarchal language. Each of the main female protagonists engages in a different type of activity along these lines.

Both Nívea and Clara take their daughters on gift-giving missions to the poor in an attempt to compensate for economic inequality, although they recognize the inadequacy of their actions. This can be thought of as a silent act or ritual that is counterpoised to Esteban's view of poverty and economic difference, since the practice of these expeditions is passed down from mother to daughter across various generations.

Clara's spiritism, which becomes a major aspect of Blanca's education, also acquires a ritualistic character, becoming a regular Friday ceremony. Clara's ever-increasing involvement with the spirits is accompanied by a decreasing involvement in the domestic order relegated to her by patriarchal ideology. She assigns all household duties to the servants and abandons herself to a silent, psychic, inner world, which serves as a rebellion against the traditional domestic role assigned to women (135).

Blanca uses another medium, sculpture, as a form of silent expression and social protest. As we already observed, Blanca's classes on how to make clay figures turn into a form of social organization for women (347). Similarly, Blanca's daughter Alba, the most concrete political activist in the novel, starts off as a childhood painter drawing frescoes on her bedroom wall. There she painted "all the wishes, memories, sorrows, and joys of her childhood" (240–41). Swanson suggests that these activities represent a rebellion against the dichotomies established by patriarchal ideology, because they all depict hybrid figures, which symbolize the binary divisions that separate human beings (Swanson 1994, 227). These examples show that the protagonists' so-called wild zone is not a space of passive escapism, but rather one that is coupled with active subversion of both the social and patriarchal orders.

The theme of silence implicitly contends against patriarchal ideology in Allende's works by emphasizing the value of a female union that at times stretches across generations, or what Nina Auerbach terms a "community of women." Auerbach acknowledges the basis of such a community on a silent (implicit or nonverbal) code, which she refers to as "more a buried language than a rallying cry" (Auerbach 1978, 9), in contrast to the explicit, verbalized codes of male societies.

Allende illustrates the functioning of such a code among her female characters in *The House of the Spirits*. Indeed, Clara's telepathic abilities can be seen as a hyperbolic realization of this secret, silent bond between pairs or groups of women. For example, prior to Clara's marriage to Esteban, Férula, her future sister-in-law, wants to ask Clara if she can live with them, but cannot find a way to formulate the question. Clara anticipates Férula's query by inviting her to live with her and Esteban, thus confirming to Férula her mind-reading ability.

Several other episodes suggest a similar unvoiced dialogue between female characters. For example, when Blanca was pregnant, "she was convinced that her baby would be a girl. As her mother had done with her, she developed a whole system for communicating with the silent, uninterrupted dialogue" (251).

Perhaps the most important example of this unvoiced dialogue and silent code is found toward the end of the novel, when Clara's granddaughter Alba is imprisoned as a political subversive after the fall of the Allende government. When she is placed in solitary confinement she wishes to die, until Clara appears to her with the key to life in the shape of a mental or silent writing: "Clara also brought the saving idea of writing in her mind, without paper or pencil, to keep her thoughts occupied and to escape from the doghouse and live" (414).

Finally, in *The House of the Spirits*, Allende portrays silence as a source of strength for women. This attitude once again implicitly enters into combat or agon with the traditional male ideology that equates words with power. When Clara is pregnant, silence allows her to replenish the energy sapped by her physical state: "She wanted to rise to a level that would allow her to leave behind the discomfort and heaviness of pregnancy . . . She entered one of her long periods of silence—I think it lasted several months" (113). When Alba is being tortured, her silence attests to the strength of her determination and character, because she bravely weathers extreme physical pain that renders her unconscious, rather than betray her fellow citizens (409).

The House of the Spirits maintains a constant battle between patriarchal and feminist views that sustains the play of the novel until the end, when the family patriarch, Esteban Trueba, finally acknowledges the error of his sociopolitical philosophy and the reader can resolve the play into an ultimate meaning. Although some critics (Boyle 1995; A. A. Nelson 2002) feel that Trueba's apology and sudden portrayal as fundamentally good at the novel's conclusion negates the novel's implicit criticism of authoritarianism, such a change of heart on the part of the novel's chief proponent of right-wing ideology can be seen as the result of a process of evolution that many Chileans underwent because of the Pinochet coup and its devastating effects on their friends, families, and Chilean society as a whole.

The agonistic plot structure of *The House of the Spirits* studied above loosely conforms to Pratt's archetype of the novel of social protest (which is a variant of the novel of patriarchal enclosure) (Pratt 1981, 59). Allende does not follow the exact structure of this archetype in the way that Pratt outlines it in her study of British and American fiction (where women seek social equality exclusively through socialism and communism). Nonetheless, she does focus on character evolution through political circumstances that inform the general relationship between the two sexes. We already observed how hyperbolic silence is an important element in the construction of the polarization of these two types of discourses in *The House of the Spirits*. Ironic and hyperbolic constructions nurture the characters' interactions with each other within the context of the Allende and Pinochet governments. This sociopolitical backdrop foregrounds these relationships, which tend to dichotomize themselves in the following manner: pro-Allende, socially conscious women are abused by pro-Pinochet, violent men. These dichotomies motivate the plot movement, notably through the events surrounding Esteban and Clara's marriage, as well as Alba's interactions with Esteban García. Consequently, characterization, plot development, and irony and hyperbole as implicit constructions ultimately reinforce each other.

We already studied the agon established between Clara and Esteban's discourses in the novel. Although we observed Clara's hyperbolic silence as a subversive reaction to Esteban's abuse and philosophy of social inequality, we did not study how Esteban himself represents a hyperbolized portrait of right-wing political ideology. Prior to Allende's election, Esteban's conservative ideas are so exaggerated that his own political party is embarrassed by him. The narrator claims, "He was fanatical, violent, and antiquated, but he represented better than anybody else the values of family, tradition, private property, law and order" (307–8). Prior to the election of the Allende government, when Esteban cites statistics on the growth of communism, his own party suspects "they were just the senile rantings of an old man" (306). This exaggerated anticommunist stance also proves ironic in light of the subsequent political events of the dictatorship in which Esteban Trueba's own family members suffer at the hands of the government and he comes to recognize the flaws of the Pinochet dictatorship and his own ideology.

In *The House of the Spirits*, the social activist Alba is also pitted against Esteban García, representative of the military government. García is constructed as a hyperbolic portrait of social resentment and evil, from the time he first visits the Trueba mansion to ask for a recommendation to the police academy during Alba's childhood (286). On this early occasion, when García first meets the innocent Alba, the narrator informs us that although Esteban García has never before met Alba, he vehemently hated her and wished to destroy her because Alba had everything that he desired but could never obtain. He even entertains thoughts of sexually abusing little Alba. The Esteban García / Alba subplot is developed through a series of hyperbolic encounters such as this one, from which García evolves into his subsequent role as a torturer under the Pinochet dictatorship. García's portrayal as a twisted, vengeful man, who takes out his frustrations under the guise of performing governmental duties through such acts as dunking Alba's head into a bucket of excrement, is as hyperbolic as Alba's silence when she is faced with rape, torture, and solitary confinement in the "doghouse." Hyperbole is a direct instrument of both characterization and the various subplots that structure general plot development in *The House of the Spirits*.

Silence in *Of Love and Shadows*

Allende's second novel, *Of Love and Shadows*, similarly presents a constant collision of patriarchal and feminist perspectives that eventually resolve into a site of feminist perception. Silence, once again, is not portrayed as a form of patriarchal oppression, but rather as a subversive weapon against imposed societal norms for women. The novel focuses on the lives of several women from distinct social classes: Beatriz Alcántara and her daughter Irene Beltrán, from the upper class (although they are no longer wealthy); Hilda Leal, from the intellectual middle class (now impoverished as well), and Digna Ranquileo and her daughter Evangelina, from the poverty-stricken, working class. Despite their many differences, these women all use silence and silent ritual as forms of rebellion that collide with the patriarchal ideology that attempts to suppress them.

Beatriz Alcántara is portrayed as a superficial person whose main aspirations in life are to be wealthy and beautiful. She lives for years in an unhappy marriage to Eusebio Beltrán, who eventually abandons the family. However, Beatriz's negative portrayal is attributed to the patriarchal forces with which she has been obliged to contend. Irene reflects upon her father's psychological abuse of her mother thus: "With time she came to realize that the man she adored could be despotic and cruel. He tormented his wife unmercifully, calling attention to each new wrinkle, to the unwanted pounds at her waist" (Allende 1988, 144). Moreover, Eusebio is the agent of Beatriz's financial ruin. He disappears, leaving Beatriz responsible for innumerable debts. The text counterpoises this traditional male-female marital relationship to Beatriz's affair with a younger man. Beatriz's new relationship takes the form of a secret biannual rite of purification, and thus a silent rebellion against societal norms:

> Michel represented the hidden and, at the same time, the brightest side of her life. She could not possibly share her secret; no one would have understood her passion for a man so much younger than her. She could imagine her friends' comments: Beatriz has lost her head over some boy, a foreigner; of course, he will exploit her and take all her money; at her age, she should be ashamed. No one would believe the tenderness and shared laughter, the friendship; he never asked for anything, and would not accept her gifts. They met twice a year, anywhere on the globe, for a few perfect days. She returned with her body gratified and her soul refreshed. (175–76)

Beatriz simultaneously voices her own perspective on her relationship with Michel and that of patriarchal society. In this implicit dialogue, Beatriz opposes her view of her affair with Michel to society's by repeating the "voice" of society itself through her friends' imagined comments. In this manner, Beatriz mocks societal miscomprehension of her relationship.[9] Her affair is a silent ritual that combats patriarchal stereotypes about male/female relationships (that it is okay for older men to love younger women, but not vice versa). In addition, this relationship is counterpoised to Beatriz's unsuccessful marriage, thus creating a relation of agon between forms of love respectively condoned and condemned by society.[10]

Hyperbolic silence is also a feminist weapon for Hilda Leal, wife of the Spanish Civil War exile Professor Leal. Hilda suffered an injury to her head during the war, and it resulted in a period of amnesia. She never speaks of her past tragedies in Francoist Spain, but it is not clear that this silence is due to any real forgetfulness on her part. She silently accompanies her husband in his political activities: "Those who knew her attributed her selective memory to the blow that had split open her skull when she was young, but Professor Leal could interpret the small signs and suspected that she had forgotten nothing. She simply did not want to burden herself with ancient woes, and for that reason, she never mentioned them, nullifying them through silence . . . She marched steadfastly [and silently] beside him in street demonstrations" (27).[11]

Hilda's silence can be seen as a subversive weapon. Silence is described in positive and assertive terms. The word "nullifying" suggests destruction, abolition, and obliteration, all of which are aggressive actions. Furthermore, Hilda was just as much in the public eye as her husband in the street demonstrations, where her silence was accompanied by her steadfast march, suggesting strength and determination, rather than passivity.[12]

Hilda's silence and silent rituals enter into direct battle both with patriarchal values as espoused by the authoritarian Pinochet dictatorship and the traditional forms of political activism enacted by her husband and sons (who find Hilda's efforts laughable). Hilda combats the government through what Saville-Troike terms an "institutionally-determined silence" (Saville-Troike 1995, 16) in the form of religious services or "mystical vigils" that occur twice weekly:

> As for Hilda, she used a unique method to resist the dictatorship. Her opposition was concentrated specifically against the General, who, according to her, was possessed by Satan and was the very incarnation of evil. She thought it possible to defeat him through systematic prayer and faith in her cause. Toward this goal, she attended mystic evening sessions twice a week. . . .
>
> Her family teased her so unmercifully that Hilda began going to her meetings in tennis shoes and slacks, hiding her prayer book under her sweater. She told them she was going out to jog in the park, and continued serenely in her laborious task of toppling authority with a rosary. (Allende 1988, 98–99)

This passage illustrates the subversive intent of silence and ritual as well as their existence as a political strategy in a relationship of agon or combative play with the patriarchal discourses of the novel. Silent ritual is characterized as a "laborious" task and hence as active, hard work, as opposed to a passive submersion in oppression. Just as the male members of the Leal family must disguise their more traditional forms of subversive activity (the printing press used to disseminate subversive pamphlets), Hilda must disguise her religious rituals, by pretending to engage in sporting events. However, Hilda's battle is twofold: she simultaneously fights the oppressive government and the patriarchal values of her own household. Hilda's religious rites are akin to Clara's spiritualist activities in Allende's first novel. They both are nontraditional, magical, or quasi-magical acts that are associated with public (political or social) rebellion.

The agon between patriarchal discourse and silent, rebellious feminine ritual is epitomized by the figure of Evangelina Ranquileo. Evangelina suffers daily fits of an unknown nature. During these fits she goes into a trance, has superhuman strength, and is said to make objects move telekinetically as well as heal the sick. Her mother, Digna Ranquileo, brings Evangelina to both priests and doctors (notable representatives of patriarchal authority) in an attempt to cure these hysterical fits. When the fits prove incurable, Evangelina "entered a stage of sadness that kept her silent and sleepless both day and night" (Allende 1988, 58). The silent fits also have a ritualistic character, as they occur every day at twelve noon. One afternoon, during this midday spectacle, which much of the town attends, a group of soldiers under the direction of Lieutenant Juan de Dios Ramírez appears. The soldiers shoot at the house and Ramírez attempts to arrest Evangelina. However, before they can touch her, Evangelina attacks and overpowers the lieutenant (74). Silent ritual is seen as a source of hyperbolic strength and empowerment. Evangelina's magical fits parallel Hilda's "mystical vigils" and Clara's spiritualism. These nontraditional talents or powers are counterpoised to traditional patriarchal power—in this case, the army. The important point is that these magical, ritualistic elements are equally weighted and valid positions in Allende's fiction, and are not summarily dismissed by a traditional, masculinist perspective.[13]

Subsequent to Evangelina's encounter with Ramírez, she is kidnapped, raped, and murdered by the lieutenant. Her body is eventually uncovered in a secret cave along with fifteen other cadavers of Chilean citizens murdered by the police. This event historically corresponds to the discovery in Lonquen of cadavers of disappeared Chilean citizens. Thus, Evangelina indirectly leads to the uncovering of a scandalous political crime. Evangelina is a force of resistance against Ramírez and eventually serves as the instrument used to bring him to justice. Her death is a silent catalyst that has repercussions in the public, political sphere and forces the government to take action against Ramírez and his men.

The plot structure of *Of Love and Shadows*, just like that of *The House of the Spirits*, can be thought of as a variation of Pratt's category of novels of social protest (Pratt 1981, 59). *Of Love and Shadows* enacts the same hyperbolic polarity between socially conscious, silent women and hyperbolically violent men through the relationship between Evangelina Ranquileo and Lieutenant Ramírez. Evangelina represents the victims of the Pinochet regime, while Lieutenant Ramírez encapsulates military repression under Pinochet. Evangelina's hyperbolic, silent attack on Ramírez is used to advance the historical aspect of the plot, since her burial in the mass grave of Lonquen leads to the discovery of the abuses of the Pinochet government by the Chilean people and Francisco and Irene's subsequent attempts to achieve punishment for these crimes. Hence, just as characterization and plot structure are intertwined in *The House of the Spirits*, so hyperbole, characterization, plot structure, and political discourse are all inextricably connected in *Of Love and Shadows*. Although Allende does represent women from different social classes in both novels, such as Beatriz, Hilda, Digna, and Evangelina (who are respectively from the wealthy, bourgeois, and working classes) and describes differences in their jobs and living conditions, Allende does not distinguish in any significant way between the silences or other feminist manifestations of these protagonists from different socioeconomic groups. Political affiliations, rather than class associations, are what unite the protagonists in Allende's novels. Political alliances tend to override all other differences in *The House of the Spirits* and *Of Love and Shadows*.

Ironic and Hyperbolic Appropriation of Stereotyping, Compensation, and Collusion in *The Stories of Eva Luna*

In contrast to Allende's novels, *The Stories of Eva Luna* rely less on agon fueled by silence and more on the use of irony and hyperbole as silent strategies to suggest a feminist reading. In order to understand how Allende constructs the stories through irony and hyperbole, we must first discuss the techniques used by the author to portray women in her tales. As we saw in the first chapter, there are four male-dominated processes used for female literary characterization: stereotyping, compensation, collusion, and recuperation. Stereotyping refers to the tendency to portray women according to a fixed, traditional model. Compensation is defined as imagery and ideas that "elevate the moral value of femininity," and collusion as "attempts to parade women's consent to their subordination" (Greene and Kahn 1985, 21–29). Finally, recuperation is the process by which men oppose attempts to challenge the historically dominant meaning of gender (28–29).

At first glance, many of the stories of Allende's *The Stories of Eva Luna* appear to subscribe to the dominant male ideology, presenting stereotyped female protagonists who consent to their own subordination and who are of an exaggerated moral fiber. However, upon closer examination, it becomes clear that stereotyping, compensation, and collusion are converted into a feminist tool in Allende's texts, principally through their ironic employment. Since irony is a "silent" technique, one that is developed strictly through an implied but never explicitly stated rejection of a declaration, its use by Allende supports the notion of the primacy of subversive silence in her texts.

In almost all of Allende's stories, the use of the figure of hyperbole goes hand in hand with the development of ironic situations. Frequently, silence is exaggerated to achieve the processes of stereotyping, compensation, collusion, and recuperation, which are then magnified to such a point that the reader begins to question their role in the narrative and suspect the possibility of ironic intent. Since Allende's narrators use hyperbole to construct conflicting visions of the female protagonists (who are first presented as extraordinarily passive and then as aggressive), the reader (particularly the reader who belongs to the feminist "discursive community") will be likely to attribute ironic intent to one of the portrayals.[14] This is particularly true because these conflicting visions occur within a context of ironic plot twists and situations. The fact that the hyperbolic portrayal is inherently the less credible one by virtue of its exaggeration will lead the reader to interpret the hyperbolized image as ironically constructed. Since hyperbole, like irony, is an implicit technique, not formally stated within the text, we can thus refer to hyperbolic silence (both exaggerated silence and hyperbole as a "silent" figure) when speaking of Allende's work.

It is important to note here that hyperbole (and the magical realism it frequently leads to within a text) is not in and of itself ironic. Indeed, many authors associated with hyperbole and magical realism, such as Gabriel García Márquez, with whom Allende has often been compared, employ hyperbole as a tool for creating fantasies or questioning the relationship between fiction and reality (and the impossibility, at times, of distinguishing between the two). What sets Allende's use of hyperbole apart is its consistent employment with regard to feminine roles within a context of situational irony. The exaggeration of traditional female roles and attitudes within the backdrop of these ironic contexts may suggest to some readers the possibility of a feminist-oriented reading in which the hyperbole in question is ironically interpreted as signaling just the opposite of what it appears to say.

Stories that Focus on Female Stereotyping

Although most of the stories from *The Stories of Eva Luna* include elements of at least two of the ideological techniques outlined above, Allende's tales may be categorized according to which of these ideological devices predominates in the text. The three stories that primarily portray and invert female stereotyping are "Dos palabras" [Two Words], "La mujer del juez" [The Judge's Wife] and "Niña perversa" [Wicked Girl]. The first of these, "Two Words," presents Belisa Crepusculario as a self-made woman from a poor family who supports herself "selling words" (i.e., writing things for other people). Belisa initially appears to be the victim of the feared civil war hero, the Colonel, whose henchman, el Mulato, abducts her under the Colonel's orders. The Colonel wants Belisa to write a political speech for him that will transform his reputation as a feared and brutal man, and convert him into a popular and beloved presidential candidate. Despite the brutality of her abduction, Belisa adopts a compassionate attitude toward the Colonel that fits with the traditional model of the understanding and love-struck female: "She felt the urge to help him because she felt a powerful desire to touch that man (Allende 1991, 15). The fact that Belisa feels pity for the man responsible for kidnapping her also suggests elements of female compensation and collusion as well.

However, despite Belisa's original casting as victim in the story, it is she who ironically triumphs over the Colonel in the end, dominating him through the two free words she awards him for the purchase of his speech. The reader is never explicitly told what these words are. He or she is left to infer their content on the basis of the effect they produce on the Colonel in the story:

> And every time he thought of those two words, he thought of Belisa Crepusculario. . . . The men knew then that their leader would never undo the witchcraft of those accursed words, because the whole world could see the voracious-puma eyes soften as the woman walked to him and took his hand in hers. (18–20)

From the reader's perspective, these words that constitute the story's prime catalyst and most potent force are completely silent, meant to remain a secret. Thus, they emphasize not only the power of words, but also the idea of the power of silence.

The hyperbolic power of Belisa's words makes them act like a spell with magical effects on the Colonel (Carullo 1997, 127). The subsequent union of Belisa and the Colonel leads the reader to question Allende's intention of portraying a traditional, idyllic romance between Belisa and her former captor. The exaggeration of the spell-like effect of Belisa's words (which the reader may infer as a declaration of love in the form of the two words *te amo*, or "I love you") underscores the power of women, which in turn subverts the traditional stereotype of the passive female waiting for identity to be bestowed on her by the love of a man. Normally, the man's declaration of love converts female existence into mere male appendage. Allende's portrayal of the love affair between Belisa and the Colonel is an inversion of the traditional male/female romantic roles in which the man "conquers" the female. Moreover, Belisa cannot at once be both a helpless, love-struck victim and a dominant conqueror. The simultaneous existence of these two postulated personalities within "Two Words" clearly leads the reader to an incongruity that he or she must resolve through rejection of one of these perforce ironic images.

Usually, as we shall see in later stories, the reader seizes upon the incredibility of the hyperbolic image to reject it and resolve the contradiction by assuming it is ironically constructed. However, in this particular story, both the vision of Belisa as captive colluding in her own victimization, falling in love with her oppressor, and Belisa as controlling lover who dominates the Colonel with her spell-like words are equally hyperbolic. This makes the reader's task of determining which interpretation to accept more challenging than in some of the other stories, where the exaggerated position logically leads to its rejection. In this case, the reader must make a decision about the implicit author's belief system in order to resolve the conflict. Is the author posited through textual structures more likely to think that women are love-struck females who contribute to their own victimization, or that women can be dominant and empowered by words? The feminist-oriented reader will certainly choose the second, feminist interpretation of the story, which is also reinforced by other narrative comments concerning women's social situation. For example, we are told that Belisa chooses her career because, as a poor woman, the only other options open to her are becoming a prostitute or a servant (Allende 1991, 12). This fact emphasizes the idea that Allende is contextualizing the story within a feminist framework focusing on the rights and condition of women. Allende's text thus ironically appropriates the strategies of stereotyping and compensation from traditional male ideology and silently converts them into cues that may be read from a feminist perspective by certain readers.

A second good example of Allende's appropriation of the technique of stereotyping is found in the story "The Judge's Wife." First, the title itself suggests that Casilda, the woman it refers to, is not a person in her own right, but merely her husband's appendage, "the Judge's wife," without her own identity. She is initially presented as a silent, weak, and passive figure. Second, she is hyperbolically described as silent and almost invisible on the text's very first page. She was " . . . as colorless and silent as a shadow . . . she seemed weightless, on the verge of dematerializing in a moment of carelessness. She gave the impression of not being there" (Allende 1991, 205).

This original casting of Casilda within the traditional female stereotype is subsequently contradicted by a number of other elements in the story. For example, we are told that after the Judge marries her he becomes less stern and more just, and that everyone noted that her influence caused great changes in his personality. These changes include some legal decisions that might be deemed feminist. For example, the Judge decides not to punish an adulterous wife on the grounds that her husband kept a concubine and therefore had no right to demand her fidelity, thus eliminating the sexual double standard.

Moreover, when the Judge imprisons the mother of the infamous criminal Nicolás Vidal, Casilda is the only one who can persuade the Judge to feed the starving woman, whose fast is intended to lure Vidal out of hiding and achieve his capture. This episode leads to the Judge's death and Vidal's relentless pursuit of Casilda and her children for revenge. Casilda devises a plan to gain time until the authorities can arrive and capture Vidal. Knowing that Vidal will rape her, she decides to dazzle him with her lovemaking abilities and thus stall him until the police catch up with him. This strategy leads to the story's incredible final paragraph in which Casilda and Vidal appear to fall in love: "She did not forget for one instant throughout that memorable afternoon that her objective was to gain time, but at some point she let herself go, marveling at her own sensuality, and somehow grateful to Vidal. That was why when she heard the distant sound of the troops, she begged him to flee and hide in the hills. Nicolás Vidal preferred to hold her in his arms and kiss her for the last time, thus fulfilling the prophecy that had shaped his destiny" (215).

This final paragraph is predicated on a romantic hyperbole: Casilda's sexual gratification is so great that she forgets her revenge on Vidal and urges him to flee, while he corresponds in kind by sacrificing his life for the privilege of a last kiss and final few moments in her arms. Thus, *The Stories of Eva Luna* once again appropriates the techniques of female stereotyping (Casilda becomes the woman who is dominated by her love of a man) and compensation (her moral superiority allows her to pardon her victimizer). Patricia Hart interprets the ending as an example of the latter, viewing it as one of the many instances of female forgiveness in Allende's stories, which is a way in which the chain of senseless male violence and revenge is broken by the moral superiority of women. Hart terms this technique "magic feminism," which she defines as a juxtaposition of real and impossible events narrated matter-of-factly in order to convey truths about the world beyond the fictional work (Hart 1993, 105).

The story's absurd and surprising conclusion is a hyperbole that fulfills Radner and Lanser's function of "distraction," which, as we saw in chapter 2, is the creation of a stylistic "noise" that prevents the feminist message from being heard (Radner and Lanser 1987, 417). In the case of "The Judge's Wife," that message is explicitly stated in the final paragraph when the narrator tells us that Casilda never even momentarily forgot that her goal was to gain time for an ultimate revenge. Her incredible moment of forgiveness coupled with Vidal's equally incredible self-sacrifice for love serve as a form of interference in the perception of this message. Once again, the reader is presented with two contradictory images of the protagonist. Casilda is either the silent, passive, female who falls in love with her rapist, or the strong, influential woman who controls her husband and leads to her enemy's downfall. Since Casilda cannot be both, the reader must infer that one of the images is ironically constructed. The hyperbolic, passive description of Casilda is more likely to be rejected by the reader on the basis of its incredibility. This will lead him or her to accept the construction of Casilda as the strong, clever, triumphant female. The text parodies romantic stereotypes in which women routinely fall in love with their rapists. Allende thus ironically appropriates an ideological device of patriarchy and uses it in an implicitly critical manner. The story's ultimate message is that Casilda is stronger and smarter than the male counterpart she has outwitted and triumphed over in the story.

Casilda's victory over Vidal is emphasized by Vidal's initial underestimation of Casilda's power. At the very beginning of the story we are told that Vidal did not find her attractive and that she had "delicate fingers useless for pleasuring a man. . . . Casilda seemed so insignificant and remote to him that he took no precautions against her" (Allende 1991, 203–4). Vidal's fate as read by a fortuneteller is to die for a woman. It is thus highly ironic that Casilda, whom he judged totally harmless and unappealing, turns out to be the one who causes his death and who ends up conquering him precisely with the sexual prowess in which he deems her totally lacking. Vidal suffers from the poor judgment men stereotypically attribute to women. Thus, the man who initially appears more intelligent and powerful ends up the victim who will lose his life at the end of the story. This ironic plot twist suggests Allende's ironic inversion of traditional stereotypes, which in turn serves to deconstruct them and to potentially situate the reader within a feminist perspective.

The description of Elena Mejías in the third story, "Wicked Girl," evokes the stereotyped image of a silent, invisible adolescent. The reader is told that Elena "moved in an aura of silence vanishing in the shadows of a room" and felt no need to communicate with her mother, since each was "immersed in her silent routine" (Allende 1991, 24–25). Despite this silence, Elena's mother knows what her daughter is thinking and is always able to sense when she is hiding things from her (25). Elena develops a passion for a new lodger in her mother's boardinghouse, Juan José Bernal, who becomes her mother's lover. Elena cannot express her budding adolescent sexual feelings through words and turns instead to ritual, a form of nonverbal, silent expression. Every night, when she knows Bernal is out of his room, she goes through his drawers, sucks his toothbrush, uses his comb, and touches his clothing in what is described as "the ceremonies she invented," "magic ceremonies" and a "lover's ritual" (30–32). One night, after secretly witnessing her mother and Bernal making love, Elena sneaks into Bernal's room while he is asleep and attempts to replace her mother. Bernal rejects her advances, and after this episode, Elena is sent off to boarding school while Bernal and her mother marry. Ironically, after Bernal rejects Elena, he becomes obsessed with her. Years later, when Elena is grown and about to marry, she visits her mother and stepfather. The latter, who has lived all these years tormented by desire for her, confronts her about the episode, but her response is an ironic and silent lack of recall of the incident.

Once again, Allende's story provides an ironic inversion of traditional stereotypes through an appropriation of them. She employs the stereotype of the female ruled by her passion for a man, only to invert it and create an obsessive male passion that translates into an unhappy life for Bernal. Elena goes on to lead a normal existence, but Elena's memory torments Bernal for the rest of his life.

Stories that Focus on Female Compensation

Three stories suggest an ironic appropriation of female compensation: "La venganza" [Revenge], "Clarisa," and "El oro de Tomás Vargas" [The Gold of Tomás Vargas].

The first of these tales, "Revenge," initially presents Dulce Rosa, the orphaned daughter of a murdered senator, as the weak, silent, stereotypical female victim. She is raped by Tadeo Céspedes, her father's political opponent, whom she "suffered in silence" (Allende 1991, 307). Despite her subsequent sworn revenge, years later Tadeo and Dulce fall in love and Dulce forgives him for his past deeds in a hyperbolic act of female compensation. However, this apparent compensation is used as a stepping-stone toward Dulce's ultimate revenge and triumph over Tadeo. Since the rape years ago, Dulce's memory has haunted Tadeo. Despite her forgiveness, Dulce is torn between avenging her father and her desire to marry Tadeo. She kills herself, thus condemning Tadeo to a long life of misery without her: "And he [Céspedes] knew he would live to be ninety and pay for his guilt with the memory of the only woman who had ever touched his heart" (311). In other words, Allende's story does not carry a message of forgiveness of the rapist (which would have resulted in the Dulce's marriage to him and a so-called happy ending), but rather results in the execution of revenge and punishment for Tadeo Céspedes. The reader is presented with two contradictory images of Dulce Rosa. On the one hand, she is the sweet, passive female who loves and forgives her rapist; on the other, she is the strong, determined woman who takes revenge on him through her suicide. The necessary execution of the promised revenge is underscored by the text's repetition of its certainty. When Dulce's father agrees not to kill her (a measure intended to avoid her rape by Tadeo), we are told that "there was unflinching fortitude in Dulce Rosa's clear eyes, and he knew she would survive and punish his executioner" (304). Similarly, the narrator informs us that revenge was "her one mission in this world" (307). This constant insistence on Dulce's desire for revenge makes her supposed transformation from revenge seeker to her rapist's lover so exaggerated and incredible that the reader, forced to choose between these two competing images, will be led to reject the passive, forgiving one and interpret it as an ironic portrayal that questions rather than confirms traditional gender ideology. The very method used to suggest forgiveness (love of the enemy) is ironically the instrument used to achieve revenge (tormenting him with her memory after her suicide).

The entire story "Clarisa" is an ironic twist on the notion of female compensation. Clarisa is the self-sacrificing wife and mother par excellence. She supports and cares for her insane husband and two mentally retarded children without ever complaining or feeling pessimistic, at that same time that she does good deeds in the town and is viewed by her neighbors as a saint. Clarisa is supposedly so traditional and old-fashioned that the narrator attributes her death to the shock she experiences during the pope's visit upon witnessing a group of men dressed as nuns carrying signs in favor of abortion, divorce, and other controversial matters. Once again, Allende uses hyperbole to subvert an image. The reader begins to doubt the validity of Clarisa's staid and perfect behavior, when he or she is faced with the incredible idea that her death was due to shock at seeing the homosexuals dressed like nuns. The ironic nature of this appropriation of female stereotyping and compensation is further supported by the discovery of Clarisa's infidelity with Diego Cienfuegos at the end of the story. She is not the traditional woman who perfectly subscribes to society's moral rules, but rather establishes her own version of morality, justifying her affair, which produced two normal children, as a balance for the two retarded children born through her marriage.

Clarisa's saintliness is also subverted and shown to be ironic by the result of some of her good deeds. For example, at the beginning of the story we are led to believe that she reforms a robber who attempted to steal from her and sent her Christmas presents every year thereafter. However, we later learn that the robber continued to steal, that he "had not mended his ways, but instead become a true professional" (54). He tells Clarisa when he visits her on her deathbed that he robs only wealthy people which is not a sin. The robber, like Clarisa, subscribes to his own moral rules, not society's. Thus, the text treats Clarisa's supposed ability to heal and reform ironically, which contradicts the image created of Clarisa as a flawless human being.

The ironic presentation of Clarisa as saint is not intended as a condemnation of the protagonist, but rather of society that imposes such norms and expectations. Clarisa's logic and values prove compelling, and the contrast between these and the appropriated female stereotyping and compensation serves to situate the reader within a feminist textual perspective. It is the ironic counterpoint of hyperbolic extremes, sainthood versus marital infidelity, that leads the reader in this direction.

The construction of an ironic interpretation of "Clarisa" is aided by the narrator's often ironic tone. For example, when speaking of her relationship with Clarisa, the narrator, Eva Luna, states that their friendship overcame death "which has put a slight crimp in the ease of our communications" (43). Such an ironic tone supports the overall ironic interpretation of the story, as does Clarisa's use of irony to achieve a series of good deeds. She obtains scholarships for atheists from the Jesuits, musical instruments for the Hebrew choir from the German Institute, and a refrigerator for the Teresian Sisters from the politician Diego Cienfuegos, even though they are his political enemy (48).

The last story that ironically highlights female compensation, "The Gold of Tomás Vargas," is also based on an ironic plot twist. In this story, Allende not only appropriates female stereotyping and compensation, but also relies heavily on other techniques of indirection, such as implication. The story initially presents Vargas's wife, Antonia Sierra, as her husband's passive victim. The narrator describes her as toothless and black-and-blue from Vargas's beatings (Allende 1991, 73). Antonia's moral capacity is elevated through her generosity toward Concha Díaz, Vargas's pregnant concubine who ends up living with them and for whom, rather than anger, Antonia entertains a "secret compassion" (78). Of course, Concha is simply another of Vargas's victims, which leads to an ironic bonding between the two women who were formerly enemies. The story goes on to narrate how Vargas loses a gambling debt but cannot pay it, because when he goes to dig up his hidden gold, it is not where he put it. Vargas is subsequently killed for his failure to pay his debt, while Antonia and Concha go on to live a happy life together.

The reader is never explicitly told what happened to Vargas's gold. However, the story implies that Antonia and Concha dug up the gold and used it to purchase farm animals and clothing, and thus establish a better life for themselves. Ironically, it is the supposedly weak and victimized women who outwit and triumph over the miserly and abusive Vargas. Once again, the reader is forced at the story's conclusion to choose between contradictory portrayals of the two women. Are they silent, innocent, all-forgiving victims, or strong, clever women who unite to defeat Vargas? The hyperbolic portrayal, in this case the forgiving victim, is the less credible option and hence the one rejected by most readers. Moreover, the supposed moral superiority of the two women is questioned through their stealing of Vargas's gold, with the obvious consequence of his murder by the lieutenant, to whom he owes the money. The story uses both appropriation and silent implication to make its point and situate the reader within a feminist perspective.

Stories that Focus on Female Collusion

There are two stories that illustrate Allende's ironic appropriation of the technique of female collusion: "Si me tocaras el corazón" [If You Touched My Heart] and "María la Boba" [Simple María]. In the first of these two stories, Amadeo Peralta seduces Hortensia, a young girl of fifteen. He abandons her after a brief sexual encounter, but Hortensia shows up on his doorstep the next day. Peralta, on the brink of marrying another, decides to keep Hortensia as his concubine. He hides her in an underground pit, but soon forgets about her, leaving an Indian woman in charge of her care. After forty-seven years, Hortensia is discovered by some children playing near the pit and Peralta is arrested. However, Hortensia is not angry with him and plays her psaltery every day outside his prison.

On the surface, it may appear that Hortensia colludes with Peralta to effect her own mistreatment. After all, it is she who sought out Peralta after their initial encounter "with the terrifying submission of a slave" (Allende 1991, 92). However, upon closer examination, we see that the narrator has strewn clues throughout the text that negate Hortensia's responsibility for her own victimization. The most compelling contradiction is found in the story's first paragraph, when we learn that Hortensia does not have a normal mental capacity: "The girl was simple and even though she may have been enchanted by the tone of his voice she did not understand the meaning of his words" (91). Similarly, at the end of the story, we are told that Hortensia "with the faltering step of a madwoman," brought Peralta food daily while he was in prison (100). Hortensia only colludes with her own victimization because she is mentally incapacitated, not because she is a woman who accepts a passive, abused role. Indeed, her supposed collusion is so hyperbolic that it implicitly leads the reader to reject its validity. Consequently, the ideology behind collusion is subverted and Hortensia exonerated from any real responsibility for her victimization, since she cannot control her own mental status.

Furthermore, the story's conclusion ironically inverts the roles of victim and victimizer. Amadeo Peralta ends up in jail, just as he had incarcerated Hortensia for forty-seven years. The torture she suffered in the form of neglect is paralleled by the torture Peralta suffers while hearing an overly solicitous Hortensia play her psaltery every day outside his prison. The sound of her psaltery courses through "every nerve in his body." It is referred to as a "daily castigation," although Peralta cannot recall why he is in prison and simply remains "lost in his misfortune" (Allende 1991, 101). Hortensia's inability to forget about Peralta (in the form of her music) causes Peralta to suffer. This is a deliberate inversion of the neglect that made Hortensia suffer. Thus, the female protagonist unwittingly and ironically triumphs over her male victimizer at the end of the story, preventing the reader from lending any credence to notions of female collusion and situating him or her within a feminist perspective.

Hortensia is a "silent" protagonist in many ways. She is locked away from the world and unable to communicate with anyone for forty-seven years. When she is finally rescued by her neighbors, we are told that she had lost the use of words. The way in which Hortensia communicates is through her music: "Only her hands, forever occupied with the psaltery ... now extracted from the instrument the unvoiced sob trapped in her breast" (96). Indeed, as we have seen, it is through her psaltery playing that Hortensia "communicates" with the imprisoned Peralta in the end, grating on his nerves and making his incarceration unbearable. The use of instrumental music (like its use in "Soledad de la sangre" and "El árbol") can be seen as a form of ritualistic and nonverbal communication through which Hortenisa achieves an ultimate revenge on Peralta.

Similarly, the story "Simple María" presents an ironic enjoyment of prostitution by its protagonist and consequently, a negation of her collusion in the construction of her own demeaned state. María, like Hortensia, is not mentally intact. When she was twelve, she had been hit by a cargo train, which "had transported the girl into a state of innocence from which she would never return" (Allende 1991, 171). María (once married and now widowed) shared a passionate relationship with a drunken Greek sailor who later abandoned her. She innocently seeks to repeat this experience with a string of men, thus converting herself into a prostitute. Although the story describes "her enthusiasm for each new encounter with a man" (179), María is dissatisfied with her life and wishes to die. The text implies (but never states) that María commits suicide by drinking a poisoned cup of hot chocolate. The story ironically and thus silently negates the stereotype of enjoyable prostitution and the female collusion it implies, first by emphasizing María's mental incapacitation, and second, by intimating her suicide. The hyperbolic vision of María enjoying an endless round of sexual partners is ultimately nullified through the text's conclusion.

Silence and Narrative Framing

In addition to the ironic employment of stereotyping, compensation, and collusion, Allende frames *The Stories* of *Eva Luna* within an ironic juxtaposition of two quotations from *A Thousand and One Nights*. The first quotation explains how the King has a virgin brought to him every night and killed in the morning until Scheherazade, the vizier's daughter, who "was very eloquent," is selected to accompany him.

After the text's last story, the following epigraph appears: "And at this moment in her story, Scheherazade saw the first light of dawn, and discreetly fell silent." Anyone familiar with *A Thousand and One Nights* knows that Scheherazade narrates a series of tales as a means to stay alive through the night, knowing that she will not be killed if she is able to entertain the king until morning (he will keep her alive to continue telling stories each night). Her verbal ability parallels that of the narrator of the *The Stories of Eva Luna*, and is a way of combating her victimizer, the abusive king. However, once she no longer needs to speak, we are told that Scheherazade chooses silence, the weapon used by women throughout *The Stories of Eva Luna*. This juxtaposition of two quotations from *A Thousand and One Nights* is interesting, because it ironically negates the dichotomy established by patriarchal society between speech and silence. Allende juxtaposes traditional ideology (speech as power) with a subversive ideology (silence as power), and shows the invalidity of speech's exclusive claim to authority as developed by patriarchal society. Allende illustrates how both speech and silence are powerful weapons that can and should be employed by women. Hence, the placement of these epigraphs dialogues with the content of the stories in a way that enhances their message and emphasizes the power of women over their male abusers (whether through verbal or nonverbal strategies), which is the ultimate message of Allende's stories.

Silence, Characterization, and Plot in *The Stories of Eva Luna*

There is a striking similarity among many of the tales included in Allende's *The Stories of Eva Luna*. Almost all of the stories studied here initially appear to conform to Pratt's archetype of "novels of Eros" (although, of course, these are short stories and not full-length novels). "Novels of Eros" revolve around love (between either a man and a woman or two women) (Pratt 1981, 73–132). As we have seen, the female protagonists of "Two Words," "The Judge's Wife," "Clarisa," and "Simple María" all engage in passionate relationships with men who are not their husbands. Nonetheless, upon careful analysis, most of these stories turn out to be ironic portrayals of hyperbolic romance that actually wind up developing a series of themes very distinct from the topic of love. Besides the theme of female revenge against patriarchy already examined, many of Allende's stories also focus on female social consciousness. This theme organically springs out of both hyperbolic silence and the hyperbolic feminine portraits that were shown to be ironic within these texts. Such exaggerated silences/portraits inevitably aid the female protagonists in their achievement of social justice within these tales and hence are vital to both characterization and plot development in *The Stories of Eva Luna*.

The reader of "Two Words" is distracted from its sociopolitical context by the romantic relationship that evolves between Belisa and the Colonel. The reader must not forget, however, that the plot element that brings these two characters together is the Colonel's desire to transform himself from being a feared, barbaric, local caudillo into being the respected president of the nation. In pursuit of this goal, he hires Belisa to write a political speech for him, which is a great success. Through both the reciting of the speech and the two free words Belisa offers him as a bonus, the Colonel is gradually transformed from an inspirer of terror into the hope and joy of his people. Whereas at the outset of the text he is described as "linked to devastation and calamity" (Allende 1991, 13), he has now "captured the nation's heart" (18). The reader is so captivated by his transformation through love of Belisa that he or she may tend to ignore the concomitant sociopolitical transformation. However, the story's political commentary is definitely present and developed through hyperbole: the Latin American countries need to break the cycle of violence and create peaceful candidates with substantive ideas. Since the Colonel owes his conversion to the hyperbolized effect of Belisa's words (both in his political speech and the private, secret words he must keep unsaid), women thus appear as the sociopolitical conscience of the continent and the catalyst of sociopolitical change.

Similarly, "The Judge's Wife" does not appear to offer any social commentary at first glance. The reader tends to focus on the development of relationships: first between Casilda and the Judge, and then between Casilda and Nicolás Vidal. The implicit theme of social consciousness evolves through the character Casilda. Her silence, which initially appears passive, is shown to be both powerful and subversive. She influences her husband to release a boy who stole from an employer who underpaid him, and to refuse to punish an adulterous woman with an equally unfaithful husband. These are both judgments that foster social equality. Similarly, Casilda silently makes the judge feed the starving Juana la Triste by quietly attempting to do so herself. The use of Juana's torture as a tool to achieve the arrest of her criminal son is hence exposed as unjust and barbaric. The implicit irony of the power of one as quiet and silent as Casilda is used to develop the implicit social message behind the tale's love story. Although the fact that Casilda's husband is a judge may initially appear incidental to the story, the reader subsequently realizes that her husband's profession is crucial both to the plotline and to the elements of social justice it helps to evolve.

Clarisa's bid for social justice is somewhat more explicit than that of the women of the first two stories, in the sense that she is characterized as a woman of high moral fiber and a general do-gooder from the very start. We are told that Clarisa has obtained monies for needy groups from a series of unlikely and ironic sources (such as scholarships for atheists from the Jesuits) (Allende 1991, 48). Her ability to transcend preestablished social dichotomies (Jews versus Germans, Teresian sisters versus Communists, etc.) and achieve what the needy require springs from her own ironic characterization as a saint who simultaneously engages in an extramarital affair. Clarisa's social justice is as hyperbolic and ironic as she is. A synergistic relationship exists between her characterization and the social work with which she is inextricably associated.

Finally, "Simple María" herself does not truly achieve social justice, but rather puts an end to the degradation caused by her own personal prostitution through her suicide. This suicide negates the hyperbolic portrait of the happy prostitute that María initially evokes and hence achieves an implied condemnation of the ancient social ill of prostitution. Despite María's simplemindedness, she intuitively perceives that her life has been demeaned and achieves a form of social criticism through her death. Her implied suicide parallels the implicit character of the text's social commentary, which springs once again from the employment of both irony and hyperbole to characterize María throughout the story.

It is interesting that these four stories all appear to follow the archetype of Eros, but simultaneously develop an implicit plotline surrounding the need for social reform. This surreptitious plot element tempts the reader into classifying these texts, along with Allende's two novels, according to the archetype of social protest. However, in contrast to the texts in that category, the characters in *The Stories of Eva Luna* bear no explicit connection to any particular political party or movement and generally lack sociopolitical contextualization. The hyperbolic love stories overshadow the implicit element of social justice, and the stories remain under the rubric of "Eros."

6
Symbolic Silence: Rosario Ferré's Equation of Women and Puerto Rico

ROSARIO FERRÉ WAS BORN IN 1942 IN PONCE, PUERTO RICO. HER father, Luis A. Ferré, was a former governor of the island. She obtained a bachelor's degree from Manhattanville College in New York, a masters from the University of Puerto Rico, Río Piedras, and a PhD from the University of Maryland in 1986. Ferré married Benigno Trigo in 1960 and had three children; they later divorced, and she married Agustín Costa, a Puerto Rican businessman. She founded the journal *Zona de Carga y Descarga* in Puerto Rico (1972–75), which was a vehicle for her earliest publications (Smith 1997, 310). While Ferré lived in the United States she worked as a professor of Latin American literature at such prestigious institutions as Harvard, Berkeley, and Johns Hopkins. She currently resides in Puerto Rico and dedicates herself exclusively to writing (Gutiérrez 2001–2, 133). Her works include four novels: *Maldito amor* [*Sweet Diamond Dust*] (1989), *La casa de la laguna* [*The House on the Lagoon*] (1995), *Los barrios eccéntricos* [*Eccentric Neighborhoods*] (1997), and *Vuelo del Cisne* [*The Flight of the Swan*] (2002). She has also published several collections of short stories: *Papeles de Pandora* [*Pandora's Papers*] (1976), *Los cuentos de Juan Bobo* [*The Stories of Juan Bobo*] (1981), *La mona que le pisaron la cola* [*The Monkey with the Stepped-on Tail*] (1981), *La caja de cristal* [*The Crystal Box*] (1982), and *Las dos Venecias* [*The Two Venecias*] (1992). Ferré is also known for her poetry—*Fábulas de la garza desangrada* [*Fables of the Bleeding Heron*] (1982) and *Sonatinas* [*Sonatinas*] (1989)—and various collections of essays, which include *Sitio a Eros: Trece ensayos literarios* [*Siege upon Eros: Thirteen Literary Essays*] (1980) and *Coloquio de las perras* [*Colloquium of the Dogs*]

(1990), among others. Ferré is also very interested in the art of translation, and has translated many of her own works from Spanish to English and vice versa. Frequently her English translations do not directly correspond to the Spanish versions and are closer to re-writings in English of the original texts. Consequently, I will frequently provide my own translations of the Spanish texts when discussing her works.

Rosario Ferré's fiction is thematically feminist, centering on the rejection of bourgeois societal norms for women. Stylistically, the author's work is characterized by the employment of indirect narrative techniques, notably those that are significant in the development of symbolic meanings. This chapter will examine the collection of short stories *Papeles de Pandora*, the short novel *Sweet Diamond Dust*, and the full-length novel *The House on the Lagoon*. I will use Tveztan Todorov's critical work, *Symbolism and Interpretation*, as a springboard for analysis of Ferré's symbolic use of silence.

Ferré believes that women do not possess a different language, but do convey different meanings largely based on the polysemy of their texts (Hintz 1995, 39). This position clearly coincides with Todorov's idea of emphasis on the indirect associations of discourse. Ferré exploits the use of ambiguous discourse to make language convey a feminist meaning. The author employs silence in the sense that she does not explicitly take a feminist stance in her texts, but indirectly implies it through various textual strategies that I discuss below.

Paradigmatic Indices of Symbolic Interpretation in Ferré's Works

Ferré constructs silent, symbolic associations in her works through textual incoherencies that motivate the reader to refer to unstated symbolic associations of the collective memory. Todorov calls such connections "paradigmatic" (Todorov 1982, 30). Although Ferré employs this strategy throughout her works, the two stories that rely most heavily on paradigmatic associations are "La muñeca menor" [The Youngest Doll] and "Amalia."

In the opening story of *Papeles de Pandora*, "The Youngest Doll," the third-person omniscient narrator recounts the life of a woman who was bitten by a parasite (a river prawn) while swimming in the river. Her swollen leg could have been cured by the doctor, but instead he deliberately allowed the parasite to fester in the woman's leg over a period of years, so that he could earn enough money to send his son to medical school. The woman, with no possibility of marriage due to her swollen leg, dedicates herself to making dolls for her nieces every year for their birthdays and eventually for their weddings. The youngest niece marries the doctor's son, who is mercenary and superficial like his father. He treats the youngest niece as if she were a doll, displaying her on the balcony as a member of the almost extinct Puerto Rican aristocracy. As the doctor ages, he is puzzled by the fact that his wife does not, but rather has the same "porcelain-like" skin of her youth. One day, he discovers that his wife has turned into the doll. The story ends with "frenzied river prawns" emerging from the eye sockets of the niece/doll.

The story begins with the following paragraph about the aunt, which contains a number of paradigmatic indices that point the reader toward the shared knowledge of a community for textual interpretation: "As a young woman, she had often bathed in the river, but one day when the heavy rains had fed the *dragontail* current, she had a soft feeling of melting *snow* in the marrow of her bones. With her head nestled among the black rock's reverberations, she could hear the slamming of salty foam on the beach mingled with the sound of the waves, and she suddenly thought that *her hair had poured out to sea at last*. At that very moment, she felt a sharp bite in her calf. (Ferré 1991, 1, my emphasis).

This passage describes the feelings of the aunt as she bathes in the river. When we first examine the literal or direct meaning of the sentences, they convey very little actual coherent sense. For example, as the aunt bathes in the water, she feels in her bones "the soft sensation of snow." In order to comprehend what the aunt is experiencing, we must follow Todorov's principle of pertinence, by appending additional, indirect paradigmatic meanings to the concrete object snow.[2] Cirlot states that snow is usually symbolic of the mystical or numinous because of its association with the sky (Cirlot 1978, 324). Also, if we examine the traditional associations for the attributes of snow (white, cold), we find that these point to celestial elevation as well. White symbolizes a heavenly state, while "cold" corresponds to a desire for elevation and silence (101, 208). Chevalier and Gheerbrant suggest that white is the color associated with initiation rites and hence the process of death and rebirth (Chevalier and Gheerbrant 1996, 1105–6). Thus, "snow" is a paradigmatic element whose relationship to collective knowledge suggests it has a second, indirect meaning, that of the aunt's desire to achieve some type of silent, spiritual elevation or ritual death and rebirth.

We are also told that as the aunt bathes she thinks that her "hair had poured out to sea at last." According to Cirlot, "A full head of hair represents *élan vital* and *joie de vivre*, linked with the will to succeed" (Cirlot 1971, 135).³ Moreover, the sea itself is "seen . . . as the source of life" (281). Chevalier and Gheerbrant note that hair has a number of symbolic associations that include heaven, the dwelling place of the soul, and sunbeams, all suggesting a similar spiritual or elevated dimension (Chevalier and Gheerbrant 1996, 460–63).⁴ Walker indicates that women's hair is particularly symbolic. In Eastern religions, hair was thought to control the cosmic powers of creation, while the hair of the goddess Isis "carried magical powers of protection, resurrection, and reincarnation" (Walker 1988, 313). All of these paradigmatic associations suggest that the aunt finally feels a sense of freedom, vitality, spirituality, and rebirth as she swims in the ocean. In an intertextual reading with Gabriela Mistral's poem "Todos íbamos a ser reinas," María Lagos notes that the idea of reaching the sea symbolizes dreams of freedom that go unfilled both in Mistral's poem and Ferré's short story (Lagos 2003, 173–75). This interpretation reinforces the symbolic association between the aunt's swim in the river and her attempts to enjoy life and attain liberation. However, on this particular day, the current is in the shape of a dragon's tail. The dragon symbolizes "a kind of amalgam of elements taken from various animals that are particularly aggressive and dangerous, such as serpents, crocodiles, lions. . . . The dragon . . . stands for 'things animal' *par excellence*, and here we have a first glimpse of its symbolic meaning related to the Sumerian concept of the animal as the 'adversary'" (Cirlot 1971, 85–86). Chevalier and Gheerbrant state, "[T]he dragon may be identified with the serpent as a diabolical symbol" (Chevalier and Gheerbrant 1996, 307). Thus, the aunt's freedom and vitality are interrupted by the presence of an enemy. The dragon's tail is also phallic, thus suggesting that the woman's adversary is man (the patriarchal order). It is precisely at this moment that the aunt is bitten by the river prawn, which, as we shall see, is later identified with the male doctor who exploits her.

The analysis of this first paragraph shows how Ferré relies on indirect or silent associations from the collective memory to establish a potentially feminist meaning in her text. The aunt is not merely swimming in the river, but symbolically attempting to assert her freedom as a woman. Just as she feels as if she is achieving her union with the water, she is bitten by the parasite that destroys this very freedom.

Another example of the story's use of associations with the collective memory is the phrase that describes the youngest niece's motives for marrying the doctor's son: "She was deathly curious to find out what dolphin flesh was like" (Ferré 1991, 5). There are at least two possible associations connected with the word "dolphin." In Spanish a "dolphin" (in addition to the mammal), refers to the firstborn son of a king. Hence, the use of the word dolphin might serve as a reference to the father-son relationship between the doctor and the man the youngest niece marries. Another possibility is that the dolphin is a sexual allusion, since it is associated with erotic, pagan deities (Cirlot 1971, 85). This would lead us to interpret the niece's motive for marrying the doctor as sexual curiosity.

The second story, which extensively invites symbolic interpretation based on paradigmatic indices, is "Amalia." The story presents the identification between a girl and her doll, Amalia. The girl is the product of an incestuous relationship between her mother and her uncle. The uncle is a corrupt military man who, upon the mother's death, moves into the girl's house with three prostitutes and his chauffeur and entertains U.S. fellow officers there. The uncle also attempts to initiate an incestuous relationship with the girl, who appears to have been raped by the chauffeur Gabriel. At the end of the story, the three prostitutes and Gabriel set fire to the house and expel the girl and her doll Amalia to the patio. As we shall see, most of this information is communicated indirectly to the reader through allusion rather than statement.

At the beginning of the story, the narrator/protagonist tells us that she is out on the patio "sweating white horses and seagulls that vomit salt. Now I begin to rock in my arms this repugnant melting bundle which used to be you, Amalia, as well as me, together we were one inseparable being" (Ferré 1976, 64, my translation).[5] This sentence makes no sense on the propositional level. How can someone sweat "white horses and seagulls that vomit salt"? The reader is obliged to find an indirect meaning for these words. "White horses" and "seagulls" are potentially paradigmatic indices. Various possible associations for the horse include the forces of primogenital chaos, the natural, unconscious, instinctive zone, and a sign of death (Cirlot 1971, 110). Chevalier and Gheerbrant note that the horse as a symbol of "unconscious psychosis" can be either dark or light. The white, celestial horse "stands for the control, mastery and sublimation of the instincts" (Chevalier and Gheerbrant 1996, 517). Thus, the fact that the girl was "sweating white horses" might refer to any of these indirect meanings. She may be attempting to suppress unconscious desires or envisioning her death, which, we learn in the following paragraph, is likely to occur, since she appears to have a rare skin condition that restricts her from exposure to the very sunlight that is pouring down on her on the patio. At the same time that she sweats white horses, the seagulls, or birds in general, "are symbols of thought, of imagination and of the swiftness of spiritual processes and relationships" (Cirlot 1971, 28). Chevalier and Gheerbrant concur that birds generally represent spiritual states (Chevalier and Gheerbrant 1996, 87). Consequently, the narrator/protagonist of "Amalia" simultaneously rejects (an action suggested by the verbs "sweat" and "vomit") her sublimation of instincts (white horses) and affirms her spirituality (seagulls).

Thus, one possible interpretation of this passage might be as a manifestation of the girl's internal conflict between instinctual desires for the prohibited on the one hand, and spiritual relationships, on the other. Also, if horses are thought to signify death, the passage might suggest that the girl's demise implies something positive: the spiritual and the imaginative (connoted by seagulls) in contrast to the base existence she has led in the house, which is apocalyptically destroyed by fire at the story's end.

Another example of paradigmatic indices is the narrator's description of her relationship with her mother and father/uncle: "They talk to me but I know they're using me as a sounding board to talk among themselves, I'm just a whitewashed wall to bounce off tennis balls" (Ferré 1991, 49). A wall expresses the idea of impotence and resistance (Cirlot 1971, 316). The girl is both powerless and yet combative about her familial situation.

Syntagmatic Indices of Symbolic Interpretation in Ferré's Work

Almost every one of Ferré's texts analyzed here, with the possible exception of *The House on the Lagoon*, invites the construction of silent, indirect, symbolic meanings on the basis of syntagmatic associations.[6] The repetition of elements that suggest a parallel between the nieces and the dolls fabricated by the aunt in "The Youngest Doll" is an excellent example of a syntagmatic symbolic link based on indices of excess. The dolls are repeatedly personified or continually exhibit characteristics also attributed to the nieces. For example, the narrator informs the reader that "*the birth* of a new doll was always cause for a ritual celebration, which explains why it never occurred to the aunt to sell them for a profit" (Ferré 1991, 2, my emphasis). The choice of the word "birth" (versus fabrication) personifies the dolls, as does the fact that they live in their own room: "There were nine of them, and the aunt would make one doll for each per year, so it became necessary to set aside a room in the house for the dolls alone to inhabit" (Ferré 1976, 10, my translation).⁷ Once again, the word "inhabit" personifies the dolls and emphasizes their identity with the nieces. Moreover, we are told that the nieces' dolls were "made in their image and likeness" (Ferré 1991, 4). The youngest niece and the doll also exhibit identical postures. Both sit with their eyes lowered on the balcony and piano, respectively (5, 15). Finally, at the end of the story, the niece and the doll become interchangeable. The niece is described as having "porcelained skin" (like that of the porcelain doll), while the doll occupies the niece's place in the bed with the frenzied antennae of the river prawns emerging from her empty eye sockets (15).

This continuous repetition of the identification of the niece and the doll and the emphasis on the personification of the dolls function as signs to the reader that he or she should interpret dolls as having an indirect, symbolic meaning in the text. The silent, symbolic message behind the text is that men treat women as if they were dolls—decorative objects to be displayed, and not real human beings. Thus, the niece becomes the doll at the story's end. This transformation, however, is not a passive acceptance of one's fate, but rather a subversive element, since the doll's eye sockets are filled with the very parasites that originally bit the aunt. The silent doll rises up to confront and frighten the doctor's son, ironically inverting its traditional meaning of passivity (Rivera 1994, 96).

The story "Amalia" also evidences syntagmatic connections based on an excess in the form of the repetition of both forbidden gardens and biblical allusions. The story begins with an epigraph from Genesis that narrates man's ejection from the garden of Eden: "So he drove out the man; and he placed a Cherubim at the East of the Garden of Eden; and a flaming sword which turned every way, to keep the way of the tree of life" (Ferré 1991, 47). This epigraph is immediately followed by the words of the first-person narrator (the girl) of "Amalia" in reference to her presence on the patio: "At last I am inside the *forbidden* garden" (47, my emphasis). The use of the term "forbidden" emphasizes the attempt to set up a parallel between these two situations. Man was forbidden to eat from the tree of knowledge, while the girl was formerly forbidden to stay out on the patio. Thus, the girl is associated with rebellious, transgressive behavior through this syntagmatic repetition of forbidden gardens (namely, the Garden of Eden and the patio referred to by the girl as the forbidden garden). The symbolic relationship between patio and paradise is an ironic one, since, as I mentioned, the girl suffers from a rare skin condition which makes sun exposure on the patio a deadly proposition for her. Nonetheless, in comparison with her previously abused existence in the house, death on the patio is seen as a preferable fate.

The girl projects her prohibition to go out into the sunlight on to her doll Amalia, who is made of wax: "As soon as their attention is distracted by something she flies out into the sunlight like a moth; . . . she lies down on the floor like a common slut . . . because she wants to know what happens, she says she wants to know what it's like" (48). Just like man with regard to the tree of life/knowledge, the girl/doll seeks the forbidden because of her curiosity or desire to "know what happens." The biblical allusions are syntagmatic indices through repetition or excess that signal the need to interpret their indirect sense within the story and point to the protagonist's rebellion against the horrible conditions of her life.

A third story, "The Seed Necklace," also forces the reader to append additional, indirect meanings to the text through its repetition of certain syntagmatic elements. The tale begins with the figure of a wife who has an affair with a roaming guitarist. Her husband and family are scandalized by her behavior and try to declare her insane. Eventually the guitarist disappears, leaving her pregnant with her son Arcadio and the gift of the seed necklace, which are the rosary beads the guitarist always wore. Arcadio's mother becomes mute as a result of her treatment by her family. Her silence is a rebellion against her societal role as dutiful wife and mother, which she is forced to resume upon her lover's abandonment.

There are multiple narrators in the story. The primary first-person narrator is also an important character: the family's servant, Armantina, who eventually marries Arcadio. Arcadio also briefly narrates, as does a third-person omniscient narrator.

"The Seed Necklace" is entirely predicated on implicit meanings. The reader is left to deduce most elements of the action through the establishment of syntagmatic connections. For example, Arcadio's opposition to his stepfather's political career and Arcadio's subsequent murder are never explicitly stated in the text. Ferré silently suggests these events through the repetition of certain elements. First, Armantina states, "Your father began to have an enormous success in his campaign; . . . until the day he got the telegram . . . DON'T YOU DARE, MONEY AND POWER—IT'S TOO MUCH, YOU'VE TOO MANY IRONS IN THE FIRE, and soon after that the endless telephone calls to New York began" (Ferré 1991, 74). The reader must make a connection between this passage and the following one in which Arcadio leaves the family: "I'm leaving Armantina; I can't stand it a minute longer in this house now that Mother, God, how they fouled her up, I'm going off to New York, as soon as I find a job I'll send you the ticket" (71). These two passages that repeat the mention of New York constitute syntagmatic indices (through excess) of the need to symbolically interpret the discourse. Arcadio leaves for New York, and his family members call New York repeatedly after they receive the anonymous telegram. They obviously believe Arcadio to be the sender of the telegram and a danger to the father's political ambitions. Ferré never states these details but implies them indirectly through syntagmatic associations.

Ferré's story "Sleeping Beauty" also makes use of syntagmatic indices through excess. The story's protagonist, María de los Angeles, expresses herself through dance, and her goal in life is to be a first-class ballerina. However, she is controlled by a series of other people who have different aims for her. The Mother Superior of the Catholic school she attends wants her to be a nun, while her father wants her to marry and provide him with male heirs for his fortune. When her father prohibits her from dancing, she becomes ill and is hospitalized. Near death, her boyfriend, Felisberto, promises to marry her and allow her to continue her career as a ballerina. María de los Angeles, in a coma, hears this and miraculously awakens. However, once married, Felisberto also attempts to control her. He forces her to have a child, although she does not want one because it will impede her career as a dancer. María de los Angeles becomes alienated from everyone. She expresses this alienation by dressing like a prostitute, picking up a stranger, and having sex with him in a hotel room. She also sends anonymous notes to Felisberto about her presence at the hotel, so that she will be discovered. Felisberto walks in on her dancing in the hotel room while her lover is asleep and murders her and himself. Most of the story is narrated through letters from the Mother Superior to the father, the father to the Mother Superior, a letter from Felisberto to the father which he never sends, the two anonymous letters to Felisberto, and a few clippings from the society pages. We only hear María de los Angeles's voice in the two "anonymous" notes to Felisberto and in a few italicized passages that present her stream-of-consciousness interior monologue by a third-person omniscient narrator. One of these passages, María de los Angeles's narration of the ballet *Giselle*, is converted into a symbol of María de los Angeles's relationship with Felisberto through the overlapping of events from the ballet and María de los Angeles's own life:

like Giselle after she buries Loy's dagger in her chest, because she suspects he wasn't a simple peasant, as he had told her, but was going to turn into a Prince with vested interests at any moment. . . . Loys always succeeds in his objectives and he's not about to let Giselle get away from him, he's bent on finding her hiding place in the woods so as to take away her dewdrop lightness, so she can never be a Willy again, but no, Giselle is mistaken, Loys truly loves her he won't get her pregnant, he'll put on a condom light and pink, he promised next to her deathbed. (Ferré 1991, 106–7)

This passage is notable because it introduces the idea of Loys/Felisberto as a "simple peasant." This motif is later repeated several times in Felisberto's letter to María de los Angeles's father, in which he indicates that he never knew that María de los Angeles did not want to have children, and confesses that he raped his own wife:

You can't imagine the turmoil her request threw me into. Loving María de los Angeles as I do, I had always wanted a child from her. I felt it was the only way to make her mine. Don Fabiano, perhaps because I come from a humble background and I've always had a terrible fear of losing her . . . *Although I may be from a humble background, that doesn't mean I don't have my dignity. . . . But when she continued being obstinate, refusing me, don Fabiano, in the end . . . I forced her, shit, don Fabiano, I made her a big stomach by force.* (Ferré 1991, 113, except italicized portion, which I have translated from Ferré 1976, 175)[8]

Hence, the idea of Felisberto as simple or humble may be seen as a syntagmatic index by excess, whose repetition clearly signals the need to interpret its indirect sense. Although Felisberto claims to be from a modest background in contrast to María de los Angeles's prominent family, "humble" is a relative term (in comparison with the extraordinary wealth of María de los Angeles's family) whose emphasis implies that it is ironically employed in the text to characterize Felisberto's nature. Since he is a self-made millionaire who, by his own admission, rapes his own wife, forcing her to have his child, it is hard to view him as "humble." His money may not be as old as María de los Angeles's father's, but his patriarchal values surely are. The reader is thus led to reject the literal meaning of "humble," and accept an ironic interpretation of the term.

The story provides contradictory versions of the deaths of María de los Angeles and Felisberto, which may be seen as a sign to interpret this event symbolically based on syntagmatic indices of lack. The first and correct version is to be inferred by the interruption of María de los Angeles's sexual encounter with a stranger by Felisberto: "She didn't even turn around when she heard the door of the hotel room burst open, but went on carefully placing one foot in front of the . . . " (115). The reader assumes that Felisberto enters and murders her, and commits suicide shortly afterward. The second version is provided by María de los Angeles's father and serves as a lie to preserve social appearances. He writes to the Mother Superior that Felisberto walked in on María de los Angeles's meeting with a choreographer and started insulting María de los Angeles for her desire to dance. When the choreographer defended her, Felisberto took out a pistol, accidentally shot María, and then presumably shot himself when he realized what had happened. This textual contradiction serves to suggest an indirect meaning concerning the subject of the utterance, María de los Angeles's father, rather than its object (the death of María de los Angeles). It indirectly conveys the message that María de los Angeles's father is superficial, primarily concerned with social appearances, rather than truth or the reality of his daughter's death.

The story "El regalo" [The Gift], included in the same volume, *Sweet Diamond Dust*, also employs syntagmatic indices based on excess to develop the indirect meaning of the mango, which is the gift alluded to by the title. The story relates the friendship between Carlotta and Merceditas at the Sacred Heart Catholic School. Carlotta is a mulatto who is racially discriminated against by Mother Artigas. Merceditas is the girl from a privileged background who stands by her friend.

Once again, Ferré relies heavily on syntagmatic repetition of the mango to create an indirect meaning that conveys a feminist perspective. As carnival queen, Carlotta receives a mango as a present and gives it to her friend Merceditas. When the mango is discovered by Mother Artigas, she tells Merceditas that her punishment is to display the mango on her desk at all times. At first, a sweet aroma emanates from the fruit, but eventually it rots and fills the school with a horrible smell. At the end of the story, Merceditas gives the mango to Mother Artigas. "'Here it is, Mother,' she said, curtsying before Mother Artigas for the last time. 'Here's your Sacred Heart. It's my gift to you'" (Ferré 1996, 118). The constant repetition of the presence of the mango throughout the text suggests its symbolic value. The putrefying mango can be seen as a symbol of decaying religion. Mother Artigas, rather than displaying a sense of charity and kindness that one would associate with authentic religious faith, is mean and vindictive. Thus, her betrayal of the genuine sentiments of a "sacred heart," which is the name of the religious school, is embodied in the rotten fruit.⁹ Although she is a woman, Mother Artigas (like Mama Elena in *Like Water for Chocolate*), as a figure of religious authority, can be seen as representative of the patriarchal order through her attempts to dominate and control the women at her school according to the traditional precepts of patriarchal society.

Ferré's short novel *Sweet Diamond Dust* is an excellent example of how the author employs syntagmatic contextual indices based on lack. There are five narrators: don Hermenegildo, friend of don Ubaldino de La Valle, who is writing a novel about Ubaldino as one of Puerto Rico's prominent figures; Titina, Ubaldino's black servant, Arístides, Ubaldino's second-oldest son; doña Laura, Ubaldino's wife; and finally Glora Camprubí, Ubaldino's nurse and wife of Ubaldino's eldest son, Nicolás. As the reader reads these different narrations, various contradictions arise between the five versions of the history of the La Valle family. These contradictions either force the reader to reject each individual statement and construct a composite version, or oblige him or her to try to deduce, if possible, which version is correct.¹⁰ For example, one element of the story that varies from narrator to narrator is who fathered Gloria's son. Titina tells us: "Nicolasito was born before his grandfather's demise and some eleven months after his father's airplane accident."¹¹ This comment directly states that Nicolás is the baby's father, but indirectly implies that he is not, since a baby is normally born nine months after conception, and thus could not be fathered by someone who died eleven months before his birth. This version is confirmed by Arístides, who tells us, "Father thinks the baby's his. . . . Gloria made love to Father every morning, as soon as I left to oversee the cane fields" (Ferré 1996, 48–49). However, doña Laura, the family matriarch, provides another version, indicating that Nicolás, whose marriage to Gloria was supposedly one of convenience, is indeed the father: "But as soon as they married, the bride became pregnant and exhibited her shame to the four winds. Nicolás, in a moment of weakness, ceded to the temptation of the flesh, and Gloria was once more the victim of the family" (Ferré 1999, 79, my translation).¹²

Finally, Gloria casts further doubt on the versions of her son's paternity provided by Titina and Arístides, as well as Laura's contention that her marriage to Nicolás was one of mere convenience, when she indicates that they shared a passionate physical relationship: "Because . . . she knew that married or not we'd always be together. . . . It was all the same to us, so powerful was the love that consumed us" (Ferré 1998,

84). How is the reader to know which discourse to believe? The narrators, with the exception of don Hermenegildo (whose discourse is exposed, as we shall later on see, as romanticized and utopian), are presented in a Bakhtinian dialogical manner. In other words, each discourse is equally weighted without a subsuming third-person authorial voice to indicate whom we should believe and whom we should discredit. Consequently, the reader's participation is critical to the formation of signification. He or she must provide the silent meaning behind the contradictions. In this particular instance, the reader might be led to examine the ulterior motives of each speaker before forming a conclusion. Arístides, Laura, and Gloria all potentially have reasons to lie about Nicolasito's paternity. Arístides sets out in his discourse to discredit his ex-love Gloria, because she spurned him; Laura, as Ubaldino's wife, may be unaware of his true relationship with Gloria or desirous of concealing it to maintain the family's reputation; while Gloria is concerned about her own public image. Titina, however, is the most disinterested character; her only goal is to obtain the house that she claims was promised to her by Ubaldino. Although it is always possible that she has made some error in her narration, it seems likely that her specification of birth date is accurate, and that Ubaldino is really Nicolasito's father. Ultimately, the silent sense communicated by the numerous contradictions points to the fundamental corruption of the majority of inhabitants of Guanamí, particularly the La Valle family, which is the motivation of the novel's apocalyptic ending.

Another example of contradiction is found in the conflicting accounts of the death and sexuality of Nicolás de La Valle. According to his brother Arístides, Nicolás was a homosexual and died by suicide or was murdered by the workers whom he forced to have sex with him as payment for the employment benefits he offered them (Ferré 1998, 53–87). Gloria's version of the events is completely different. She suggests that Nicolás was murdered by either his father or his brother. Moreover, she claims that he was not a homosexual, and that they shared a passionate physical relationship (Ferré 1998, 84–85).

Once again, the reader cannot know for certain which, if any, of the versions of the story to believe. However, since Arístides is portrayed as jealous of his brother, both for his superior educational opportunities and marriage to his girlfriend, this is reason enough to incline the reader to favor Gloria's version and to view Arístides's tale as an attempt at defaming his brother's character. Moreover, it makes sense that doña Laura would have to have a powerful motivation to disinherit Arístides and leave the Central Justicia ("Diamond Dust" in the English translation) to Gloria and her son. These deductions are all silently appended to the text by the reader, instead of directly stated by the words of the text itself. Ferré uses unreliable narration that functions as a syntagmatic index based on lack to write through silence and implicitly criticize woman's role as victim of patriarchal society via the figure of Gloria.

Gender Naturalization

The constant employment of syntagmatic indices of lack in the form of conflicting narrations presents an interesting question that relates to the interpretation of *Sweet Diamond Dust* and its employment of silence. In the examples discussed above, the reader must go through a process of assumptions and deductions to determine whose narration to believe. Invariably, we saw how the discourses of various female protagonists seemed more reliable. This granting of authority to female discourses results in a discrediting of the process of gender naturalization used in the discourses of male narrators, a process that Sara Mills describes in *Feminist Stylistics*. Mills, as discussed in the first chapter, evolves a theory of the feminist affiliation of a text based on the theory of "a feminist affiliation complex" promulgated by Gilbert and Gubar, as well as Lynne Pearce's idea that this affiliation can be communicated through a series of textual cues (Mills 1995a, 58). When Mills discusses these ideas, she indicates that there are three kinds of texts: "First, for women to write they can adopt a supposedly masculine voice and align themselves with a male voice and tradition; or, second, they can adopt a stereotypically female voice and align themselves with the same set of values, since they are not challenging the status quo. The third position is one where women writers, mainly feminists, signal their alignment with a female tradition by a range of cues within the text." (58).

According to Mills, texts communicate gendered information (stereotypes) in a variety of forms. Certain phrases, such as "it is known that" and the use of axioms, present gendered information as natural and thus force the reader to accept it as true (Mills 1995, 66-67). Ferré uses such techniques in the discourses of her male characters, notably Don Hermenegildo and Arístides. However, since the discourses of these two characters are largely (although not entirely) discredited, these statements end up functioning ironically to expose the technique of naturalizing gendered information which patriarchy uses to reinforce its gendered stereotypes. Ferré's deconstruction of the process of gender naturalization is another factor that creates a possible feminist perception on the part of the reader. For example, at the novel's beginning, Hermenegildo narrates the background of Guamaní: "At that time Guamaneños of the upper crust all belonged to the same clan. There were blood ties among the most distant families, and we always gave one another financial and moral support, so as better to manage our sugarcane haciendas. Our sons studied in Europe and our daughters were taught the sacred virtues of the home" (Ferré 1996, 6).

Hermenegildo's narration is an idealized version of the town that presents everyone as one big happy family. Within this utopian framework, we are told that the men studied abroad while women were trained how to be mothers. The narrator provides this context of a perfect world so that the reader will accept this division of gender roles as the natural and correct order of things. It is only later on, when the propagandistic nature of Hermenegildo's discourse is revealed, that the reader learns to reject Hermenegildo's narration and thus the gender stereotypes he attempts to perpetuate.[13]

Similarly, Arístides uses popular sayings to naturalize his gender stereotypes and to portray Gloria's submissive behavior as the normal rule for male/female relationships: "When you itch it's best to scratch, and so she moved in with me and kept house, becoming quiet and demure, eager to please me in every way" (Ferré 1996, 41).[14] Although Arístides attempts to convince the reader to accept the traditional female submissive role through his use of axiomatic language, the reader is ultimately led to reject the stereotypes he creates upon comprehending the unreliable nature of his discourse.

Mills suggests that texts can signal their feminist affiliation through relatively simple techniques, such as presenting female characters whose nontraditional behavior is not explicitly judged (or who take pride in themselves), focusing on the relationship between female characters, using informal speech registers rather than formal prose (associated with men in the public sphere), and the implicit presupposing of certain background knowledge when the text addresses a female audience. Narrative perspective (can a passage be rewritten from a traditional male viewpoint?) and verbal transitivity choices (which characters act and are acted upon) are sometimes also important factors in determining whether a text affiliates with a traditional male or feminist perspective (Mills 1995a, 68). When we reexamine *Sweet Diamond Dust* in these terms, it becomes clear that despite the conflicting versions of the truth and a general focus on questioning different versions of reality, the text favors the female viewpoint through a series of techniques designed to create a feminist perspective. The novel emphasizes the friendship or "community of women" (Auerbach 1978, 6) created between Gloria and Laura. The implicit/nonverbal nature of this connection is emphasized throughout the novel. For example, when Laura is narrating Gloria's calming effect on her husband, she states that she and Gloria had a "tacit understanding" that Gloria would make Ubaldino fall in love with her to "tame his fury," in exchange for a monetary payoff in Laura's testament (Ferré 1986, 78). The reader is told that Gloria and Laura understand each other without words, at least partially because they are both women. For example, Laura states: "Because she [Gloria] is a woman like me and I consider her my friend" (Ferré, 1996, 78). This emphasis on women's friendship and mutual comprehension is clearly a sign that the text is situating the reader within a feminist perspective.

Ambiguous Discourse

In many instances, the paradigmatic and syntagmatic indices of symbolic interpretation create ambiguous discourse, which Todorov defines as words whose literal and figurative meanings exist simultaneously on the same level (Todorov 1982, 54–55).[15] For example, the reader of Ferré's "The Youngest Doll" will perceive both the story's direct meaning (the tale of an aunt who makes dolls for her nieces and how one of the nieces turns into the doll) and its indirect meaning (men treat women like dolls, which are decorative and passive objects) at the same time, yet will have missed the point of the story if he or she fails to perceive its second, indirect sense. The conventional, indirect, paradigmatic associations of the identification woman/doll are silently implied but never directly stated by Ferré, constituting the text's silent and figurative meaning.

In "Amalia," the scene in which the North American military men are entertained at the uncle's house by the prostitutes María, Adela, and Leonor is an excellent example of ambiguous discourse: "Are these girls daughters of the American Revolution? All. But much more exotic of course, the flesh and fire of tropical fiestas . . . let's start screwing together the erector set girls, mi daddy wanted me to be an engineer and every year he gave me for Christmas a yellow erector set" (Ferré 1991, 72). Here the head or most readily apparent meaning (screwing together the erector set = putting together an erector set) gives way to the passage's chief meaning[16] ("screwing" is a slang term for sexual intercourse, while "erector" evokes "erection" and thus the sentence's sexual innuendo). The discourse is comprehended on two levels, but only the second truly makes sense within the story's context.

Similarly, a sexual relationship between Gabriel and the narrator is implied through their doll play in the following scene in which the chauffeur violates the norms of their game by grabbing the doll Amalia:

> That day I had become very angry because Gabriel had dared to take Amalia out of her box and had wanted to play with her; I don't want you to, don't touch her, I said, leave her alone, but he was much stronger than I; he began to rock her in his arms, singing to her all the time under his breath, until Amalia, oh oh oh, began to lose control of herself; she began to break the laws of the game, oh oh oh, she ran up and down the galleries lifting and lowering her skirts, oh oh oh, as if she had lost her mind, shaking the skirt's black silk folds between the balconies' banisters, oh oh oh, laughing for the first time with her tiny teeth shibamshibam, stepping on the garlic and onion with bare heels, shibamshibam, oh oh oh, Mother, how I like the smell of scrub, the scrub of rub, oh oh, oh, and then fleeing, Amalia running and screaming like a she-devil, like a dervished shrew, tripping over your skirts and rising again without caring about anything, because now you knew the price you'd have to pay. (53–54)

Once again, Ferré creates an ambiguous discourse. The discourse's literal meaning (the actual doll play) rapidly gives way to an indirect meaning. We already know from the story's prior context that the girl identifies herself totally with Amalia and projects her feelings onto the doll. For example, when her mother dies, she dresses the doll in mourning. Thus, when Gabriel grabs the doll, the reader is to infer that it is the narrator whom he really accosts, and the struggle that ensues resembles that of a rape in which the victim first resists and then is finally overpowered.[17] Ambiguous discourse also characterizes "Sleeping Beauty." In part 2 of the story, María de los Angeles is in a coma provoked by her father's prohibition of dancing. The reader is presented with her stream-of-consciousness interior monologue during the coma. The monologue fuses the stories of *Sleeping Beauty* and *The Red Shoes*. The discourse can be simultaneously understood on both a direct and indirect level: "She recognized his voice, it was Felisberto coming, he was nearing the castle, she tried to get up but the heavy gold lamé of her dress wouldn't let her rise, dance DANCE! that's what was forbidden! . . . you'll dance forever because you'll marry me and I'll take you faraway, talk to me, I can see you tiny, as though you were a little girl at the bottom of a well, you're getting bigger, closer, coming up from the depths, my gold dress falls away, I feel it tugging at my toes, I'm free now, light" (Ferré 1991, 100–101). The fact that the protagonist is draped in a heavy gold lamé can be perceived both in a literal and figurative sense. We can literally understand this to be her costume in the ballet, but we can also indirectly comprehend that the heavy gold is symbolic of her family's money and societal position. Her father's desire to have an heir to his fortune and the limited societal norms for a girl from a rich family preclude María de los Angeles's following a career in dance and favor the traditional role of matrimony.

THEMATIC SILENCE

Ferré's employment of stylistic indirection is frequently accompanied by a marked thematic, nontraditional silence, a characteristic shared by all the authors studied here. In "The Youngest Doll," silent ritual becomes a "language" used to express women's feelings and desires in a manner similar to that of Allende's characters in *The House of the Spirits*. For example, the aunt is a silent figure who rarely speaks in the story, but rather expresses herself through doll-making. Yvette López points out that this doll-making process is described in the story as a form of ritual behavior. There is also a connection between the aunt's wedding gift of a honey-filled doll to each niece when she marries and rites of initiation in which honey is a symbol of rebirth or personality change and is also associated with the acquisition of wisdom (López 1982, 50–54). In other words, honey is a paradigmatic index that points to marriage as a ritual in which the nieces (women) will be forced to change and become knowledgeable about their situation as females subjugated by the patriarchal order. The aunt does not communicate this information through words, but rather through the silent ritual of doll-making.

There are many other instances of the aunt's silent communication through dolls. For example, before the aunt places the doll's eyes on the figure, she submerges them in the ocean so that they learn to recognize parasites. This action indirectly reveals the aunt's anguish faced with her situation and her desire that her nieces (as represented by the dolls) avoid a similar circumstance.

Silence and ritual are also forms of communication in "Amalia." Doll playing is a silent ritual upon which the narrator projects all unverbalized feelings and emotions. The narrator's silence is not passive, since she rebels against her uncle in the actions attributed to the doll and obtains freedom from his corruption at the story's end, albeit in the form of death on the patio. We can see how dolls function to express the narrator's feelings in the episode in which she receives a present from her uncle. It is a male doll dressed in military uniform who is supposed to be Amalia's (the female doll's) boyfriend. This doll is presented to the narrator at the same time that the uncle sexually propositions her. Although it is the narrator who makes the boyfriend doll resemble Gabriel the chauffeur instead of the military uncle, she attributes the doll's defacing to Amalia. Through this action, the protagonist/Amalia rebels against her uncle's exploitation (and hints at her real relationship with Gabriel), as do Gabriel, María, Leonor, and Adela at the end of the story, when they kill the uncle and set fire to his house. The decadence and corruption of the household members leads to an apocalyptic ending.

A third story where silence is an explicit theme is "The Seed Necklace." As we saw earlier, the mother in this story becomes mute after her affair with a roaming guitarist: "When the street urchins came and put the seed necklace in her hand, here they said, he left you this before he went away, and so she got up, walked back home, and from then on became a model wife *but didn't speak anymore*" (Ferré 1996, 70, except italicized portion, which is my translation and emphasis).[18] Once the mother is abandoned by her lover, she decides to comply with her societal role of wife and mother. However, she indicates her rebellion against this role through her silence. The emphasized words are highly ironic, because they state that she was an exemplary wife but never spoke, thus implying that a good wife does not, or need not, speak! The narrator offers the reader an implied social commentary on marriage in these words.

Armantina, the family servant and later Arcadio's wife, also becomes mute and fuses with the character of the mother. Upon the mother's death, Arcadio abandons the family and goes to New York. He plans to send for Armantina in six months. When his father (the mother's husband who passes for Arcadio's father) decides to run for public office, he receives a threatening letter from New York, which the reader deduces is sent by Arcadio. Arcadio is later murdered under strange circumstances, allegedly while attempting to rob someone. Once again the reader deduces that the father is responsible for Arcadio's murder. Before Arcadio's demise, the father and brothers question the pregnant Armantina about his whereabouts, physically torturing her in the process. Although it is never explicitly stated, the reader is left to infer that her subsequent muteness is the physical result of their actions (Ferré 1991, 74). Armantina states: "All of a sudden my mouth starts working, struggling for breath, trying with all my might to speak, to break off the invisible muzzle" (75).[19]

It is not a coincidence that both female protagonists (the mother and Armantina) end up mute. However, this inability or refusal to speak is not passive. Armantina triumphs over the family in the end by poisoning the father and brothers responsible for the mother's unhappiness, Arcadio's death, and her own mistreatment. The story begins and ends with the same phrases: "Now I see them seated for the last time around the table eating and drinking from my hand with absolute confidence" (Ferré 1976, 122, my translation)[20] referring at first to the mother and then to Armantina. This repetition emphasizes the fusion of the two female protagonists.

In "Sleeping Beauty," María de los Angeles, like Ferré's other protagonists, communicates her feelings exclusively through nonverbal acts. Dance, like doll-play or doll-making, can be seen as a form of ritual or silent communication in the text.[21] Kathleen Glenn points out that María de los Angeles's rebellion against society can be seen in her act of improvisation during the ballet *Coppélia*, in which she refuses to follow the ballet's script and eventually flees the scene of the ballet in medias res (Glenn 1996, 211).

Moreover, shortly after the birth of her son, María de los Angeles attends a circus performance in which she sees Carmen Merengue, her father's former mistress, perform on a tightrope. Carmen, like María de los Angeles, is dedicated to her profession, and abandoned María de los Angeles's father to pursue her work. Felisberto tells us that after viewing Carmen's performance, María de los Angeles attempts to imitate it by dancing on a tightrope. Her tightrope dance is accompanied by a steadfast silence: "What grabbed my attention most was the expression on her face. She seemed empty of all thought. I spoke to her and she didn't answer, as if she weren't listening to me. . . . She . . . refuses to answer me" (Ferré 1976, 178, my translation).[22] Dance is María de los Angeles's only form of true expression in a society in which her wishes are systematically ignored and her autonomy violated. After making love with the stranger at the end of the story, we are told: "She felt like dancing. . . . She thought with relief that for the first time she was going to be able to be herself . . . to be a dancer, although a second-or third-rate one" (Ferré 1976, 179, my translation).²³

A number of female protagonists in Ferré's *Sweet Diamond Dust* are also associated with silence. For example, the silence imposed by don Julio Font upon his wife, doña Elvira, is converted by the latter into a form of protest. Don Julio beats his wife for speaking up and insisting that he pay a stipend to an injured worker, after which Elvira retreats into a "foggy silence,' refusing to attend to her domestic chores, in a manner similar to that of Clara in *The House of the Spirits* (Ferré 1996, 14).

Doña Elvira's response is not simply the desired silence, but rather a silence accompanied by her relinquishment of her so-called wifely duties. Not only does she stop interfering in her husband's business, but also simply refuses to talk to him at all or engage in any household activities. This is clearly not an outwardly imposed silence, but a self-imposed silence of protest against don Julio's abusive treatment.

Gloria's final protest against don Hermenegildo's narration and the abuses of the La Valle family is symbolized by her silent destruction of doña Laura's final testament. The testament, which leaves the Central Justicia (Diamond Dust), the family's sugarcane business, to Gloria and her son, is wordlessly destroyed by Gloria: "And then I saw Gloria walk out of a dark corner . . . . *She didn't say a word* or even look at me. She slid her hand brazenly under the lace pillowcases and took out Laura's will from under them. Then she slowly, deliberately tore it in half and threw it into the wastepaper basket" (Ferré 1996, 80, my emphasis).

The novel concludes with Gloria's setting fire to the house, thus putting an end to the La Valle family and the abuse perpetrated by them on the workers of the Central Justicia. This apocalyptic ending engineered by a silent, female character is similar to the ones already seen in "Amalia" and "The Seed Necklace." The patriarchal order must be destroyed in order for a new, egalitarian society to be created. Silent, submissive women, normally part of the naturalized gender information provided to the reader by the male narrators, are converted into silent, subversive women. This inversion deconstructs the gendered stereotype of silence and helps to position the reader within a feminist perspective.

Ferré's short story "El regalo" [The Gift] shares many of the characteristics of Ferré's novel. Just as racial prejudice is a major theme in *Sweet Diamond Dust* (Gloria is treated by many members of the La Valle family as inferior for being mulatto; the family is ashamed of their racial mixture and hides the fact that Ubaldino's father, don Julio, was part black), Carlotta Rodríguez is discriminated against because of her race. Carlotta is voted carnival queen, a role seen as unfit for a girl who attends the religious Sagrado Corazón School. The strict Mother Superior, Mother Artigas, wants to have Carlotta expelled for participating in the carnival and wearing makeup. However, the real motive behind her objection to these activities is her own racial prejudice. Carlotta is the first mulatto accepted to the school, for purely financial reasons, and Mother Artigas does not approve of her being there.

The themes of silence, ritual, and a community of women are clearly developed in "The Gift." Carlotta is best friends with Merceditas Cáceres, daughter of an illustrious family that does not see the need for women to be educated (Ferré 1996, 96). Merceditas's desire to attend college, to do something other than marry and stay home, is a sign of the text's feminist orientation. Moreover, the focus on Merceditas's friendship with Carlotta and the former's sacrifice of her own well-being in order to defend her friend (the notion of a true community of women) are further signs of the text's nontraditional perspective. Mother Artigas attempts to control Carlotta by prohibiting her use of makeup and imposing a wall of silence upon her. No one in the school is allowed to speak to her or vice versa. When Carlotta refuses to adhere to Mother Artigas's orders and continues her ritual of makeup application, her wearing of makeup becomes a wordless protest flaunted in the face of the religious school authorities:

> Carlotta obeyed without complaint and returned to her desk with face sparkling clean. But meekness could become, in her case, a powerful weapon, as is often the case with gentle souls. As soon as she found herself alone the next day at recess, she took out a stick of mascara, a lipstick, and a tube of heavy pancake makeup, and applied them generously to her face. Her features, shaded by the thick layers of paint, acquired a grotesque aspect.... It was at this point that Mother Artigas decided to intervene, forbidding everyone in the school from talking to Carlotta, under pain of expulsion. (Ferré 1996, 111–12)

After this silence is imposed, although Merceditas does not dare to speak to Carlotta, she always saves her a place at lunch and includes her in the games at recess. The story ends with Carlotta's expulsion from the school. However, as she is leaving, she is accosted by Mother Artigas, who violently rips her clothing and shaves her head. Merceditas comes to her friend's defense, pushing Artigas away and leaving the school with Carlotta in an act of solidarity.

Finally, Ferré's novel *The House on the Lagoon* (1995) repeats many of the themes and techniques already observed in *Papeles de Pandora* and *Sweet Diamond Dust*. The novel takes the form of a supposed family history, narrated by the character Isabel. Her narration is frequently interrupted and "corrected" by comments in the form of a counternarration by her husband, Quintín. This format is similar to the contradictory versions of the same story already analyzed in *Sweet Diamond Dust* and may also be viewed as a manifestation of syntagmatic indices based on lack. Isabel narrates the lives of a number of women, whom, as we shall see, express themselves and their dissent with the patriarchal order through nonverbal forms of communication. Quintín's mother, Rebecca Arrigoitia, is one of the novel's main characters. Rebecca is married to Buenaventura, a rich but uncultured man who has no appreciation of the things that Rebecca enjoys—namely, poetry and dance. For Rebecca, just as for María de los Angeles in "Sleeping Beauty," dance is a form of wordless communication of her feelings: "Rebecca . . . didn't want children. She felt she was a free spirit; if she had children, she'd never be able to dance and be one with nature the way she wanted" (Ferré 1995, 39–51).

Rebecca adopts a feminist perspective, elevating her dancing career over maternity, which pits her against the patriarchal order. However, in words identical to those of don Julio Font in *Sweet Diamond Dust*, Rebecca's husband tells her to be quiet, using axiomatic language that naturalizes the traditional gender stereotype that women should be silent ("women may speak out when chickens get to pee"). Buenaventura's words and actions (the patting of Rebecca's backside) are chauvinistic gestures that the text indirectly repudiates through the subsequent portrayal of Buenaventura as a violent wife-beater. Rebecca defies Buenaventura's prohibition of dance by staging a version of Oscar Wilde's play *Salomé* at her home in which she appears dancing virtually naked. She knows the performance of the dance is a "risky decision," yet decides to be "faithful to her vocation" and challenge patriarchal authority through her silent art. When Buenaventura walks in on the scene, he beats her with a leather belt and leaves her unconscious (Ferré 1995, 65). Just as don Julio Font beat Elvira in *Sweet Diamond Dust*, so Buenaventura physically abuses Rebecca in *The House on the Lagoon*. This physical violence leads most readers to disassociate themselves from Buenaventura's ideology and adopt a feminist perspective.

After this episode, Rebecca is forced to give up dance, which for her is equivalent to becoming invisible or mute: "Rebecca . . . put away her dancing shoes, her silk tunics, and her poetry books and slowly faded from view like one of the forgotten nenuphars at the back of the terrace" (Ferré 1997, 85, my translation).[24]

Almost all of the women in *The House on the Lagoon* express themselves through their participation in some type of ritualistic or nonverbal behavior. Just as Rebecca lives through dance, Madeleine, Rebecca's mother, dedicates herself to growing orchids, a project portrayed in the novel as a silent act that gives Madeleine power over her own destiny: "Orchids were her hobby. . . . She liked the sense of privacy the nursery gave her . . . one was at peace and in total control of one's self. . . . Madeleine never learned to speak Spanish. She spoke English at home with her father and with her husband, and sign language with everyone else" (Ferré 1995, 93–94). Madeleine expresses her discontent with living in Puerto Rico and her nostalgia for Boston through a self-imposed silence. By refusing to learn Spanish, she essentially secludes herself from the rest of the world, and expresses herself through silent activities such as sports and gardening.

Isabel, the principal narrator, like Rebecca, her mother-in-law, associates dance with communication. Isabel tells us, with regard to the Kerenski dance school, that when she danced she "was just venting the woes I was suffering at home" (Ferré 1997, 173).[25]

Isabel's mother, Carmita Monfort, and her grandmother, Gabriela Antonsanti, are two nontraditional female characters. Gabriela, the mother of six children, is characterized by her antichildbearing stance. She rebels against motherhood and forbids her daughters from having more than one child every five years. Gabriela forces her daughter Carmita, who became pregnant with a second child while Isabel was still a baby, to abort her second pregnancy. After this episode, Carmita could not have any more children and became severely depressed. She spent the rest of her life gambling, another silent ritualistic act designed to combat her feelings of loss and depression. Moreover, when her husband Carlos commited suicide, Carmita "never spoke again" (Ferré 1995, 217). Faced with an unhappy life, silence is Carmita's refuge.

Textual Voice

In addition to this thematic silence, Ferré employs "textual voice," which, as we saw with regard to Bombal, refers to the use of unusual print or punctuation in a text. These elements offer a silent deviation from the norms of the text, and thus are a form of nonverbal signification (Ross 1979, 306–7). *The House on the Lagoon* presents a very interesting use of textual voice. The novel is structured as the narration of the respective family histories of Quintín and Isabel, who have been married for some twenty-five years. Isabel is secretly writing a novelistic version of the families, which she hides from Quintín. Quintín discovers the novel, reads it, and, as someone who has studied history and considers himself a historian, is offended by what he terms inaccuracies in the narration. Quintín's version of the events and commentaries on Isabel's narration, all recounted by an omniscient third-person narrator, appear in italic print that sets his thoughts off from the rest of the text. It is only in the novel's final section, "Cuando las sombras se avencinan" [A Whirlpool of Shadows], that Isabel's narration also partially appears in italic type.

Julie Barak suggests that the sections attributed to Quintín are in fact created by Isabel and are part of her novel, because they do not appear in first-person narration and are frequently destroyed right after he has supposedly composed them. Moreover, she points out that often these sections are written from Isabel's (a female's) perspective. Thus, according to Barak, Isabel casts doubt on her own narration, and the purpose of Quintín's sections is to question the relationship between history and fiction (Barak 1998, 31–38). Although history versus fiction is undoubtedly one of the novel's principal themes, Ferré is also unquestionably concerned with presenting an opposition of feminist viewpoints and nonfeminist viewpoints that is encapsulated and underscored through the use of textual voice to offset Quintín's perspective. Despite an occasional lapse in perspective (Barak cites Quintín's comment that "like most men, he could barely find the socks in his own drawer") (Barak 1998, 33), the italicized comments tend to portray what Mills would call a traditional male affiliation. For example, in one section, Quintín's marginal comments include this:

> Worse still was the way the manuscript was tainted with feminist prejudices. Obviously, Isabel wanted to be in tune with the times, but really, it was deplorable. Feminism was the curse of the twentieth century! . . . Was Isabel writing this novel because she wanted to have control over their lives? She was imposing her opinions and making decisions; creating or destroying characters, *but in the real world this could not be. As head of the family, it was his job to remain at the head of the household.* (Ferré 1995, 108, except italicized portion, which is my translation)[26]

Quintín espouses traditional patriarchal viewpoints such as that the man is the head of the household and that feminism is a curse. In other instances, he is condescending and disbelieving with regard to Isabel's potential for writing something good on her own (186–87). The implication once again is one of male superiority. The author uses textual voice (in this case, italic print) as a tool to situate the reader within a feminist perspective. Ferré cleverly inserts the traditional patriarchal perspective within a distinctive typeface. This viewpoint is that of Quintín, the historian, who affiliates himself within a traditional male genre: formal, public discourse ("history"). Isabel, as an unpublished novelist who is writing a fictionalized version of family memoirs, situates herself within the private, personal sphere. Quintín sees her novel as a private diary that, once written, should remain silent and unpublished: "If it remained unpublished, it would be even more perfect, because it would remain an ideal work.... If Isabel still loved him, she could make that sacrifice. It would be a sublime proof of her love for him" (Ferré 1997, 201 my translation).[27] Quintín egotistically sees the publication of Isabel text's as something she should give up for his sake, another example of traditional, patriarchal ideology that dictates that women should sacrifice their own interests for love of men.

Ferré's text underscores the chauvinistic nature of these comments and offsets them precisely through textual voice. The author counterpoises text (regular print) and countertext (italic print), thus facilitating reader identification with Isabel's narration in the main body of the novel (the nonitalic print). At the end of the novel, this affiliation is cemented by Quintín's role as a violent wife-beater. Isabel's rebellion is seen in her final abandonment of Quintín (who also dies at the end of the novel) and her publishing of the novel, which is explained in the final italicized portion, this time attributed to Isabel. Such conversion to italic print is significant, because it signal's Isabel's entrance into the public realm through the publication of her novel. This communication is silent, conveyed solely on the visual plane through italic print.

The Equation Woman / Puerto Rico in Ferré's Texts

Another important indirect association that various critics have pointed out with regard to Ferré's work is the symbolic connection Ferré establishes between her female protagonists as victims of patriarchal society and Puerto Rico as the victim of U.S. imperialism.[28] In her essay *Coloquio de las perras* [Colloquium of the Dogs], which is a feminist parody of Cervantes's exemplary novel, *Coloquio de los perros*, Ferré explicitly states the presence of this association in her novel *Sweet Diamond Dust*. The author notes that, just as Puerto Rico is dependent upon the United States and fragmented by the political divisions surrounding its commonwealth status, so are women divided between who they are and what patriarchal society tells them they should be. Ferré states: "In *Sweet Diamond Dust* state colonialism is related to what could be called the colonialism of women, who live a fragmented life, dependent on the patriarchal order. Therefore, the island is often described in a feminine and poetic light" (Ferré, 1990, 109–10, my translation).[29]

To carry this parallel one step further, we could say that just as Puerto Rico strives to gain its independence from the United States, so the female characters of Ferré's fiction fight for their independence from patriarchy. As we shall see, at times this battle becomes directly linked to the Puerto Rican political pro-independence movement and Puerto Rican feminism.

Many of the stories of *Papeles de Pandora* develop within a framework of the transformation of the Puerto Rican economy, which directly relates to U.S. imperialism. As a result of the United States occupation of Puerto Rico in 1898 after the Spanish-American War, the Puerto Rican economy gradually changed from the hacienda system to the predominance of large U.S. capitalist corporations. Landowners eventually sold their property to these corporations as the economy evolved into a full-fledged capitalist system through the influx of U.S. monies to spur industrialization and the implantation of "Operation Bootstrap" in the 1940s and 1950s (Acosta-Belén 1986a, 10–11). Ferré sees capitalism as a U.S. import and thus one of the many consequences of Puerto Rico's colonial status. The colonial status of Puerto Rico vis-à-vis the United States is interpreted as a mirror of women's status vis-à-vis men and the patriarchal order. Consequently, female characters in Ferré's texts associate themselves either implicitly or explicitly with anticolonial Puerto Rican political movements. According to Norma Valle Ferrer, historically these political parties have tended to support feminist ideals, whereas the conservative parties have reinforced traditional values: "The leftist parties in Puerto Rico, the Puerto Rican Independence Party (PIP) and Puerto Rican Socialist Party (PSP), believe in the integration of women in all levels of the revolutionary struggle and their postulates are feminist. They support the elimination of the total juridical and economic structure which oppresses women and the consciousness raising of women, as well as men, in a struggle to eradicate not only *de facto* discrimination, but also male chauvinist attitudes that permeate our society" (Ferrer 1986, 85).

In *Papeles de Pandora*, Ferré alludes to the capitalist/colonial transformation through her portrayal in "The Youngest Doll" of the impoverished aristocratic family whose youngest niece marries the son of the aunt's doctor. Just as the old Puerto Rican hacienda economy withers away under U.S. imperialism, so does the niece languish as an individual through her conversion into a doll or mere decorative object under the dominance of her husband. Similarly, in "Amalia," the U.S. colonial presence is captured through the uncle's association with the U.S. military officers and the interjection of English phrases within the text. The uncle tries to dominate his niece through his suggestive gifts and actions, but she fights for independence by escaping to the forbidden patio. In "Sleeping Beauty," the society pages that trace the marriage of the protagonist, María de los Angeles, reflect colonialism both through the use of English terms (such as the BPs or the Beautiful People), as well as the mention of American music (the wedding songs include such tunes as "Love Is a Many-Splendoured Thing"). These norms dictate traditional behaviors to women, those upheld by María de los Angeles's father and her husband, Felisberto, behaviors that she attempts to rebel against through her silent dance.

These subtle indices gradually become more apparent in Ferré's next text, *Sweet Diamond Dust*, which exposes the corruption of both the hacienda system and the U.S. capitalism that replaced it. This evolution is documented through the efforts of the La Valle family to retain their sugarcane business, and Arístides's threat to sell it to his American brothers-in-law upon his mother's death. The rebellion against both inequitable systems is expressed through Gloria's act of arson, which destroys the entire hacienda, thus removing it from both the hands of the landowning aristocracy and of U.S. capitalists, as well as freeing her from the tyranny of the abusive men of the La Valle family. Moreover, when doña Laura defends her decision to disinherit Arístides and her daughters, her words echo those of an important representative of the Puerto Rican independence movement, Pedro Albizu Campos. Her discourse about her family's refusal to preserve what belongs to Puerto Rico and their desire to allow the sugarcane industry to be taken over by the enemy, the United States, is similar to the rhetoric of those who favored independence in the early part of the twentieth century (Silva 2003, 58).

As Ferré herself noted in *Coloquio de las perras* [Colloquium of the Dogs], Puerto Rico is frequently personified in feminine terms in *Sweet Diamond Dust*. We are told that Guamaní's houses spread "their balconied verandahs upon the slopes like a debutante's brightly colored skirts" (Ferré 1996, 3). The North American imperialists sing the glories of Puerto Rico's "emerald reefs pinned on the sapphire breast of the sea" (68). Ferré also cites José Gautier Benítez's poem within the text, in which he describes Puerto Rico as "voluptuous and light/sweet, placid, complimentary and tender,"[30] which the narrator terms a "peace-loving, feminine, and childlike" description of Puerto Rico (75).

In addition to these descriptions, Laura's narration explicitly equates Gloria's sexuality with Puerto Rico's prostituted status in relation to United States imperialism. She refers to Gloria as a "legendary prostitute" who offered herself to "the new entrepreneurs who came from the north" (76). Moreover, "In her body . . . both races, both languages, English and Spanish, grew into one soul. . . . She's the priestess of our harbor; pythia of our island's future" (76).

Finally, the alignment between anticolonialism and feminism has an equally explicit dimension in *The House on the Lagoon*, where, as we have seen, the protagonist, Isabel, is an active member of the Puerto Rican independence movement (as are many other female characters), whereas Quintín, her authoritative husband, favors union with the United States. Indeed, the majority of women in the novel favor Puerto Rican independence. Puerto Rico's relationship to the United States is also articulated in the novel in terms of silence. However, this silence appears in its traditional sense of oppression. For example, we are told with regard to Arístides's religious school: "The history of the United States was taught thoroughly at their school, yet Puerto Rican history was never mentioned. In the nun's view, the island *had* no history. In this, they were not exceptional: it was forbidden to teach Puerto Rican history at that time, either at private or public schools" (Ferré 1995, 91).

If Puerto Rico becomes a state, it will be "silenced" through the loss of the Spanish language. Isabel establishes a specific relationship between Puerto Rico and women: "The way I see it, our island is like a betrothed, always on the verge of marriage. If one day Puerto Rico becomes a state, it will have to accept English—the language of her future husband" (84).

Abby, one of Isabel's grandmothers, was an active participant of the Nationalist Party. The Nationalist Party was founded in 1922 under Pedro Albizu Campos and stood firmly against U.S. colonialism in Puerto

Rico. According to Edna Acosta-Belén, "Women played an important role in the Nationalist Party particularly during the 1950s" (Acosta-Belén 1986a, 11). Similarly, when Rebecca's friends "argued that the island should be a sovereign nation and cease being a territory of the United States, she agreed wholeheartedly. If she couldn't be independent herself, she would say, at least her country should have control over its own destiny" (Ferré 1995, 97). Quintín tells us that every four years he votes for Puerto Rico to become a state (assimilated to the United States and thus patriarchal ideology), whereas Isabel votes for independence (61). Ferré equates women and Puerto Rico (and hence feminism and national independence) in the novel, which forms another indirect, symbolic association upon which Ferré's texts are constructed.

Symbolism and Characterization

Ferré's works are difficult to categorize within archetypal plot structures. Several ("The Youngest Doll," "Sleeping Beauty," and *The House on the Lagoon*) follow the archetype of the marriage plot, and "The Gift" is similar to the narratives described as "novels of Eros," a variety of which is friendship between two women (Pratt 1981, 95). However, most of the other texts studied here defy classification. Despite their originality of plot development, all of these texts share similar techniques of characterization. Regardless of the plot structure, Ferré employs an emphatic polarization between male characters and female characters that directly corresponds to her use of symbolic, indirect discourse. Polarization, or the exaggeration of extremes to present male and female protagonists, is frequently constructed through symbolic discourse. Men become symbols of evil in Ferré's texts, and this is largely achieved through indirect, symbolic associations appended to the literal meanings of her words.

Both the doctor and his son in "The Youngest Doll" are completely corrupt characters. The doctor breaks the Hippocratic oath by willfully refusing to cure the aunt's swollen leg, so that he can earn money to put his son through medical school. Such actions suggest his parasitic nature, and establish an indirect parallel (symbolic association) with the river prawn that bites the aunt. Similarly, the uncle in "Amalia" is morally bereft, guilty of both an incestuous relationship with his sister and an attempted incestuous relationship with his niece/daughter. His incestuous character is never explicitly stated, but rather hinted at through indirect discourse. The character is further demeaned through his sexual orgies with the three prostitutes he houses. The story suggests that the only way to combat the evil represented by the uncle is through his total destruction, which occurs in the apocalyptic ending to the tale. The father and the brothers in "The Seed Necklace" are guilty of Arístides's murder, as well as the physical abuse of his wife, Armantina, both of which are suggested through indirect, syntagmatic associations. The text implies that these characters are politically corrupt as well.

María de los Angeles's father and husband in "Sleeping Beauty" are also portrayed in a completely negative manner. The father has no regard for his daughter's wishes, and shows himself to be concerned only with superficial, social appearances, a characteristic we observed through symbolic evocation related to the subject of the utterance. Her husband, Felisberto, is shown to be a liar and rapist. The male characters of *Sweet Diamond Dust* are mostly liars (Arístides), wife-beaters (Julio Font), or sexually diseased and insane (Ubaldino). Many of these characteristics (notably, their lack of truthfulness) are suggested through syntagmatic indices based on lack (or implicit narrative contradictions). The two main male characters of *The House on the Lagoon*, Quintín and his father, Buenaventura, are both wife-beaters, and Quintín is an attempted murderer as well. None of the aforementioned characters has any redeeming qualities. They are completely negative, designed to symbolize the corruption and injustice of patriarchy.

In contrast, Ferré's female characters are largely sympathetic to the reader, principally because they are portrayed as innocent victims of hyperbolically evil males in most of the texts. Such is the case of the aunt and the youngest niece in "The Youngest Doll," the unnamed narrator in "Amalia," the mother in "The Seed Necklace," María de los Angeles in "Sleeping Beauty," Gloria in *Sweet Diamond Dust*, and many of the female characters (notably Isabel and Rebecca) in *The House on the Lagoon*. The only exception to this rule is Armantina in "The Seed Necklace," who, although otherwise positively portrayed, ends up murdering the father and brothers in the story (which is seen as a justifiable revenge). The most negative female character of all is Mother Artigas in "The Gift," but, as we already discussed, she functions mainly as a symbol of patriarchal values, and hence substitutes for the male characters that are totally absent from this story.

Ferré includes as characters women from all different racial and socioeconomic classes. In stories like "Sleeping Beauty" and "The Youngest Doll," Ferré contemplates the exploitation of upper-class women by their husbands. Although Ferré's working-class characters frequently exhibit the same types of situations and protests as do their wealthier counterparts, in some instances their behaviors are markedly distinct. Ferré's minority and/or working-class protagonists tend to engage in more dramatic, apocalyptic forms of protest than their bourgeois counterparts, such as Armantina poisoning the family at the end of "El collar de camándulas," or Gloria (the working-class mulatto) setting fire to the house at the end of *Sweet Diamond Dust*. Although Ferré does emphasize the exploitation of Gloria by the La Valle family in *Sweet Diamond Dust*, and the racial discrimination against Carlotta by the nuns of the Sacred Heart school in her story "The Gift," in other instances the silence these protagonists employ to protest their circumstances is not appreciably different from that of her middle-class protagonists. For example, Carlotta in "The Gift" uses makeup as a silent ritual of protest, and this is very similar to actions by other middle-class protagonists, such as María de los Angeles in "Sleeping Beauty," who uses dance as a form of implicit protest. Similarly, both the bourgeois mother and the servant Armantina become mute as forms of protest against patriarchal abuse in Ferré's story "The Seed Necklace."

In sum, Ferré's symbolic discourse and symbolic characters are inextricably intertwined in her works. Although other techniques are also used to construct the hyperbolically evil characters, there is a definite connection between symbolic technique and characterization. The fact that male characters are almost universally negative reinforces the feminist-oriented reading of these texts.

7
Parodic Silence: Ritual and Genre in Laura Esquivel

LAURA PALOMARES ESQUIVEL WAS BORN ON SEPTEMBER 20, 1950, IN Mexico City. She worked as a schoolteacher and published her first novel, *Like Water for Chocolate*, in 1989, gaining enormous success with both the book and a film version. The latter was produced by her former husband, Antonio Arau, with whom she has one daughter. Esquivel, also a screenplay writer, has since published three more novels: *The Law of Love* (1995), *Swift as Desire* (2001), and *Malinche* (2006). Although much has been written about *Like Water for Chocolate*, the bibliography on Esquivel's other novels is sparse due to the recent time frame of their publication.

Like Water for Chocolate and *The Law of Love* both play with the novel's traditional form by including elements that are not normally found in novels. Each chapter of *Like Water for Chocolate* begins with a cooking recipe, while *The Law of Love* is a science fiction novel that includes illustrations and a compact disk whose tracks are designated to be listened to at certain moments in the novel. These elements create meaning not only through traditional verbal signs (the words of a recipe or song), but also through other nonverbal signs (for example, the visual disposition of the words of a recipe or an illustration).

In *Between Two Fires: Intimate Writings on Life, Love, Food and Flavor*, Esquivel presents a series of short stories and brief essays about life, cooking, and mankind's need for a new worldview. In this collection, Esquivel suggests that an alternative form of expression can be found in the relationship between cooking and language. She refers to kitchens as "sacred places" and the women who cook in them as "priestesses." Moreover, she insists upon their modest attitude toward the great act of food preparation: "And the most surprising thing is that they did it [cooking] in the most humble manner; as if they weren't doing anything. . . . *As if they didn't know that the foods they prepared and the rest of us ate remained in our bodies for many hours . . . giving us an identity, a language,* a legacy" (Esquivel 2000, 13, my emphasis). Here Esquivel establishes two important connections: she points out the relationship between cooking and ritual, and designates cooking as a "language" and thus a form of expression. These are also the primary elements the characterize Esquivel's first novel, *Like Water for Chocolate.*

Archetypes of the Sentimental Romance Novel in *Like Water for Chocolate*

Esquivel employs the silent, indirect technique of parody of the sentimental romance novel in *Like Water for Chocolate* to situate the reader within a feminist perspective.[1] Esquivel's choice of the sentimental romance novel as the genre of *Like Water for Chocolate* (as well as her imitation of the science fiction genre in *The Law of Love*) can be seen as an enactment of the principle of "trivialization" (the use of genres considered inferior by the dominant culture). Trivialization, just like incompetence and other encoded forms, suggests a covert rebellion against patriarchal society (Radner and Lanser 1987, 412–25).

Although the parodic aspect of the novel has been much studied, the silent or implicit dimension of parody has been ignored.[2] Gérard Genette emphasizes the importance of this implicitness in his study of transtextuality, *Palimpsestes*, where he defines any aspects that connect a text to a specific genre as architextuality. According to Genette, a text does not usually declare its own genre. Such connections tend to be mute and depend upon the text's reception by the reader, who must make a series of associations between the text in question and other similar texts that have been read in the past (Genette 1982, 11). Genre associations are based on a series of thematic and formalistic conventions (such as verse versus prose and extension of the text) that can vary according to the historical era. The implicit nature of these connections in part explains why *Like Water for Chocolate* has been interpreted by some critics as a mere replication of the clichés of the sentimental romance, while others consider the novel a critical parody of them.[3] Several important books focus on the constituent elements of the sentimental romance novel. An early study from the 1960s by Andrés Amorós concentrates on the popular romances written in Spain by Corín Tellado, which are a more contemporary version of the nineteenth-century *novela por entregas* (serial novels) and are similar to Harlequin romances in English. Janice Radway in *Reading the Romance: Women, Patriarchy, and Popular Literature* also identifies important archetypes in romantic fiction through her analysis of the reading habits of a group of woman in the Smithton community.[4] These two studies will serve as a departure point for the identification of the characteristics of the romance genre. I will then show how these elements are imitated and their ideologies subverted in *Like Water for Chocolate*. Finally, this chapter will illustrate how thematic silence is used to enhance the development of the mimicked sentimental romance novel traits that create a silent parody of this genre.

Both Amorós and Radway specify that the first and foremost element of the romance novel is its focus on a couple who is madly in love (Amorós 1968, 17; Radway 1991, 120). The relationship between Tita and Pedro in *Like Water for Chocolate* certainly fulfills this requirement. The hero is usually extremely masculine, and frequently cruel and indifferent to women because of past hurts, but has a secret, nurturing side (Radway 1991, 128). Although Pedro of *Like Water for Chocolate* does not fit this description, the traits associated with the prototypical female protagonists accurately characterize Tita. The heroine of the romance novel is traditionally innocent, and beautiful, yet rebellious and even boyish (she participates in nonfeminine activities) and, characterized by special or unusual talents (Radway 1991, 131–33). In the early pages of the novel, Esquivel sets up Tita's parallel with the romantic heroine in a flashback in which Tita recalls how she played hooky from school with the boys and beat them all at a swimming race, as well as how she brought four startled horses under control during a carriage ride (Esquivel 1992, 37). Of course, Tita's special talents in the kitchen, albeit a traditional female activity, also set her apart from her nondomestic sisters, particularly in the hyperbolized form in which these talents are described in the novel. Nonetheless, despite this initial presentation of nonfeminine behavior, the romance novel reinforces traditional notions of femininity by portraying its heroines as unusually compassionate and caring (Radway 1991, 127). This may be said of Tita, who dutifully returns to her home to care for Mama Elena when she is ill. Generally speaking, the heroines of these novels are ultimately portrayed as useless outside the domestic realm (Amorós 1968, 16–24).

As for plot structure, a key element identified by both Amorós and Radway is the presence of a love triangle or one or two foils to the romance between the hero and heroine. In *Like Water for Chocolate*, these foils are Tita's sister Rosaura, who marries Pedro (an arrangement to which Pedro agrees so he can be close to Tita), and John, the doctor who saves Tita when she is on the verge of insanity. The domineering Mama Elena, although not a romantic interest, also serves as a foil to the romance between Tita and Pedro and may be seen as the evil character who causes a problem or conflict, as cited by Amorós (Amorós 1968, 60–61). It is interesting that Radway notes that there are two kinds of male foils in romantic fiction: the truly evil, dangerous villain and the sensitive, expressive males who are overtly appreciative of the heroine's qualities (Radway 1991, 131). This latter kind of foil is the type that John Brown plays in Esquivel's novel. Esquivel constantly emphasizes his generosity and dedication to Tita (Esquivel 1992, 108), and his tender loving care nurses her back to health after the death of her beloved nephew, Roberto.[5] In contrast, the demanding and calculating female foil is characterized by a self-interested pursuit of social position (Radway 1991, 131). Rosaura fills this prescription through her insistence on her privileged role as Pedro's wife, despite her knowledge that her husband desires Tita. The fact that these rivals are suspected rather than actual is almost invariably revealed to the reader, but not to the heroine herself of romantic fiction (Radway 1991, 122). Rosaura, the female foil in *Like Water for Chocolate*, is never a real threat to Tita, but there are jealous moments in which Tita is unaware of this, and Pedro inadvertently makes her suffer (which is another classic characteristic of the romance genre). For example, when Pedro first agrees to marry Rosaura, Tita is not cognizant of the fact that he does this only to be near her and anguishes over the inconstancy of his love, which produces "icy feelings" in her (Esquivel 1992, 15).

Finally, Radway notes that the traditional ideology behind the romance novel fosters a realization of female selfhood defined both in relation to the hero (self-fulfillment through his love) and the mother figure (reestablishment of the symbiotic union with the mother) (Radway 1991, 135–38). In *Like Water for Chocolate*, Tita's problematic relationship with her mother is the catalyst for all the conflicts that occur throughout the novel. Mama Elena's domineering, authoritarian nature prohibits Tita from marrying Pedro in the first place. Tita's initial acceptance of her role within the traditional family (the youngest daughter must care for her mother in her old age), as well as her adherence to patriarchal norms of behavior (she must respect her sister's marriage to Pedro), motivates the novel's actions and causes her unhappiness. The novel presents an interesting twist on the idea of reencountering union with the mother to find one's true self and ultimate happiness. In Tita's case, it is just the opposite. When Tita is finally able to confront her dead mother's ghost and confess her hatred, she at last achieves a sense of liberation and identity by severing their final ties: "Tita had said the magic words that would make Mama Elena disappear forever" (Esquivel 1992, 199). This example illustrates how Esquivel mimics the formula of the romance novel, but plays with its elements to create something different than just another romantic text that reinforces traditional patriarchal ideology. Moreover, Tita's rebellion against Mama Elena can be seen as a rejection of the patriarchal norms she upholds, such as women's self-sacrifice and sexual denial.

The final element of the romance novel is its inevitable happy ending, a notion Esquivel also plays with in *Like Water for Chocolate*. Although her protagonists are united at the novel's end for all eternity, this occurs through a simultaneous death that both mimics and subverts the "love conquers all" message of the sentimental romance.

This implicit parody of romance novels raises the question of how to determine whether Esquivel is merely mimicking the genre or actively parodying it with critical intent. As was the case with Isabel Allende, Esquivel's use of hyperbole fosters an incredulous, questioning attitude that leads the reader to doubt the author's acceptance of the ideology of the romance fiction genre, which normally aims at achieving literary realism to foster the escapism of these texts (Radway 1991, 109). Furthermore, her representation of women as powerful characters contradicts the clichés inherent in romance fiction and suggests that she is mocking them through their exaggeration. What particularly interests us here is the way in which Esquivel uses thematic silence in the text to reinforce the novel's parodic dimension and implicitly criticize the sentimental romance genre. The passages in which silence appears especially emphasize the characteristics delineated above and hence contribute to the novel's parodic construction.

Silence as Constructive Tool of Parody in *Like Water for Chocolate*

The first category of silences corresponds to the parodic development of an evil character that represents an obstacle to the lovers' union. Thus, the novel begins with Mama Elena's silencing of her youngest daughter,

Tita, when the latter broaches the possibility of marriage to her boyfriend Pedro:

> Tita knew that discussion was not one of the forms of communication permitted in Mama Elena's household, but even so, for the first time in her life, she intended to protest her mother's ruling.
> "But in my opinion . . ."
> "You don't have an opinion, and that's all I want to hear about it. (Esquivel 1992, 11)

This passage illustrates how Muriel Saville-Troike's taxonomy of silences illuminates the use of rhetorical silence as a form of communication in *Like Water for Chocolate*. It exemplifies the functioning of individually determined silence (Saville-Troike 1995, 16). Tita's original silence is dictated by the norms of the household. In other words, it is the status-indicative type of silence, which is a subcategory of the sociocontextual variety, because it is based on Tita's position as youngest daughter vis-à-vis her mother as family matriarch. Thus, this first silence (which Tita unsuccessfully attempts to break) establishes Mama Elena as an evil authoritarian figure who represents a patriarchal order that must not be transgressed.

Mama Elena uses another subcategory of individually determined silence, symbolic and tactical silence (Saville-Troike 1995, 16) to communicate her anger and disapproval of Tita: "Tita knew perfectly well that all these questions would have to be buried forever in the archive of questions that have no answer. In the De la Garza family, one obeyed—immediately. . . . Mama Elena left the kitchen, and for the next week, she didn't speak a single word to her" (Esquivel 1992, 12). In the family, questions are routinely unanswered (met with silence). In other words, the disapproval of questions (a form of rebellion) is communicated through the silence with which such questions are "answered," hence converting silence into a tactic used to reinforce obedience to authority.

Another example is when Tita and Pedro witness Gertrudis's flight with the Mexican revolutionary, after eating Tita's quails in rose petals. Gertrudis's passion inspires Tita's rebellion, and we are told that she tries to call out to Pedro to take her away with him, but that no sound would come out of her mouth (Esquivel 1992, 57). This passage represents a psychological silence rather than a sociocontextual one (Saville-Troike 1995, 17), indicative of Tita's fear of her mother. She tries to speak to Pedro to communicate her rebellion against societal norms, but is unable to speak any actual words. All of these passages serve to reinforce Mama Elena's role as a hyperbolically evil character. Up until this point, silence conveys traditional associations of repression and passivity. Since words fail Tita, she must devise another form of expression, which, as we shall see, turns out to be cooking. The novel evolves from traditional connotations of silence to silent, ritualistic cooking as a feminist marker.

The most obvious silence in the novel is the muteness that Tita adopts when her beloved nephew, Roberto, dies. Tita takes refuge in the pigeon house and refuses to speak. Mama Elena wants to have her committed to an insane asylum and calls Dr. Brown for this purpose. Dr. Brown refuses to commit Tita and takes her to his house, where she remains silent for a long period of time:

> Some day, when she felt like talking, she would tell John that, but now, she preferred silence. There were many things she needed to work out in her mind, and she could not find the words to express the feelings seething inside her since she left the ranch. She was badly shaken. The first few days she didn't even want to leave her room; her food was brought to her there by Katy, a seventy-year-old North American woman. . . . Going to the window facing the patio, she raised her hands to heaven; she wanted to escape from herself, didn't want to think about making a choice, didn't want to talk again. She didn't want her words to shriek her pain. (Esquivel 1992, 109)

This description of Tita's silence suggests that it is self-imposed. Tita can talk, but she chooses not to. Her silence can be interpreted as either interactive and psychological (it is a form of neurosis brought about by the shock of her nephew's death) or as noninteractive and contemplative (silence as a meditative refuge used by Tita to recuperate her energy and decide what course to follow in the future) (Saville-Troike 1995, 16–17). Although the text initially leads us to interpret Tita's silence as a form of mental illness, the above passage clearly signals its therapeutic, restorative powers. This period of silence coincides with the time that Tita remains under Dr. John Brown's protection. Thus, Tita's recuperative silence underscores Dr. Brown's helpfulness in the restoration of Tita's mental state, and hence his role as sensitive, expressive male foil, which as we have already seen, is another of the characteristics attributed to the sentimental romance.

It is interesting that Tita finally decides to speak when Chencha brings her a beef-tail broth. After eating this dish, Tita verbally communicates for the first time in six months. This provoking of speech through food suggests the relationship between food and language that will be developed later. This same relationship is suggested by the words "she couldn't find the words to express what was *cooking* inside her" (Esquivel 1989, 108, my translation and emphasis), which underscore the connection between cooking and self-expression.[6]

Romantic fiction's emphasis on a young couple who are madly in love is also emphasized through the communicative, silent gestures observed in the relationship between Tita and Pedro. When Mama Elena forbids Pedro's marriage to Tita, Pedro decides to marry Tita's sister Rosaura in order to be near his love. Their interaction is clearly limited by Mama Elena's ever vigilant eye. Thus, Pedro and Tita have few opportunities to speak. However, the silence that exists between them does not severely limit their communication, which is largely carried out through their nonverbal gestures. Saville-Troike terms this form of silent communication "nonvocal/nonverbal proemics" (Saville-Troike 1995, 17).

For example, during the courtship between Rosaura and Pedro, Pedro's family's first visit to Tita's house is an anguishing experience for Tita. During the visit, Pedro expresses his passion for Tita exclusively through glances and eye-contact which are silent communicative acts: "She turned her head and her eyes met Pedro's. It was then she understood how dough feels when it is plunged into boiling oil. The heat that invaded her body was so real she was afraid she would start to bubble—her face, her stomach, her heart, her breasts—like batter, and unable to endure his gaze" (Esquivel 1992, 16). Moreover, the glances are described in cooking terminology, once again suggesting the communicative power of food.

Similarly, when Tita is preparing the banquet for her nephew's baptism, the glances she exchanges with Pedro express their mutual erotic feelings: "Tita looked up without stopping her grinding and her eyes met Pedro's. At once their passionate glances fused so perfectly that whoever saw them would have seen but a single look, a single rhythmic and sensual motion, a single trembling breath, a single desire" (66–67).

The setting for this amorous communication between Tita and Pedro is also significant, because it takes place in the kitchen while Tita is cooking.[7]

When Pedro and Tita finally consummate their love, there is no verbal communication between the two (other than Tita's initial questioning of why Pedro is in the room). The focus is on "Pedro's accursed gaze" (158). In the face of their extreme passion, even the voluble Chencha is rendered speechless: "Chencha was struck dumb with surprise for the first time in her life; not a single sound escaped her lips" (159).

Physical gestures, such as passionate glances, the movement of Tita's breasts, and the sexual act, not words, are the true communicators of feelings in *Like Water for Chocolate*.[8] The hyperbolic narration of these silent gestures comically reconstructs the intensity of the love between the male and female protagonists of the sentimental romance novel in a tone bordering on the tongue-in-cheek.

The presentation of women as useless outside the domestic realm and within the public sphere is both parodied and subverted in *Like Water for Chocolate*. First, it is subverted through Gertrudis's role as a general in the Mexican revolution. Second, it is contested through the negation of the traditional values of cooking/knitting. In other words, the novel first parodies the traditional presentation of women through its emphasis on these two typical female domestic activities. However, these two activities are then hyperbolically presented as silent rituals that serve as an alternative form of expression for women. Hence, upon imitating them, Esquivel divests them of their traditional passive connotations and invests them with a new, powerful, communicative function. The new meaning with which Esquivel infuses these activities suggests an emphasis on female empowerment that contradicts the submissive ideology of traditional romance fiction and indicates the novel's parodic character.[9] The implications of cooking and knitting are explored below.

Silent Rituals in *Like Water for Chocolate*

The establishment of cooking as a ritual is important for the study of the role of silence as a way of creating a feminist perspective in the text. As we saw in the first chapter, Ardener suggests ritual as a possible communicative alternative for women to male-dominated language, and Saville-Troike points out the connection between ritual and silence as part of an integrated communicative system. Most rituals, such as religious services, funerals, and public performances, are accompanied by an institutionally determined silence, with the exception made for one or two duly authorized speakers (Saville-Troike 1995, 16). *Like Water for Chocolate* has cleverly established a new location for ritual, the kitchen. As with most rituals, this sacred location implies the necessity of silence for its participants, who instead of communicating through words, do so through the ritualized act of cooking. Some passages even explicitly designate cooking as ritual. For example, "On Mama Elena's ranch, sausage making was a real ritual.... All the women in the family had to participate" (Esquivel 1992, 9).[10]

The encounter between Tita and the spirit of John's dead grandmother, Luz del Amanecer, emphasizes the many interrelationships between food, cooking, silence, and ritual. Here silence is explicitly designated in the text as a form of communication between the two women, who are drawn together by the food that Luz del Amanecer cooks:

> [S]he decided to go see who was cooking. It couldn't be Katy. The person who produced this kind of smell really knew how to cook. Never having laid eyes on her, Tita felt she knew this person, whoever she was. ... she met a pleasant woman around eighty years old. She looked a lot like Nacha....
>
> She looked up and smiled kindly, inviting Tita to sit down next to her. Tita did so. The woman immediately offered her a cup of the delicious tea....
>
> She stayed with the woman for a little while. The woman didn't speak either, but it wasn't necessary. From the first, they had established a communication that went far beyond words. (110)

The relationship between Tita and Luz del Amanecer is established on the basis of the delicious foods the latter cooks. Neither one speaks, but in the ritualistic space of the kitchen, speech is unnecessary. A silent form of communication "beyond words" characterizes their interaction. Tita and Luz del Amanecer share a social marginality that emphasizes their union. Tita is a woman alone, forbidden to marry and thus to integrate into society. Luz del Amanecer was an Indian woman who married a white man and was ostracized by his family for a long period of time. Their relationship once again recalls Auerbach's community of women united by a silent code (Auerbach 1978, 5). Luz del Amanecer joins Tita, Nacha, and Chencha (another servant in the house) as silent figures who express themselves through the cooking ritual, which functions as a symbolic language.

This connection between cooking and language is made explicit in various passages of *Like Water for Chocolate*. Cecilia Lawless notes that since food/recipes are considered primarily a feminine discourse, they are not normally associated with empowerment. Nonetheless, Tita inverts this traditional connotation and develops her own language from these elements, one that "combines erotics with independence" (Lawless 1997, 262).

Esquivel purposely selects a "gendered discourse" (recipes) and subverts its traditional connotation (a woman's place is in the kitchen) to convert it into an instrument of communication and power, rather than passivity, for women. In *Like Water for Chocolate*, cooking is constructed as a form of nonverbal communication that effectively expresses Tita's emotions when words cannot. Whatever sentiment Tita experiences when cooking a recipe, whether it be anger, passion, or sadness, that emotion is communicated through the food to whoever eats it, and the recipient experiences that same emotion:

> It was as if a strange alchemical process had dissolved her entire being in the rose petal sauce, in the tender flesh of the quails, in the wine, in every one of the meal's aromas. That was the way she entered Pedro's body, hot, voluptuous, perfumed, totally sensuous.
>
> With that meal it seemed they had discovered a new system of communication, in which Tita was the transmittee, Pedro the receiver, and poor Gertrudis the medium, the conducting body through which the singular sexual message was passed. (Esquivel 1992, 52)

In another section, we are similarly told that Tita mixes cooking ingredients in the same manner that a poet plays with words (69). The cooking ingredients and recipes are Tita's vocabulary. Quotidian language is insufficient to express her feelings. Thus, when Tita prepares Rosaura's wedding cake, her tears permeate the dessert with her sadness, and all the wedding guests end up forlorn and vomiting. When she prepares the quails in rose petals, her passion penetrates the dish and affects her sister Gertrudis, who runs away with a soldier from the Mexican revolution. Tita's happiness upon her nephew's birth is communicated to everyone through the stew she prepares for his baptism. Finally, when Esperanza weds Alex, the food acts as an aphrodisiac that is reflective of Tita's own amorous feelings. Cooking is a silent communicative alternative to traditional, male-dominated language.[11]

Cooking is not the only ritual presented in the novel. Esquivel also incorporates the act of knitting as a ritualistic behavior on Tita's part. Tita's anguish, loneliness, and unrequited love are expressed by the coldness she feels. She attempts to remedy these sentiments and sensations through the knitting of an enormous blanket (19). The knitting of the blanket is never really finished, as we are later told: "And that's what she specified in the cookbook she started writing that night, after crocheting a big section of bedspread, as she did every night" (59). And in another section: "In despair, at night—after she had knit a little section of bedspread, of course—she would invent new recipes, hoping to repair the connection that flowed between them through the food she prepared" (69). Thus, Tita simultaneously enacts two rituals: the writing of the recipe book and the knitting of her blanket. At the end of the novel, the symbolic communicative content of the act of blanket knitting becomes apparent. When Pedro dies while making love to Tita, she experiences a tremendous chill. She drapes herself with the enormous blanket that "covered . . . all three hectares" (245) of the ranch. After swallowing the matches that she lights through recalling passionate moments with Pedro, the sparks ignite the blanket, which in turn sets fire to the entire ranch. Through the symbolic, ritualistic act of knitting a blanket, Tita succeeds in communicating both her desolation and her passion. At the end of the novel Tita and Pedro are joined in death, and thus Tita is no longer in need of the blanket that she made to combat her sadness and isolation. The blanket burns up in the flames when all of Tita's matches are lit. The ritual (blanket knitting) disappears when its need is extinguished by the warmth of the eternal union of Tita and Pedro. Esquivel appropriates knitting, a traditional domestic act, only to invert its traditional sense through hyperbole and transform it into a sign of female expression. The two silent rituals of cooking and knitting/weaving are used to simultaneously mimic and subvert the notion of the useless, powerless, domestic woman fostered by traditional romantic fiction.[12] In this way, the novel constructs a parody of the romantic fiction genre, a parody that serves as a silent and implicit marker of a feminist position from which the novel may be read.

Like Water for Chocolate also subverts the sentimental romance genre through hyperbole and magical realism, both of which point to its unrealistic character. Among these elements are the contrast between sublime love and banal cooking ingredients, the nostalgia of Rosaura's wedding guests for their greatest love counterpoised to their collective vomiting, and the use of comical, rhyming strings of adjectives to describe the characters, among others (Glenn 1994, 42–43). Some other hyperbolic elements much cited by the criticism on Esquivel include the amount of salt produced by Tita's tears when she was born, Tita's ability to breast-feed her nephew Roberto, the incredible length of the woven blanket, the igniting through passion of the matches Tita swallows at the novel's end, and the effects of Tita's cooking on those who eat it—notably, the flames exuding from Gertrudis when she consumes the quails in rose petals. All of these hyperbolic elements suggest that Esquivel comically and subversively appropriates the romance genre instead of reproducing its ideology (Ibsen 1995, 7–20).[13]

It is interesting to note that the one element of the sentimental romance genre that Esquivel does not exactly parody in *Like Water for Chocolate* is the total absence of political issues and social problems, which are normally supplanted by all-powerful love in these novels. The main portion of the novel takes place during the 1910 Mexican revolution. Although Esquivel does not explicitly focus on the social and political significance of the revolution, she accurately portrays the situation of women during the revolution both through the figure of Gertrudis and Tita's life in general. During the revolution, women served as arms runners, spies, and nurses. Escandón tells us "their combat related activities represented a profound change in their usual confined roles" (Escandón 1994, 200). Shirlene Soto in her book on women's participation in the Mexican revolution indicates that some women even came to occupy military ranks, which is the case with Gertrudis in *Like Water for Chocolate*: "While most *soldaderas* remained virtually anonymous, a few achieved some recognition. Several soldaderas established reputations for their fighting prowess. One of the most famous was Margarita Neri, from southern Mexico. Many stories surround Neri's life, making it almost impossible to separate myth from reality. Neri rapidly became a high-ranking revolutionary officer, assuming command over large numbers of Indians. Neri, supposedly a Dutch-Maya from Quintana Roo, was noted for her dancing as well as her fighting" (Soto 1990, 45).

It is possible that Esquivel modeled Gertrudis upon Neri, since she is not only referred to as *la generala* (a high military rank), but also is depicted as a good dancer in the novel: "She began to dance gracefully to the polka 'Jesuita in Chihuahua,' which Juan was playing brilliantly on the norteño accordion" (Esquivel 1992, 180). Gertrudis's freedom is placed in opposition to Tita's limited opportunities, which generally characterized women during that era. Although there was some reform of women's legal status (such as the authorization of divorce and remarriage) during the period of the revolution, women generally led confined lives and experienced no change in their political status during that time (Escandón 1994, 200). The fact that Esquivel does not adhere to the romance novel's sociopolitical contextual void also suggests to the reader that her work is not a mere replication of the romance genre but rather a critical engagement with the potentially stultifying effects of this type of fiction.

The use of implicit stylistic techniques, such as parody/architextuality in *Like Water for Chocolate*, combined with Esquivel's emphasis on thematic silence in the novel, illustrates how the writer subversively converts silence from a patriarchal marker of passivity into a feminist marker of rebellion. Esquivel continues this poetics of subversion through parody in her second novel, *The Law of Love*.

Textual Voice and Parody in *The Law of Love*

Catherine Perricone designates *The Law of Love* an "eclectic" novel (Perricone 1999, 295). The novel's cover defines it as a "novel with music." The book includes a compact disk taped to the back and multiple illustrations by the artist Miguelanxo Prado. The novel is set in a futuristic world of reincarnated beings in which the main character, Azucena, is searching for her "twin soul," Rodrigo. In other words, the novel mixes the science fiction, quest, and romance genres. To call it "eclectic" seems to understate the case.

To understand *The Law of Love*'s relationship with silence, we need to consider three fundamental concepts: paratextuality, textual voice, and parody/architextuality (which we have already examined with regard to *Like Water for Chocolate*). Genette defines paratextuality as "autographic or allographic accessory signs" such as a work's title, subtitle, preface, postface, footnotes, epigraphs, and illustrations that comment on the text. Thus, *The Law of Love*'s compact disk and illustrations are paratextual elements.[14]

As we saw in chapter 6 on Rosario Ferré, Stephen Ross refers to Genette's paratextual elements as examples of "textual voice."[15] Genette's paratextuality and Ross's "textual voice" overlap. However, paratextual elements may have semantic content, whereas elements of textual voice signify purely on the visual plane, and therefore can be thought of as nonverbal or "silent" elements of a text.

Thus, Esquivel's first uses silence in *The Law of Love* through nonverbal elements in the form of cartoonlike illustrations. These illustrations occupy a significant role in the novel's development. The main character, Azucena, is an astroanalyst, a futuristic psychiatrist or psychologist. All characters in the novel have led several lives, but are not always capable of remembering them. Characters are reincarnated to expiate sins of their past existence. To achieve this goal, characters must frequently undergo astroanalysis and remember their past. They often listen to music (some of which is reproduced on the compact disk), which evokes mental images (depicted by the novel's illustrations) of their past lives. These images are then recorded on a special camera so that the astroanalyst can view them and help patients to understand their significance. Azucena herself undergoes this process to find her "twin soul." The characters' reliance on illustrations as an alternative form of expression again underscores the positive value of silence.

Esquivel's second use of silence brings us back to Genette's concept of architextuality. In *The Law of Love*, Esquivel relies heavily on the conventions of three distinct novelistic genres (science fiction, quest novel, romance novel) to articulate a feminist position for the reader. Below I will examine how Esquivel uses implicit genre parody to subvert traditional patriarchal ideology in *The Law of Love*.

Anne Cranny-Francis points out that the merging of science fiction and quest structure (in which the relationship between a tough male hero and a passive female victim/prize is portrayed) is a common practice of traditional science fiction. Consequently, Cranny-Francis argues, feminist science fiction writers are confronted with the challenge of using an inherently "masculinist story-telling mechanism to tell a feminist story" (Cranny-Francis 1990, 67).[16]

The Law of Love subverts this convention of the traditional science fiction / quest novel by inverting its terms. A female heroine (Azucena) seeks a male victim/prize (Rodrigo). Rodrigo is portrayed as a helpless individual, trapped on a primitive planet, Korma, from which Azucena eventually rescues him. He is also accused of assassinating a candidate for the world presidency, and his pursuit by the authorities only ends when Azucena arranges the transference of his soul to the body of Cuquita's husband. Thus, Esquivel inverts traditional roles associated with this genre.

The Law of Love also "silently" relies on genre conventions to convey implicit meaning through futuristic science fiction elements. In the story, male and female characters are often reincarnated as beings of the opposite gender. In other words, the fluidity with which one can pass between genders abolishes gender differences. This ultimately proposes a genderless society in which men and women are totally equal. For example, Rodrigo, in one of his reincarnated lives, was a raped woman, while one of Isabel's henchmen assumes Azucena's body in the novel.[17]

The novel simultaneously achieves an implicit parody of the traditional romantic fiction with which it shares many traits. The traits of the sentimental novel defined in Amorós and Radway and exemplified by *Like Water for Chocolate* also characterize *The Law of Love*. Esquivel uses these elements in a highly parodic fashion. The novel incorporates many of the clichéd characteristics of such novels at the same time that it purposefully excludes others. Esquivel hyperbolically incorporates elements of popular fiction to expose its alienating effects on women. At the same time she clearly inverts or contradicts other standard elements of this fiction for the same purpose. This mixture at times may confuse the reader with regard to the text's message.

A good example of Esquivel's mocking parody of romance fiction is the first scene in which Azucena and Rodrigo appear. They are madly in love because they are "twin souls" who have finally been united. The narrator describes their physical and spiritual union in terms of the activation of each of the seven "chakras" or "energy receptors" they possess. Each chakra corresponds to "a note on the musical scale and to a color in the rainbow" (Esquivel 1996, 20–21). Consequently, their mutual activation in the twin souls produces a marvelous melody and an amazing splash of color that coincide with their sexual union. This physical coupling is simultaneously described as a "reciprocal penetration" in which the atoms of each body fill the other. This amorous description mimics the notion of all-powerful or perfect love common in popular romance. However, instead of the focus on the male lover's penetration of the female, Esquivel describes a mutual penetration of body and soul. Esquivel's erotic description is totally egalitarian, thus negating patriarchal ideology's emphasis on male sexual dominance, an emphasis typically implied in popular romantic fiction.

Esquivel's description of this union of souls is also notable for its emphasis on color and music, two nonverbal forms. The union of souls is not characterized by semantic communication between the lovers, but rather is achieved through energy that is converted into a rainbow and a "marvelous melody," reminiscent of the illustrations and compact disk in the novel. Music and colors communicate through nonverbal signifiers, reinforcing the concept of expression through silence rather than words.

Despite Lisbeth Gant-Britton's affirmation that *The Law of Love*'s connection with the romance genre hampers its critical stance vis-à-vis patriarchal ideology (Gant-Britton 2000, 261), the work's highly parodic nature does not diminish its critical power, but rather enhances it. *The Law of Love* parodies the sentimental romance genre to expose and subvert its sexist ideology. Esquivel's hyperbole indicates the absurdity of such staples of traditional romantic fiction as the love triangle, female reliance on men for happiness, and the emphasis on physical beauty. For instance, the novel makes fun of these elements in the passage in which Azucena, now in the decrepit body of Cuquita's grandmother, is depressed by Rodrigo's involvement with Citlali. Azucena regains her happiness through a physical relationship with Teo, who is really an undercover guardian angel acting by order of Anacronete (Azucena's regular guardian angel) to help Azucena regain her equilibrium and focus on her mission. In this passage (Esquivel 1996, 189–90), the novel satirizes the notion of a perfect mate or "twin soul" that is at the core of all romantic fiction. Both Rodrigo and Azucena, supposedly the perfect match, ignore their supposed spiritual connection and engage in purely physical relationships with others. Rodrigo lets himself "be carried away by Citlali's swaying hips," while Azucena, after expressing her anguish and lamenting Rodrigo's fickleness, engages in a passionate sexual relationship with Teo in the spaceship's bathroom. This sexual encounter immediately lifts her depression and feelings of unworthiness, thus revealing her own parallel lack of constancy. The scene's tongue-in-cheek tone is underscored by the comically detailed description of Azucena's labored efforts to make love in an old woman's body,[18] at the same time that Azucena's passionate encounter is interrupted by Cuquita's urgent need to use the bathroom. *The Law of Love* exposes the male dependency and female lack of identity perpetuated by the sentimental or serial novel through this highly comic portrayal of supposedly lofty relationships turned carnal. Moreover, within this deconstruction of the romance novel's notion of "true love," Esquivel deftly posits an egalitarian position for women, since Azucena does not bemoan her temporary abandonment, but rather happily engages in a sexual relationship on a par with Rodrigo's flirtations. Although at the end of the novel Rodrigo and Azucena are reunited (one would expect nothing less of a romantic parody), Esquivel has successfully deconstructed the notion of a perfect love contained in the idea of "twin souls."

Esquivel also parodies romantic clichés when Azucena is finally reunited with Rodrigo on the planet Korma. Her dreams of a passionate encounter with her twin soul are dashed when Rodrigo does not even recognize her, since her soul has been transplanted into a new body. Rodrigo is also suffering from amnesia. Esquivel pokes fun at the traditional representation of such romantic reunions in the following:

> She had dreamed of a romantic meeting in the best movie tradition, where Rodrigo, seeing her from a distance, would run toward her in

slow motion: she, in a white chiffon gown undulating in the wind; he dressed like a twentieth-century heartthrob in elegant linen slacks and a silk shirt half unbuttoned to reveal his strong muscular chest. The background music could only be the theme from "Gone with the Wind." As they met, they would throw themselves into each other's arms, like Romeo and Juliet, Tristan and Isolde, Paolo and Francesca. And then the music of their bodies would become one with the music of the spheres, turning their encounter into an unforgettable moment in the lore of famous lovers. Instead, there she stood, facing a man who showed not the slightest flicker of life. (Esquivel 1996, 132)

Esquivel's hyperbolic description of the anticipated encounter underscores the unrealistic nature of such romantic expectations. Both the physical descriptions of the lovers (the woman's dress blowing in the wind; the man with his chest exposed) as well as the use of the theme music from *Gone with the Wind* are stereotypes straight out of Hollywood film production. The comparison of Azucena and Rodrigo with the most famous lovers of all time emphasizes the element of exaggeration in the description. The text's rejection of these romantic stereotypes and clichés is implicit in the technique of parody.

A final example of romantic parody is the novel's ending, in which all novelistic conflicts are resolved and everyone lives happily ever after. Rodrigo and Azucena are reunited, and Azucena recovers her young body and her baby. Citlali and Cuquita are joined with their twin souls. Carmela and Julito get married. Anacreonte, Azucena's guardian angel, his mission completed, marries Pavana and departs for his honeymoon. Even the evil devil Mammon happily marries Lilith at the end. Thus, we see in exaggerated form how everyone falls in love and all problems are solved.

Feminism in *The Law of Love* and Beyond

The question of parody and the fundamental difference between Esquivel's novels and those that she imitates leads us to a discussion of the incorporation of Mexican history and world events in *The Law of Love*. Like *Like Water for Chocolate*, this novel cannot be accused of the social and political void associated with sentimental romance novels. In particular, Esquivel focuses on the Mexican conquest and the 1985 Mexico City earthquake as seminal historical events. The 1985 earthquake marked an important moment in the development of the Mexican women's movement. Escandón states: "The effects of this natural disaster on the Mexican political system could not have been anticipated. Specifically, for the women's movement, the increased political participation in spontaneously organized groups meant a new alliance among women of different classes" (Escandón 1994, 210). Since much of the garment industry, largely composed of female workers, was destroyed during the earthquake, these women, later joined by middle-class counterparts, became very active in lobbying for female rights in industry (Escandón 1994, 211).

Esquivel parodies this new alliance between women of different social classes in *The Law of Love* through the relationship between the characters Azucena and Cuquita. Azucena represents the bourgeoisie in the futuristic society portrayed in the novel. She belongs to the class of the "evolved ones" who are granted all sorts of privileges because they have evolved to a higher state of expiation of their past lives and sins. In contrast, Cuquita belongs to the PRI, or Partido de revindicación de los involucionados (Party for the Vindication of the Unevolved), a working-class group whose name is satirically modeled on the other Mexican PRI, the Partido revolucionario institucional (Institutional Revolutionary Party). At the beginning of the novel, the two women are enemies who distrust one another. However, as the novel progresses, Azucena and Cuquita become friends who learn to help each other. In addition to their individual gains through unity, they work together for a common cause: the exposure of the evil nature of the candidate for the world presidency, Isabel González. Although at times comedic, this alliance parodies the new alliance between Mexican upper-class women and working-class women after 1985. It is interesting that Esquivel emphasizes the silent bond between the two women, thus uniting once again the implicit technique of parody with the explicit theme of silence.

This parody of the new association between middle-class women and lower-class women in *The Law of Love* reflects a general connection between Esquivel's parodic silence as a postmodern phenomenon and the popularization of feminism in Mexico during the late 1980s and early 1990s. The predominance of genre parody and use of elements of popular narrative such as the sentimental romance, cooking recipes, and science fiction suggest a link to postmodernism in its nonelitist character. According to Linda Hutcheon, postmodern practice is self-reflexive, highly parodic, and ironic; blurs the borders between high and low genres and disciplines such as history and fiction; and questions both authorial originality and the separation of politics and aesthetics, revealing the ideological nature of all human knowledge (Hutcheon 1988, 3–21). This emphasis on popular or mass culture in Esquivel reflects a similar popularization or nonelitist tendency of the women's movement in Mexico. Escandón notes that since the 1980s, there has been a mutual influence between feminism and lower-class, urban movements. This intermingling has given rise to a new, popular feminism, in which "women express their class demands with a feminist perspective" (Escandón 1994, 213). Hence, Esquivel's popularization of fiction through its parody of mass culture correlates with a corresponding popularization of the Mexican women's movement during the 1980s and 1990s. By employing familiar elements of mass culture such as recipes or romance novels, Esquivel has made her fiction less elitist and more accessible to people, especially women, from less-privileged backgrounds. It is precisely for its popular appeal that Esquivel's fiction has frequently been criticized. Nonetheless, Esquivel's work reflects an important cross-fertilization between upper-class readers, lower-class readers, and the feminist movement.

Inverted Gender Roles and Silent Communication in *Swift as Desire*

The theme of communication is at the center of Esquivel's third novel, *Tan veloz como el deseo* [*Swift as Desire*] (2001). Superficially, the novel appears to differ significantly from Esquivel's other two, because it presents a male protagonist, Júbilo Chi. Júbilo is a character whose essence is reflected by his symbolic name. His mission in life is to bring joy to others and to enjoy himself. Júbilo repeatedly serves as an interpreter of other peoples' language and feelings. He thus becomes a telegraph operator, a job that allows him to serve as a vehicle of communication between individuals.

Although Júbilo is a male character, he does not incarnate patriarchal values in most instances. The traditional male hero is usually portrayed as unemotional, pragmatic, and extremely focused on professional and economic success, whereas traditional female characters are usually described as emotional, impractical, and exclusively involved with home and family. In *Swift as Desire*, Júbilo and his wife, Lucha, reverse stereotyped gender roles. Júbilo is almost exclusively guided by his emotions. His job is not particularly lucrative, and he is not ambitious about earning more money. His biggest priority is spending time with his wife and his children. In contrast, Lucha is a very pragmatic and ambitious character. She decides to go to work to supplement her family's income. This inversion of male/female roles is symbolized by the characters' names: Júbilo, or "Joy," reflects the protagonist's desire to make everyone happy; he chooses the self-sacrificing role usually attributed to women. Lucha, or "Fight," suggests men's struggle in the workforce to earn a living and provide for their families. These traditional gender stereotypes are implicitly challenged through their inverted parody.[19]

Women are traditionally portrayed as the great communicators within the private domain, the ones who openly express emotions that are usually repressed by their male counterparts. Thus, Júbilo, who carries out the role traditionally assigned to women, is the person in charge of communication in the novel.

It is no surprise that Júbilo's communicative acts question the validity of language as an expressive vehicle. This questioning starts in his childhood, when Júbilo, the only bilingual member of his family, serves as interpreter between his Mayan grandmother and his Spanish mother. The relationship between these two women is initially characterized by silence. This silence communicates the tensions between two distinct cultures and viewpoints: "For many years, she [the grandmother] had avoided visiting her son's home.... Her rejection of her daughter-in-law was so great that for years she refused to speak to her, arguing that she couldn't speak Spanish" (Esquivel 2001a, 13). Júbilo's birth forces his grandmother to visit the house and establish communication with her daughter-in-law. This communication shows the incapability of words to fully express certain concepts and emotions, and the need to focus on nonverbal gestures to adequately understand the real truth behind language: "[F]rom the age of five, the child became the family's official interpreter.... *So, as Júbilo translated, not only did he have to be aware of these subtleties, but he also had to pay attention to his mother's and grandmother's tone of voice, the tension in their vocal cords, as well as the expression on their faces and set of their mouths*" (14, my emphasis).

In another passage, we are directly told that words do not express the grandmother's true feelings, which are instead communicated through a "silent voice" that only Júbilo can hear: "Even to an innocent child like Júbilo, it was obvious that his grandmother was making an effort to swallow her words. But, as strange as it sounds, Júbilo heard the silent words clearly, even though they had never been spoken. And he understood that this 'voice' that remained silent was the one that truly represented his grandmother's desires. So Júbilo ... frequently translated those imperceptible murmurings instead of the words she spoke out loud" (15). This passage suggests the communicative value of silence and emphasizes that Júbilo's special talent lies in his ability to perceive and interpret this silence for others. Júbilo's special communicative talent is portrayed as a telepathic power. The thoughts of others are somehow transferred to Júbilo, without direct mediation through words. Words are portrayed throughout the novel as "traitors" to true thoughts. Unlike most people, Júbilo can directly hear the silent thoughts of others and translate them into an authentic "language."

When Júbilo, a victim of Parkinson's disease, finally becomes unable to speak, his daughter Lluvia perpetuates the idea of the communicative value of silence. She says: "I would have to learn to listen to his silence to find the answers" (66). At the end of the novel, Lluvia acquires her father's uncanny ability to interpret the silent thoughts of others. When Júbilo and Lucha meet again after thirty years of silence, Júbilo communicates his thoughts to her through an old telegraph machine. The darkness of the room impedes Lucha's comprehension of his message (transformed into words on a computer screen), so Lluvia is called upon to interpret. Lluvia, just like her father before her, instead of translating the exact words, communicates her father's true feelings "behind" these words. She tells her mother that Júbilo knows that his duty was to love her, take care of her, and fill her life with laughter, and he was sorry that he failed to do so, although he will always love her best. The narrator informs us: "That isn't what don Júbilo had signalled at all, but he loved hearing his daughter interpret his words in that way. He made a sign of complicity and gave a deep sigh" (196). It is significant that Júbilo's ability to translate people's true feelings behind their words is passed on to his daughter, Lluvia. Since Júbilo functions more like a mother than a father in the text, we can see the passage of his talent as a matrilineal inheritance that emphasizes the imperfections of male-centered language and women's need to go beyond it for authentic expression.

In a variety of instances, the novel suggests the importance of alternative, symbolic forms of communication. For example, the novel begins with the Mayan hieroglyphics etched in the stone, which Júbilo attempts to interpret. The instrument of Júbilo's chosen profession, the telegraph, is based on Morse code, a symbolic code that arbitrarily assigns a system of dots and dashes to the alphabet. Júbilo relishes his job as telegraph operator precisely because it gives him the power to interpret a code that no one else can understand. This gives Júbilo an absolute freedom to interpret these signs at his discretion, and thus to communicate the "true" meaning behind them and to bring love and happiness to everyone: "Since only he would know what was said to him in the messages that he was to transmit, he would be able to translate them in his own way! . . . He knew perfectly well that his ability to 'hear' people's true feelings wasn't shared by everyone" (22).

Of course, there is a certain comic irony in Júbilo's translations, which always accentuate the positive and omit the negative, particularly when he translates between his mother and grandmother. Nonetheless, Esquivel underscores the communicative value of silence and the presence of a nonverbal meaning beyond one's actual words. Despite Júbilo's male identity (because of the gender role-reversal), once again, the emphasis placed on silence and the pitfalls of male-dominated language serves as a signal to the reader of the text's feminist orientation.

Parody, Plot, and Characterization in Esquivel's Fiction

The plot structure of Esquivel's *Like Water for Chocolate* loosely conforms to Annis Pratt's single-woman plot, while *Swift as Desire* has some elements of the married-woman plot. The same synergistic connection between plot, characterization and form observed with regard to the previous writers can also be noted in Esquivel's work. The principal male characters of *Like Water for Chocolate*, *The Law of Love*, and *Swift as Desire* may be viewed as weak, in varying degrees, in comparison with their female counterparts. This portrayal of strong female characters and weak male figures is a direct inversion of the societal stereotypes for men and women. Such stereotypes inform much of the sentimental romance fiction that Esquivel has been shown to parody in her works. Consequently, silent parody is intimately connected to the characterization that advances the plot in all three books mentioned.

For example, Pedro in *Like Water for Chocolate* is far from the ideal novelistic hero. Instead of attempting to run away with Tita, or marrying her against her mother's prohibition, he settles for marriage to Tita's sister, Rosaura. Although he continues to desire Tita, he makes no attempt to divorce his wife. Pedro is by no means a social rebel, and his lack of forcefulness, which motivates most of the novel's action, is an inversion of the traditional male hero of romantic fiction.

John Brown is an equally colorless suitor for Tita. Despite his kindness and solicitude, he lacks Pedro's passion and the ability to convince

Tita that he would be a superior choice to his rival. Similarly, the revolutionary who weds Gertrudis follows in her shadow, as she becomes a general and he continues as mere soldier.

In *The Law of Love*, the male lead, Rodrigo, is an unimpressive figure. He is portrayed as both fickle (abandoning his twin soul, Azucena, for Citlai) and weak (he is kidnapped and abandoned on the planet Korma, where he is sexually attacked by a female inhabitant), while Azucena takes the initiative in rescuing him and reestablishing their romance. Finally, in *Swift as Desire* we observed the role reversal between Lucha and Júbilo. Despite Júbilo's good intentions and communicative abilities, he shows himself to be weak on a number of occasions. He loses his job, becomes severely depressed, and falls into a deep sleep the night his infant son, Ramiro, suffocates himself with his blanket. In contrast, Lucha is portrayed as a strong woman who stands up to don Pedro's sexual abuse and financially supports her family.

This characterization by inversion of gender stereotypes directly ties into Esquivel's choice of parodic silence. Such inversions aid the parodic constructions that rely on silent associations between the text and genre norms for their development. As we observed earlier in this chapter, parody may be defined as imitation with a difference. One of the principal differences between Esquivel's texts and the romance novels she mimics is the inversion of stereotyped gender roles that is crucial to her development of parody. This parodic inversion also favors the construction of strong female characters. Hence, such characterization posits a potentially feminist perspective for certain readers.

8
Cultural Silence: Naive Narrators, Inverted Icons, and Bilingual Gaps in the Works of Sandra Cisneros

SANDRA CISNEROS WAS BORN IN CHICAGO, ILLINOIS, ON DECEMBER 20, 1954, to a Mexican father, Alfredo Cisneros del Moral, and a Chicana mother, Elvira Cordero Anguiano. Cisneros, unlike the other writers studied in this volume (who were raised in bourgeois or wealthy families and largely portray middle-class or upper-class characters), grew up in a working-class environment. Her father was an upholsterer, while her mother worked in a factory. Sandra was the only female in a group of seven siblings (Brackett 2005, 13).

Cisneros graduated from Loyola University in 1976 and was accepted into the prestigious University of Iowa writers' workshop that same year. It was during her tenure in that program that Cisneros began to discover her own unique writing style, closely associated with her personal ethnic and economic class experiences. When she graduated with a master of fine arts in creative writing degree in 1978, she accepted a job as a school counselor in Chicago at the Latino Youth Alternative High School. During this period, she listened to the experiences of her students, which provided her with material for her writing, and helped her to hone her working-class, Latina voice (36).

In 1982, Cisneros won a grant from the National Endowment for the Arts. This enabled her to complete her first novel, *The House on Mango Street*, published in 1984 by Arte Público Press. That same year, Cisneros also moved to San Antonio, Texas, and shortly thereafter won another important grant, the Dobie Paisano Fellowship. In 1987, Cisneros won a second NEA Fellowship, and published *My Wicked, Wicked Ways*, a poetry collection. Four years later, Cisneros's first book of short stories, *Woman Hollering Creek* (1991), appeared with Random House, a mainstream press (as opposed to a small, specialty press, like Arte Público), and won the Lannan Literary Award for Fiction. In 1993, she won the Anisfield-Wolf Book Award, a prize granted for works that help broaden the public's understanding of cultural diversity (64–86). Cisneros published another book of poetry, *Loose Woman*, in 1995. Her most recent piece of fiction, the novel *Caramelo*, based on her father's life, appeared in 2002.

Although Cisneros was born in the United States and is an American, rather than a Latin American writer, her work is characterized by its strong connection to Mexican culture and by its bilingual writing. In other words, in all of her texts, Cisneros focuses on the unique experience of growing up both Mexican and American, within two cultural identities, and with two languages, Spanish and English. Consequently, as a prominent Chicana and Latina writer, she also represents an important aspect of Latin American women's writing, as I hope to show in this chapter. Indeed, critics such as Sonia Saldívar-Hull have emphasized the unity and commonalities between Latin American and Chicana feminism. In her book *Feminism on the Border*, Saldívar-Hull underscores the connections between Cisneros's Chicana feminism and the *feminismo popular* movement in Mexico (Saldívar-Hull 2000, 55).[1]

As in the middle-class and upper-class writers studied in the previous chapters, silence as both technique and theme is omnipresent in Cisneros's works. However, in contrast to the silences of these other writers, Cisneros's silences are inextricably linked to the cultural heritage and/or socioeconomic status of her protagonists in a more pronounced way. Although in isolated instances we previously observed how silence corresponded to the socioeconomic condition of the female characters of these other authors' works (e.g., the protagonist of "Ruth Werner" or the elderly woman in "El espejo," both by Marta Brunet), these silences were not emphatically tied to specific cultural elements or practices. However, in Cisneros's works, silence is inevitably associated with either a poor, Chicana character, Mexican cultural icons—such as La Malinche or the Virgin of Guadalupe—or the inescapable bilingualism of the protagonists. Consequently, I term Cisneros's silences "cultural silence," because they are specifically linked to a unique, working-class, Chicana cultural heritage. It is important to note here that Cisneros's strong representation in her texts of her ethnic and working-class roots results in narratives that simultaneously employ silence not only as a feminist weapon, but also as a communicative element for Chicanos and the poor, working-class segment of the population. Thus, many of the passages related to silence in this chapter are not exclusively feminist, but rather focus on silence as it relates to minority voices in general. This is perhaps the primary difference between Cisneros and the other women writers studied here. Cisneros's socioeconomic and ethnic status (Mexican heritage) with regard to mainstream Anglo society position her to represent the specificity of poor, Hispanic minority experience. Consequently, Cisneros's characters and their silences clearly differ from those of the other writers in this volume, despite their common employment of subversive silence.

SILENCE AND NAIVE NARRATORS IN *THE HOUSE ON MANGO STREET*

Cisneros's *The House on Mango Street* (1984) employs a child or adolescent narrator, who provides a unique vision of the world. In this section, I will demonstrate that child narration leads to gaps in the text that create silences specific to the cultural and socioeconomic reality of the young, female protagonists. These gaps or silences help to emphasize the plight of poor Chicana women throughout the text by obliging the reader to actively construct the narrative's missing commentary.

The protagonist and narrator of Cisneros's first novel, *The House on Mango Street*, is Esperanza Cordero, whose age is never specified in the work. At the outset of the novel, Esperanza appears to be around ten to twelve years old, although she seems to age and grow throughout the work, because, as Beth Brunk notes, her narrative perspective evolves into a more mature, insightful voice in certain sections of the text (Brunk 2001, 141). Since there are many situations that a young person cannot yet understand, her youth inevitably creates textual silences, particularly in terms of her ability to evaluate the narrated events. When we speak of "evaluation," we are borrowing a linguistic term, one that has been discussed at length by such linguists as William Labov and Dell Hymes. According to William Labov, narrative evaluation is

> [t]he means used by the narrator to indicate the point of the narrative: its *raison d'être*: why it was told and what the narrator is getting at. . . . Every good narrator is continually warding off this question; when his narration is over it should be unthinkable for a bystander to say, 'So what?' . . .

Evaluative devices say to us: this was terrifying, dangerous, weird, wild, crazy, or amusing, hilarious, wonderful; more generally that it was strange, uncommon, or unusual—that is, worth reporting. It was not ordinary, plain, humdrum, everyday, or run-of-the-mill. (Labov 1972, 366–71)

Labov also identifies three types of narrative evaluation strategies: (1) external evaluation, when the narrator interrupts his narrative to address the listener and inform him of the point of his narration; (2) evaluative embedding, when the narrator either attributes to himself a sentiment that expresses the evaluative point as occurring to him when the event is happening, or introduces a third person in the narration who provides such an explanation; (3) evaluative action, when the narrator dramatizes the evaluation, briefly suspending narration of the action itself to indicate through dramatization its connection to the evaluative point (370). For us, the key point in Labov's study is his association of evaluative ability in narrative with age: "In reporting their own experience, adults have developed the ability to evaluate their own behavior with more complex linguistic devices. . . . The late development in the use of evaluative syntax appears to be general to all subcultures" (395–96).

Dell Hymes builds upon Labov's work in his book *Ethnography, Linguistics, Narrative Inequality*. Although Hymes attempts to show that children can exhibit some forms of narrative evaluation through their use of what he terms verses, stanzas, and dialogic scenes, Hymes agrees that, at best, children's narrative evaluations are more implicit in comparison with the explicit evaluations of adult discourse.[2] Consequently, Hymes theorizes that children's narratives are seen as lacking narrative competence, and thus are perceived as inferior. This renders children's voices socially powerless (Hymes 1996, 192).

These linguistic theories have interesting implications with regard to the relationship between silence and Cisneros's works, particularly *The House on Mango Street*. Many of the vignettes narrated by Esperanza implicitly convey the poverty and oppression of the Chicanos who live on Mango Street, especially the women. This oppression is emphasized through Esperanza's status as a child powerless to control the circumstances surrounding her. However, Esperanza's narrative voice rarely provides an explicit evaluation of the events she narrates. Consequently, the denunciation of these realities remains undelivered. It is only implicitly exposed through her discourse.

For example, in one of the early chapters of the book, "Cathy Queen of Cats," Esperanza tries to become friends with her neighbor, Cathy:

> You want a friend, she says. Okay, I'll be your friend. But only till next Tuesday. That's when we move away. Got to. Then as if she forgot I just moved in, she says that the neighborhood is getting bad.
> Cathy's father will have to fly to France one day and find her great great distant grand cousin on her father's side and inherit the family house. How do I know this is so? She told me so. In the meantime they'll just have to move a little farther north from Mango Street, a little father away every time people like us keep moving in. (Cisneros 1991a, 13)

Esperanza's words offer a matter-of-fact description of Cathy's desire to move away because people like Esperanza's family are moving into the neighborhood. Her words offer no explicit denunciation of the racism implicit in Cathy's comments. Cathy is obviously portrayed as a girl of European descent (her family claims to be related to the queen of France), while the reader knows from previous chapters, such as "My Name," that Esperanza's family is of Mexican origin. Esperanza does not overtly criticize Cathy's attitude; indeed, she attempts to excuse it by saying that she must have forgotten that Esperanza's family had just moved in. Although Esperanza does not directly explain that the point of her narration is the racial discrimination against Chicanos, of which she is made victim, the reader is perfectly capable of extracting this theme from her discourse. The silent articulation of the theme forces the reader to append an evaluation of the episode. Esperanza's failure to directly articulate Cathy's racism and her innocent attempt to excuse it enhance the sympathetic impact of this passage on the reader. Consequently, the reader's narrative evaluation will evince even stronger emotional identification and a more forceful critique of discriminative practices than a direct textual denunciation. In this instance, the silence is mainly linked to ethnicity and culture (Chicano reality), rather than explicitly related to gender, although frequently these elements cannot be separated from one another, both inside and outside the text. This point is aptly made by Lynn Chancer and Beverly Watkins in *Gender, Race, and Class* where they argue that race, ethnicity, class, and gender are not discrete elements in any analysis (Chancer and Watkins 2006, 67).

Similarly, "Louie, His Cousin & His Other Cousin" presents the escapades of one of Louie's cousins on Mango Street. Although Esperanza explains, "We only saw him once," she also tells us, "but it important" (Cisneros 1991a, 24). Louie's cousin drives down the street in a yellow Cadillac and then takes all the neighborhood children for a ride. At the end of the section, Esperanza tells the reader:

> The seventh time we drove into the alley we heard sirens . . . real quiet at first, but then louder. Louie's cousin stopped the car right where we were and said, Everybody out of the car. Then he took off flooring that car into a yellow blur. We hardly had time to think when the cop car pulled in the alley going just as fast. We saw the yellow Cadillac at the end of the block trying to make a left-hand turn, but our alley is too skinny and the car crashed into a lamppost. . . .
> Louie's cousin was okay. They put handcuffs on him and put him in the backseat of the cop car, and we all waved as they drove away. (Cisneros 1991a, 24–25)

Esperanza makes no explicit mention of the fact that Louie's cousin has stolen the car, although this becomes rapidly apparent to the reader when he is pursued and arrested by the police. However, whether Esperanza and the other children of Mango Street fully understand the implications of this episode remains ambiguous, especially when they innocently wave as the police car carries Louie's cousin off to jail. In either case, the subtext of crime and poverty in the Chicano neighborhood, affecting both its male and female inhabitants (no one has ever been inside a Cadillac before, and Louie's cousin is clearly guilty of stealing it), is implicitly present and quite comprehensible to the reader.

There are many other episodes that reflect Esperanza's youthful innocence, and lack of narrative evaluation, and there is a consequent implicit evaluation on the part of the reader. "A Rice Sandwich" illustrates the racism and prejudices of the nuns at Esperanza's school, who assume that she lives in the ugly flats that "even the raggedy men are ashamed to go into" (45). They humiliate Esperanza by associating her with these houses, and she bursts into tears. In "The Earl of Tennessee," Esperanza naively refers to all the women whom the character Earl brings into his apartment as his wives, though the reader clearly understands that these women are prostitutes, another segment of exploited women.

While the above episodes focus largely on the poverty and discrimination faced by Chicano men and women, there are other significant episodes that specifically relate to gender and women's plight. In these episodes, the protest against women's inferior condition and their status as sexual objects is silently rendered through Esperanza's innocent narrative perspective.

In the first of these episodes, "The Family of Little Feet," someone from the neighborhood gives Esperanza, Lucy, and Rachel a bag of high heels with which they can play "dress-up." The girls put the heels on and parade through the streets. They enjoy themselves until a drunken bum on the corner offers them a dollar for a kiss, at which point Esperanza declares:

> We have to go right now, Lucy says taking Rachel's hand because she looks like she's thinking about that dollar.
> Bum man is yelling something to the air but by now we are running fast and far away, our high heel shoes taking us all the way down the avenue and around the block. . . .
> We are tired of being beautiful. Lucy hides the lemon shoes and the red shoes and the shoes that used to be white but are now pale blue under a powerful bushel basket on the back porch, until one Tuesday her mother, who is very clean, throws them away. But no one complains. (42)

Once again, Esperanza is silent about how to evaluate this episode. There is no explicit denunciation of the danger of rape or the threat sexuality can imply for young women in the neighborhood, but the reader can articulate these themes on the basis of Esperanza's narration. Silence (or implicit evaluation) is the technique employed to suggest such themes and criticize this reality. Moreover, as Leslie Gutiérrez Spencer points out, this episode is an inverted parody of the Cinderella theme. In this well-known fairy tale, Cinderella acquires the famous glass slippers from her fairy godmother, and this eventually leads to her meeting and marrying Prince Charming. Cisneros silently and indirectly subverts this fairy tale and the romantic myth it implies by showing how the heels/slippers that make the girls on Mango Street feel like princesses can only lead to danger and possibly sexual abuse. Cisneros exposes the myth of happily-ever-after implied by Cinderella, and shows how the women on Mango Street are controlled, beaten, raped, and generally abused by men (Spencer 1997, 286). There is a silent feminist content that the reader must append to the episode.

Similarly, in "The First Job," an elderly Asian man befriends a now slightly older Esperanza on her first day of work. She is very nervous until this man begins to speak with her and invites her to sit with him in the lunchroom in the future. This initial friendship turns into a scene of sexual harassment. Esperanza tells us: "Then he asked if I knew what day it was, and when I said I didn't he said it was his birthday and would I please give him a birthday kiss. I thought I would because he was so old and just as I was about to put my lips on his cheek, he grabs my face with both hands and kisses me hard on the mouth and doesn't let go" (Cisneros 1991a, 55). The chapter ends on this note, and there is no explicit evaluation of the event on the narrator's part. There is a silent indictment of sexual abuse of women that pervades the episode and is indirectly communicated to the reader. Indeed, the protest against sexual abuse is perhaps greater because it is innocently rendered through a child's voice incapable of direct criticism of the event. The reader is left to construct not only a possibly stronger evaluation of the episode, but also a greater amount of sympathy for the protagonist than might have occurred if explicit evaluation had been provided.

A final example from *The House on Mango Street*, "Edna's Ruthie," is perhaps the most ambiguous of the episodes that lack explicit narrative evaluation. The reader is provided with a series of strange facts about Ruthie: "She wears one blue sock and one green because she forgot, is the only grown-up we know who likes to play" (67). She cannot make simple decisions on her own, like whether or not she should play bingo with Edna's friends (she asks her mother's opinion); she claims she cannot read because she gets headaches, but that she used to write children's books; and she insists she is married, although she lives with her mother and sleeps on a couch in the living room. These details have been interpreted in a variety of ways by different critics. Some think that Ruthie is an example of a woman whose life was ruined by her husband; she either left or was kicked out, and lost her career of writing children's books and other job opportunities that Esperanza claims she once had.[3] Although this is possible, the details also may suggest that Ruthie may be mentally deficient in some way, and that is why she likes candy and likes to play with the children. If she is mentally backward, that would explain her sudden appearance (was she previously institutionalized?), her failure to match socks, her inability to read, her uncomfortable feeling inside stores, her invention of stories about her husband, and so forth. If this is the case, Esperanza adds one more type of victim to her list: the mentally disabled woman. There is no place for Ruthie in the world. She is rejected by adult society and treated with contempt and impatience by her mother, upon whom she remains dependent. Silence is the vehicle employed to expose social ills. Edna is one more type of victimized woman on Mango Street.

Inverted Icons in
Woman Hollering Creek

The second type of silence frequently employed by Cisneros is an implicit inversion of the meaning of cultural symbols and icons that have traditionally presented women in passive and stereotyped roles. Although this characteristic has been previously studied by the existing criticism on Cisneros, no one has yet examined the relationship of inverted cultural icons to silence as a subversive technique.[4] The employment of cultural symbols has two potential silent valences: First, as we saw in the chapter on Rosario Ferré, symbolism, through its reliance on indirection, is an inherently silent, nonverbal technique. Second, this symbolic silence is magnified when the symbols in question are cultural, because such cultural symbols imply a necessary familiarity with cultural context; otherwise, one could not interpret them. Hence, these symbols are rendered "silent" or invisible to those readers who are not acquainted with their cultural values.

There are at least four stories in the collection *Woman Hollering Creek* that are predicated on the inversion of cultural icons. The first and most widely discussed of these stories is "Woman Hollering Creek," the tale that shares the title of the collection. This story presents the plight of Cleófilas, a young woman who grows up in Mexico watching *telenovelas* (soap operas) that glorify romance and female self-sacrifice. She marries Juan Pedro Martínez Sánchez, and they move to Seguín, Texas, where Juan Pedro has a job. Juan Pedro physically abuses Cleófilas, who is miserable at her husband's side. Together they have a son, and shortly thereafter, Cleófilas finds herself pregnant again. Cleófilas is fascinated by the name of the creek, La Gritona (The Hollering Woman), that runs through the town behind her house, and this constitutes a major motif of the story:

> *La Gritona.* Such a funny name for such a lovely *arroyo*. But that's what they called the creek that ran behind the house. Though no one could say whether the woman had hollered from anger or pain. The natives only knew that the *arroyo* one crossed on the way to San Antonio, and then once again on the way back, was called Woman Hollering, a name no one from these parts questioned, little less understood. *Pues, allá de los indios, quién sabe*—who knows, the townspeople shrugged, because it was of no concern to their lives how this trickle of water received its curious name. (Cisneros 1991b, 46)

In a subsequent passage, Cleófilas links Woman Hollering Creek to the Mexican myth of La Llorona (The Weeping Woman), which is only partially explained in the following passage:

> The stream sometimes only a muddy puddle in the summer, though now in the springtime, because of the rains, a good-size alive thing, a thing with a voice all its own, all day and all night calling in its high, silver voice. Is it *La Llorona*, the weeping woman? *La Llorona*, who drowned her own children. Perhaps *La Llorona* is the one they named the creek after, she thinks, remembering all the stories she learned as a child.
>
> *La Llorona* calling to her. She is sure of it. . . . Wonders if something as quiet as this drives a woman to the darkness under the trees. (51)

This second passage about the creek is interesting for two reasons. First, it sets up a counterpoint between the sounds of shouting (La Gritona) and weeping (La Llorona), both associated with bodies of water, and in particular, the town's creek. Second, there is an implicit parallel established between the myth of La Llorona and the character Cleófilas. In the Mexican myth, La Llorona is a woman whose husband cheats on her. In rage and frustration, she drowns her children in the river. Significantly, the narrator omits the fact of La Llorona's husband's betrayal in her reference to the myth. This omission constitutes an important cultural silence within Cisneros's text. The episode in which Cleófilas takes her son to the riverbank and contemplates the myth of La Llorona immediately follows the ensuing narrative passage, which implies Juan Pedro's marital infidelity while Cleófilas is in the hospital giving birth:

> A doubt. Slender as a hair. A washed cup set back on the shelf wrong-side-up. Her lipstick and body talc, and hairbrush all arranged in the bathroom a different way.
>
> No. Her imagination. The house the same as always. Nothing. . . .
>
> Smudged finger print on the door. Crushed cigarette in a glass. Wrinkle in the brain crumpling to a crease. (50)

Through this passage's indirect implication of Juan Pedro's infidelity (which clearly parallels the Llorona myth, although the betrayal element is omitted from Cisneros's version of the myth in her story), the text sets up a potential parallel between Cleófilas and La Llorona. However, when Juan Pedro hits Cleófilas with her book, her beloved romance novel, Cleófilas does not retaliate by drowning her son. Instead, she insists upon Juan Pedro taking her to the doctor so that her unborn child can be properly examined. This request turns out to be a subterfuge, so that Cleófilas can communicate her abused state to the authorities and get help. The technician, Graciela, who performs the sonogram, witnesses Cleófilas's bruises. She then calls her friend Felice to enlist her help and obtain a ride for Cleófilas across the border, in order that she may return to her father. Felice's reaction as she crosses the creek is an implicit explanation of how La Llorona becomes La Gritona in the story "Woman Hollering Creek":

> But then again, Felice was like no woman she'd ever met. Can you imagine, when we crossed the *arroyo* she just started yelling like a crazy, she would say later to her father and brothers. Just like that. Who would've thought?
> Who would've? Pain or rage, perhaps, but not a hoot like the one Felice had just let go. Makes you want to holler like Tarzan Felice had said.
> Then Felice began laughing again, but it wasn't Felice laughing. It was gurgling out of her own throat, a long ribbon of laughter, like water. (56)

Felice (whose name is close to the Spanish word *felicidad*, meaning "happiness"), evokes pure joy through her shout as she crosses the water. This is paralleled by Cleófila's own laughter. The weeping originally associated with the water through La Llorona has been transformed. The formerly self-sacrificing Cleófilas inverts the meaning of La Llorona, who becomes a figure associated with victorious shouts and laughter, instead of tears and murder, owing to Cleófilas's ability to take positive action and escape. It is interesting to note that this conversion is achieved in large part through silent associations (the implicit connections to the Llorona myth) and nonverbal sounds. Weeping, shouting, and laughing, although vocal processes, are all nonverbal actions that lack semantic content. Thus, the women are empowered through an inversion of an implicit cultural allusion and not through direct language or words.

A second story that involves the inversion of implicit cultural symbols, as well as other nonverbal expression, is "Never Marry a Mexican." The protagonist, ironically named Clemencia (she offers anything but clemency as she pursues revenge on the lover who abandoned her and returned to his wife), is a Chicana artist involved in a long-term affair with a white man named Drew. Despite their passionate relationship, Drew refuses to leave his wife, and Clemencia ultimately seeks revenge by seducing Drew's teenage son. Clemencia, like so many of the protagonists of earlier feminist writers, expresses her feelings and controls her destiny through a form of nonverbal expression—in this case, painting. It is through her talent as a painter that Clemencia can possess and manipulate Drew to create the future that she wishes to have:

> You're nothing without me. I created you from spit and red dust. And I can snuff you between my finger and thumb if I want to. Blow you to kingdom come. You're just a smudge of paint I chose to birth on canvas. And when I made you over, you were no longer a part of her, you were all mine. . . .
>
> I paint and repaint you the way I see fit, even now. After all these years. Did you know that? You think I went hobbling along with my life, whimpering and whining . . . when you went back to her. But I've been waiting. Making the world look at you from my eyes. And if that's not power, what is? (75)

On one occasion before Clemencia and Drew separate, Clemencia is at Drew's house while his wife is out of town. She uses this opportunity to enact two forms of nonverbal protest against Drew for refusing to leave his wife. First, Clemencia drops a trail of gummy bears in "places where I was sure she would find them. One in her Lucite makeup organizer. One stuffed inside each bottle of nail polish. I untwisted the expensive lipsticks to their full length and smushed a bear on the top before recapping them" (81). Once again, the trail of gummy bears constitutes a silent form of protest, in which Clemencia hopes to endanger Drew's relationship with his wife by making her suspicious of their affair. Moroever, she purposely chooses to destroy expensive makeup in the process, thereby also silently expressing a form of social resentment against the rich, upper-class, white wife of her lover. According to Harreyette Mullen, "[T]he candy bears are an example of the ambiguous signification of coded hidden or double messages. . . . According to the author, an 'upside-down gummy bear' resembles 'a Mexican statue of Coatlicue.' Thus, by inversion, the sugar sweet candy that the artist-protagonist plants like a poison pill in the boudoir of her rival connects her to the creative/destructive potential invested in the Aztec phallic mother goddess Coatlicue" (Mullen 1996, 8).

In other words, Cisneros converts the gummy bear into a Mexican cultural symbol (Coatlicue) whose significance will only be apparent to those familiar with Mexican culture (and Cisneros's particular interpretation of it). Coatlicue is the Aztec solar and war goddess who gave birth to the moon (Nebel 1995, 88). She is associated with the Earth, and consequently is both the loving and devouring mother (Lindemans n.d.).

This added dimension of feminist creativity and aggressiveness will only be perceived by a limited number of readers, and thus remains to a certain degree implicit or silent within the text.

Clemencia's second form of protest manifests itself when she steals a tiny Russian doll from a set of dolls of different sizes (belonging to Drew's wife), each one contained inside a larger doll. The doll is then used to invert the myth of La Llorona, previously discussed with regard to the story "Woman Hollering Creek." On her way home from Drew's house, Clemencia drops the small doll into a dirty river: "I stopped the car ... and dropped the wooden toy into that muddy creek where winos piss and rats swim. The Barbie doll's toy stewing there in that muck. It gave me a feeling like nothing before and since" (Cisneros 1991b, 82). Mullen also points out that in this passage, Clemencia essentially reenacts the myth of La Llorona, who drowned her children in the river (Mullen 1996, 8). However, by using a doll belonging to her enemy, Drew's wife, Clemencia, implicitly inverts the myth. In the original story, the wife (La Llorona) finds out that her husband is unfaithful and destroys her own life by drowning her children. In the version of the myth presented in "Never Marry a Mexican," Clemencia, the lover, symbolically destroys her opponent (Drew's wife) by drowning her doll in the dirty creek. The protagonist, unlike the original Llorona, refuses to embrace her role of victim, and chooses instead the active role (silently expressed through actions and not words) of drowning the iconic "child" of her adversary, instead of her own. Both the cultural symbolism and its inversion add a significant dimension of feminist protest lacking in the myth's original form.

The story "Little Miracles, Kept Promises" is filled with inversions of female stereotypes and mythical figures who incarnate them. The story consists of a number of messages left at the foot of the statue of the Virgin of Guadalupe, a Mexican cultural symbol connoting the pure, self-sacrificing woman. However, despite the focus on such a traditional image, Cisneros manages to invert the symbolism of the figure and invest it with new meanings. The story implicitly contrasts the messages of traditional woman who express traditional thoughts about their gender, such as the mother who proclaims that her eldest daughter should forget about finishing school because "her place is at home helping us out" (Cisneros 1991b, 117), to the messages of women who reject their traditional passive role and search for new, more egalitarian relationships. Such is the case of Barbara Ybañez, who asks San Antonio to send her

[a] man man. I mean someone who's not ashamed to be seen cooking or cleaning or looking after himself. . . . In other words, don't send me someone like my brothers who my mother ruined with too much chichi or I'll throw him back. . . . *I'll turn your statue upside down until you send him to me*. I've put up with too much too long, and now I'm just too intelligent, too powerful, too beautiful, too sure of who I am finally to deserve anything else. (Cisneros 1991b, 117, my emphasis)

In the above passage, it is significant that Ms. Ybañez threatens to invert the statue of San Antonio in order to obtain a feminist man. Its inversion implicitly suggests a reversal of traditional gender roles and the newly found strength of women.

Similarly, Teresa Galindo requests that the Virgin invert her previous wish to send her "a guy who would love only me" and should now "lift this heavy cross from my shoulders and leave me like I was before, wind on my neck, my arms swinging free, and no one telling me how I ought to be" (122). In this instance, it is the woman's wish that is inverted as she longs for her previous freedom.

However, the most central figure of the story is the final letter writer, Rosario Chayo de León. Rosario, like the protagonist, Clemencia, from "Never Marry a Mexican," is a painter. She thanks the Virgin for granting her request of not being pregnant because, she says, "I don't want to be a mother. I wouldn't mind being a father. At least a father could still be an artist, could love something instead of someone, and no one would call that selfish" (127). Rosario expresses herself through her painting, a form of nonverbal, silent communication, and this leads her to a feminist stance in which she rejects motherhood in favor of her career. In this process, she also initially rejects the figure of the Virgin of Guadalupe, whom she associates with the silent, self-sacrificing attitudes of her mother and grandmother: "Virgencita de Guadalupe. For a long time I wouldn't let you in my house. I couldn't see you without seeing my ma each time my father came home drunk and yelling, blaming everything that ever went wrong in his life on her. . . . Couldn't look at you without blaming you for all the pain my mother and her mother and all our mothers' mothers have put up with in the name of God. . . . I wasn't going to be my mother or my grandma. All that self-sacrifice, all that silent suffering" (127).

However, Chayo inverts the traditional image of Guadalupe and female passive silence by associating her with "our mother Tonantzín," an Aztec goddess, who has been fused with the Virgin of Guadalupe and has similar symbolic value to Coatlicue. According to Chayo, Guadalupe's church is built on the site of Tonantzín's temple, and through this connection Chayo learns to appreciate the powerful aspects of the traditional female figure Guadalupe: "That you could have the power to rally a people when a country was born, and again during civil war, and during a farmworker's strike in California made me think maybe there is a power in my mother's patience, strength in my grandmother's endurance. Because those who suffer have a special power, don't they? The power of understanding someone else's pain. . . . When I could see you in all your facets, all at once. . . . I could love you, and finally learn to love me" (128).

Chayo is ultimately able to reconcile the figures of the indigenous Tonantzín (associated with sin, serpents, and sexuality) and the Christian Virgin of Guadalupe (linked with motherhood and self-sacrifice), the two sides to every woman, through recognition of the power of silence (its transformation from passive to powerful). The story never explains exactly who Tonantzín is, and consequently she constitutes a silent cultural symbol, the significance of which remains unclear for many readers. In "Little Miracles, Kept Promises," Chayo restores what Jacqueline Doyle calls the previously lost dimensions of the Aztec deity Tonantzín to the Guadalupe figure, hence converting her into a modern, feminist symbol of action, acceptable female sexuality, and social protest (Doyle 2004, 272). However, the transformation of the traditional Guadalupe figure is largely effected through implicit cultural associations and inversions that bring a silent dimension to the story's content.

The final story that relies heavily on nonverbal silent inversion of implicit cultural symbols is *"Bien* Pretty," whose protagonist is ironically named Guadalupe, after the Virgin focused upon in the previous story. Lupe, as she calls herself, is also a painter, and clearly expresses herself through her artwork. The main plot of the tale revolves around Lupe's romances, first with Eddie, the Chicano boyfriend who leaves her for a blonde white woman, and then Flavio, her Mexican lover, who turns out to have a family back in Mexico to whom he must return. When Lupe is abandoned by Flavio, she is initially devastated and takes to watching the mind-numbing *telenovelas* populated by passive and love-struck females. However, in time, Lupe returns to her painting, and uses it as a vehicle to recover her self-respect and identity, and to overcome Flavio's betrayal. She primarily achieves this through an inversion of the myth that inspired the names of the two Mexican volcanoes, Prince Popoctépetl and Princess Ixtacchíhuatl. Although Lupe does not relate the entire myth, she tells us that in the original story "Prince Popo, half-naked Indian warrior built like Johnny Weismuller, [is] crouched in grief beside his sleeping princess Ixtacchíhauatl" (Cisneros 1991b, 144). Cisneros's subsequent novel, *Caramelo*, offers a version of this myth of the twin volcanoes, which provides the details missing in *"Bien* Pretty." In *Caramelo*, the main character's (Celaya's) grandfather explains that Prince Popo murders Princes Ixta for a reason he cannot recall, and then is so overcome with grief he kneels in tears by her side (Cisneros 2002, 57).[5] This description appears to give the active role to Prince Popo and the traditional, passive role to Princess Ixta. Prince Popo is clearly associated with Lupe's ex-boyfriend Flavio, since he previously posed for the male figure in the painting. However, after their breakup, when Lupe repaints the picture, she symbolically reverses the role of the two volcanoes: "Went back to the twin volcano painting. Got a good idea and redid the whole thing. Prince Popo and Princess Ixta trade places. After all, who's to say the sleeping mountain isn't the prince, and the voyeur the princess, right? So I've done it my way. With Prince Popocatepetl lying on his back instead of the Princess. Of course, I had to make some anatomical adjustments in order to simulate the geographical silhouettes. I think I'm going to call it El Pipi del Popo. I kind of like it" (Cisneros 1991b, 166).

Of course, the symbolic role reversal between the male and the female in the painting suggests that Lupe is not going to just lay down and die after her breakup with Flavio (who "killed" her by leaving her), but rather stand on her own two feet, live on, and triumph. There is no sleeping princess in her final painting, only a humorous allusion the sexual organ of the reclining prince. The implicit meaning is the triumph of Lupe over Flavio, and hence women over men, in the story. These significations are silently appended to the text through the nonverbal painting and the inversion of the Mexican myth, whose content is never explicitly stated.

Bilingual Silences in *Caramelo*

A third important aspect of Cisneros's fiction is the bilingualism that characterizes all of her works, but especially her last novel, *Caramelo*. Cisneros takes some first steps toward defining the two languages in which she simultaneously writes in her dedication of *Woman Hollering Creek* to her parents: "For my mama, Elvira Cordero Anguiano, who gave me the fierce language. Y para mi papá, Alfredo Cisneros Del Moral, quien me dio el lenguaje de la ternura" (Cisneros 1991b, n.p.), [For my mama, Elvira Cordero Anguiano, who gave me the fierce language. And for my father, Alfredo Cisneros Del Moral, who gave me the language of tenderness] (my translation). In this dedication, Cisneros distinguishes between the "main" language in which she writes—English—which she categorizes as "fierce" (her language of power, of social criticism, of gender and racial protest), and Spanish, which she refers to as "the language of tenderness," the language she uses to express feelings and emotions. This interesting dichotomy not only suggests that the two languages with which Cisneros was raised are used for different purposes, but also implies that one or the other may sometimes be inadequate to express what Cisneros wishes to say. Many linguists have identified this dilemma as the fundamental challenge that faces bilingual speakers. Since these speakers live in the space between two languages, they are frequently faced with the "untranslatability" of their sentiments, because sometimes words or concepts from one language cannot exactly be translated into the other. At other times, these bilingual writers require a combination of words from both languages to try to give an accurate expression of what they are experiencing. The bilingualism of Chicanas has been linked to their specific identity by writers like Gloria Andalzúa, who claims that the simultaneous employment of both Spanish and English constitutes a fundamental need and characteristic of Chicana self-expression:

> For a people who are neither Spanish nor live in a country in which Spanish is the first language, for a people who are not Anglo; for a people who cannot entirely identify with either standard (formal, Castillian [*sic*]) Spanish nor standard English, what recourse is left to them but to create their own language . . . a language without terms that are neither *español ni inglés*, but both. We speak a patois, a forked tongue, a variation of two languages. . . . Until I am free to write bilingually and to switch codes without having always to translate while I still have to speak English or Spanish when I would rather speak Spanglish, and as long as I have to accommodate English speakers rather than having them accommodate me, my tongue will be illegitimate. (Andalzúa 1999, 77–81)

Andalzúa points to one of two important aspects of bilingualism that relate it to the topic and technique of silence that permeates Cisneros's work. Andalzúa insists that when Chicana writers write in "Spanglish," they should not have to translate Spanish words for English-only speakers. This technique creates a form of "silent" expression for nonbilingual readers, many of whom do read Cisneros's work.

However, the second, and perhaps more significant, silence created by bilingualism is that of the expressive gaps that inevitably appear when the speaker lives and writes within two languages. The current research on bilingual memoirs suggests that both emotions and memories can be lost in communication when a person associates or experiences these events in one language, but attempts to recount them in another. Mary Besemeres's work suggests that "outside the [original] language it becomes harder to talk about these feelings, to have them recognized. Emotions as seen by these authors, then, are both culturally shaped and individually experienced. Insofar as they write the absence of direct counterparts in English to the emotion words they use in their other language, their narratives lend support to a view of emotions as culturally relative, rather than universal" (Besemeres 2006, 36).

Similarly, Robert Schrauf and Ramón Durazo-Arvizu state that the narrative absence of the original language in which an event took place may lead to the inexpressibility of certain emotions or details connected with that event:

> In the case of bilinguals, a second problem with post-hoc coding of emotion is that the step from retrieval to report-in-words involves employing narrative conventions of spoken language. This introduces a cross-linguistic compound. Considerable research now shows that languages differ in how their particular morphological, lexical and syntactic conventions shape the expression of detail in narrative. . . . By implication, some information may well be retrieved from memory but not be narratively expressed, because the language spoken (or written) does not provide the obligatory expression of details. (Schrauf and Durazo-Arvizu 2006, 292)

This inexpressibility or emotive communicative failure is best expressed by Doris Sommer in the introduction to her collection *Bilingual Games*. Sommer insists that bilingual code switching leads to "overloaded systems [that] unsettle meaning. When more than one word points to a familiar thing, the excess shows that no one word can 'own' or 'be' that thing. Several contending words point, each imperfectly" (Sommer 2003, 1). In other words, despite the agglomeration of multiple words, even in multiple languages, there is somehow a semantic slippage that leads to a silent or nonverbalized meaning. This silence or inability to fully express a concept is explicitly developed throughout Cisneros's novel *Caramelo*.[6] *Caramelo* is narrated by Celaya Reyes from the perspective of both a little girl and an adolescent, who describes her father's family. She thus often exhibits the naive, youthful narrative vision already studied in detail with regard to Esperanza in *The House on Mango Street*. The main protagonists are Celaya herself, her father, and the Awful Grandmother (the father's mother), and the novel focuses on the relationship between the three. Although based on Cisneros's own life, the author weaves a tale that goes beyond family history and a tribute to her father (who died during the writing of the novel). It comes to encompass feminist themes and a history of Chicano ethnic identity in the United States. These three topics (family, feminism, ethnicity) interweave through the constant employment of bilingualism in the novel and particularly through the cultural symbol of the *caramelo rebozo* (the caramel-colored shawl) that gives rise to the novel's title and is an element repeatedly associated with the Awful Grandmother's and Chicana identity. I will return to the importance of the *caramelo rebozo* below, once I have illustrated the basic functioning of the silent gaps of bilingualism throughout Cisneros's work.

Let us now examine the two types of bilingual silence present in *Caramelo*: untranslatability and insufficient word agglomeration. The first, untranslatability, can be supported through numerous novelistic passages. For example, when Celaya describes how her grandmother met and fell in love with her grandfather, Narciso Reyes, she describes her grandfather thus: "So let us take a closer look at Narciso Reyes, a beautiful boy blessed with a Milky Way of *lunares* floating across his creamy skin like arrows instructing,—On this spot kiss me. Here I must insist on using the word *lunares*, literally 'moons,' but I mean moles, or freckles, or beauty spots, though none of these words comes close to capturing the Spanish equivalent with its sensibility of charm and poetry" (Cisneros 2002, 103).

Here Celaya offers several possible English equivalents for the word *lunares*, but rejects them as inadequate because they fail to capture the "charm and poetry" conveyed by the Spanish word. Indeed, there may culturally be connotations associated with the word *lunares* that make it not only untranslatable to the English speaker, but also not fully comprehensible to one who understands Spanish but did not grow up speaking that language. Either way, there is clearly a meaning or emotive content attached to the word *lunares* that remains silent for the English-only and/or native English speaker. The narrator explicitly states this in her discussion of the term *lunares* and its so-called equivalents in English.

Another good example is found in Celaya's description of her family's new house when they move from Chicago to San Antonio: "*Rascuache*.

That's the only word for it. Homemade half-ass. Our house is one of those haphazard, ramshackle, self-invented types, as if each room was added on as the family who built it got bigger, when they could afford it, layer upon layer of self-improvement, somebody trying their very best, even if that best isn't very much" (305).

In this passage, Celaya enumerates several English words or definitions (haphazard, ramshackle, self-invented) to attempt to convey the meaning of *rascuache*, while acknowledging that *rascuache* is "the only word for it." None of the English translations can quite capture the emotive sense or connotations of *rascuache*, which is why Celaya is forced to offer several possible English equivalents. The non-native Spanish speaker or nonbilingual speaker ends up missing something in this passage that remains for him or her a "silent" or incommunicable semantic content. This passage is also a good example of how silent linguistic gaps tie into Cisneros's social criticism. Here, *rascuache* is clearly pointing to the economic difficulties faced by working-class Chicanos in the United States.

A final example is the scene in which Celaya's grandfather offers several compliments to the grandmother while he is courting her. In this passage, Celaya reflects upon the lack of English equivalent for the Spanish word *piropos*:

> Like all novitiates, Soledad sincerely believed the *piropos* Narciso tossed her, a word in Spanish for which there is no translation in English, except perhaps "harassment" (in another age, these were called "gallantries"). —Ay Mamacita, if I die who will kiss you? —How sad there isn't a *tortilla* big enough to wrap you up in, you're that *exquisita*. . . . She'd never had anyone say such things to her. Who could blame her for feeling grateful to the man she looked up to as honorable and well educated, her social superior.
>
> —Don't tell anyone, but you're my favorite!
>
> It made her heart *ping*! How was she to know it was just a *piropo*? Something a man says to one, and then to several others. (156)

It is interesting that Celaya places the word *piropos* between the English terms "harassment" and "gallantries," which are two completely distinct concepts in English. *Piropos* are a type of persistent, flowery, somewhat insincere compliment that lies between these two points. It is impossible for the English-only speaker to capture the linguistic implications of the word *piropos* here. Cisneros attempts to illustrate it through the ensuing words of the grandfather, but once again, there is a meaning or connotation that remains silent for some readers. At the same time, the gaps between the words and definitions communicate a silent feminist protest by showing how women of previous generations were manipulated through the words and actions of men. In this case, the *piropo* leads to the grandmother's unwed pregnancy and shows her vulnerability as both a woman and a social inferior (she was a servant in the grandfather's house). Cisneros indirectly exposes and criticizes female exploitation through this passage.

The second type of bilingual silence is illustrated through bilingual word conglomerations that the textual narrator or characters frequently use in an effort to convey incommunicable meanings. The first good example of this is found on page 84 of the text, when Celaya's mother becomes angry with her father upon learning that he had had a child out of wedlock before he had met her. Her bilingual insults convey the sense of inexpressible anger, of a feeling that lies somewhere beyond the meaning of any one of the words she employs in her diatribe: "In two languages Mother hurls words like weapons, and they thump and thud their target. . . . Mother is calling [father] a big *caca*, a goat, an ox, a fat butt, a shameless, a deceiver, a savage, a barbarian, *un gran puto*" (84). There is a force of feeling beyond any one word or term here that can only be approached by the string of insults, both in Spanish and English. The mother's inability to verbally communicate her anger in its entirely is part of a bilingual feminist silence that protests the male double standard and secrecy regarding the earlier part of his life.

Similarly, the father's image of Chicanos is an impression that goes beyond a simple English or Spanish description. When Celaya describes the closing of a deal between her father and his friend Mars, she describes their interaction thus: "Then Mars does the funky *raza* handshake with Father, like Chicano power, and Father, who is always ranting and raving about Chicanos, the same Father who calls Chicanos *exagerados*, *vulgarones*, zoot-suiting, wild-talking *mota*-smoking, forgot-they-were-Mexican Mexicans, surprises us all. Father handshakes the funky handshake back" (281). This particular passage, rather than being specifically feminist, relates to ethnic connotations that cannot be adequately expressed. The father's negative image of Chicanos lies somewhere between the Spanish words *exagerados* and *vulgarones*, and the English zoot-suiting, wild-talking, forgot-they-were-Mexicans.

Perhaps the most interesting of the bilingual silences in *Caramelo* occurs when Celaya describes the scene on a Mexican calendar: "On the kitchen door we've kept a 1965 Mexican calendar, a picture called *El rapto*. A white horse, a handsome *charro* and in his rapturous arms, a swooning beauty, her silk *rebozo* and blouse sliding off one sexy shoulder . . . *El rapto*. I wonder if that means The '*rape*' and I wonder if 'rapture' and 'rape' come from the same word" (312–13).

This passage is a bit different from the previous ones, because it offers a series of associations for the word *rapto*, which is never directly translated. Celaya does not appear to know that *rapto* would most commonly be translated into English as "kidnapping." Nonetheless, she seems to comprehend the possible implications of this kidnapping (rape) and then goes on to associate the Spanish *rapto* with a false English cognate, the word "rapture." By presenting the calendar from Celaya's youthful, naive, viewpoint, the bilingual silence (the omitted principal meaning of *rapto*) succeeds in conveying how popular images and the media glamorize rape and present it as something positive (rapture, or being carried away with love, ecstasy, and pleasure). Hence, the passage contains an implicit feminist criticism of such techniques, a criticism that is never directly voiced in the text.

Caramelo's most central cultural symbol, the *caramelo rebozo* (caramel-colored shawl), is developed within a bilingual description that illustrates not only the construction of bilingual gaps, but also how nonverbal cultural objects, such as the shawl, function as a communicative language for women. In the novel, Celaya narrates the Awful Grandmother's youth, when she was simply known as Soledad. Soledad's mother, a skilled shawl maker, died when Soledad was a child. After her father's remarriage, her father lost interest in Soledad and sent her off to live with his cousin. Her mother, Guillermina, left a beautiful, unfinished shawl, which Soledad inherits and uses as a form of self-expression. The following bilingual description attempts to capture the beauty and significance of the *caramelo rebozo*:

> Even with half its fringe hanging unbraided like mermaid's hair, it was an exquisite *rebozo* of five *tiras*, the cloth a beautiful blend of toffee, licorice, and vanilla stripes flecked with black and white, which is why they call this design a *caramelo*. The shawl was slippery-soft, of an excellent quality and weight, with astonishing fringe work resembling a cascade of fireworks on a field of sunflowers, but completely unsellable because of the unfinished *rapacejo*. Eventually it was forgotten, and Soledad was allowed to claim it as a plaything . . . .
>
> Poor Soledad. Her childhood without a childhood. . . . and now Soledad's fingers took to combing this fringe of the unfinished shawl, plaiting, unplaiting, over and over, the language of the nervous hands.

Stop that, her stepmother would shout, but her hands never quit, even when she was sleeping....

Because she didn't know what else to do, Soledad chewed on the fringe of her *rebozo*. Oh, if only her mother were alive. She could have told her how to speak with her *rebozo*. How, for example, if a woman dips the fringe of her *rebozo* at the fountain while fetching water, this means I am thinking of you. Or, how if she gathers her *rebozo* like a basket, and walks in front of the one she loves and accidentally lets the contents fall, if an orange and a piece of sugarcane tumble out, that means, — Yes, I accept you as my *novio*. Or if a woman allows a man to take up the left end of her *rebozo*, she is saying I agree to run away with you.... But who was there to interpret the language of the *rebozo* to Soledad? (94–105)

This passage will not be totally comprehensible to the English-only reader, since he or she will not comprehend words like *tiras* (strips of cloth) and *rapacejo* (fringe) used to describe the shawl. Moreover, the shawl is clearly portrayed as a nonverbal, feminine language, with which women can express their innermost feelings and desires. The timid and emotionally abandoned Soledad cannot express herself through words. Instead, she attempts to communicate her feelings by braiding and unbraiding the fringe of the shawl, although she lacks the specific "vocabulary" associated with the shawl language (what it means to dip the shawl in water, use the shawl as a carrier, and so forth). The important point here is that the female expression is nonverbally represented through a cultural symbol that is bilingually portrayed in the novel. In this passage, Cisneros successfully combines three different types of "silences": female nonverbal expression (the shawl as a language); silent cultural symbol (although she explains the cultural significance of the shawl, some of its connotations remain hidden for non-Mexicans or non-Chicanos); and the bilingual description, which leads to a nonverbalized meaning for English-only speakers. According to Gutiérrez y Muhs, another way in which the *caramelo rebozo* relates to silence is through the meaning of the verb *rebozar*, which signifies "to muffle up." This definition thus connects the shawl to Chicana identity, because in Gutiérrez y Muhs's view, "they who are to be muffled up give multiple meanings to the instrument of their muffling ... the *caramelo rebozo* becomes the personified voice of the past through one of the main protagonists, the Awful Grandmother" (Gutiérrez y Muhs 2006, 32–33). In other words, the silent language of the *caramelo rebozo* is not just a form of nonverbal expression, but specifically a form of Chicana nonverbal expression. As we shall see later on, Cisneros constructs this association through the hybrid character of the *caramelo rebozo*, which also relates it to postmodern feminism.

OTHER TYPES OF SILENCES IN CISNEROS'S WORKS

The above three categories of silence (namely, naive narrators, cultural symbols, and bilingualism) are fairly unique to Cisneros's work understood within the context of the other feminist writers studied here.[7] In addition, Cisneros repeats certain forms of silence that we have previously observed with regard to other women writers in Latin America, notably the paradoxical silence employed by Marta Brunet and María Luisa Bombal and described in the earlier chapters of this book. In this section, I will examine the additional silences that can be found in Cisneros's works, and how they relate to the fiction of other women writers.

The House on Mango Street includes various direct thematic references to silence as well as several nonverbal, symbolic forms of silent protest. For example, in the chapter "No Speak English," the unhappy protagonist, Mamacita, refuses to learn English and has her husband paint her house pink like the one she left behind in Mexico. The pink house is a nonverbal signifier of the woman's discontent and protest against her life in the United States, as is her silence in English. Similarly, toward the end of the novel, "A House of My Own" highlights a form of nonverbal protest through the image of the silent house and the blank page before Esperanza writes down the words: "Not a man's house. Not a daddy's. A house all my own.... Only a house quiet as snow, a space for myself to go, clean as paper before the poem" (Cisneros 1991a, 108). In "Beautiful and Cruel," Esperanza uses silent gestures to protest female subservience to men: "I have begun my own quiet war. Simple. Sure. I am one who leaves the table like a man, without putting back the chair or picking up the plate" (Cisneros 1991a, 89).

Finally, both Sally in "What Sally Said" and Esperanza in "Red Clowns" refuse to completely verbalize their abuse by males. In "What Sally Said," although Sally's father beats her, Esperanza tells us: "But Sally doesn't tell about that time he hit her with his hands just like a dog, she said like I was an animal.... Just because I'm a daughter, and then she doesn't say" (Cisneros 1991a, 92). In "Red Clowns" Esperanza's rape by a group of boys at the carnival is implied but never directly stated, and she clearly manifests her desire not to talk about the episode: "I don't remember. Please don't make me tell it all. Why did you leave me alone? . . . Only his dirty fingernails against my skin, only his sour smell again" (Cisneros 1991a, 100). The silence on the part of Sally and Esperanza in these last two episodes, as well as the silent figures of the women sitting by the window, accepting their lives of entrapment (such as Esperanza's grandmother and Rafaela, who drinks mango and papaya juice), project a passivity or acceptance of their fate that contrasts with the first three silences in which Mamacita and Esperanza employed silence as a protest against patriarchal society.

Woman Hollering Creek also evinces both passive and combative silences. In the story "Eleven," a little girl who is turning eleven has her birthday ruined by her teacher, who insists that an old, ugly, raggedy red sweater found in the classroom belongs to the girl. The girl silently protests this attempt by the teacher to humiliate her by quietly placing the sweater by the edge of her desk, as a sign of rejection and protest. However, later on, when the teacher makes her wear the sweater, she simply cries in a helpless fashion, exhibiting a passive acceptance of her fate. Similarly, although Clemencia in "Never Marry a Mexican" achieves silent revenge on her lover, Drew, in various forms throughout the story (the trail of gummy bears, the Russian doll thrown into the river, and her affair with Drew's teenage son, already discussed), she also exhibits a passive, ineffectual silence when she is finally introduced to Drew's wife during an art exhibition and can only muster a "Hello Megan":

> Then he is walking toward me, and I didn't know what to do, just stood there dazed like those animals crossing the road at night when the headlights stun them.
>
> And I don't know why, but all of a sudden I looked at my shoes and felt ashamed at how old they looked. And he comes up to me. . . . "Ah, Clemencia! *This* is Megan" . . .
>
> I grinned like an idiot and held out my paw—"Hello Megan"—and smiled too much the way you do when you can't stand someone. Then I got the hell out of there. (Cisneros 1991b, 79)

When finally faced with the opportunity to confront her rival, Clemencia is essentially silent, unable to articulate the words necessary to tell the truth about her relationship with Drew or challenge Megan's role as his wife in any way. She simply disappears from the exhibition as quickly as possible.

Caramelo also exhibits some paradoxical silences. We have already seen combative or expressive silences in the novel, such as the *caramelo rebozo*. In addition, other passages depict silent, passive females who quietly accept their fate, such as Celaya's mother when she is abandoned by her first love, Enrique Aragón: "With the clock ticking toward and then past the hour Enrique used to telephone. The clock, the calendar, the hours, weeks, months. The silence. The silence like an answer. The silence an answer. There was a little hole in her heart where he'd once been.... '*I do not love you*,' Enrique said. You said. I said nothing" (Cisneros 2002, 222–26). Celaya's mother makes no attempt to respond or combat this rejection, but simply marks the hours of Enrique's absence in silence.

Celaya's silence is portrayed in stark contrast to that of her mother. For example, she hates sleeping on a couch in the living room and longs for her own silent space where she can be alone, as a form of self-expression: "Sleep in a place where they can't find you. A place you can go to be alone. Why would you want to be alone? . . . It's a way of being with yourself, of privacy in a house that doesn't want you to be private.... People ... force you to talk when you don't feel like it" (364).

Here silence is a form of identity-affirmation for the young Celaya. Similarly, Celaya's refusal to cook or do other household chores may be thought of in much the same terms as that of the protagonist of Castellanos's "Cooking Lesson." Her coded use of incompetence may indeed be a silent rebellion against a chore stereotypically ascribed to woman: "How my mother says I am no good for anything in the kitchen except burning rice. How I can't even iron my own clothes without scorching them. How I need strict supervision anytime I sew anything. Did I tell you I once sewed my shirt to my pants leg when I was trying to sew a button? I am not meant for the kitchen even though I'm an only daughter" (Cisneros 2002, 322).

Finally, the silent reappearance of Celaya's grandmother serves as a powerful force of determination in Celaya's life. In one episode, when a group of rough Chicana girls beat Celaya up for being smart and talking "like a white girl," Celaya flees across the interstate. While she is running away, she hears a voice in her mind that is never actually verbalized, but which reminds her of her own personal strength and the essence of her identity by repeating her full name as opposed to her nickname, Lala:

> Celaya. Somebody or something said my name. Not 'Lala.' Not 'La.' My real name. Who the hell was that, I think to myself. Who was that? . . . Celaya. I'm still myself. Still Celaya. . . .

> When I don't expect it. When I'm alone. When I don't want it to. The Grandmother comes and gets me. Like light, or a dance, or a tattoo needle, because there is no name for what I am naming. And it's like a doorbell or a fire alarm without a sound. . . .
>
> I know when I open my eyes she'll be there. . . . The Grandmother. (357–62)

The grandmother is inextricably tied to Celaya's identity for two reasons: first, they share a great love of Celaya's father, and second, the Grandmother symbolizes the silent struggle of all women who must rise from a position of subservience and exploitation. It is interesting that the force of the grandmother is described in terms of silence. There is no word to convey her appearance and effect on Celaya. It is like "an alarm without sound." Silence, as in the previous works, can be either combative or passive in *Caramelo*. Within the context of contemporary postmodern feminism, this vacillation between different positions can be seen as a function of feminist postmodern performance, in which submissive and aggressive roles are constantly changing, and agency is a variable in constant flux that women can adopt or abandon depending upon the particular situation in question. I explore the topic of postmodern feminism in the following section.

Cisneros and Postmodern Feminism

As we saw in chapter 7, Laura Esquivel's work in the 1980s and 1990s specifically related to certain tendencies in the Mexican postmodern feminist movement. Similarly, numerous parallels can be observed between Cisneros's works from the same time period and U.S./Mexican postmodern feminism with its "performance turn," as discussed in the preface to this book. Many critics have signaled the relationship between Cisneros and postmodernism, notably Ellen McCracken. McCracken says: "Eventually, as Cisneros becomes a postmodern ethnic commodity for the mainstream with the publication of *Woman Hollering Creek* (1991), both her public persona and her writing display a larger degree of hybrid ethnicity as spectacle" (McCracken 2000, 3). Cisneros is writing during a time period in which women's silence is not just a combative weapon or expressive tool, but in which the audience is receptive to the critique of neoliberal assumptions (the unity of identity), and silence as a facet of gender is "performed" in ways that make it part of the postmodern destabilization of the subject, language, and society (Krolokke and Sorensen 2006, 34).

In order to comprehend exactly how Cisneros's work is postmodern and written for a postmodern audience, we must first define what postmodernism in literature means. Ian Gregson stresses that postmodernism emphasizes the disbelief in language (illustrating the gap between signifier and signified), exposes norms and categories that are perceived as natural to be ideological constructs, reveals reality as not a unitary fact but rather as a multiplicity of signs and representations, and shows identity to be inherently unstable and ultimately constituted through performance (what the self does). Although sometimes realist techniques may be used in this postmodern fiction, such techniques ultimately are employed to deny "the uniformity at the base of human experience" (Gregson 2004, 135). Krolokke and Sorensen add, "Third-wave feminism constitutes a significant move in both theory and politics toward the 'performance turn' we introduced earlier. The performance turn marks a move away from thinking and acting in terms of systems, structures, fixed power relations and thereby also 'suppression'—toward highlighting the complexities, contingencies, and challenges of power and the diverse means and goals of agency" (Krolokke and Sorensen 2006, 21).

At least two of the three types of silences discussed in this chapter correspond to the ideas of a new, postmodern feminism. The first, Cisneros's employment of silent, cultural symbols, is frequently predicated upon the postmodern desire to deconstruct categorization and expose the ideology behind it. As we saw in the section on *Woman Hollering Creek*, Cisneros inverts many cultural figures, such as La Malinche and the Virgin of Guadalupe. In this process, Cisneros invests these figures with new, feminist meanings, converting them from passive, self-sacrificing women or negative icons (as in the case of La Malinche) into positive, assertive figures. Consequently, according to Susan Griffin, Cisneros destroys the monolithic categories of the pure woman versus the fallen one, good versus evil, and so forth (Griffin 1997, 86). For example, in the story "Woman Hollering Creek," the negative symbol of La Llorona, who drowns her own children out of despair and frustration, becomes the positive figure of La Gritona, who rebels against her submissive and abused state. This transformation of the cultural symbol simultaneously deconstructs the categorization of woman as passive or aggressive, as submissive or dominant, and illustrates how women need not be one or the other, since La Llorona and La Gritona in the story are one and the same.

Similarly, Clemencia, the protagonist of the story "Never Marry a Mexican," is described as La Malinche, Cortés's Indian translator during the Conquest (Cisneros 1991a, 74). This figure is frequently viewed as that of the traitor in Mexican culture, yet in Cisneros's story, Clemencia is not portrayed exclusively in that light. Although perhaps she is partially seen as a traitor to other women, since she has sexual relations with their men while the women give birth (as is the case with regard to Drew's wife, Megan), she is also seen as the figure betrayed by her lover, who despite their passionate, long-term affair refuses to leave his upper-class, white wife, because, after all, one should "never marry a Mexican." This ambiguity deconstructs the dichotomy traitor/betrayed previously constituted by the Malinche icon, and suggests the fluid nature of these roles. Finally, Chayo in "Little Miracles, Kept Promises" shows how the Virgin of Guadalupe can simultaneously be a figure of maternal self-sacrifice and Tonantzín, a passionate, sexual, nontraditional woman. Chayo is not seen negatively as the fallen woman, despite her sexual activity (she prays to the Virgin that she is not pregnant); nor is she viewed as the pure, sweet virginal girl who follows the self-sacrificing path of her mother and grandmother. Chayo deconstructs these two categories to create her own specific identity as a painter, and as a woman who sees the subversive value of both silent self-sacrifice and more vocal societal protest. Rose Marie Cutting suggests that in such stories as "One Holy Night" and "*Bien* Pretty" Cisneros also deconstructs essentialist characteristics attributed to men and women. In the first of these tales, Cutting claims that the female protagonist does not subscribe to traditional attitudes of shame associated with premarital sex, while in the second, Lupe's role reversal of the two volcanoes in her painting deconstructs traditional associations of masculine dominance and female passivity (Cutting 2003, 65). McCracken points out that *Caramelo* similarly deconstructs categories through its use of such devices as scholarly footnotes and a chronology at the end of the text. These techniques destroy the distinction between the genres of history and fiction, as well as between fiction and truth (McCracken 2000, 6).

Bilingualism is the second technique presented here that Cisneros employs in her texts to construct postmodern silences designed for a postmodern audience. In the section on *Caramelo*, I illustrated how bilingual gaps were constructed in the novel. Cisneros's use of both Spanish and English in her texts to suggest an inexpressible space between the two languages exactly coincides with the postmodern project of deconstructing language by showing the gaps between signifier and signified.

Such bilingualism also aids in Cisneros's deconstruction of a unified identity. Since neither she nor her characters exist within a single language, this duality between Spanish and English indicates a hybrid identity that is borne out through other narrative techniques. Gutiérrez y Muhs suggests that in the novel *Caramelo*, the *caramelo rebozo* is a symbol of cultural hybridity, because its various colors symbolize the many hybrid Mexican figures that the novel highlights. Gutiérrez y Muhs discusses Cisneros portrayal of numerous "cultural Chicanas" (women who were from other countries but were accepted as Mexicans), such as Toña La Negra and María Antonieta Pons (Gutiérrez y Muhs 2006, 28). These bicultural women constructed through bilingual language underscore the notion of hybrid identity.

Moreover, the very Chicana identity of all of Cisneros's protagonists is shown to be a cultural hybrid of American and Mexican cultures. *The House on Mango Street* is also in form a hybrid text, which some see as a cross between the novel and the short story (McCracken 1989, 64), while others consider it to be a mix of poetry and fiction (Doyle 1994, 12), or of autobiography and fiction (Valdés 1992, 68). Similarly, Jayne Marek notes that Cisneros's first novel is "a complicated take on Mexican-American heritage, not a clear affirmation or rejection of either Chicana/o or Anglo acculturation but of the combination of both that denies Esperanza's autonomy" (Marek 1996, 184).

These examples illustrate that despite some similarities between Cisneros and the other women writers studied in this book, Cisneros's work is specifically oriented toward the reader of her time, one who is steeped in the postmodern culture of class, cultural difference, and racial difference. Cisneros's texts deconstruct traditional categories of heterosexuality/homosexuality, male/female, Mexican/American, and the like. In this process, Cisneros employs silence more diffusely than the previous writers, using it not just as woman's subversive weapon, but also as a technique employed in conjunction with the voice of Chicanos and the poor in general. Moreover, at times these various groups and their specific needs are fused into one character or narrative situation.

Plot and Postmodern Protagonists

At least two of the three narratives written by Cisneros fall under Annis Pratt's category of "novels of development," or the female bildungsroman (Pratt 1981, 13).[8] Just like Rosario Castellanos's novel *Ini-*

tiation Rite, studied in chapter 4, Cisneros's novels focus on the search for identity of her young, female protagonists. Esperanza in *The House on Mango Street* and Celaya Reyes in *Caramelo* are preteens or adolescents who wish to combat society's stereotyped role for women. Although the traditional female bildungsroman plot presents women who are forced into submissive roles as part of a process of marital grooming (with the ultimate denouement of marriage), these two narratives expressly invert the roles of women and the original purpose of the novel of development. Esperanza and Celaya are constructed as women who are aware of gender discrimination; who actively combat traditional, passive, female roles; who want to have careers; and who either do not want to marry at all (as in the case of Esperanza), or are specifically groomed away from marriage and domestic occupations (Celaya escapes an early marriage to the boyfriend with whom she runs away and rejects all household duties in the course of the novel, including a job as a housekeeper for a group of priests).[9] These characterizations are another example of Cisneros's technique of inversion, which we observed with regard to her use of cultural symbols. Although Cisneros maintains the link between female development and identity, she subverts both the ultimate purpose of the traditional female bildungsroman (marriage) as well as the notion of fixed identity through her postmodern emphasis on hybridization in both language (Spanish/English) and cultural identity (American/Mexican). Cisneros's focus on deconstructing the dichotomies and categories that limit human beings posits a potential flux in self-identification based on the particular moment and situation in which one finds oneself. Identity becomes an action or performance. For example, Celaya can relate to different events either as an American, a Mexican, or a Chicana (i.e., both), depending upon the imposed circumstances. As we saw in the section on bilingualism, she reacted to the word *rapto* like an American (native English speaker), by not recognizing its meaning of "kidnapped." She reacts in the same way to the group of Chicana bullies. However, in other situations, such as the description of the communicative value of her grandmother's *caramelo rebozo*, Celaya underscores her Mexican identity, or, as in the case of the many bilingual descriptions, as a Chicana exposed to both languages. A good example of this is the transcription of the song "Júrame" in both Spanish and English in chapter 39 of the novel. Similarly, protagonists such as the children in the story "Mericans" pretend to be non-English speaking, Mexican natives in front of a group of American tourists. Although Cisneros's works express the concept of a nontraditional female identity, the construction of such an identity is never a monolithic, fixed idea in her narratives.[10] Moreover, the importance of class, race, and ethnicity in Cisneros's fiction shifts the focus of her narratives from women understood as a universal category to women understood on the basis of their ultimate differences.

9
Conclusions: Toward a Feminist Poetics of Silence

THIS BOOK BEGAN IN THE SUMMER OF 1999 WHEN I WAS ASKED TO prepare a course on Latin American women writers. I spent the entire summer reading novels and short stories authored by Latin American women, and was surprised to discover that many of them shared a technical and/or thematic focus on silence. Was it a mere coincidence that the protagonists of such diverse works as Isabel Allende's *The House of the Spirits*, Laura Esquivel's *Like Water for Chocolate*, and Rosario Ferré's *Papeles de Pandora* were all mute? Was there any significance in the common motif of knitting as a communicative act on the part of the protagonists in María Luisa Bombal's *The Shrouded Woman*, Allende's *The House of The Spirits*, and Esquivel's *Like Water for Chocolate*? Was the fact that so many female characters are painters or sculptresses in the works by Allende, Castellanos, Ferré, and Cisneros important in any way? So many questions regarding the role of silence, nonverbal actions and rituals, and implicit narrative techniques came to mind that I began to think and read extensively about silence in literature. I discovered that other theorists had also noticed and contemplated these and similar commonalities. However, none had clearly articulated a theory elucidating specific patterns of silence in the works of Latin American women writers. This void motivated a research project spanning almost a decade. So many years of reading Latin American and Latina writers, of immersing myself in feminist literary criticism, and of examining the feminist use of silence have led me to the following conclusions about this topic.

My central conclusion, which I hope to have proven in this book, is that it is indeed possible to identify a poetics of combative silence among many Latin American and Latina writers. Since silence has been an element long associated with women's oppression, many female writers have either consciously or subconsciously (since some feel we cannot impute intention to authors with regard to their texts) appropriated this element of silence in both their narrative form and their thematic exposition. These writers have inverted the original passive meaning of silence to create a subversive instrument against patriarchal dominance. Furthermore, such appropriation varies in nature according to the era, country, and personal background (race, age, socioeconomic status) of each writer and will be interpreted differently by differing readers according to the readers' own characteristics. Consequently, in the course of this book I have identified and illustrated six distinct types of silences. The first type, paradoxical silence, is attributed to the early twentieth-century Chilean writers Marta Brunet and María Luisa Bombal, who wrote during the presuffrage era when audiences were not primed for a totally combative use of silence and women still suffered a passive silence at home. The second silence is coded silence. Rosario Castellanos employs coding strategies in her works, because she wrote on the cusp of second-wave feminism, during a moment in which feminist attitudes still frequently needed to be disguised through such strategies. The third type is hyperbolic silence, which is found in the novels and short stories of Isabel Allende, who begins to exhibit postmodern techniques through an ironic appropriation or exaggeration of female stereotypes designed to question rather than to accept such outmoded female images. Symbolic silence is the fourth variety. It is found in the texts written by Rosario Ferré. Ferré's indirect discourse suggests a powerful indictment of patriarchy is possible through silent symbol and narrative implication. The fifth silence is parodic silence, which is found in Laura Esquivel's texts. Esquivel's works continue to move toward postmodern feminism through their mimicry of romance novels and parody of other forms, such as science fiction, that propagate patriarchal ideology. Finally, the sixth form of silence is cultural silence, which is found in the works by the Latina writer Sandra Cisneros. Cisneros's work epitomizes postmodern, popular feminism because of the author's employment of silence linked to the working-class, Chicana, cultural specificity of her protagonists. The silence emphasizes their difference and varying degrees of agency vis-à-vis Anglo culture. Both Esquivel and Cisneros works show how subversive silence continues to be operative in women writers in the twenty-first century.

My second conclusion, upon reviewing this topic, is that I am, necessarily, myself enacting a type of the silence—that of omission—throughout the pages of this book. There are surely other Latin American and Latina writers who would nicely fit into the paradigms I have established, and others whose works might suggest the construction of additional paradigms. Yet, I have failed to mention them and analyze their works within this book. In the course of my research, I discovered many other women writers who employ silence subversively, and a variety of interesting articles that discuss some aspects of the manifestation of silence in these other writers' works. However, unless I wish to spend another decade working on this book, I can only mitigate this omission by relegating a few lines to each of these important writers in these concluding remarks. The following discussion is by no means all-inclusive, and is merely intended to briefly identify several other significant twentieth-century and twenty-first-century women writers whose use of silence will, I hope, inspire others to explore their works and perhaps build upon the paradigms suggested here. This overview also reinforces my thesis that a poetics of subversive silence applies to many twentieth-century Latin American and Latina writers, but is too pervasive to allow for a totally comprehensive analysis here.

In the first half of the twentieth century, the Costa Rican writer Yolanda Oreamuno (1916–56) wrote several novels and many short stories, including the novels *Nuestro silencio* [Our Silence] (1947) and *La ruta de su evasión* [The Path of their Evasion] (1949). In the short story "Valle alto" [High Valley], the protagonist is a lonely woman who travels to a foreign country. During this journey, the woman lives an erotic fantasy in which she makes love with a stranger with whom she shares a cab along the way. This silent fantasy fulfills her life, and seems to provide a refuge or weapon against her unarticulated concerns and preoccupations (Gold 1990, 202). *La ruta de su evasión* presents a similar valuation of silence in the form of the quiet complicity between the female protagonists, Teresa and Aurora. Together these two characters silently overcome their sense of entrapment (Chaverri 1997b, n.p.). Oreamuno's use of silent female fantasy and interior monologue suggests similarities to María Luisa Bombal's work, since Bombal also uses these techniques as weapons against patriarchy and a means of fulfillment for women trapped in lives that they cannot escape because of social constraints. Oreamuno's work requires further study, and may well be another example of early twentieth-century works that fit the paradigm of paradoxical silence.

Another woman writer who employs silence subversively is Elena Garro (1920–98) of Mexico. Garro, married and divorced from the famous Nobel Prize–winning author Octavio Paz, was overshadowed by her former husband, and her work did not receive much acclaim during her lifetime. However, she wrote many novels and short stories, spanning four decades (the 1960s to the 1990s), the most famous of which are *Recuerdos del porvenir* [*Recollections of Things to Come*] (1963) and *Testimonios sobre Mariana* [Testimonies about Mariana] (1981). In *Recuerdos del porvenir*, the female protagonists stage a protest against the repressive military caudillo, Francisco Rosas, toward the end of the Mexican revolution, using silence and a highly codified language as weapons against patriarchal forces (García 1990, 98). Similarly, the main point of Garro's *Testimonios sobre Mariana* is the presentation of Mariana's silent resistance to her husband's domineering personality (Rubio 1997, 362). Garro's work may fit into the paradigm of silent protest through coding techniques established here with regard to the works of Rosario Castellanos.

Another Mexican writer who has been much associated with silence is Elena Poniatowska. Poniatowska is well known for her novels *Hasta no verte Jesús mío* [*Here's to You, Jesusa!*] (1969), *Tinísima* (1991), and *Paseo de la Reforma* [Walk of Reform] (1996), as well as her famous historical account of the Tlatelolco student massacre, *La noche de Tlatelolco* [The Night of Tlatelolco] (1971). Several articles have been written about Poniatowska's use of silence, which appears to oscillate between a subversive silence in such stories as "La felicidad" [Happiness] and an imposed silence of marginality in such works as *Querido Diego, te abraza Quiela* [Dear Diego, Quiela Embraces You] (1978). Janet Gold points out that in "La felicidad," Poinatowska presents a woman's long interior monologue as a means of combating solitude and death (Gold 1990, 199), while Rubén Rodríguez speaks of a passive silence in Poniatowska's novel (Rodríguez 2000, 296). Poniatowska's works are of great complexity, and her use of silence clearly merits further inquiry.

The Argentine writer Sylvia Molloy is famous for her novel *En breve cárcel* [*Certificate of Absence*], published in 1981. Molloy constructs a muted plot of feminist protest against incest behind the dominant plot of a woman who has been humiliated by her lesbian lover by being forced to listen to a detailed description of her lover's amorous encounter with another woman. Molloy employs symbolism and silent implication throughout the text to suggest the protagonist's incestuous relationship with her father (Norat 1995, 112–20). Molloy's reliance on symbolism and implication place her soundly within the paradigm of symbolic silence established in my discussion of Rosario Ferré's work.

Moreover, her theme of lesbian love suggests a movement toward post-structuralist feminism, in which feminist difference is emphasized in literary portrayals.

Another Argentine writer, Luisa Valenzuela, is known for both her short stories and novels. Among her short-story collections are *El gato eficaz* [The Efficient Cat] (1972), *Aquí pasan cosas raras* [Strange Things Happen Here] (1975), *Cambio de armas* [Exchange of Arms] (1982); her novels include *Cola de lagartija* [*The Lizard's Tale*] (1983) and *Novela negra con argentinos* [*Black Novel: With Argentines*] (1990). Valenzuela has acquired great fame through her use of fantasy and political themes. Her short-story collection *Cambio de armas* is an excellent example of the use of feminist silence. Three tales—"Cuarta versión"[Fourth Version], "Cambio de armas" [Exchange of Arms], and "De noche soy tu caballo" [At Night I Am Your Horse]—suggest female protest against the political reality of Argentine dictatorship (the dirty war) through narrative gaps and silences that require the reader to participate in the construction of the repressive political circumstances. Narrative implication in these texts both suggests silence imposed and rebellion against this imposition. In "De noche soy tu caballo," the narrator's silence (refusal to betray her revolutionary boyfriend when she is incarcerated) is an example of how silence constitutes a protest or subversive weapon, although it is not exclusively feminist. In the story "Ceremonias de rechazo" [Ceremonies of Rejection] the boyfriend of the protagonist, Amanda, is also a revolutionary, but here Amanda's silent protest is more personal than political. Her boyfriend comes and goes as he pleases, and this leads Amanda to feel a general lack of control in her life. She finally decides to break off the relationship, and engages in numerous silent beauty rituals (facial mask, cleansing bath, and leg shaving) to reestablish her sense of purpose and control of her destiny. These are the "ceremonies of rejection" alluded to in the story's title, and they clearly constitute a feminist rebellion. Although Valenzuela does repeat some of the techniques seen in the other writers studied here, her works might suggest a new paradigm, possibly that of political silences.

Marjorie Agosín of Chile and Margo Glantz of Mexico, both contemporary writers whose works span from the 1970s to the present, offer the experience of growing up Jewish in Latin America. Both Agosín and Glantz have written memoirs about this topic: Agosín's *Sagrada memoria* [Sacred Memory] was published in 1994, while Glantz's *Las genealogías* [*The Family Tree*] appeared in 1991. Paul Goldberg asserts that both writers use subversive silence in their works. Silence is a source of security, a coping mechanism, as well as a psychological condition resulting from persecution (Goldberg 2000, 319). Goldberg's discussion of these works leads me to believe that they might fit my paradigm of paradoxical silence; however, since these are memoirs and not novels, upon further study they may also suggest a unique paradigm associated with this type of autobiographical writing. Furthermore, since Glantz and Agosín represent the Jewish minority voice, their works sometimes parallel the postmodern tendencies of Cisneros, where silences are not always purely feminist, but also a protest against minority discrimination.

Similarly, Esmeralda Santiago of Puerto Rico wrote a fictionalized memoir of her immigrant experiences in the United States entitled *When I Was Puerto Rican*. Santiago's work illustrates some uses of nonverbal expression as a form of communication for women. Negi, Santiago's main character, describes how her knitting needles made "patterns with thread that might have told a story" (Szadziuk 1999, 99). Santiago, like Sandra Cisneros, is a Latina writer who uses bilingualism in her texts. Although she provides a glossary of Spanish terms at the end of *When I Was Puerto Rican* that facilitates comprehension for the nonbilingual reader, the portrayal of working-class and bicultural concerns suggests that Santiago's work might be another example of the cultural-silence paradigm.

The contemporary Mexican writer Sara Sefchovich, who is both a historian and a sociologist, has written various novels to date: *Demasiado amor* [Too Much Love] (1990), *La señora de los sueños* [The Lady of Dreams] (1993), *La suerte de la consorte* [The Fate of the Consort] (1999), and *Vivir la vida* [To Live Life] (2000). Sefchovich's *La señora de los sueños* provides an excellent example of the communicative and subversive values of silence. First, the novel consists primarily of the interior monologues of the four main characters: a housewife (Ana Fernández) and her husband, son, and daughter. Ana is very bored with her role of housewife. She does not know what to do with herself during the day, while the other family members are at school or work. One day she enters a bookstore and starts spending her mornings and afternoons reading. She reads books about an Arab bride, a Russian princess, a Cuban revolutionary who is Castro's lover, and a family on an Israeli kibbutz, just to name a few of her texts. In each case, after reading the book, Ana reenacts the role of the book's protagonist in her everyday life. She tries out different roles until she establishes a lucrative baking business, imitating the domestic role of one of her protagonists on the kibbutz. Although this role ironically seems to mimic one of her primary tasks as housewife, Fernández has clearly used her silent reading activity to find fulfillment and to create positive action in her life. Although to some her reading activity has been interpreted as passive fantasy, in reality it is a transformative action with important life-changing implications for all her family members. Thus, Fernández's silence provides a twist on the use of escapist fantasy in early twentieth-century feminist literature. Although Sefchovich's fantasy seems similar to that found in such early works as *La última niebla*, the silent fantasy of her protagonist impinges on reality in a new, contemporary way. Perhaps Sefchovich's use of silent fantasy is a parody of earlier, more inactive, escapist fantasy. That would liken her work to Esquivel's parody of romance and science fiction and relate it to that postmodern paradigm.

For every author I have mentioned here, I have surely omitted ten others who employ silence subversively in their works. Nonetheless, this overview illustrates that the use of feminist, combative silences is a pervasive phenomenon in the works of Latin American and Latina writers. Silence in the form of narrative theme and indirect stylistic techniques such as parody, hyperbole, irony, metaphor, symbolism, and textual voice constitutes what Jean Franco terms a "subversive mythology" (Franco 1992, 75) aimed at situating the implied reader within a feminist perspective. In this analysis, we have observed many "speaking silences," and thus how silence has clearly evolved from a marker of feminine suppression to a sign of feminist expression in the works of many Latin American and Latina women writers.

Notes

Preface

1. Krolokke and Sorensen 2006 provide an excellent overview of the three waves of feminism. First-wave feminism has widely been recognized as corresponding to the early feminist movement, from the fight for women's suffrage to the late 1960s; second-wave feminism has traditionally been associated with the more radical women's liberation movement of the late 1960s and 1970s, possibly extending through the 1980s and 1990s; and third-wave feminism coincides with shifts in the movement toward poststructuralist analysis from the mid-1990s until the present.

2. A recent issue of *PMLA* 121, no. 5 (2006) includes a subsection entitled "Feminist Criticism Today." The articles included in this section, by such noted scholars as Jane Elliot, Marianne DeKoven, and Susan Gubar, debate the notion that feminism is dead and signal productive avenues for future feminist study. Both Astrid Henry and Toril Moi discuss how feminism became "a bad word," while Elliot indicates how current poststructuralist debates have marginalized literary studies. My book hopes to recover the use of feminist theory for the study of literary texts. In particular, Gubar signals how literary studies have suffered from the contemporary poststructuralist bent, which moves away from the notion of women as a group and focuses upon other categories that intersect with women, such as queer and postcolonial theories. See Gubar 2006, 1714.

1. Language and Silence

1. In the field of Hispanic literary criticism, Marta Traba also seems to subscribe to the notion that a different or separate style characterizes women writers. Traba (in contrast to the French feminists) sees women's writing as less symbolic, explicative rather than interpretative, sportive of an oral character, and focused on reality. See Traba 1985, 21–26.

2. Sara Castro-Klarén states: "To deny them access and use of the written word is to deny them history, knowledge, and as a corollary, power. Thus it is not true, as Guber and Gilbert indicate, that the West is mistaken in confusing literary authorship with patriarchal authority; on the contrary, the West recognizes without any ambiguity the coincidence between writing, knowledge, and power" (Castro-Klarén 1985, 41, my translation).

3. For more on dialogism, see Bakhtin 1981 and Bakhtin 1984.

4. Guerra provides a very interesting history of attempts to define "woman" throughout the ages in Guerra-Cunningham 1995.

5. Mills 1995 refers to Wolfgang Iser's notion of the implied reader postulated by the author, as distinct from the text's actual reader (who may not coincide with the implied reader, a completely hypothetical and ideal construct). See Iser 1978 and Iser 1974 for more information on the implied reader.

6. Mills is once again following Iser's ideas on reader-reception theory.

7. I borrow the term "textual voice" from Stephen Ross, whose theory I will discuss in more detail in subsequent chapters. See Ross 1979.

8. Debra Castillo's book *Talking Back* (1992) discusses silence at length, but only examines its employment in the works of Helena María Viramontes. Castillo's approach is different from my own; it focuses more on such concepts as surfacing and negation that relate to silence in a tangential way. Nonetheless, my own analysis owes a profound debt to Castillo's groundbreaking work. See D. Castillo 1992.

9. Note that this collection contains thirty articles on the topic of silence, many of which focus on poetry and theater. I have limited myself here to discussing some of the more pertinent articles on prose writings. Moreover, although I cite the entire volume in my reference list, I specifically mention there only those articles that I directly use in this book.

10. A comparison between the use of silence in male and female writers would be an interesting and worthwhile undertaking, but unfortunately remains outside the scope of the present book.

11. The same can be said of Rosario Castellanos's fusion of the subordinate status of women and Indians, although we do not focus here on Castellanos's indigenist texts.

2. Paradoxical Silence, Part I

1. Koski's idea of distraction relates to the techniques of indirection discussed by Radner and Lanser in the first chapter. These techniques are applied to the works of Castellanos and Allende in chapters 4 and 5, respectively. According to Radner and Lanser, distraction refers to "strategies that draw out or draw attention away from the subversive power of a feminist message" (Radner and Lanser 1987, 417). Carreño Bolívar also notes that Brunet used *criollismo* as a "mask" for her social criticism (Carreño Bolívar 2002, 49).

2. Note that all English translations of Brunet's short stories are my own. I will include the original Spanish in the note corresponding to each passage. The original Spanish passage reads: "la mujer apegaba convulsivamente el delantal a la boca para hacerlo [un sollozo] morir allí sin ruido alguno. Porque le habían dicho que 'no querían oírla'" (Brunet 1962, 105).

3. "La casa fue primero de quincha con revoque de barro. Pero, al correr del tiempo, el hombre empezó a subir lajas del río y alrededor de las paredes ya existentes hizo otras de piedra. Era como una casa metida dentro de otra casa" (ibid., 100).

4. "La voz estaba dentro de ella perdida" (ibid., 122).

5. "transfiriendo a la hija su amor por el padre" (ibid., 124).

6. "Sigue mirándose, pero escucha ahora *en su interior el denso silencio de su sangre*. Rodeada de frío, inmóvil. ¿Esa es ella? ¿Ella misma?" (ibid., 299, my emphasis).

7. "no puede ser sino como es. Lo vive intensamente, en profundidad, con la sabiduría específica de su condición de mujer" (ibid., 300).

8. "una forma de callar en voz alta" (ibid., 301).

9. In Spanish, these last two quotations are "infinitamente desamparados en su respectiva soledad" and "un doloroso insomnio interior" (ibid., 298).

10. "desvaída lepra amarillenta del tiempo" (ibid.).

11. "Poseía un marido" (ibid., 42).

12. "no admitía vasallajes" (ibid.).

13. "hembra sumisa al macho en el rapto violento" (ibid., 46).

14. "Era una figura ambigua como las que estilizara Chana Orloff" (ibid., 42).

15. "El amor, mientras fuera manifestación platónica, entraba en su vida de cerebral a la cual le era sólo necesario el perfume del licor para crear la embriaguez" (ibid., 43).

16. "Aquel [el fonógrafo] era lujo suyo, [. . .] Tenía que guardar su recuerdo, cuidar su ensueño y tan solo en un país de silencio podía hacerlo" (ibid., 110–13).

17. "La mujer los miraba, quieta. Que no se acercaran de nuevo a su fonógrafo, era suyo, allí residía su vida interior, su evasión a los días incoloros" (ibid., 116–17).

18. "Nunca mentaba a la hija" (ibid., 87).

19. "La vieja apretó los labios [. . .] y no dijo nada" (ibid., 90).

20. [Eufrasia] "Hacía sigilosos viajes por el sendero hasta enfrentar el puente. [. . .] El hombre puso el pie en el puente. [. . .] de súbito vaciló, herido por la piedra en la frente; vaciló, osciló y desapareció entre las paredes del tajo, sumido en lo húmedo. [. . .] Agora gané yo [. . .] y pa siempre [. . .] ¡Je! —lo dijo creyó decirlo *pero de la boca cerrada, como trancada el labio inferior, no se movió un músculo ni salió un sonido*" (ibid., 99–100, my emphasis).

21. "Otro mundo, rodeada de silencio" (ibid., 265).

22. "Lo de las narices" (ibid., 269).

23. "Pensaba: 'Esto es lo que yo quería, sí, esto. Estar sola, no hablar'" (ibid., 269).

24. "Buscaron todo este día, todo el siguiente: troncos, pedazos de raíces engrifadas [. . .] piedras, cerradas en su mudez de siglos a las que era preciso golpear, manosear, para que adquirieran sentido y 'dijesen' algo. [. . .] las manos autoritarias manejaban y vencían la tenaz oposición de la larga liana de un alambre, fijando una rama con otra, una raíz a una piedra. Al ver de pronto al padre, mostró triunfalmente su obra. —No dirás que no es tu retrato [. . .] —Ahora yo sé porque me gustan las narices [. . .] También lo sabía ahora el padre. Era como si deletreara símbolos sin sentido. Que Margarita aprendiera a leerlos. A leerlos de corrido. *Y a escribir en ese idioma*" (ibid., 272–73, my emphasis).

25. "Desde un ángulo nuevo" (ibid., 70).

26. "Cada tejado era un problema que resolver" (ibid.).

27. "Abarcar más horizonte" (ibid.).

28. "una pobre loca" (ibid., 263).

29. "Con la boca sensual y dura y la barbilla cuadrada de voluntarioso" (ibid.).

30. This is my translation, as are all other citations in English from *María Nadie*. The Spanish reads: "Eres una chiquita bien mala de la cabeza [. . .] mereces unos buenos azotes" (Brunet 1997, 124).

31. "Creaba su ambiente: un rincón para su cama, para su ropa, para sus libros. Un rincón, el más propicio al silencio, para leer y soñar" (ibid., 107–8).

32. "después de estos monólogos dirigidos a tal o cual persona, quedo convencida de que se lo he dicho y mi sorpresa es dar con la realidad de mi silencio" (ibid., 129).

33. "inmediatamente la sumaron al juego. [. . .] No hay que decírselo a nadie. Lo que pasa en el abra es secreto de tres. Ahora somos tres para un secreto. Tres: Tres. Tres—y solemnemente extendían las manos sellando una y otra vez el pacto. [. . .] Cacho y Conejo fueron mis adorables compañeros en un recinto de cuento. Ellos me aceptaban como salida de un sombrero de prestidigitador, sin pasado, sin porvenir y por eso fueron mi parcela de felicidad" (ibid., 65–66).

34. "Me iré. María Nadie también tendrá ante sí una puerta abierta. Seré de nuevo María López. Una puerta abierta ante mí. Puede que hacia una vida radiante. Puede que hacia *inenarrables* sufrimientos. Pero será la vida" (ibid., 138, my emphasis).

35. "Me iré a esa hora en que una mala pájara debe regresar a su nido" (ibid., 138).

3. Paradoxical Silence, Part II

1. Bombal published another novel titled *House of Mist* in 1947 which is loosely based on *La última niebla*. Since Bombal rewrote both *La última niebla* and, to a lesser degree, *La amortajada* in English, these English versions do not exactly correspond to the original Spanish, and I will thus provide all my own translations. For an in-depth discussion of the relationship between the Spanish-language novel *La última niebla* and the English-language novel *House of Mist*, see Rubio 1998.

2. For a more detailed biographical account of María Luisa Bombal, see Gligo 1985.

3. See the studies on Bombal in Boyle 1993; Carreño Bolívar 2002; Guerra-Cunningham 1980; Gutiérrez Mouat 1987; Levine 1974; Salas 1997; Sepúlveda-Pulvirenti 1987; and Trovatto 2001.

4. See the studies by Agosín 1985; Bastos 1985; Bianchi 1985; Braun 1994; and Lagos-Pope 1997.

5. As Diane Marie Braun notes, women use silence and dreams "to simultaneously dramatize women's marginalization and refute it" (Braun 1994, 45).

6. "Silencio, un gran silencio, un silencio de años. De siglos, un silencio aterrador que empieza a crecer en el cuarto y dentro de mi cabeza" (Bombal 1988, 12). Also note that Trovatto discusses other possible symbolic associations for this episode that connote an idealized sexual encounter rather than an actual occurrence. See Trovatto 2001, 70.

7. "la mirada displicente de Daniel tropieza con la mía" (Bombal 1988, 25).

8. "Hoy he visto a mi amante" (ibid.).

9. "Mi único anhelo es estar sola para poder soñar, soñar a mis anchas" (ibid., 23).

10. "—¿No te habló? Ya ves, era un fantasma [. . .] Esta duda que mi marido me ha infiltrado; ¡esta duda absurda y tan grande!" (ibid., 31–31).

11. Dolores DeLuise focuses on this battle between the protagonist and Daniel in a different but analogous way. She sees it as a conflict between two distinct fictions: Daniel tries to live the fantasy that the protagonist is his first wife, while the protagonist lives in the dreamworld of her imaginary lover (DeLuise 1993, 134–41). M. Ian Adams views *La última niebla* as a battle between the protagonist and the mist, rather than a battle between her and her husband, Daniel. Adams clearly sides with the viewpoint that silence is a form of passivity and alienation in the novel (Adams 1975, 15-35).

12. " se le antojaba el presagio de una catástrofe" (Bombal 1988, 136).

13. "En vano había agotado los inconscientes métodos de la pasión para reconquistar a Antonio; ternura, violencia, reproches, *mutismo*, asedio amoroso" (ibid., 142–43, my emphasis).

14. "un odio *silencioso* que en lugar de consumirla, la fortificaba" (ibid., 145, my emphasis).

15. "Solía abismarse en la contemplación de aquella muchacha silenciosa que tejía extendida en una larga mecedora de paja. [. . .] *Si solamente hubieras tirado de hilo mi lana, si hubieras, malla por malla, deshecho mi tejido [. . .] a cada una se enredaba un borrascoso pensamiento y un nombre que no olvidaré*" (ibid., 133, my emphasis).

16. See E. W. Nelson 1987 for an excellent analysis of some cases of narrative ambiguity in *The Shrouded Woman*. Also see Mezei 1996 for more on free indirect discourse and narrative authority.

17. "Ahora sólo queda, cerca de ella, el marido de María Griselda. ¡Cómo es posible que ella también llame a su hijo: el marido de María Griselda! ¿Por qué? ¡Porque cela a su hermosa mujer! ¡Porque la mantiene aislada en un lejano fundo del sur! [. . .] De pronto aquellos párpados bajos comienzan a mirarla fijamente, con la insondable fijeza con que miran los ojos de un demente. ¡Oh abre los ojos, Alberto! [. . .] Ahora pega a la llama de uno de los cirios la imagen de María Griselda y se dedica a quemarla. [. . .] ¿No entrega acaso un poco de su belleza en cada retrato? Sí, pero ya el fuego deshojó el último. Ya no queda más que una sola María Griselda; la que mantiene secuestrada allá en un lejano fundo del sur. ¡Oh, Alberto, mi pobre hijo!" (Bombal 1988, 117–18).

18. "Pasaron años. Años en que se retrajo y se fue volviendo día a día más limitada y mezquina. ¿Por qué, por qué la naturaleza de la mujer ha de ser tal que tenga que ser siempre un hombre el eje de su vida? Los hombres, ellos, logran poner su pasión en otras cosas. Pero el destino de las mujeres es remover una pena de amor en una casa ordenada, ante una tapicería inconclusa" (ibid., 142).

19. "parecían no querer reconocerle ya ningún derecho a vivir" (ibid., 96).

20. "La había traicionado en sus planes ¡tan bondadosa y torpemente como lo hubiera hecho su propio padre!" (ibid., 144).

21. "piense que hay medidas que una señora no puede tomar sin rebajarse" (ibid., 144).

22. This quotation and all others from "El árbol" are my translation. The original Spanish reads: "clara, estrecha y juiciosamente caprichosa" (Bombal 1988, 46).

23. "Ha quedado aprisionada en las redes de su pasado, no puede salir del cuarto de vestir. De su cuarto de vestir invadido por una luz blanca aterradora. [. . .] Le habían quitado su intimidad, su secreto; se encontraba desnuda en medio de la calle, desnuda junto a un marido viejo que le volvía la espalda para dormir" (ibid., 55). Note that Guerra-Cunningham also relates the music to Brígida's different life stages, indicating that Mozart's hedonistic quality prefigures the lost innocence and vitality of Brígida's youth; Beethoven's music, expressive of loneliness and a tormented love life, symbolizes the unsatisfied passion of the stage of Brígida's marriage; and Chopin's music, evocative of exalted feelings and emotions, signals Brígida's desire for love at the story's end, when she finally decides to divorce Luis (Guerra-Cunningham 1980, 111–31).

24. "esgrimiendo rabiosamente el arma aquella que había encontrado sin pensarlo: el silencio" (Bombal 1988, 51).

25. Note that owing to the symbolic connection between the story and the myth of the "rowan tree," I have chosen to translate *gomero* as rowan tree. There are many other possible translations for *gomero*.

26. Andrew Debicki also develops the story's symbolism through its opposition of darkness and light. For Debicki, the tree is a symbol of illusions and their fate. See Debicki 1971 for further details.

4. The Encoded Silence of Rosario Castellanos

1. See Steele 1996 for an interesting discussion of the circumstances surrounding Castellanos's death. Steele maintains that Castellanos had been prone to depression her entire life, and thus committed suicide when her son, Gabriel, returned to Mexico to live with his father. She also speculates about the possibility that she had either been murdered by the Mexican government or by her chauffeur.

2. See the epilogue to Castellanos 1996, 370–83.

3. Note that this translation is my own. The Spanish appears thus: "La respiración de Enrique estaba hinchada de cólera. Sacudió con desprecio a Emelina. —¡Has deshonrado tu apellido! ¡Y con un cualquiera! ¡Con un extranjero aprovechado! [. . .] Enrique echó a andar sin rumbo por las calles desoladas. De lejos le llegaba el eco de las marimbas, de los cohetes de la feria. Pero no se apagó siquiera cuando Enrique golpeó con los aldabonazos convenidos, la puerta del burdel" (Castellanos 1964, 95).

4. For a very interesting comparison of this story to its film version, see Mennell 1999.

5. All translations of this text are my own. The Spanish reads: "El lugar adecuado para un marido era en el que ahora reposaba su difunto Juan Carlos" (Castellanos 1971, 49).

6. "entendió por prudencia el silencio, el asentamiento, la sumisión" (ibid., 53).

7. "Pocos tenían la suerte de la señora Justina que se encontró un hombre bueno y responsable" (ibid., 62).

8. "Por fortuna su pobre padre estaba muerto y enterrado en una tumba a perpetuidad en el Panteón Francés"; "El lugar adecuado para un marido era en el que ahora reposaba su difunto Juan Carlos" (ibid., 48–49).

9. I borrow this idea from Warhol 1996, 21–39.

10. All English translations of this text are my own. The Spanish reads: "las sonrisas aprobatorias fueron congelándose en un gesto de antipatía" (Castellanos 1996, 18).

11. "Porque no se elige ser soltera como una forma de vida, sino que, la experiencia ya lo dice, se queda una soltera, esto es, se acepta pasivamente un destino que los demás nos imponen. [. . .] Y por qué las necesidades de los demás son verdaderas y las de la soltera son apenas caprichos? Porque lo que ella necesita lo necesita para sí misma y para nadie más y eso, en una mujer, no es lícito. Tiene que compartir, dar. Sólo justifica su existencia en función de la existencia de los demás" (Castellanos 1995c, 32).

12. "Compró muebles sólidos, desempacó antiguas vajillas, colgó cortinas y cuadros. Sus familiares [. . .] no dejaron de expresar su desaprobación. Pero no pudieron impedir que Beatriz acabara por tener una casa acogedora" (Castellanos 1996, 34).

13. "Cerró los ojos para que no la vieran y los labios para que ninguna la invocara. Ciega, muda, invisible, y sorda. Bastó un paso más y en el mismo sitio donde antes estuvo Cecilia Rojas, ahora estaba nadie" (ibid., 51).

14. "Este silencio ¿Es sabiduría o falta de feminidad?" (ibid., 73).

15. "Un hecho se anula no mencionándolo" (ibid., 106).

16. "Su problema eran las palabras [. . .] de esa mansión [de la escritura] el único habitante ahora era el silencio" (ibid., 189–90).

17. "Lo que iba a decidirse o confirmarse en el acto sexual era algo mucho más importante que aquello sobre lo que legislaba su vanidad o su gazmoñería: era su existencia misma. [. . .] Este sector de su relación había sido declarado zona de silencio. Porque Mariscal no disponía, para aludir a ella, más que de la terminología corriente que Cecilia se rehusaba a escuchar. Simulaba que lesionarían su delicadeza esas mismas palabras con que su madre la hubiera calificado de puta, aunque, en verdad, estaba en desacuerdo no sólo con su matiz condenatorio sino también con su significado meramente descriptivo" (ibid., 233).

18. "se sentía distante, sobrecogida y totalmente feliz" (ibid., 368).

19. For more information on the female bildungsroman in Latin American, see the excellent books by Lagos (1996); Lutes (2000); and Kushigian (2003).

20. "esa luz que exponía a los objetos, indefensos, a una mirada que ya no acertaría nunca más a desviarse. El objeto desnudo ante la mirada fija. Entre ambos antagonistas ningún obstáculo que impidiera observar la arista más mínima de una realidad sin atenuantes" (Castellanos 1996, 138).

21. "Incidente que Cecilia interpretó (para explicarlo, para justificarlo, para perdonarlo) como la revelación y patentización ante una mirada ajena y hasta en cierto modo desinteresada de su feminidad" (ibid., 138).

22. "Quiero que el otro me mire, como dicen los hindúes, con mirada favorable" (ibid., 177).

23. "Una de esas miradas que dan a cada acción el peso de un juicio" (ibid., 149).

24. "Cecilia se aplicó, encarnizadamente, a instruirse en las artes de agradar [. . .] se adelantaba a adivinar sus fantasías y se esmeraba en cumplirlas. Esta aplicación, además de su utilidad inmediata, la ayudaba a mantenerse al margen, como una observadora atenta, no como una participante enajenada" (ibid., 233–34).

25. "Yo quiero ser yo, oscura, quieta, anónima. Para *mirar* únicamente, para entender algo, por pequeño que sea, para decirme en secreto a mí misma eso que he entendido" (ibid., 322, my emphasis).

26. See the following pages of the novel for examples of explanatory and clarifying parentheses: 54, 59, 63, 721, 75, 77, 85, 90, 91, 93, 96, 106, 108, 109, 130, 131, 134, 139, 143, 147, 166, 189, 192, 194, 219.

5. HYPERBOLIC SILENCE

1. No articles offer a comprehensive analysis of silence, however, there are mentions of the topic in the following studies: Agosín 1993; Bartholomew 1993; Boschetto 1989; Camacho-Gingerich 1992; Dupláa 1989; Frenk 1996; García-Johnson 1994; Koene 1998; Perricone 1991; and Swanson 1994.

2. Koene's study is perhaps the most thorough one that exists on the topic of silence in Allende. Although Koene theorizes in her introduction that silence in Allende can indeed be subversive in nature, most of the examples given in her analysis of *Eva Luna* and *The Stories of Eva Luna* actually run counter to her hypothesis and underscore silence as a negative, passive condition imposed upon women by patriarchal society. Koene's study, with the exception of a few well-placed examples (e.g., her discussion of "The Gold of Tomás Vargas"), is an analysis of the evolution of Allende's characters from silence to

the appropriation of the word as a form of power (Eva Luna achieves her identity through her role as a writer in the novel *Eva Luna*, while characters like Belisa Crepusculario in "Two Words" from *The Stories of Eva Luna* also assert authority through words). Although I agree with Koene's emphasis on the importance of words and writing in these narratives, I disagree with its opposition to silence seen as only a form of passivity imposed by patriarchy. See Koene 1998, 150-215.

3. For a more detailed account of Chilean feminism prior to the Allende and Pinochet governments, see Kirkwood 1986.

4. Alice Nelson interprets the female characters' names as indicative of the desire for restored innocence. This is in keeping with her theory that both *The House of the Spirits* and *Of Love and Shadows* are romances that foster neoliberal politics through their presentation of a philosophy of postcoup reconciliation. She ignores the possible historical association between the color white and the white handkerchiefs of the *arpilleristas*. Nelson alleges that Allende's allegorical interpretation of history as a conflict between Trueba and the García males erases women as historical agents (A. A. Nelson 2002, 211). Although I agree with Nelson's assertion that there are some unfortunate passages in Allende's novels that either conflict with or attenuate a possible feminist message (such as Alba's blithe acceptance of her pregnancy as a possible result of rape), I believe that Nelson ignores a series of important factors that contradict her thesis. She dismisses the potentially subversive value of silence and magic in both novels. Women are associated with these elements precisely because of the combative dimension they acquire within the context of the two narratives, as illustrated by my analysis.

5. For information regarding the development of the Chilean women's movement since the fall of Pinochet, see Schild 1998. Schild examines the link between efforts of the Chilean neoliberal state to redefine citizenship and the activities of Chilean women's movements. According to Schild, the elections of 1990 led to a general demobilization of social movements in Chile and exposed important differences among feminists, who are split between *políticas* (political ones) and *autónomas* (autonomous ones). The *políticas* feel that the struggle for women's equality should be fought from within party politics, while the *autónomas* believe that the approach of the *políticas* will lead to the loss of women's autonomy (Schild 1998, 99).

6. Note that the English version changes "all women" to "most women." I have slightly altered the translation in the last sentence here to correspond more exactly to the Spanish: "Supo que a pesar del aparente abismo que las separaba, podía contarle la verdad porque en esencia eran hermanas, como finalmente lo son todas las mujeres" (Allende 1985a, 125).

7. Mora, among others, has indicated that characters such as Alba in *The House of the Spirits* do not achieve a truly feminist political consciousness, because she becomes involved in politics chiefly because her boyfriend is a political radical (Mora 1987, 53–61). A. A. Nelson 2002 makes similar arguments regarding Allende's female characters in both *The House of the Spirits* and *Of Love and Shadows*. However, I argue that Allende's female characters become politically involved through their men precisely because this is historically how most Chilean women became involved in politics in Chilean history. Through this involvement, as I have shown, a feminist consciousness subsequently developed among Chilean women.

8. The other play strategies are as follows: Alea is play based on chance and the unforeseeable. The game functions through de-familiarization, which according to Iser "it

achieves through storing and telescoping different texts, thus outstripping what their respective, identifiable segments were meant to mean." Alea frustrates the reader's expectations based on reading conventions. The third game is mimicry, "a play pattern designed to generate illusion," while the fourth is illinx, a game in which various positions are subverted or canceled as they interact with one another. Iser states that illinx "aims at bringing out the rear view of the positions yoked together in the game" (Iser 1989, 333).

9. This passage is a perfect example of what Mikhail Bakhtin calls "double-voiced discourse." According to Bakthin, a dialogic relationship can exist even within a single word, as long as someone else's semantic position is reflected within it. We may think of this as Bakhtin's "repetition of someone else's words with a different accent" (in this instance, the "someone else" is patriarchal society). According to Bakhtin, one speaker can invest another's words with "expressions of doubt, indignation, irony, mockery, ridicule and the like" (Bakhtin 1984, 194–95).

10. For more on Bakhtin's dialogism in Allende's work, see Meyer 1988, 151–57.

11. Note that the English translation omits the word "silently," which I have reintroduced into the translation through the word in brackets: "Quienes la conocían atribuían esa memoria selectiva al golpe que le partió la cabeza en su juventud, pero el profesor Leal podía interpretar los pequeños signos y sospechaba que ella nada había olvidado. Simplemente no deseaba cargar con antiguos pesares, por eso no los mencionaba, anulándolos mediante el silencio. [. . .] *Silenciosamente* iba a su lado con pasos firmes en las manifestaciones callejeras" (Allende 1985ab, 36, my emphasis).

12. In contrast, Moya-Raggio 1991, 120 views Hilda's silence as indicative of oppression. Catherine Perricone agrees with my interpretation of Hilda's silence as subversive and examines how Allende silently communicates meaning to the reader through the characters' attire and selected nonverbal actions. See Perricone 1991, 90.

13. Minc 1987, 185–86 comments on Evangelina's nonsubmissive behavior. Perricone also examines this episode in terms of its number symbolism. See Perricone 1991, 88–89. Also see Frenk's excellent discussion of magical discourses (Frenk 1996, 79). This theory of the subversive power of magic once again contradicts Nelson's idea that agency is denied to working-class individuals in Allende's novels. See A. A. Nelson 2002, 214.

14. In *A Rhetoric of Irony*, Wayne C. Booth establishes and defines different categories of irony. According to Booth, the development of what he terms "stable irony" is a four-step process: (1) The reader is required to reject the literal meaning of a discourse; (2) the reader will try out alternative interpretations that are incongruous with the literal statement; (3) the reader must make a decision about the author's knowledge or beliefs; (4) the reader chooses a new meaning for the literal statement (Booth 1974, 35). Booth summarizes the mental process by which the reader concludes that there is ironic intent in the following manner: "Thus I do not reject a printed statement because of any literal untruth. I reject it because I refuse to dwell with anyone who holds this whole set of beliefs. And then, because I cannot believe that the author of the statement can be that kind of person, I am forced (through psychological and intellectual pressure which I will not even pretend to understand or explain) to make sense out of this statement by concluding that it is ironic" (Booth 1974, 35). Essentially, this is what happens to the feminist reader of Allende's *The Stories of Eva Luna*, who fails to believe that Allende could possibly subscribe to such hyperbolic portrayals of women according to notions of

stereotyping, collusion, and compensation. Similarly, in *Irony's Edge: The Theory and Politics of Irony*, Linda Hutcheon explains that irony is not simply a rhetorical tool present within a text, but rather an "event" that occurs depending upon the specific "discursive community" to which the interpreter of a text belongs. Discursive communities are groups that share certain common experiences. For example, people of the same gender or race might constitute a specific discursive community. Of course, there is much overlap between these categories, and hence one can simultaneously belong to various discursive communities. The important point is that the decision to attribute irony (or the failure to do so), despite authorial intentions, will to a large degree depend upon the discursive community to which one belongs (Hutcheon 1994, 4–18). As we shall see, the conflictual textual evidence of a simultaneously aggressive and passive female image in *The Stories of Eva Luna* is what leads the reader to interpret Allende's text ironically.

6. Symbolic Silence

1. Note that although individual stories from this collection have been translated under the title *The Youngest Doll*, this book has never been translated in its entirety. The title of the collection can be interpreted and hence translated in two ways: papel means either "paper" or "role." Consequently, Ferré's title is a perfect example of the ambiguous discourse I study in this chapter. Papel refers to the different societal roles that women are forced to occupy and simultaneously it refers to the "papers" or writing of women writers.

2. According to Todorov, any discourse that seems incoherent will invite the construction of additional, indirect meanings. Todorov defines "paradigmatic indices" as those elements of a text that cannot be understood without either reference to a grammar book or a dictionary, or that suggest associations from the collective memory (or shared knowledge of a community) to achieve their interpretation. See Todorov 1982, 30–31.

3. Wherever possible, I will cite from the English edition of Cirlot, although certain symbols only appear in the Spanish version.

4. Chevalier and Gheerbrant also discuss a series of other meanings for hair, such as virility or mourning, that seem less applicable to this particular context. See Chevalier and Gheerbrant 1996, 459–63.

5. Note that the phrase "sudando caballos" (sweating horses) is omitted from the sentence in Ferré's own English translation. I have added it back in here. The Spanish reads as follows: "Sudando caballos blancos y gaviotas que vomitan sal. Ahora empiezo a acunar entre los brazos esta masa repugnante que eras tú, Amalia y era también yo, juntas éramos las dos una sola" (Ferré 1976, 64).

6. According to Todorov, "syntagmatic" refers to the relationship between various segments of a text (utterances or assertions belonging to the same context), and syntagmatic indices can be based on either lack or excess. In the first case, if two elements of a text contradict each other, "the interpreter will be tempted to transform the meaning of one or the other" (Todorov 1982, 31). If an element is repeated (indices based on excess), it will also tend to be interpreted symbolically.

7. Note that this is my translation; unfortunately, the word "inhabit," which is key to my interpretation, is omitted in Ferré's own English translation. The original Spanish reads thus: "Como eran nueve y la tía hacía una muñeca de cada niña por año, hubo que

separar una pieza de la casa para que la *habitasen* exclusivamente las muñecas" (Ferré 1976, 10, my emphasis).

   8. Note that I add some words back into the translation (from "Although" to "force") that Ferré omitted in the English translation of the story. These words can be seen in the original Spanish: "insistió que mi promesa de dejarla bailar abarcaba el acuerdo de que no tuviéramos hijos. Me explicó que a las bailarinas una vez que salen encintas, se les ensanchan las caderas y [. . .] no pueden jamás llegar a ser bailarinas excelentes. No puede imaginarse la confusión en que esta declaración me amojó. Queriendo a María de los Angeles como la quiero, un hijo de ella era mi gran ilusión. Ud. sabe Don Fabiano que soy de origen humilde y quizás por esto siempre he tenido temor de perderla. Aunque ya sea de origen humilde no quiere decir que no tenga mi dignidad. [. . .] Pero cuando se me siguió emperrando, negándoseme, don Fabiano, al final. [. . .] La forcé carajo Don Fabiano le hice barriga a la fuerza" (Ferré 1976, 174–75). Ferré's translation appears in the bibliography under *The Youngest Doll.*

   9. Jill Albada-Jelgersma traces the fluctuating symbolic meaning of the mango in Ferré's story. Her article asserts that the mango symbolizes Carlotta, the forbidden fruit/punishment, and finally society's decaying social values. See Albada-Jelgersma 1998, 13–27.

   10. Susan Divine states that due to these contradictory voices, the only truth that can be established in the novella is that Puerto Rico was a paradise only for the rich landowners. In contrast, I argue that the contradictory voices engage the reader in a complex series of deductions that lead to the establishment of certain truths and frequently the valuing of female discourses over those of the male protagonists. See Divine 2004.

   11. Ferré 1996, 20 is the source for most of this translation. Note that I have altered Ferré's translation by translating "unos once meses" as "some eleven months," which corresponds to the Spanish version: "Nicolasito nació seis meses después de la muerte de su abuelo y unos once meses después de la muerte de su padre" (Ferré 1998, 31). In the English translation, Ferré changes "some eleven months" to "a few days," which totally alters the meaning of the passage.

   12. Note that this is my translation. Ferré has omitted this section from her own translation. The original Spanish quotation is as follows: "Pero no bien se casaron [Gloria y Nicolás] la novia salió encinta y exhibió su vergüenza a los cuatro vientos. Nicolás, en un momento de debilidad cedió a la tentación de la cama y Gloria fue una vez más la víctima de la familia" (Ferré 1998, 79).

   13. Gutiérrez Mouat points out that Hermenegildo's comments here are later contradicted by other segments of the narration, such as the relation of Elvira's return from studies in Europe, a fact that contradicts Hermenegildo's statement that the men studied abroad while the women learned how to be mothers. See Gutiérrez Mouat 1994, 283-306. Montes Garcés also touches upon some of the ideological aspects of the novel's contradictory viewpoints (Montes Garcés 2002, 131–38).

   14. "Como bien dice el dicho, sarna con gusto no pica y si pica no mortifica, y al enamorarse de mí se transformó de un día para otro, en una muchacha morigerada y decente, atenta a mi menor capricho y sumisa a mi voluntad" (Ferré 1998, 50).

   15. Todorov speaks at length about the notion of a "hierarchy of meanings" throughout discourse. Textual meanings range from literal (direct discourse that does not evoke anything beyond the literal meaning) to transparent discourse (the literal meaning is totally ignored and only the indirect meaning is taken into account). In between the two,

we find ambiguous discourse, which posits several meanings that exist simultaneously on the same level. The added meanings can refer either to the content of the utterance (the object discussed) or the subject of the utterance (it can provide additional information about the speaker) (Todorov 1982, 53–60).

16. Todorov uses the terms "head" and "chief," meaning to refer respectively to the first and second levels of meaning in ambiguous discourse (ibid., 55).

17. Sharon R. Wilson interprets this scene differently. According to Wilson, this scene symbolizes the protagonist/Amalia's rebellion against gender and class rules, for now the doll engages in unladylike behavior by lifting her skirt and visiting floors in the dollhouse other than the one assigned to her. See Wilson 2001, 143–63.

18. The English translation omits the words "but didn't speak anymore," which I have added back into the translation so that it more directly corresponds to the original Spanish, which reads thus: "Uno de los niñitos mugrientos se le acercó él le dejó esto antes de irse le dijo y puso el collar de matos y camándulas en el suelo entonces ella cogió el collar con las manos y se levantó de la esquina y regresó a la casa y desde entonces fue una esposa ejemplar *pero no volvió a hablar más*" (Ferré 1976, 123–25, my emphasis).

19. Note once again that the English version omits much of what the Spanish version tells us regarding Armantina's muteness. The original Spanish reads: "No llores Armantina te mando el pasaje seguro tú eres mi mujer [. . .] porque ella era salvaje se escapaba todo el tiempo de la casa antes de que le quebraran el espinazo y cuando se lo quebraron ya era demasiado tarde ya ella había saltado la valla había dado sin miedo su carne al blanco. [. . .] Ahora todos se acercan a la caja arrastrando los pies y yo también me acerco apretando los puños extendiendo una mano que adelgazo sobre la curva fría del aluminio entonces muequeando boqueando tascando la serreta que me parte los labios tratando de romper la boca muda" (Ferré 1976, 127–30). The English version only states: "[d]on't cry, Armantina, I'll send you the ticket, I promise, you're my wife now, God . . . now everybody draws near to the coffin: they take out their hankerchiefs to wipe the perspiration from their faces; they trail their feet diffidently; I also draw near with my fists clenched; I put out my hand to touch the cold-metal curve of the lid; all of a sudden my mouth starts working, struggling for breath, trying with all my might to speak" (Ferré 1991, 72–75).

20. Once again, this is my English translation because the published English version significantly alters the sense of the Spanish text, which reads: "Ahora los veo sentados por última vez alrededor de la mesa comiendo y bebiendo absolutamente confiados de su mano" (Ferré 1976, 122).

21. Kathleen Glenn states: "Each of the three divisions of the story—Coppelia, Sleeping Beauty and Giselle—takes its title from a famous ballet, a nonverbal text" (Glenn 1996, 209). Also see López 1983, 41-52, for an excellent discussion of this story.

22. This translation is mine, because, once again, Ferré entirely omitted this section from his English version. The original Spanish of the text reads: "Lo más que me llamó la atención fue la expresión de su cara. Parecía vaciada de todo pensamiento. *Le hablaba y no me contestaba, era como si no me estuviera escuchando [. . .] se niega a contestarme*" (Ferré 1976, 178, my emphasis).

23. This translation is mine because much of the Spanish text was omitted from the English version: "Sintió deseos de bailar. [. . .] Pensó con alivio que por primera vez iba a poder ser ella [. . .] a poder ser bailarina, aunque fuera de segunda o tercera categoría" (Ferré 1976, 179).

24. Note that once again I have slightly altered Ferré's English version of the text in order to reproduce words that appear in the original Spanish: "Guardó sus zapatillas de baile, sus túnicas de seda y sus libros de versos al fondo del ropero, y se fue apagando poco a poco como uno de los nenúfaares olvidados al fondo de la terraza" (Ferré 1976, 85).

25. Note that this is my translation. The English version reads "I was just trying to forget my troubles at home," a translation that does not strongly reflect the use of dance as a form of communication (Ferré 1995, 186). The Spanish states: "No podía adivinar que cuando yo bailaba con aquella vehemencia, no estaba cultivando ningún estilo, me estaba desahogando de las penas que sufría en mi casa" (Ferré 1997, 186).

26. Note that I have translated the last part of the final Spanish sentence ("but [. . .] household"), which is omitted in Ferré's English version. The Spanish reads: "Peor aún, era la manera como el manuscrito estaba plagado de prejuicios feministas. Isabel quería estar a tono con los tiempos, pero sus esfuerzos eran patéticos. El feminismo era la maldición del siglo XX. [. . .] ¿Estaría escribiendo Isabel la novela para demostrarle que en la casa de la laguna ella estaba al timón? En el mundo de la ficción, ella imponía sus opiniones, pero en el mundo real no podía ser así. Como jefe de la familia su deber era permanecer a la cabeza del hogar" (Ferré 1997, 122–23).

27. This is my translation. Ferré replaces the line "Si se quedaba inédita, sería todavía más perfecta, porque permanecería una obra ideal" (Ferré 1997, 201) [If it remained unpublished, it would be even more perfect, because it would remain an ideal work] with the following: "What mattered was that it existed, that it had been born and could compete with the rest of creation" (Ferré 1995, 88).

28. See Gutiérrez Mouat 1994, 286 for this interpretation: "Para Ferré estas prescripciones tradicionales, transmitidas por la familia, son homólogas a las imposiciones alienantes de la metrópolis colonial." [For Ferré, these traditional precriptions, transmitted by the family, are homologous to the alienating impositions of the colonial metropolis (my translation)]. Also see Palmer-López's study on the Puerto Rican Generation of 1970, in which she discusses the relationship between Ferré's work, feminism, and anticolonialism, as well as her explicit role in the Puerto Rican independence movement (Palmer-López 2002).

29. The entire quotation in Spanish is as follows: "El conflicto político puertorriqueño es un espejo convexo en otro sentido: en él se reproduce también el conflicto de la mujer, escindida entre lo que es y lo que diariamente escucha que debería ser, porque las instituciones sociales (la patria en el primer caso, la familia en el segundo), se beneficiarían de ello. Por eso en *Maldito amor* el colonialismo de estado se encuentra emparentado a lo que podría llamarse el colonialismo de la mujer, que vive una vida fragmentada y dependiente del orden patriarcal. Por eso la isla es descrita a menudo bajo una luz femenina y poética." (Ferré 1990, 109–10).

30. Note that the English translation cites the poem in Spanish. This is my translation.

7. PARODIC SILENCE

1. In the past, parody, generally understood as imitation of another work, was always associated with ridicule or satire, whereas, as Linda Hutcheon points out, "unlike what is more traditionally regarded as parody, the modern form does not always permit one of the texts to fare better or worse than the other. It is the fact that they differ that

this parody emphasizes and indeed, dramatizes" (Hutcheon 1985, 31).

2. See Monet-Viera 2004 and Sánchez Flavian 2004 (who studies *Like Water for Chocolate* as a parody of the male bildungsroman) for studies that focus on parody from a different angle.

3. See Bilbija 1996; Bird 1999; Glenn 1994; Grant 1995; Ibsen 1995; Johnson 2002; Lillo and Sarfat-Arnaud 1994; Marquet 1997; Monet-Viera 2004; Potvin 1995; Price 2005; Valdés 1996; and Zapata 1997 for this debate.

4. Also see Modleski 1984. Modleski analyzes gothic romance, soap operas, and Harlequin romance novels.

5. For an interesting interpretation of the role of John Brown in the novel as "gringo scientist," see Hoeg 1997, 112–27.

6. Note that the original Spanish states that Tita "no encontraba palabras para expresar lo que se estaba cocinando en su interior" (Esquivel 1989, 108). The word "cocinando" is translated as "seething" in the published English version (Esquivel 1992, 108), but literally means "cooking," a meaning which has added significance within the context of the novel.

7. Escaja 2002 provides an interesting analysis of how the novel employs Foucault's concept of territories of sexual confinement, such as the brothel, insane asylum, and psychiatrist's chair. Escaja shows how Tita subverts and rebels against these elements of bourgeois repression.

8. In addition to Pedro and Tita, other characters communicate through gesture. For example, Mama Elena alienates a series of cooks through her gestures. In one case the chef was "[a] deaf mute. She put up with it for fifteen days but she left when Mama Elena told her in signs that she was an idiot" (Esquivel 1989, 136).

9. Fernández-Levin 1996 uses Mircea Eliade's categories to study in detail the conversion of Tita's kitchen into a sacred space. Her analysis shows how repetition, Tita's goddesslike behavior, magical or mythical elements, chronological negation, and Tita's empowerment to control lives through the food she cooks create the cooking ritual. Clara Ramón-Odio also notes the ritualistic nature of cooking. See Ramón-Odio 1996, 44.

10. Tony Spanos notes that in the novel, the kitchen is a sacred space of creation and rebellion from which Tita ultimately controls her own destiny through her recipes (Spanos 1995, 29–36).

11. Salkjelsvik 1999 shows how the cooking recipe is employed in the novel as a subversive discourse that is constantly in flux and that is opposed to other fixed and unchangeable discourses in the novel, such a Dr. Brown's chemical formula and Manuel Antonio Carreño's *Manual de urbanidad y buenas maneras*, cited several times in the text.

12. Dobrian 1996, 57–62 discusses other parodic elements in *Like Water for Chocolate*.

13. See Fox-Anderson 2000–01 for a study of the magical dimension of the novel through its employment of alchemy.

14. For a discussion of how some of these paratextual elements function to create meanings in *The Law of Love*, see Bados-Ciria 1996, 38–42 (who discusses the role of opera and dance within the novel); M. González 1996, 43–47; and Rodríguez-Vivaldi 2003, 25–32.

15. See Ross 1979, 306–7.

16. Ryan Prout also discusses the use of science fiction elements in *The Law of Love* and how they contributed to the novel's negative reception. See Prout 2000, 43–54.

17. Perricone also notes that this gender fluidity negates the traditional male aggressor / female victim dichotomy of patriarchal fiction (Perricone 1999, 298).

18. "Azucena's jaws had to open much farther than usual to receive Teo's tongue in her mouth. Her dry, wrinkled lips had to stretch, though they were aided in this by saliva from her astral companion. Her leg muscles had neither the strength nor the flexibility required for the act of love, but nearly miraculously, they acquired them in short order" (Esquivel 1996, 190).

19. Ibsen 1995, 13 notes a similar role reversal between Pedro and Tita in *Like Water for Chocolate*.

8. Cultural Silence

1. Saldívar Hull states: "The feminism of the 1970s simply did not address the situations of working-class and peasant women in Mexico and other Third World countries.... In the 1980s, however, the Women's Movement made a huge impact on working-class women when feminist activists went into the factories to discuss women's specific problems in the workplace. The tremors that reverberated from this new alliance between working-class, peasant, and 'traditional' feminists ironically came as a result of the 1985 earthquake in Mexico City.... The Mexican usage of the *popular [feminismo]* underscores what Lynn Stephen ... calls 'common marginalization.' ... The invisible 'life of work' that Chicanas and Mexicans share on both sides of the Mexico/U.S. border brings to light a new formulation of Chicana feminism.... Cisneros identified with a group of Chicana 'popular' feminists who struggled to change the literary scene and the lives of less privileged women around them" (Saldívar-Hull 2000, 104–5).

2. An example of this type of passage is the section "Hips" from *The House on Mango Street*, in which Rachel, Lucy, Esperanza, and Nenny engage in a rhyming competition centered around the theme of hips. According to various critics, in this process, the girls arrive at an implicit evaluation of the role hips play in a woman's life. See Saldívar-Hull 2000, 97–98, where she discusses how the girls celebrate their ability to play with words and various languages to produce an evaluation of the female body/sexuality as something positive. Also see Doyle 1994, 15, who similarly views the girls' improvisation of songs about hips as a sign of their ability to "write beyond the ending of the cultural scripts confining the women around them, rejecting that old song that Nenny repeats." This is also a good example of how the girls, in a postmodern vein, "perform" their gender, an aspect of Cisneros works that I discuss later in this chapter. Finally, see Mary Louise Pratt (1977), who also disccusses the applicability of Labov's theory and the notion of evaluation to literary discourse.

3. See Sánchez 1995, 237, where he speaks of Ruthie as "only one of many symbols in *The House on Mango Street* of the trapped female."

4. Haryette Mullen states that Cisneros's text *Woman Hollering Creek* "includes frequent references to the specificity and difference coded into any and all languages; to the violence of inadequacy of translation and interpretation; to the translator's and by extension writer's unfaithful role of betrayer of the culture's inside secrets and to the existence of encoded messages which are more accessible to readers familiar with various insider codes and cryptographic devices employed in the text" (Mullen 1996, 3). Also see Carroll and Maher 1997; Doyle 2004; Figueroa 2000; Fiore 1994; Saldívar-Hull 2000; and Thomson 1994, all of whom discuss the use of cultural symbols.

5. Other sources claim that since Popo and Ixta were from feuding families, the gods were angry with their love and punished them by causing Princess Ixta to fall ill and die. See M. Castillo.

6. D. Castillo (1992, 260–62) alludes to this phenomenon when she discusses the bilingual/bicultural texts of Denise Chávez and Maxine Hong Kingston: "When two languages and two cultures are involved, this double-voicing is forced into the foreground, making it somewhat easier to mark in the bicultural work the textual site of the functioning of translation-as-violation. We could call the study of these interstices semiology or phantasiology, or, following Nicolas Abraham and María Torok, cryptonomy. . . . I choose to begin with the Whorfian hypothesis: briefly, that the perspective of each individual language determines (and over-determines) our view of reality. . . . From their very different perspectives, Whorf and Abraham and Torok join Derrida in emphasizing the function of what Whorf calls the covert—in other terms, the resistances to analysis which in their obstructiveness serve to situate evaluation." Thus, Castillo also recognizes the "covert" or "silent" aspect of bilingualism.

7. Although there are other Chicana writers who use some of these techniques, these are not characteristics we have observed in the Latin American writers examined in the previous chapters.

8. For more information on the relationship between the bildungsroman and Cisneros's work see Bolaki 2005 and Gutiérrez-Jones 1993.

9. See Doyle 1994 for a discussion of how *The House on Mango Street* constitutes a *Kunstlerroman* that avoids the closure of the traditional marital plot. Doyle uses Rachel DuPlessis's ideas in her book *Writing Beyond the Ending*.

10. Although the general critical consensus has been that Cisneros posits a postmodern sense of identity in her works, there are critics who disagree, such as Juan Daniel Busch. See Busch 1994, 123–34.

References

Acosta-Belén, E. 1986a. "Puerto Rican Women in Culture, History and Society." In *The Puerto Rican Woman: Perspectives on Culture, History, and Society*, ed. E. Acosta-Belén, 1–29. New York: Praeger.

———, ed. 1986b. *The Puerto Rican Woman: Perspectives on Culture, History, and Society*. New York: Praeger.

Acosta Cruz, M. I. 1990. "Historia, ser e identidad femenina en 'El collar de camándulas' y *Maldito amor* de Rosario Ferré." *Chasqui*: 19, no. 2:23–31.

Adams, M. I. 1975. *Three Authors of Alienation: Bombal, Onetti, Carpentier*. Austin: University of Texas Press.

Agosín, M. 1983. *Las desterradas del paraíso, protagonistas en la narrativa de María Luisa Bombal*. New York: Senda Nueva de Ediciones.

———. 1984. "La mimesis de la interioridad: 'Soledad de la sangre' de Marta Brunet y 'El árbol' de María Luisa Bombal." *Neophilologus* 68:380–88.

———. 1985. "Espacio y lenguaje feminocéntrico en tres obras de María Luisa Bombal." In *El Cono Sur: Dinámica y dimensión de su literatura*, ed. R. S. Minc, 161–67.

———. 1986. "Marta Brunet: A Literary Biography." *Revista Interamericana de Bibliografía / Inter-American Review of Bibliography* 36:452–59.

———. 1987. *Scraps of Life: Chilean Arpilleras*. Trans. C. Franzen. Trenton, NJ: The Red Sea Press.

———. 1993. "Isabel Allende: *La casa de los espíritus*." In *Las hacedoras: Mujer, imagen, escritura*, 143–158. Santiago: Cuarto Propio.

Ahern, M., ed. and trans. 1988. *A Rosario Castellanos Reader*. Austin: University of Texas Press.

———. 1994. "Domestic Space as Creative Forum." *Latin American Literature and Arts* 48:23–26.

Ahmed, S., ed. 2000. *Transformations: Thinking Through Feminism*. London: Routledge.

Albada-Jelgersma, J. 1998. "El mangó: Función poética de un signo en 'El regalo' de Rosario Ferré." *Anclajes: Revista del Instituto de Análisis Semiótico* 2, no. 2:13–27.

Allende, I. 1985a. *De amor y de sombra*. Buenos Aires: Editorial Sudamericana.

———. 1985b. *La casa de los espíritus*. Buenos Aires: Editorial Sudamericana.

———. 1986. *The House of the Spirits*. Trans. M. Boden. New York: Bantam Books.

———. 1988. *Of Love and Shadows*. Trans. M. S. Peden. New York: Bantam Books.

———. 1989. *Cuentos de Eva Luna*. Barcelona: Plaza & Janés.

———. 1991. *The Stories of Eva Luna*. Trans. M. S. Peden. New York: Bantam Books.
Alvarez, M. A. 1996. "El discurso / los discursos. Tradición / subversión en la escritura de Laura Esquivel." *Celehis: Revista del Centro de Letras Hispanoamericanas* 5, no. 6–7:5–11.
Amago, S. 2000. "Isabel Allende and the Postmodern Literary Tradition: A Reconsideration of *Cuentos de Eva Luna*." *Latin American Literary Review* 28, no. 56:43–60.
Amorós, A. 1968. *Sociología de una novela rosa*. Madrid: Taurus.
Andalzúa, G. 1999. *Borderlands La Frontera: The New Mestiza*. 3rd ed. San Francisco: Aunt Lute Books.
Anderson, H. 1983. "Rosario Castellanos and the Structures of Power." In *Contemporary Women Authors of Latin America*, eds. D. Meyer and M. F. Olmos, 22–32. Brooklyn, NY: Brooklyn College Press.
Ardener, E. 1975a. "Belief and the Problem of Women." In *Perceiving Women*, ed. S. Ardener, 1–17. London: Malaby Press.
———. 1975b. "The Problem Revisted." In *Perceiving Women*, ed. S. Ardener, 19–27. London: Malaby Press.
Ardener, S., ed. 1975. *Perceiving Women*. London: Malaby Press.
Auerbach, N. 1978. *Communities of Women: An Idea in Fiction*. Cambridge, MA: Harvard University Press.
Bados-Ciria, C. 1996. "*La ley del amor*, de Laura Esquivel: ¿Por qué la ópera, el danzón y el comic?" *Revista de Literatura Mexicana Contemporánea* 1, no. 3:38–42.
Bakhtin, M. 1981. *The Dialogic Imagination*, ed. M. Holquist. Trans. C. Emerson and M. Holquist. Austin: University of Texas Press.
———. 1984. *Problems of Dostoevsky's Poetics*, ed. C. Emerson. Minneapolis: University of Minnesota Press.
Baldez, L. 2002. *Why Women Protest: Women's Movements in Chile*. Cambridge, MA: Cambridge University Press.
Barak, J. 1998. "Navigating the Swamp: Fact and Fiction in Rosario Ferré's *The House on the Lagoon*." *Journal of the Midwest Modern Language Association* 31, no. 2:207–18.
Barr, M. S., ed. 2000. *Future Females: The Next Generation; New Voices and Velocities in Feminist Science Fiction*. Lanham, MD: Rowman and Littlefield.
Barrett, M. 1980. *Women's Oppression Today: Problems in Marxist Feminist Analysis*. London: Verso.
Barthes, R. 1974. *S/Z*. New York: Hill and Wang.
Bartholomew, K. 1993. "Name and Character in Allende's *La casa de los espíritus*." *Selecta: Journal of the Pacific Northwest* 14:83–87.
Bastos, M. L. 1985. "Relectura de *La última niebla*, de María Luisa Bombal." *Revista Iberoamericana* 51, no. 132–33:557–64.
Bautista, G. 1989. "'El realismo mágico en *La casa de los espíritus*." *Discurso Literario* 6, no. 2:299–310.
Baxter, J. 2003. *Positioning Gender in Discourse: A Feminist Methodology*. London: Palgrave.
Baym, N. 1997. "The Madwoman and Her Languages: Why I Don't Do Feminist Theory." In *Feminisms: An Anthology of Literary Theory and Criticism*, eds. Robyn R. Warhol and Diane Price Herndl, 279–92. New Brunswick, NJ: Rutgers University Press.

Bennett, C. 1998. "The Other and Other-Worldly: The Function of Magic in Isabel Allende's *La casa de los espíritus*." *Bulletin of Hispanic Studies* 25, no. 1 (1998): 357–65.

Berg, M. G. 1998. "The Short Stories of Marta Brunet." *Monographic Review / Revista Monográfica* 4:194–206.

Bernal, A. A. 1984. "Notas sobre la evolución de la mujer en los cuentos de Marta Brunet." *Chiricú* 3:19–25.

Besemeres, M. 2006. "Language and Emotional Experience: The Voice of Translingual Memoir." In *Bilingual Minds: Emotional Experience, Expression and Representation* ed. A. Pavlenko. 34–58. Clevedon, England: Multilingual Matters.

Bianchi, S. 1985. "María Luisa Bombal o una difícil travesía." *Atenea* 451:175–92.

Bilbija, K. 1996. "Spanish American Women Writers: Simmering Identity Over a Low Fire." *Studies in Twentieth Century Literature* 20, no. 1:147–65.

Bird, R. J. 1999. "Ausencia y arquetipos en tres novels mexicanas contemporáneas." *Revista de Literatura Mexicana Contemporánea* 4, no. 10:15–19.

Bolaki, S. 2005. "'The Bridge We Call Home': Crossing and Bridging Spaces in Sandra Cisneros's *The House on Mango Street*." *eSharp: Electronic Social Sciences, Humanities, and Arts Review for Postgraduates* 5:1–14.

Bombal, M. L. 1988. *La última niebla / La amortajada*. Barcelona: Biblioteca de Bolsillo.

Booth, W. C. 1974. *A Rhetoric of Irony*. Chicago: University of Chicago Press.

Boschetto, S. M. 1989. "Dialéctica metatextual y sexual en *La casa de los espíritus* de Isabel Allende." *Hispania* 72, no. 3:526–32.

Boyle, C. 1993. "The Fragile Perfection of the Shrouded Rebellion (Re-reading Passivity in María Luisa Bombal)." In *Women Writers in Twentieth-Century Spain and Spanish America*, ed. C. Davies, 27–42. Lewiston, NY: Edwin Mellen Press.

———. 1995. "Frameworks and Contexts in *La casa de los espíritus*: A Chronicle of Teaching." *Journal of Latin American Cultural Studies* 4, no.1:105–12.

Brackett, V. 2005. *A Home in the Heart: The Story of Sandra Cisneros*. Greensboro, NC: Morgan Reynolds Publishers.

Braun, D. M. 1994. "Silence and Dream as Textual Strategies in Selected Works of Sor Juana Inés de la Cruz, María Luisa Bombal and Angeles Mastretta." PhD diss., Flordia State University.

Brunet, M. 1962. *Obras completas de Marta Brunet*. Santiago: Zig-Zag.

———. 1997. *María Nadie*. Santo Domingo: Pehuén.

Brunk, B. L. 2001. "*En otras voces*: Multiple Voices in Sandra Cisneros' *The House on Mango Street*." *Hispanófila* 133:137–50.

Busch, J. D. 1994. "Self-Baptizing the Wicked Esperanza: Chicana Feminism and Cultural Contact in *The House on Mango Street*." *Mester* 22–23, nos. 1–2:123–34.

Bustos Fernández, M. J. 1994. "Subversión de la autoridad narrativa en *Maldito amor* de Rosario Ferré." *Chasqui* 23, no. 2:22–29.

Butler, J. 1999. *Gender Trouble: Feminism and the Subversion of Identity*. New York: Routledge.

Camacho-Gingerich, A. 1992. "La mujer ante la dictadura en las dos primeras novelas de Isabel Allende." *Discurso: Revista de Estudios Iberoamericanos* 9, no. 2:13–25.

Cameron, D. 1995. "Rethinking Language and Gender Studies: Some Issues for the 1990s." In *Language & Gender*, ed. S. Mills, 31–44. London: Longman.

———, ed. 1998. *The Feminist Critique of Language: A Reader*. London: Routledge.

Cammarata, Joan F. 1996. "*Como agua para chocolate*: Gastronomía erótica, mágicorrealismo culinario." *Explicación de Textos Literarios* 25, no. 1:87–103.

Cárdenas, D. 1980. "María Luisa Bombal – El árbol." *Kanina: Revista de Artes y Letras de la Universidad de Costa Rica* 4, no. 1:55–59.

Carreño Bolívar, R. 2002. "Una escena crítica: Estereotipos e ideologías de género en la recepción crítica de Marta Brunet y María Luisa Bombal." *Anales de Literatura Chilena* 3:43–51.

Carroll, M., and Susan Maher. 1997. "'A Las Mujeres': Cultural Context and the Process of Maturity in Sandra Cisneros' *Woman Hollering Creek*." *North Dakota Quarterly* 64, no. 1:70–80.

Carullo, S. 1997. "Fetichismo, magia amorosa y amor erótico en dos cuentos de Isabel Allende." *Texto Crítico* 3, no. 4–5 (1997):125–32.

Carvalho, S. E. de. 1994. "Narration and Distance in Isabel Allende's Novels and in *Cuentos de Eva Luna*." *Antípodas* 6–7:55–62.

Castellanos, R. 1964. *Los convidados de agosto*. Mexico City: Biblioteca Era.

———. 1971. *Álbum de familia*. Mexico City: Joaquín Mortiz, Serie del volador.

———. 1988a. "Cooking Lesson." Trans. M. Ahern. In *A Rosario Castellanos Reader*, ed. M. Ahern, 207–215. Austin: University of Texas Press.

———. 1988b. "Fleeting Friendships." Trans. L. Salas. In *A Rosario Castellanos Reader*, ed. M. Ahern, 144–54. Austin: University of Texas Press.

———. 1988c. "Language as an Instrument of Domination." Trans. M. Ahern. In *A Rosario Castellanos Reader*, ed. Maureen Ahern, 250–253. Austin: University of Texas Press.

———. 1988d. "The Widower Román." Trans. R. Peacock. In *A Rosario Castellanos Reader*, ed. M. Ahern, 155–206. Austin: University of Texas Press.

———. 1995a. "La imagen de la mujer." In *Mujer que sabe latín*, 16–21. Mexico City: Fondo de cultura económica.

———. 1995b. "Notas al margen: El lenguaje como instrumento de dominio." In *Mujer que sabe latín*, 171–175. Mexico City: Fondo de cultura económica.

———. 1995c. La participación de la mujer mexicana en la educación formal." In *Mujer que sabe latín*, 22–40. Mexico City: Fondo de cultura económica.

———. 1996. *Rito de iniciación*. Mexico City: Alfaguara.

Castillo, D. 1992. *Talking Back: Toward a Latin American Feminist Criticism*. Ithaca, NY: Cornell University Press.

Castillo, M. "Iztacchihuatl and Popocatepetl" *www.uv.mx/popularte/ingles/scriptphplen.php?&len=In*.

Castro-Klarén, S. 1985. "La crítica literaria feminista y la escritora en América Latina." In *La sartén por el mango: Encuentro de escritoras latinoamericanas*, eds. Patricia Elena González and Eliana Ortega, 27–46. Río Piedras, PR: Ediciones Huracán, 1985.

———. 1989. "The Novelness of a Possible Poetics for Women." In *Cultural and Historical Grounding for Hispanic and Luso-Brazilian Feminist Literary Criticism*, ed. H. Vidal,

95–105. Literature and Human Rights, vol. 4. Minneapolis: Institute for the Study of Ideologies and Literature.

Chancer, L. S., and B. X. Watkins. 2006. *Gender, Race, and Class: An Overview*. Malden, MA: Blackwell Publishing.

Chaverri, A. 1997a. "*Como agua para chocolate*: Transgresión de límites / reinvindicación de espacios." *Taller de Letras* 25:91–116.

———. 1997b. "Estalla el silencio: Ahora en carne altiva." *Ancora: Suplemento Cultural de la Nación*. http://www.nacion.com ancora/1997/diciembre/14/ancora13.html.

Cheung, K. 1993. *Articulate Silences: Hisaye Yamamoto, Maxine Hong Kingston, Joy Kogawa*. Ithaca, NY: Cornell University Press.

Chevalier, J., and A. Gheerbrant. 1996. *The Penguin Dictionary of Symbols*. Trans. J. Buchanan-Brown. London: Penguin Books.

Chuchryk, P. 1994. "From Dictatorship to Democracy: The Women's Movement in Chile." In *The Women's Movement in Latin America: Participation and Democracy*, ed. J. S. Jaquette, 65–107. Boulder, CO: Westview Press.

Cirlot, J. E. 1971. *A Dictionary of Symbols*. Trans. J. Sage. New York: Barnes and Nobles.

———. 1978. *Diccionario de símbolos*. Barcelona: Editorial Labor.

Cisneros, S. 1991a. *The House on Mango Street*. New York: Vintage Press.

———. 1991b. *Woman Hollering Creek*. New York: Random House.

———. 2002. *Caramelo*. New York: Alfred A. Knopf.

Cixous, H. 1974. "First Names of No One." Reprinted in *The Hélène Cixous Reader*, ed. S. Sellers, 27–33. New York: Routledge, 1994.

———. 1997. "The Laugh of the Medusa," In *Feminisms: An Anthology of Literary Theory and Criticism*, 347–62. 2nd ed. New Brunswick, NJ: Rutgers University Press.

Coddou, M. 1989. "*La casa de los espíritus* y la historia." *Literatura Chilena: Creación y Crítica* 13, no. 1–4:89–100.

Craft, L. J. 1996. "Testinovela / Telenovela: Latin American Popular Culture and Women's Narrative." *Indiana Journal of Hispanic Literatures* 8:197–210.

Cranny-Francis, A. 1990. *Feminist Fiction: Feminist Uses of Generic Fiction*. Oxford: Basil Blackwell / Polity.

Cutting, R. M. 2003. "Closure in Sandra Cisneros's 'Woman Hollering Creek.'" In *The Postmodern Short Story: Forms and Issues*, eds. Farhat Iftekharrudin, Joseph Boyden, Mary Rohrberger, and Jaie Claudet, 65–76. Westport (Connecitucut): Praeger.

Debicki, A. 1971. "Structure, Imagery, and Experience in María Luisa Bombal's 'The Tree.'" *Studies in Short Fiction* 8: 123–29.

DeKoven, M. 2006. "Jouissance, Cyborgs, and Companion Species: Feminist Experiment." *PMLA* 121, no. 5:1690–96.

Delorey, D. 1996. "Parsing the Female Sentence: The Paradox of Containment in Virginia Woolf's Narratives." In *Ambiguous Discourse: Feminist Narratology and British Women Writers, ed.* K. Mezei, 93–108. Chapel Hill: University of North Carolina Press.

DeLuise, D. 1993. "The Work of the Woman Writer: From Inside to Outside in 'The Final Mist.'" *Arkansas Quarterly: A Journal of Criticism* 2, no. 2:134–41.

Disselkoen, I. M. 1989. "*De La última niebla* y *La amortajada* a *La brecha*." *Nuevo Texto Crítico* 2, no. 4:69–78.

Divine, S. 2004. "La meta-historia de Puerto Rico en *Maldito amor* de Rosario Ferré." *Divergencias: Revista de estudios lingüísticos y literarios* 2, no. 2:73–80.

Dobrian, S. L. 1996. "Romancing the Cook: Parodic Consumption of Popular Romance Myths in *Como agua para chocolate*." *Latin American Literary Review* 24, no. 48:56–66.

Doyle, J. 1994. "More Room of Her Own: Sandra Cisneros's *The House on Mango Street*." *MELUS* 19, no. 4:5–35.

———. 2004. "Faces of the Virgin in Sandra Cisneros's *Woman Hollering Creek*." In *Things of the Spirit: Women Writers Constructing Spirituality*, ed. K. K. Groover, 256–83. Notre Dame, IN: University of Notre Dame Press.

Dupláa, C. 1989. "La voz femenina frente al discurso patriarcal en *La casa de los espíritus*." *Foro Literario: Revista de Literatura y Lenguaje* 11, no. 11:19–27.

Eliade, M. 1958. *Rites and Symbols of Initiation: The Mysteries of Birth and Rebirth*. Putnam, CT: Spring Publications.

Elliot, J. 2006. "The Currency of Feminist Theory." *PMLA* 121, no. 5:1697–1703.

Escaja, T. 2002. "Alteración del espacio sociosexual: *Como agua para chocolate* y la voluntad de saber." *Ciberletras* 8: n.p.

Escandón, C. R. 1994. "Women's Movement, Feminism, and Mexican Politics." In *The Women's Movement in Latin America: Participation and Democracy*, ed. J.S. Jaquette. Boulder, CO: Westview Press.

Espadas, E. 1989. "Isabel Allende's *La casa de los espíritus*: Between the Chronicle, the Testimonial, and the Love Story." *MACLAS: Latin American Essays* 3:133–40.

Esquivel, L. 1989. *Como agua para chocolate*. New York: Anchor Books.

———. 1992. *Like Water for Chocolate*. Trans. C. Christensen and T. Christensen. New York: Anchor Books.

———. 1995. *La ley del amor*. New York: Crown Publishers.

———. 1996. *The Law of Love*. Trans. M. S. Peden. New York: Three Rivers Press.

———. 2000. *Between Two Fires: Intimate Writings on Life, Love, Food & Flavor*. Trans. S. Lytle. New York: Random House.

———. 2001a. *Swift as Desire*. New York: Crown Publishers.

———. 2001b. *Tan veloz como el deseo*. New York: Anchor Books.

Felski, R. 2003. *Literature after Feminism*. Chicago: University of Chicago Press.

Fernández-Levin, R. 1996. "Ritual and 'Sacred Space' in Laura Esquivel's *Like Water for Chocolate*." *Confluencia: Revista Hispánica de Cultura y Literatura* 12, no. 1:106–20.

Ferré, R. 1976. *Papeles de Pandora*. Mexico City: Joaquín Mortiz.

———. 1990. *El coloquio de las perras*. Harrisonburg, VA: Editorial Cultural.

———. 1991. *The Youngest Doll*. Lincoln: University of Nebraska Press.

———. 1995. *The House on the Lagoon*. New York: Plume Books.

———. 1996. *Sweet Diamond Dust and Other Stories*. New York: Plume Books.

———. 1997. *La casa de la laguna*. New York: Vintage Español.

———. 1998. *Maldito amor y otros cuentos*. New York: Vintage Español.

Ferrer, N. V. 1986. "Feminism and its Influence on Women's Organizations in Puerto Rico." In *The Puerto Rican Woman: Perspectives on Culture, History, and Society*, ed. E. Acosta-Belén, 75–87. New York: Praeger, 1986.

Figueroa, R. 2000. "Ojos de chicana: Mitos mexicanos en la obra de Sandra Cisneros Garro." In *Pensamiento y crítica: Los discursos de la cultura hoy*, eds. Javier Durán, Rosaura Hernández Monroy, and Manuel F. Medina, 389–400. East Lansing (Michigan): Michigan State University Press.

Fiore, T. 1994. "Crossing and Recrossing 'Woman Hollering Creek.'" *Prospero: Rivista di culture anglo-germaniche* 1:61–75.

Fiscal, M. R. 1979. "La mujer en la narrativa de Rosario Castellanos." *Texto Crítico* 5, no. 15:133–53.

Fishburn, E. 1995. "'Dios anda en los pucheros: Feminist Openings in Some Late Stories by Rosario Castellanos." *Bulletin of Hispanic Studies* 72, no. 1:97–110.

Fishman, P. 1998. "Conversational Insecurity." In *The Feminist Critique of Language: A Reader*, ed. D. Cameron, 253–58. London: Routledge.

Foss, K. A., S. K. Foss, and C. L. Griffin, eds. 1999. *Feminist Rhetorical Theories*. Thousand Oaks, CA: Sage Publications.

Fox-Anderson, C. 2000. "Mysterium coniunctionis: La boda alquímica de Tita y Pedro en *Como agua para chocolate: Una novela de entregas mensuales con recetas, amores y remedies caseros*." *Explicación de Textos Literarios* 29, no. 2:92–103.

Francescato, M. P. 1980. "Transgresión y aperturas en los cuentos de Rosario Castellanos." In *Homenaje a Rosario Castellanos*, ed. M. Ahern, 115–20. Valencia: Albatros.

Franco, J. 1992. "Going Public: Reinhabiting the Private." In *On Edge: The Crisis of Contemporary Latin American Culture*, ed. George Yúdice, Jean Franco, and Juan Flores, 65–83. Minneapolis: University of Minnesota Press.

Freedman, J. 2001. *Feminism*. London: Open University Press.

Frenk, S. 1996. "The Wandering Text: Situating the Narratives of Isabel Allende." In *Latin American Women's Writing: Feminist Readings in Theory and Crisis*, ed. Anny Brooksbank Jones and Catherine Davies, 66–84. Oxford: Clarendon Press.

Furman, N. 1985. "The Politics of Language: Beyond the Gender Principle?" In *Making a Difference: Feminist Literary Criticism* ed. Gayle Greene and Coppélia Kahn, 59–79. London: Methuen.

Furnival, C. 1990. "Confronting Myths of Oppression: The Short Stories of Rosario Castellanos." In *Knives and Angels: Women Writers in Latin America*, ed. S. Bassnett, 52–73. London: Zed Books Ltd.

Gant-Britton, L. 2000. "Mexican Women and Chicanas Enter Futuristic Fiction." In *Future Females: The Next Generation; New Voices and Velocities in Feminist Science Fiction Criticism*, ed. M. S. Barr, 261–276. Lanham, MD: Rowman and Littlefield.

García, K. 1990. "Comunicación y silencio en *Los recuerdos del porvenir*, de Elena Garro." *Selecta: Journal of the Pacific Northwest Council on Foreign Languages* 11:97–101.

García-Corrales, G. 2000. "Silencio y resistencia en *Los vigilantes* de Diamela Eltit." *Monographic Review / Revista Monográfica* 16:368–81.

García-Johnson, R. 1994. "The Struggle for Space: Feminism and Freedom in *The House of the Spirits*." 48, no. 1:184–92.

Geldrich-Leffman, H. 1992. "Marriage in the Short Stories of Rosario Castellanos." *Chasqui: Revista de Literatura Latinoamericana* 21, no. 1:27–38.

Genette, G. 1982. *Palimpsestes: La littérature au second degré*. Paris: Seuil.

Glenn, K. 1994. "Postmodern Parody and Culinary-Narrative Art in Laura Esquivel's *Como agua para chocolate.*" *Chasqui: Revista de Literatura Latinoamericana* 23, no. 2:39–47.

———. 1996. "Text and Countertext in Rosario Ferré's 'Sleeping Beauty.'" *Studies in Short Fiction* 33, no. 2:207–18.

Gligo, A. 1985. *María Luisa*. Santiago: Editorial Andrés Bello.

Gold, J. 1990. "Feminine Space and Discourse of Silence: Yolanda Oreamuno, Elena Poniatowska and Luisa Valenzuela." In *In the Feminine Mode: Essays on Hispanic Women Writers*, ed. N. Valis and C. Maier, 195–203. Lewisburg, PA: Bucknell University Press.

Goldberg, P. L. 2000. "Los silencios contados: The Force of Absence and the Articulation of Silence in Margo Glantz's *Las genealogías* and Marjorie Agosín's *Sagrada Memoria: Reminiscencias de una niña judía en Chile*." *Monographic Review / Revista Monográfica* 16:315–26.

González, A. 1980. "La soledad y los patrones del dominio en la cuentística de Rosario Castellanos." In *Homenaje a Rosario Castellanos*, ed. M. Ahern, 107–113. Valencia: Albatros.

González, M. I. 1996. "El efecto de la intertextualidad en la invención del mundo narrativo en *La ley del amor* de Laura Esquivel." *Revista de Literatura Mexicana Contemporánea* 1, no. 3:43–47.

Grant, A. S. 1995. "La mujer-texto en *Como agua para chocolate*." *Filología y Lingüística* 21, no. 1:47–54.

Greene, G., and C. Kahn. 1985. "Feminist Scholarship and the Social Construction of Women." In *Making a Difference: Feminist Literary Criticism*, ed. G. Greene and C. Kahn, 1–36. London: Methuen.

Gregson, I. 2004. *Postmodern Literature*. London: Oxford University Press.

Griffin, S. E. 1997. "Resistance and Reinvention in Sandra Cisneros' *Woman Hollering Creek*." In *Ethnicity and the American Short Story*, ed. J. Brown, 85–96. New York: Garland.

Gubar, S. 2006. "Feminism Inside Out." *PMLA* 121, no. 5:1711–16.

Guerra-Cunningham, L. 1980. *La narrativa de María Luisa Bombal: Una visión de la existencia femenina*. Madrid: Playor.

———. 1984. "Tensiones paradójicas de la feminidad en la narrativa de Rosario Ferré." *Chasqui* 13, no. 2–3:13–25.

———. 1987a. "Entre la sumisión y la irreverencia." In *Escribir en los bordes: Congreso internacional de literatura femenina latinoamericana*, ed. Carmen Berenguer et al., 21–27. Santiago: Cuarto propio.

———. 1987b. "Silencios, disidencias y claudicaciones: Los problemas teóricos de la nueva crítica feminista." In *Escribir en los bordes: Congreso internacional de literatura femenina latinoamericana*, ed. Carmen Berenguer et al., 73–83. Santiago: Cuarto propio.

———. 1990. "Las sombras de la escritura: Hacia una teoría de la producción literaria de la mujer latinoamericana." In *Cultural and Historical Grounding for Hispanic and Luso-Brazilian Feminist Literary Criticism*, ed. H. Vidal, 129–164. Literature and Human Rights, vol. 4. Minneapolis: Institute for the Study of Ideologies and Literature.

———. 1995. *La mujer fragmentada: Historias de un signo*. Santiago: Cuarto propio.

Guerrero, E. 2000. "The Mute Storyteller: Pedro Páramo and Silence in the Aftermath of Violence." *Monographic Review / Revista Monográfica* 16:258–67.

Gutiérrez, M. A. 2001–2. "'Amalia' de Rosario Ferré o las violencias de una cocina respetable." *Baquiana Revista Literaria* 3:133–43.

Gutiérrez-Jones, L. S. 1993. "Different Voices: The Re-*Bildung* of the Barrio in Sandra Cisneros's *The House on Mango Street*." In *Anxious Power: Reading, Writing, and Ambivalence in Narratives by Women*, ed. C. J. Singley and S. E. Sweeney, 295–312. Albany: State University of New York Press.

Gutiérrez Mouat, R. 1987. "Construcción y represión del deseo en las novelas de María Luisa Bombal." In *María Luisa Bombal: Apreciaciones críticas*, ed. E. Gascón-Vera, J. Renjilian-Burgy, and M. Agosín, 99–118. Tempe (Arizona): Bilingual Press.

———. 1994. "La 'loca del desván' y otros intertextos de *Maldito amor*." *Modern Language Notes* 109:283–306.

Gutiérrez y Muhs, G. 2006. "Sandra Cisneros and Her Trade of the Free Word." *Rocky Mountain Review of Language and Literature* 60, no. 2 23–36.

Handelsman, M. H. 1988. "*La casa de los espíritus* y la evolución de la mujer moderna." *Letras Femeninas* 14, nos. 1–2:57–63.

Haraway, D. 1991. *Simians, Cyborgs and Women: The Reinvention of Nature*. New York: Routledge.

Hart, P. 1993. "Magic Feminism in Isabel Allende's 'The Stories of Eva Luna.'" In *Multicultural Literatures through Feminist / Poststructuralist Lenses*, ed. B. F. Waxman, 103–36. Knoxville: University of Tennessee Press.

———. 1995. "Magic Feminism and Inverted Masculine Myths in Rosario Ferré's 'The Youngest Doll.'" In *Studies in Honor of María A. Salgado*, ed. M. A. Bolden and L. A. Giménez, 97–108. Newark, DE: Juan de la Cuesta.

Hedges, E., and S. F. Fishkin, eds. 1994. *Listening to Silences: New Essays in Feminist Criticism*. New York: Oxford University Press.

Henry, A. 2006. "Feminist Deaths and Feminism Today." *PMLA* 121, no. 5:1711–16.

Higuero, F. J. 2000. "Fenomenología de la mentira en *Tantos inocentes* de Guerra Garrido." *Monographic Review / Revista Monográfica* 16:190–203.

Hintz, S. 1995. *Rosario Ferré, a Search for Identity*. New York: Peter Lang.

Hoeg, J. 1997. "*Como agua para chocolate* and the Question of Viable Alternatives to Technologies of Domination." *Confluencia: Revista Hispánica de Cultura* 12, no. 12:112–27.

Holmes, D. 2003. "Decadent Love: Rachilde and the Popular Romance." *XIX* 1:16–28.

Hutcheon, L. 1985. *A Theory of Parody: The Teaching of Twentieth-Century Art Forms*. New York: Methuen.

———. 1988. *A Poetics of Postmodernism: History, Theory, Fiction*. New York: Routledge.

———. 1994. *Irony's Edge: The Theory and Politics of Irony*. London: Routledge.

Hymes, D. 1996. *Ethnography, Linguistics, Narrative Inequality: Toward an Understanding of Voice*. Abington, England: Taylor & Francis.

Ibsen, K. L. 1995. "On Recipes, Reading and Revolution: Postboom Parody in *Como agua para chocolate*." *Concerns: Women's Caucus for Modern Languages* 25, no. 2:7–20.

Irigaray, L. 1985. *This Sex Which Is Not One*. Trans. C. Porter and C. Burke. Ithaca, NY: Cornell University Press.

Iser, W. 1974. *The Implied Reader*. Baltimore: Johns Hopkins University Press.

———. 1978. *The Act of Reading*. Baltimore: Johns Hopkins University Press.

———. 1989. "The Play of the Text.." In *Languages of The Unsayable: The Play of Negativity in Literature and Literary Theory*, ed. S. Budick and W. Iser, 325–39. New York: Columbia University Press.

Jaquette, J. S., ed. 1994. *The Women's Movement in Latin America: Participation and Democracy*. Boulder, CO: Westview Press.

Jehenson, M. Y. 1995. *Latin-American Women Writers: Class, Race, Gender*. Albany: State University of New York Press.

Johnson, K. 2002. "*Como agua para chocolate*: Tita, una nueva imagen de la mujer latinoamericana." *South Carolina Modern Language Review* 1, no. 1:n.p.

Jones, A. R. 1997. "Writing the Body: Toward an Understanding of 'L'écriture féminine.' In *Feminisms: An Anthology of Literary Theory and Criticism*, ed. Robyn R. Warhol and Diane Price Herndl, 370–83. 2nd edition. New Brunswick, NJ: Rutgers University Press.

Kaminsky, A. 1993. *Reading the Body Politic: Feminist Criticism and Latin American Women Writers*. Minneapolis: University of Minnesota Press.

Kason, N. 1995. "La voz no callada: El discurso del exilio en *De amor y de sombra* de Isabel Allende." In *La nueva mujer en la escritura*, ed. J. A. Arancibia, 89–99. Montevideo: Ensayos Críticos.

Kirkwood, J. 1986. *Ser política en Chile: Los nudos de la sabiduría feminista*. Santiago: Cuarto Propio.

Koene, J. 1998. "Metaphors of Marginalization and Silencing of Women in *Eva Luna* and *Cuentos de Eva Luna* by Isabel Allende." PhD diss., University of Toronto.

Koski, L. I. 1989. "Women's Experience in the Novels of Four Modern Chilean Writers: Marta Brunet, María Luisa Bombal, Mercedes Valdivieso, and Isabel Allende." PhD diss., Stanford University.

Kramarae, C., 1981. *Women and Men Speaking: Frameworks for Analysis*. London: Newbury House Publishers.

Kristeva, J. 1984. *Revolution in Poetic Language*. Trans. M. Waller. New York: Columbia University Press.

Krolokke, C. and A. S. Sorensen. 2006. *Gender Communication Theories and Analyses: From Silence to Performance*. London: Sage Publications.

Kuramochi, Y. 1990. "Marta Brunet: Realista; Revisión crítica." *ALPHA: Revista de Artes, Letras y Filosofía* 6:47–56.

Kushigian, J. A. 2003. *Reconstructing Childhood: Strategies of Reading for Culture and Gender in the Spanish American Bildungsroman*. Lewisburg, PA: Bucknell University Press.

Labov, W. 1972. *Language in the Inner City: Studies in the Black English Vernacular*. Philadelphia: University of Pennsylvania Press.

Lagos, M. 1996. *En tono mayor: Relatos de formación de protagonista femenina en Hispanoamérica*. Santiago: Cuarto propio.

———. 2003. "Conflicting Body Signs in Rosario Ferré's 'La muñeca menor.'" *Revista de Estudios Literarios* (St. Louis, MO) 37, no. 1:167–87.

Lagos-Pope, M. 1985. "Sumisión y rebeldía: El doble o la representación de la alienación femenina en narraciones de Marta Brunet y Rosario Ferré." *Revista Iberoamericana* 51, no. 13: 731–49.

———. 1997. "Silencio y rebeldía: Hacia una valoración de María Luisa Bombal dentro de la tradición de escritura femenina." In *María Luisa Bombal: Apreciaciones críticas*, ed. M. Agosín, E. Gascón-Vera, and J. Renjilian-Burgy, 119–35. Tempe (Arizona): Bilingual Press.

Lakoff, R. 1975. *Language and Woman's Place*. New York: Harper Torch Books.

Lanser, S. S. 1992. *Fictions of Authority: Women Writers and Narrative Voice*. Ithaca, NY: Cornell University Press.

———. 1997. "Toward a Feminist Narratology." In *Feminisms: An Anthology of Literary Theory and Criticism*, ed. Robyn R. Warhol and Diane Price Herndl, 674–93. New Brunswick, NJ: Rutgers University Press.

Laurence, P. O. 1991. *The Reading of Silence: Virginia Woolf in the English Tradition*. Stanford, CA: Stanford University Press.

Lawless, C. 1997. "Cooking, Community, Culture: A Reading of *Like Water for Chocolate*." In *Recipes for Reading: Community Cookbooks, Stories, Histories*, ed. A. L. Bower, 216–35. Amhert: University of Massachusetts Press.

Lemaitre, M. J. 1992. "Deseo, incesto y represión en *De amor y de sombra* de Isabel Allende." *Letras Femeninas* 18, nos. 1–2:31–37.

Levine, L. G. 1974. "María Luisa Bombal from a Feminist Perspective." *Revista / Review Interamericana* 4:148–61.

———. 1990. "A Passage to Androgyny: Isabel Allende's *La casa de los espíritus*." In *In the Feminine Mode: Essays on Hispanic Women Writers*, ed. N. Valis and C. Maier, 164–73. Lewisburg (Pennsylvania): Bucknell University Press.

———. 2002. *Isabel Allende*. New York: Twayne Publishers.

Lillo, G., and M. Sarfati-Arnaud. 1994. "*Como agua para chocolate*: Determinaciones de la lectura en el contexto posmoderno." *Revista Canadiense de Estudios Hispánicos* 18, no. 3:479–90.

Lindemans, M. F. "Coatlicue." *Encyclopedia Mythica*. http://www.pantheon.org/articles/c/coatlicue.html

Lloyd, M. 2005. *Beyond Identity Politics: Feminism, Power and Politics*. London: Sage Publications.

Longmire, L., and L. Merrill, eds. 1998. *Untying the Tongue: Gender, Power, and the Word*. Westport, CT: Praeger.

López, I. 1982. "'La muñeca menor': Ceremonias y transformaciones en un cuento de Rosario Ferré." *Explicación de Textos Literarios* 11, no. 1:49–58.

———. 1983. "*Papeles de Pandora*: Devastación y ruptura." *Sin Nombre* 14, no. 1:41–52.

Ludmer, J. 1985. "Tretas del débil." In *La sartén por el mango: Encuentro de escritoras latinoamericanas*, ed. Patricia Elena González and Eliana Ortega, 47–54. Río Piedras, PR : Ediciones Huracán.

Lutes, L. Y. 2000. *Allende, Buitrago, Luiselli: Aproximaciones teóricas al concepto del "Bildungsroman" femenino.* New York: Peter Lang.

MacDonald, R. H. 1980. "Rosario Castellanos: On Language." In *Homenaje a Rosario Castellanos*, ed. M. Ahern and M. S. Vásquez, 41–64. Valencia: Albatros, 1980.

Marek, J. 1996. "Difference, Identity and Sandra Cisneros's *The House on Mango Street*." *Hungarian Journal of English and American Studies* 1:173–87.

Marquet, A. 1997. "¿Cómo escribir un best-seller? La receta de Laura Esquivel." *Plural* 237:58–67.

McConnell-Ginet, R. B., and N. Furman, eds. 1980. *Women and Language in Literature and Society.* Westport, CT: Praeger.

McCracken, E. 1989. "Sandra Cisneros' *The House on Mango Street*: Community-Oriented Introspection and the Demystification of Patriarchal Violence." In *Breaking Boundaries: Latina Writing and Critical Readings*, 62–71. Amherst: University of Massachusetts Press.

———. 2000. "Postmodern Ethnicity in Sandra Cisneros's *Caramelo*: Hybridity, Spectacle, and Memory in the Nomadic Text." *Journal of American Studies of Turkey* 12:3–12.

Mecheam, C. 1998. "*Como agua para chocolate*: Cinderella and the Revolution." *Hispanic Journal* 19, no. 1:117–28.

Melgar, L. 2000. "Silencios expresivos: Gamas y matices del silencio en la obra de Elena Garro." *Monographic Review / Revista Monográfica* 16:357–67.

Mennell, D. J. 1999. "El Secreto de Romelia: In Search of a View of One's Own." *Letras Femeninas* 25, nos. 1–2:49–62.

Merithew, Charlene. 2000. "'Silencios poderosos': El tema de la quietud en los ensayos de Soledad Puértulas." *Monographic Review / Revista Monográfica* 16:162–73.

Meyer, D. 1988. "Exile and the Female Condition in Isabel Allende's *De amor y de sombra*." *International Fiction Review* 15, no. 2:151–57.

———. 1990. "Parenting the Text: Female Creativity and Dialogic Relationships in Isabel Allende's *La casa de los espíritus*." *Hispania* 73, no. 2:360–65.

Mezei, K. 1996. "'Who is Speaking Here?' Free Indirect Discourse, Gender, and Authority in *Emma*, *Howards End*, and *Mrs. Dalloway*." In *Ambiguous Discourse: Feminist Narratology and British Women Writers*, ed. K. Mezei, 66–92. Chapel Hill: University of North Carolina Press.

Miller, B. 1979. "Rosario Castellanos' *Guests in August*: Critical Realism and the Provincial Middle Class." *Latin American Literary Review* 14 (1979):5–19.

Miller, F. 1991. *Latin American Women and the Search for Social Justice.* Hanover, NH: University Press of New England.

Miller, N. K. 1988. "Arachnologies: The Woman, the Text, and the Critic." In *Subject to Change: Reading Feminist Writing*, 77–101. New York: Columbia University Press.

Mills, S. 1995a. *Feminist Stylistics.* London: Routledge.

———, ed. 1995b. *Language and Gender: Interdisciplinary Perspectives.* London: Longman.

Minc, R. 1987. "Para que no lo borre el tiempo: Apuntes sobre *De amor y de sombra*." *Alba de América* 5, nos. 8–9:181–88.

Modleski, T. 1984. *Loving with a Vengeance: Mass-Produced Fantasies for Women.* New York: Routledge.

Moi, T. 2006. "'I Am Not a Feminist, But . . .': How Feminism Became the F-Word." *PMLA* 121, no. 5:1735–41.

Monet-Viera, M. 2004. "Post-Boom Magical Realism: Appropriations and Transformation of a Genre." *Revista de Estudios Hispánicos* (St. Louis, MO) 38, no. 1:95–117.

Montes Garcés, E. 2002. "Subjetividad e ideología en *Maldito amor* de Rosario Ferré." *Texto Crítico* 5, no. 10:131–38.

Mora, G. 1984. "Una lectura de 'Soledad de la sangre' de Marta Brunet." *Estudios Filológicos* 9:81–90.

———. 1987. "Las novelas de Isabel Allende y el papel de la mujer como ciudadana." *Ideologies and Literature: Journal of Hispanic and Lusophone Discourse Analysis* 2, no. 1:53–61.

Morello, C. 1978. "Un acercamiento a la novela de Marta Brunet." *Nueva Revista del Pacífico* 9:38–47.

Moya-Raggio, E. 1991. "*De amor y de sombra*: Una aproximación a su lectura." *Acta Literaria* 16: 113–24.

Mullen, H. 1996. "A Silence between Us Like a Language: The Untranslatability of Experience in Sandra Cisneros's *Woman Hollering Creek*." MELUS 21, no. 2:3–20.

Muñoz, W. O. 1991. "Enmarcando la locura en *Los convidados de agosto*." *Hispanófila* 34, no. 2:77–86.

Murphy, M. 1997. "Rosario Ferré en el espejo: Defiance and Inversions." *Hispanic Review* 65:145–57.

Nebel, R. 1995. *Santa María Tonantzin Virgen de Guadalupe: Continuidad y transformación religiosa en Mexico*. Mexico City: Fondo de Cultura Económica.

Nelson, A. A. 2002. *Political Bodies: Gender, History, and the Struggle for Narrative Power in Recent Chilean Literature*. Lewisburg, PA: Bucknell University Press.

Nelson, E. W. 1987. "Un viaje fantástico: ¿Quién habla en 'La amortajada?'" In *María Luisa Bombal: Apreciaciones críticas*, ed. M. Agosín, E. Gascón-Vera, and J. Renjilian-Burgy, 182–200. Tempe (Arizona): Bilingual Press.

Niebylski, D. C. 1998. "Heartburn, Humor, and Hyperbole in *Like Water for Chocolate*. In *Performing Gender and Comedy: Theories, Texts and Contexts*, 179–97. Amsterdam: Gordon and Breach.

Norat, G. 1995. "The Silent Child within the Angry Woman: Exorcising Incest in Sylvia Molloy's Certificate of Absence." In *Violence, Silence, and Anger: Women's Writing as Transgression*, ed. D. Lashgardi, 111–23. Charlottesville: University of Virginia Press.

Oropesa, S. A. 1992. "*Como agua para chocolate* de Laura Esquivel como lectura del *Manual de urbanidad y buenas costumbres* de Manuel Antonio Carreño." *Monographic Review / Revista Monográfica* 8:252–60.

Ortega, J. 2000. "La poética del silencio en los relatos de Juan Rulfo." *Monographic Review / Revista Monográfica* 16:253–57.

Ortiz, A.1998. "Los reflejos sobre *Una casa sobre la laguna*." *Horizontes* 40, no. 78 (1998): 127–33.

Oyarzún, K. 2000. "Género y canon: La escritura de Marta Brunet." In *Studies in Honor of Myron Lichtblau*, ed. F. Burgos, 251–64. Newark (Delaware): Juan de la Cuesta.

Palmer-López, S. 2002. "Rosario Ferré y la generación del 70: Evolución estética y literaria." *Acta Literaria* 27:157–67.

Panedas, R. M. 2003. "El sujeto camaleónico en el cuento 'La bella durmiente' de Rosario Ferré." *Alba de América: Revista Literaria* 22, nos. 41–42:249–62.

Param, C. 1968. "Soledad de la sangre: A Study in Symmetry." *Hispania* 51:252–58.

Parham, M. G. 1988. "Isabel Allende's *La casa de los espíritus* and the Literature of Matrilineage." *Discurso Literario* 6, no. 1:193–201.

Parker, G. 1990. "Michèle Perrein: The Parenthesis as a Metaphor of the Female Condition." *Contemporary French Fiction by Women: Feminist Perspectives*, ed. Margaret Atack and Phil Powriegeds Atack, 116–127. Manchester: Manchester University Press.

Peña, H. A. 1999. "Marta Brunet (1901–1967)." In *Escritoras chilenas, III: Novela y cuento*, ed. P. Rubio, 139–58. Santiago: Cuarto Propio.

Pequeño Larousse Ilustrado. 2005. Mexico City: Larousse.

Pérez, A. J. 1995. "*Como agua para chocolate*: La nueva novela de mujeres de Latinoamérica." In *La nueva mujer en la escritura de autoras hispánicas*, ed. Juana A. Arancibia and Yolanda Rosas, 41–57. Montevideo Instituto Literario y Cultural Hispánico.

Pérez, J., and G. J. Pérez. 2000. "Silence in Hispanic Literature."*Monographic Review / Revista Monográfica*, 16.

Pérez Marín, C. 1994. "De la épica a la novela: La recuperación de la voz en *Maldito amor* de Rosario Ferré." *Letras Femeninas* 20, no. 1–2:35–43.

Perricone, C. 1991. "Iconic / Metaphoric Dress and Other Nonverbal Signifiers in *De amor y de sombra*." In *Critical Approaches to Isabel Allende's Novels*, ed. Sonia Riquelme Rojas and Edna Aguirre Rehbein, 83–96. New York: Peter Lang.

———. 1999. Laura Esquivel's *La ley del amor*: The Eclectic Novel." In *LA CHISPA '99: Selected Proceedings*, ed. Gilbert Paolini and Claire J. Paolini, 293–300. New Orleans: Tulane University Press.

Pfeffer, E. 1990. "La imagen de la madre en *La casa de los espíritus* de Isabel Allende dentro del marco del machismo latinoamericano." *Beitrage zur Romanischen Philologie* 29, no. 1:65–70.

Pokorny, E. D. B. 1994. "(Re)writing the Body: The Legitimization of the Female Voice, History, Culture and Space in Rosario Ferré's 'La muñeca menor.'" *Confluencia: Revista de Cultura Hispánica* 10, no. 1:75–80.

Potvin, C. 1995. "*Como agua para chocolate*: ¿Parodia o cliché?" *Revista Canadiense de Estudios Hispánicos* 20, no. 1:55–67.

Pratt, A. 1981. *Archetypal Patterns in Women's Fiction*. Bloomington: Indiana University Press.

Pratt, Mary Louise. 1977. *Toward a Speech Act Theory of Literary Discourse*. Bloomington: University of Indiana Press.

Price, H. 2005. "Unsavoury Representations in Laura Esquivel's *Like Water for Chocolate*." In *A Companion to Magical Realism*, ed. Stephen Hart and Wen-Chin Ouang. 181–90. Woodbridge (England): Tamesis.

Promis, J. 1987. "La técnica narrativa de María Luisa Bombal." In *María Luisa Bombal: Apreciaciones críticas*, ed. M. Agosín, E. Gascón-Vera, and J. Rengilian-Burgy, 201–210. Tempe, AZ: Bilingual Press.

Prout, R. 2000. "Cosmic Weddings and a Funeral: Sexuality, Techno-science and the National Romance in Laura Esquivel's *La ley del amor.*" *Tesserae: Journal of Iberian and Latin American Studies* 6, no. 1:43–54.

Radner, J., and S. Lanser. 1987. "The Feminist Voice: Coding in Women's Folklore and Literature." *Journal of American Folklore* 100:412–25.

Radway, J. 1991. *Reading the Romance: Women, Patriarchy, and Popular Literature*. Chapel Hill: University of North Carolina Press.

Rakow, L. F., and L. A. Wackwitz, eds. 2004. *Feminist Communication Theory: Selections in Context*. London: Sage Publications.

Riquelme, S. 1987. "Notas sobre el criollismo chileno y el personaje femenino en la narrativa de Marta Brunet." *Discurso Literario: Revista de Temas Hispánicos* 4, no. 2:613–22.

Rivera, C. 1994. "Porcelain Face / Rotten Flesh: The Doll in *Papeles de Pandora.*" *Chasqui: Revista de Literatura Latinoamericana* 23, no. 2:95–101.

Rivera-van Schagen, J. 1996. "Dialogics in Laura Esquivel's *Como agua para chocolate.*" *Hispanic Journal* 17, no. 2:397–411.

Rodden, J. 1999. "Chronology." In *Conversations with Isabel Allende*, ed. J. Rodden, xv–xviii. Austin: University of Texas Press.

Rodríguez, R. 2000. "El silencio como tema en la literatura de exilio en *La nave de los locos* y *Querido Diego, te abraza Quiela.*" *Monographic Review / Revista Monográfica* 16:294–356.

Rodríguez-Peralta, P. 1977. "Images of Women in Rosario Castellanos' Prose." *Latin American Literary Review* 11:68–80.

Rodríguez-Vivaldi, A. M. 2003. "Shaking the Soul, the Mind, and the Reader: Laura Esquivel and the Multimedia Novel." *Pacific Coast Philology* 38:25–32.

Rojas, M. 1985. "*La casa de los espíritus* de Isabel Allende: Una aproximación sociolingüística." *Revista de Crítica Literaria Latinoamericana* 11, nos. 21–22:205–13.

Romaine, S., ed. 1999. *Communicating Gender*. Mahwah, NJ: Lawrence Erlbaum Associates.

Roman, C. 1994. "Female Sexual Drives, Subjectivity, and Language: The Dialogue with / beyond Freud and Lacan." In *The Women & Language Debate: A Sourcebook*, ed. Camille Roman, Susan Juhasz and Cristanne Miller, 8–19. New Brunswick, NJ: Rutgers University Press.

Roman, C., S. Juhasz, and C. Miller, eds. 1994. *The Women and Language Debate: A Sourcebook*. New Brunswick, NJ: Rutgers University Press.

Román-Odio, C. 1996. "Clarividentes, curanderas y los nuevos rituales de la literatura latinoamericana." *SECOLAS Annals: Journal of the Southeastern Council on Latin American Studies* 27:41–48.

Roses, L. E. 1993. "Las esperanzas de Pandora: Prototipos femeninos en la obra de Rosario Ferré." *Revista Iberoamericana* 162–63, no. 54:279–87.

Ross, S. 1979. "'Voice' in Narrative Texts: The Example of *As I Lay Dying.*" *PMLA* 94:300–10.

Rubio, C. 1995. "La inversión del final feliz en la cuentística de Marta Brunet." *Acta Literaria* 20:89–112.

Rubio, P. 1997. "Elena Garro." In *Encyclopedia of Latin American Literatura*, ed. V. Smith, 362–63. London: Fitzroy Dearborn.

———. 1998. "*House of Mist*, de María Luisa Bombal: Una novela olvidada." *Literatura y Lingüística* 11:181–204.

Salas, K. L. 1997. "*La amortajada* de María Luisa Bombal: La muerte como el momento en que se rompe el silencio." In *La muerte en la cultura*, 65–72. Santiago: Universidad de Chile, Facultad de Filosofía y humanidades, Centro de Estudios Judaicos.

Saldívar-Hull, S. 2000. *Feminism on the Border: Chicana Gender Politics and Literature*. Berkeley and Los Angeles: University of California Press.

Salkjelsvik, K. S. 1999. "El desvío como norma: La retórica de la receta en *Como agua para chocolate*." *Revista Iberoamericana* 65, no. 186:171–82.

Sánchez, R. 1995. "Remembering Always to Come Back: The Child's Wished-for Escape and the Adult's Self-Empowered Return in Sandra Cisneros's *House on Mango Street*." *Children's Literature* 23:221–41.

Sánchez-Flavian, P. 2004. "*Como agua para chocolate* as a Novel of Self-Discovery Formulated through Parody." *Ciberletras* 11:n.p.

Saville-Troike, M. 1995. "The Place of Silence in an Integrated Theory of Communication." In *Perspectives on Silence*, ed. Deborah Tannen and Muriel Saville-Troike, 3–18. Norwood, NJ: Ablex Publishing.

Schild, V. 1998. "New Subjects of Rights? Women's Movements and the Construction of Citizenship in the 'New Democracies.'" In *Cultures of Politics / Politics of Cultures: Re-Visioning Latin American Social Movements*, eds Sonia E. Alvarez, Evelina Dagnino, and Arturo Escobar, 93–117. Boulder: Westview Press.

Schrauf, R., and R. Durazo-Arvizu. 2006. "Bilingual Autobiographical Memory and Emotion: Theory and Methods." In *Bilingual Minds: Emotional Experience, Expression and Representation*, ed. A. Pavlenko, 284–311. Clevedon , England: Multilingual Matters Ltd.

Scott, N. M. 1987. "Verbal and Nonverbal Messages in María Luisa Bombal's 'El árbol.'" *Modern Language Studies* 17, no. 3:3–9.

Sellers, S. 1994. Introduction to *The Hélène Cixous Reader*, ed. S. Sellers, xxvi–xxxiv. New York: Routledge.

Sepúlveda-Pulvirenti, E. 1987. "María Luisa Bombal y el silencio." In *María Luisa Bombal: Apreciaciones críticas*, ed. M. Agosín, E. Gascón-Vera, and J. Renjilian-Burgy, 230–36. Tempe (Arizona): Bilingual Press.

Shayne, J. D. 2004. *The Revolution Question: Feminisms in El Salvador, Chile, and Cuba*. New Brunswick, NJ: Rutgers University Press.

Showalter, E. 1985. "Feminist Criticism in the Wilderness." In *The New Feminist Criticism: Essays on Women, Literature, Theory*, ed. E. Showalter, 243–70. New York: Pantheon.

———. 1997. "A Criticism of Our Own: Autonomy and Assimilation in Afro-American and Feminist Literary Theory." In *Feminisms: An Anthology of Literary Theory and Criticism*, ed. R. R. Warhol and D. P. Herndl, 213–33. New Brunswick, NJ: Rutgers University Press.

Sibbald, K.M. 1997. "María Luisa Bombal (1910–1980)." In *Encyclopedia of Latin American Literature*, ed. V. Smith, 131–32. London: Fitzroy Dearborn.

Silva, D. F. 2003. "Puerto Rico: una perspectiva histórica a través de la ficción ferretiana." *Céfiro* 3, no. 2:54–62.

Smith, V., ed. 1997. *Encyclopedia of Latin American Literature*. London: Fitzroy Dearborn.

Sommer, D., ed. 2003. Introduction to *Bilingual Games: Some Literary Investigations*, I–viii. New York: Palgrave Macmillan.

Soto, S. 1990. *Emergence of the Modern Mexican Woman: Her Participation in Revolution and Struggle for Equality, 1910–1940*. Denver: Arden Press.

Spanos, T. 1990. "Isabel Allende's *The Judge's Wife*: Heroine or Stereotype?" *Encyclia* 67 (1990): 163–72.

———. 1995. "The Paradoxical Metaphors of the Kitchen in Laura Esquivel's *Like Water for Chocolate*." *Letras Femeninas* 21, nos. 1–2 (1995): 29–36.

Spencer, L. G. 1997. "Fairy Tales and Opera: The Fate of the Heroine in the Work of Sandra Cisneros." In *Speaking the Other Self: American Women Writers*, ed. J. C. Reesman, 278–87. Athens: University of Georgia Press.

Spender, D. 1980a. "Defining Reality: A Powerful Tool." In *Language and Power*, ed. C. Kramarae, M. Schulz, and W. M. O'Barr, 194–205. London: Sage Publications.

———. 1980b. *Man Made Language*. London: Pandora.

Steele, C. 1990. "The Other Within: Class and Ethnicity as Difference in Mexican Women's Literature." In *Cultural and Historical Grounding for Hispanic and Luso-Brazilian Feminist Literary Criticism*, ed. H. Vidal, 297–328. Minneapolis: Institute for the Study of Ideologies and Literature.

———. 1996. "Letters from Rosario: On Power, Gender, and Canon Formation in Mexico." *Studies in Twentieth Century Literature* 20, no. 1:65–96.

Stout, J. 1990. *Strategies of Reticence: Silence and Meaning in the Works of Jane Austen, Willa Cather, Katherine Anne Porter, and Joan Didion*. Charlottesville: University of Virginia Press.

Swanson, P. 1994. "Tyrants and Trash: Sex, Class and Culture in *La casa de los espíritus*." *Bulletin of Hispanic Studies* 71, no. 2:217–37.

Szadziuk, M. 1999. "Culture as Transition: Becoming a Woman in Bi-ethnic Space." *Journal for the Interdisciplinary Study of Literature* 32, no. 3:109–30.

Tannen, D. 1989. *Talking Voices: Repetition, Dialogue, and Imagery in Conversational Discourse*. London: Cambridge University Press.

———. 1996. *Gender & Discourse*. London: Oxford University Press.

Thomson, J. 1994. "'What Is Called Heaven': Identity in Sandra Cisneros's *Woman Hollering Creek*." *Studies in Short Fiction*: 31, no. 3:415–24.

Todorov, T. 1982. *Symbolism and Interpretation*. Trans. C. Porter. Ithaca, NY: Cornell University Press.

Traba, M. 1985. "Hipótesis de una escritura diferente." In *La sartén por el mango: Encuentros de escritoras latinoamericanas*, ed. Patricia Elena González and Eliana Ortega, 21–26. Río Piedras, PR: Ediciones Huracán.

Trovatto, B. 2001. "Los espacios antagónicos en *La última niebla* de María Luisa Bombal." *Cuaderno Internacional de Estudios Hispánicos y Lingüística / International Journal of Hispanic Studies and Linguistics* 1, no. 1:69–74.

Tull, J. F. 1966. "El desarrollo de la novela de Marta Brunet." *Duquesne Hispanic Review* 5:57–62.

Umpierre, L. M.1982. "Un manifiesto literario: *Papeles de Pandora* de Rosario Ferré." *Bilingual Review / La Revista Bilingue* 9, no. 2 (1982):120–26.

Valdés, M. E. 1992. "In Search of Identity in Cisneros's *The House on Mango Street*." *Canadian Review of American Studies* 23, no. 1:55–72.

———. 1996. "Questioning Paradigms of Social Reality through Postmodern Intertextuality." *Poligrafías: Revista de Literatura Comparada* 1:227–39.

Valdivieso, M. 1976. "Social Denunciation in the Language of 'El árbol' (The Tree) by María Luisa Bombal." *Latin American Literary Review* 9:70–76.

Vallejos-Ramírez, M. A. 1997. "El arte de tejer como eje estructurante en la narrativa femenina hispanoamericana." PhD diss., University of Nebraska.

Vásquez, M. S. 2000. "Ramón J. Sender para el nuevo milenio: Silencio, clase y simbología cristera en *El lugar de un hombre*." *Monographic Review / Revista Monográfica* 16:83–93.

Velasco, M. 1992. "Evolución femenina en *La casa de los espíritus*." In *Literatura del mundo hispánico: VIII Simposio Internacional de Literatura*, ed. J. A. Arancibia, 145–159 Westminster (California): Instituto Literario y Cultural Hispánico.

Velázquez-Lara, S. 1997. "La parodia como poder subversivo feminista en la narrativa de Rosario Ferré." PhD diss., University of New Mexico.

Vélez Román, L. 2001. "Violencia y fronteras móviles en *La casa de la laguna*, de Rosario Ferré." *Alba de América: Revista Literaria* 20, nos. 37–38:167–76.

Viera, Hugo M. 2000. "El cuerpo del silencio: Héroes populares en la obra de Augusto Roa Bastos." *Monographic Review / Revista Monográfica* 16:268–80.

Villanueva-Collado, A. 1990. "(Homo) Sexualidad y periferia en la novelística de Marta Brunet." In *El descubrimiento y los desplazamientos: La literatura hispanoamericana como diálogo entre centros y periferias*, ed. J. A. Arancibia, 79–94. Westminster, CA: Instituto Literario y Cultural Hispánico, 1990.

Walker, B. 1988. *The Woman's Dictionary of Symbols and Sacred Objects*. New York: Harper Collins.

Warhol, R. 1996. "The Look, the Body and the Heroine of Persuasion." In *Ambiguous Discourse: Feminist Narratology and British Women Writers*, ed. K. Mezei, 21–39. Chapel Hill: University of North Carolina Press.

Warhol, R. R., and D. P. Herndl, eds. 1997. *Feminisms: An Anthology of Literary Theory and Criticism*. 2nd ed. New Brunswick, NJ: Rutgers University Press.

Weldt-Basson, H. C. 2000. "Silence as Narrative Strategy in Sandra Cisneros's *The House on Mango Street*." *Cuadernos de Aldeeu* 16, no. 1: 201–9.

———. 2004. "Irony as Silent Subversive Strategy in Isabel Allende's *Cuentos de Eva Luna*." *Revista de Estudios Hispánicos* 31, no. 1:183–98.

———. 2006. "La sobrelectura de los cuentos de Marta Brunet." *Alba de América* 2, nos. 47–48:273–84.

Wenzel, M. 1996. "The 'Other' Side of History as Depicted in Isabel Allende's *Of Love and Shadows*." *Literator: Tydskrif vir Besondere en Vergelykende Taal-en Literatuurstudie / Journal of Literary Criticism, Comparative Linguistics and Literary Studies* 17, no. 3:1–13.

Williams, R. G. 1993. "Reading the Parentheses." *Substance: A Review of Theory and Literary Crticism* 22, no. 1:53–66.

Wilson, S. R. 2001. "'The Poisoned Story' and Other Postcolonial Metafairy Tales in Rosario Ferré's *The Youngest Doll*." *Horizontes: Revista de la Universidad Católica de Puerto Rico* 43, no. 84:143–63.

Wodak, R., ed. 1997. *Gender and Discourse*. London: Sage Publications.

Zapata, M. 1990. "Ley y transgresión femenina en *La casa de los espíritus* de Isabel Allende." In *La narrativa de Isabel Allende: Claves de una marginalidad*, ed. Adriana Castillo de Berchenko, 69–98. Perpignan, France: Centre de Recherches Ibérique & Latinamericains.

———. 1997. "*Like Water for Chocolate* and the Free Circulation of Clichés." In *Latin American Postmodernisms*, ed. Richard A. Young, 205–19. Amsterdam: Rodopi.

Index

Acosta-Belén, Edna, 167
agency, 9–11, 220–21, 227, 241
agon, 33, 35, 104.
Agosín, Marjorie, 22–23, 29, 58, 65, 230, 231, 236 n. 4, 239 n. 1
Aguas abajo, 36, 37, 46
"Aguas abajo," 38, 40, 47–48, 54
Albada-Jelgersma, Jill, 243 n. 9
Álbum de familia, 81, 85, 92
alienation, 53, 61, 68, 95, 146, 236 n. 11
Allende, Isabel, 23, 30, 33, 104–37, 155, 174, 226, 227, 234 n. 1, 239 n. 2, 240 nn. 3 and 4, 241 nn. 10, 12, 13, and 14
Allende, Salvador, 104, 106, 107
Allende, Tomás, 104
"Amalia," 139, 142–45, 153–54, 156, 158, 165, 167, 168, 242 n. 5, 244 n. 17
Amasijo, 36
ambiguous discourse, 34, 139, 242 n. 1, 244 nn. 15 and 16
"Amistades efímeras, Las." *See* "Fleeting Friendships"
Amorós, Andrés, 34, 171–73, 185
"Amortajada, La." *See* "Shrouded Woman, The"
Andalzúa, Gloria, 210
Anguiano, Elvira Codero, 194, 209, 210
apocalyptic ending, 143, 150, 156, 158, 168, 169
appropriation, 32, 81, 122, 126, 128–32, 227
Aquí pasan cosas raras, 230
Arachne, 31, 37
"Arbol, El," 60, 61, 73–76, 78, 133, 237 n. 22
architextuality, 171, 183, 184

arpilleristas, 198, 240 n. 4
ASUMA (Association for the Unity of Women), 109
Athena, 23, 31
Auerbach, Nina, 115, 179
August Guests, The, 81, 89, 92
"August Guests, The," 82, 89
axioms, 151–52

Bakhtin, Mikhail, 23–24, 86, 100, 150, 233 n. 3, 241 nn. 9 and 10
Baldez, Lisa, 54, 105, 108, 110
Balún Canán, 80
Barak, Julie, 163
Barrios excéntricos, Los, 138
Bastos, María Luisa, 63
"Bella durmiente, La." *See* "Sleeping Beauty."
Bennett, Caroline, 114
Besemeres, Mary, 35, 211
Bestia dañina, 36
Between Two Fires: Intimate Writings on Life, Love, Food, and Flavor, 170
"*Bien* Pretty," 208–9, 222
bildungsroman, 96, 97, 102, 223–24, 239 n. 19
bilingualism, 30, 34–35, 190, 194, 195, 209–17, 222–24, 231, 248
Black Novels with Argentines. See *Novela negra con argentinos*.
blank space, 27, 62–64, 67, 68
Bombal, María Luisa, 23, 30, 32, 36, 60–79, 84, 91, 217, 226, 227, 236 nn. 1, 2, and 3
Book of Lamentations, The. See *Oficio de tinieblas*

Booth, Wayne C. 241–42 n. 14
Borges, Jorge Luis, 60
Bosque de los pigmeos, El, 105
bourgeoisie, 12, 31, 42, 75, 102, 110, 122, 139, 169, 188, 194, 246 n. 7
"Braids." *See* "Trenzas"
Braun, Diane Marie, 236 n. 5
Brunet, Marta, 23, 30–32, 36–59, 61, 74, 76–77, 84, 91, 101, 102, 195, 217, 227, 234 nn. 1 and 2
Brunk, Beth, 196

"Cabecita blanca," 88–91
Caja de cristal, La, 138
Cambio de armas, 230
Cameron, Deborah, 20–21
Campbell, Joseph, 65
Campos, Pedro Albizu, 165, 166
caramel-colored shawl. See *caramelo rebozo*
Caramelo, 35, 195, 209–18, 220, 222–24
caramelo rebozo, 212, 215–17, 223, 224
Cárdenas, Daniel, 74
Cárdenas, Lázaro, 80
Casa de la laguna, La. See House on the Lagoon, The
Casa de los espíritus, La. See House of the Spirits, The
Castillo, Debra, 22, 24, 234 n. 8, 248 n. 6
Castellanos, Rosario, 30, 32, 33, 80–103, 219, 223, 226, 227, 229, 234 n. 11 (chap. 1), 234 n. 1 (chap. 2), 238 n. 1
Castro-Klarén, Sara, 22, 233 n. 2
Centros de madre. See Mother's Centers
Certificate of Absence, 229
Chancer, Lynn, 198
Cheung, King-Kok, 27–28
Chicanos, 35, 196–99, 208, 212–14, 216, 223
Christian Democratic Party, 106
Chuchryk, Patricia, 57
Cirlot, Juan, 66, 75, 140, 141, 242 n.3
Cisneros, Alfredo del Moral, 194
Cisneros, Sandra, 11–12, 30, 31, 34–35, 194–27, 231, 247 nn. 1, 2, and 4, 248 nn. 8 and 10

City of Beasts, The. See Ciudad de las bestias, La
City of Kings. See Ciudad real
Ciudad de las bestias, La, 104
Ciudad real, 80
Cixous, Hélène, 18–19
"Clarisa," 129–31, 135, 136
Coatlicue, 205, 207
coding, 32–33, 81–82, 89–91, 100, 102, 211, 227, 229
Cola de lagartija, 230
"Collar de camándulas, El." *See* "Seed Necklace, The"
Colloquium of the Dogs. See Coloquio de los perros
collusion, 33, 122–24, 132–34, 242 n. 14
Coloquio de los perros, 138, 164, 166
communism, 117
community of women, 115, 153, 159, 179
Como agua para chocolate. See Like Water for Chocolate
compensation, 33, 122–25, 127, 129–31, 134, 242
Convidados de agosto, Los. See August Guests, The
cooking, 85–87, 90–91, 103, 170–71, 176–81, 188, 207, 219, 246 nn. 6, 9, and 11
"Cooking Lesson," 88–91, 103, 219
Costa, Agustín, 138
Cranny-Francis, Anne, 184
criollismo, 37, 38, 54, 62, 234 n.1
Crystal Box, The. See Caja de cristal, La.
Cuentos de Eva Luna. See Stories of Eva Luna
Cuentos de Juan Bobo, Los, 138
Cutting, Rose Marie, 222

Daughter of Fortune. See Hija de la fortuna.
De amor y de sombra. See Of Love and Shadows
Debicki, Andrew, 238 n. 26
deconstruction, 10, 152, 158, 186, 221–23
DeKoven, Marianne, 233 n. 2
Delorey, Denise, 99
DeLuise, Dolores, 236 n. 11
Demasiado amor, 231
development, novels of. *See* bildungsroman

discrimination, 110, 165, 169, 198, 199, 224, 231
distraction, 32, 37, 81, 127, 234 n. 1
Divine, Susan, 243 n. 10
divorce, 73, 75, 77–80, 104, 130, 138, 182, 192, 228, 237 n. 23
domesticity, 42, 70
"Dos palabras." *See* "Two Words."
Dos Venecias, Las, 138
double standard, 55, 82, 114, 126, 214
double-voiced discourse, 23–24, 28, 86, 241 n. 9
Downstream. See *Aguas abajo*
"Downstream." *See* "Aguas abajo"
Doyle, Jaqueline, 208, 247 n. 2, 248 n. 9
Dream's Root. See *Raíz de sueño*.
"Dream's Root". *See* "Raíz de sueño"
Durazo-Arvizu, Ramón, 35, 211

Eccentric Neighborhoods. See *Barrios eccéntricos, Los*
écriture féminine, 18, 20.
Efficient Cat, The. See *Gato Eficaz, El*
"Eleven," 218
Eliade, Mircea, 76, 94, 246 n. 9
Elliot, Jane, 233 n. 2
ellipsis, 26, 28, 32, 85–87, 90–91
En breve cárcel, 229
encoding. *See* coding
Eros: novels of, 89, 134, 136, 137
Escaja, Tina, 246 n. 7
Escandón, Carmen Ramos, 101, 182, 187, 189
"Espejo, El," 41–42, 47, 48, 54, 195
Eternal Feminine, The. See *Eterno femenino, El*
Eterno femenino, El, 80
evaluation, 34, 196–201, 247 n. 2, 248 n. 6
Exchange of Arms. See *Cambio de armas*

Fables of the Bleeding Heron. See *Fábula de la garza desangrada*
Fábula de la garza desangrada, 138
Family Album. See *Álbum de familia*
Family Tree, The. See *Geneologías, Las*
Fate of the Consort, The. See *Suerte de la consorte, La*

"Felicidad, La," 229
Felski, Rita, 10–11
Feminism, 9–11, 17–35, 37, 49–55, 57–59, 61, 63, 68, 70, 72, 76–77, 81–82, 85–92, 99–102, 105, 112,114, 116, 118–19, 122–28, 130–31, 133, 139, 141, 148, 151–53, 158–60, 162–64, 166, 167, 169, 171, 176, 178, 181, 183–84, 187–89, 192–93, 195, 212, 217, 220–21, 226–27, 229–32, 233, n. 1, 233 n. 2, 240 n. 3, 245 nn. 26 and 28, 247 n. 1
Feminist movement, 21, 28, 30, 31, 37, 54, 57, 101, 106–11, 189, 220, 233 n. 1
Fem Power, 107
Fernández-Levin, Rosa, 246 n. 9
Ferré, Luis, 138
Ferré, Rosario, 30, 33–34, 65, 75, 99, 101, 138–69, 183, 202, 226, 227, 229, 242–45
Ferrer, Norma Valle, 164
first-person narration, 105, 123, 181
Fishburn, Evelyn, 87
"Fleeting Friendships," 82, 89–90, 102
Flight of the Swan. See *Vuelo del cine*
Forest of the Pygmies, The. See *Bosque de los pigmeos, El*
framing, 134
Franco, Jean, 232
free indirect discourse, 32, 62, 68, 70, 72, 237 n. 16
Frenk, Susan, 112
Freud, Sigmund, 18–19
Frías, Miguel, 104
Furman, Nelly, 25

"Gabriela," 39–40, 54
Gant-Britton, Lisbeth, 185
gaps, 19, 34–35, 99, 194, 196, 211–15, 222, 230
Garro, Elena, 29, 228–29
Gato eficaz, El, 230
Geldrich-Leffman, Hanna, 84
gender, 18, 20–22, 25–26, 34, 37–38, 40–42, 48, 55–56, 68, 72, 93, 105, 107–8, 123, 129, 180, 184, 189–90, 192–93,

198–99, 206–7, 210, 220, 224, 242 n. 14, 244 n. 17, 247 n. 17 (chap. 7), 247 n. 2 (chap. 8)
gender naturalization, 151–52, 158, 160
Genealogías, Las, 230
Genette, Gérard, 34, 171, 183, 184
genre, 10, 30, 32, 34, 44, 163, 170–74, 181–85, 188, 193, 222
"Gift, The," 148–49, 158–59, 167–69
Gilbert, Sandra, 24, 151, 233 n. 2
Glantz, Margo, 29, 230–31
Glenn, Kathleen, 157, 244 n. 21
Gold, Janet, 229
Goldberg, Paul, 230–32
Gordon, William 104
Gregson, Ian, 221
Griffin, Susan, 221
Guadalupe, Virgin of, 35, 195, 206–8, 221, 222
Gubar, Susan, 24, 151, 233 n. 2
Guerra-Cunningham, Lucía, 22–23, 234 n. 4
Guerra, Ricardo, 80
Gutiérrez Mouat, Ricardo, 243 n. 13, 245 n. 28
Gutiérrez y Muhs, Gabriella, 216, 223

"Happiness." See "Felicidad, La"
Hart, Patricia, 127
Hasta no verte Jesús mío, 229
"Healer from Hualqui, The." See "Machi de Hualqui, La"
hedging, 32, 85, 86, 90
Henry, Astrid, 233 n. 2
Here's to you, Jesusa. See *Hasta no verte Jesús mío*
"High Valley." See "Valle alto"
Hija de la fortuna, 104
Hoeg, Jerry,
Holmes, Diana, 44
House of the Spirits, The, 81, 85, 92, 105–9, 111–18, 121, 122, 155, 158, 226, 240 n. 4
House on Mango Street, The, 35, 194, 196–201, 212, 217, 223, 224, 248 n. 9
House on the Lagoon, The, 34, 138, 139, 143, 160–62, 166–68

Huidobro, Ramón, 104
Humo hacia el sur, 36
Hutcheon, Linda, 242 n. 14, 245 n. 1
hybridity, 223
Hymes, Dell, 35, 196, 197
hyperbole, 30, 33, 35, 105, 111, 117–18, 122–24, 126–27, 130, 135–36, 174, 181, 185, 232

Ibáñez del Campo, Carlos, 36, 101
icons, 30, 34, 35, 194, 195, 202, 221
identity, 25, 29, 57, 65, 67, 84, 85–86, 91, 97, 98, 102, 112, 125–26, 144, 171, 174, 186, 192, 208, 210, 212, 216, 219–25, 240 n. 2, 248 n. 10
"If You Touched My Heart," 132–33
"Imagen de la mujer, La," 92
"Image of Women, The." See "Imagen de la mujer, La."
imperialism, 164–66
implied reader, 11, 26, 77, 232, 234 n. 5
incompetence, 32, 33, 81, 85, 171, 219
indirection, 24, 28, 30, 32, 34, 68, 70, 81, 85, 87, 90, 92, 94, 99, 131, 155, 202, 234 n. 1
Inés del alma mía, 105
Inés of My Soul. See *Inés del alma mía*.
Infinite, Plan, The. See *Plan infinito, El*
interior monologue, 61–62, 65, 67–70, 77, 146, 154, 228
Initiation Rite. See *Rito de iniciación*
Irigaray, Luce, 18–19
irony, 11, 24, 26, 28, 30, 32, 33, 35, 43, 70, 73, 82, 85–86, 88–91, 104–5, 107, 111, 114, 117, 122–25, 127–31, 134–36, 144, 151, 156, 188, 192, 204, 208, 227, 231, 232, 241, n. 14, 242, 247 n. 1
Iser, Wolfgang, 22, 111, 112, 234 nn. 5 and 6, 248 n. 8
"Islas Nuevas, Las," 60
italics, 162–63

"Judge's Wife, The," 124–26, 135
juxtaposition, 32, 63, 81–82, 88–90

Kaminsky, Amy, 22

Kingdom of the Golden Dragon, The. See *Reino del dragón de oro, El*
Kirkwood, Julieta, 57–58
Klimpel, Felicitas, 101
knitting, 45, 47, 69–70, 107, 110, 178, 180, 181. *See also* weaving
Koene, Jacoba, 239 n. 2
Koski, Linda, 37, 234 n. 1
Kramarae, Cheris, 20
Kristeva, Julia, 18–19
Krolokke, Charlotte, 221, 233 n. 1

Labov, William, 35, 196–97, 247 n. 2
Lacan, Jacques, 18–19
Lady of Dreams, The. See *Señora de los sueños, La*
Lagos, María, 141
Lakoff, Robyn, 20–21
language, 17–25, 33, 39–40, 49–51, 56, 65, 84, 92, 93, 95–100, 106, 115, 139, 152, 155, 160–61, 166, 170–71, 177–80, 189–92, 195, 204, 209, 216, 220–24, 229, 236, 247 nn. 2 and 4, 248 n. 6. *See also* speech
Lanser, Susan, 26–27, 32, 61–62, 70, 72, 81–82, 86, 98, 100, 127, 234 n. 2
Larco, Jorge, 61
Last Mist, The. See *Última niebla, La*
Laurence, Patricia Ondek, 27
Law of Love, The, 34, 170, 171, 183–89, 192, 193, 246 nn. 14 and 16
"Lección de cocina." *See* "Cooking Lesson"
Ley de amor, La. See *Law of Love, The*
Like Water for Chocolate, 34, 170–83, 185, 187, 192, 246 n. 2
"Little Blank Head." *See* "Cabecita blanca"
"Little Miracles, Kept Promises," 206–8, 222
Lizard's Tail, The. See *Cola de lagartija*
LLorona, La, 203, 204, 206, 221
"Loneliness of the Blood." *See* "Soledad de la sangre"
Lonquen, 121–22
looks, 97–98
López, Yvette, 155

Ludmer, Josefina, 23
Lump of Dough. See *Amasijo*.

"Machi de Hualqui, La," 49, 51–53, 58
McCracken, Ellen, 220
magic, 51, 76, 127, 128, 174, 240, n. 4, 241 n. 13
magical realism, 105, 123, 181
Maldito amor. See *Sweet Diamond Dust*
Malinche, La, 35, 170, 195, 221–22
Mámpara, La, 36
March of the Empty Pots, 106–7
Marek, Jayne, 223
"María la boba." *See* "Simple María."
María Nadie 36–38, 55–58, 102, 235 n. 30, 236 n. 34
María Nobody. See *María Nadie*
María Rosa, flor del quillen, 36
María Rosa, Flower of the Quillen. See *María Rosa, flor del quillen*
Márquez, Gabriel García, 123
Mejía, Eduardo, 81, 91
marginalization, 100, 236 n. 5, 247 n. 1
marriage plot, 48, 52, 77, 91, 167
MEMCH, 54, 105, 108
"Mericans," 224
metaphor, 24, 30–34, 38, 39, 49, 52, 70, 87, 99, 100, 232
Mexican revolution, 175, 178, 180, 182, 229
middle class, 11, 54, 106, 118, 169, 188, 194, 195
Miller, Francesca, 53, 55, 70, 101, 110
Miller, Nancy K., 31, 37, 38, 49, 51
Mills, Sara, 9–11, 25–26, 37, 68, 151–52, 162, 234 nn. 5 and 6
"Mirror, The." *See* "Espejo, El"
"Misia Marianita," 49–52, 58
"Miss Marianita." *See* "Misia Marianita"
Mistral, Gabriela, 141–42
Moi, Toril, 233 n. 2
Molly, Sylvia, 229
Mona que le pisaron la cola, La, 138
Monkey with the Stepped-on Tail, The. See *Mona que le pisaron la cola, La*
Montaña adentro, 36
Mora, Gabriela, 240 n. 7

Mothers' centers, 107
Movement of the Emancipation of Chilean Women. *See* MEMCH
Moya-Raggio, Eliana, 241 n. 12
"Mujer del juez, La." *See* "Judge's Wife, The"
Mullen, Harryette, 205, 206, 247 n. 4
"Muñeca menor, La." *See* "Youngest Doll, The.
music, 45, 47, 48, 73–74, 133, 165, 183–85, 187, 237 n. 23
muted group theory, 17, 18, 20, 23, 114

naive narrators, 34, 194, 196, 217
"Nariz, La," 49–50, 54
Nelson, Alice, 240 nn. 4 and 7, 241 n. 13
Neri, Margarita, 182
Neruda, Pablo, 60
"Never Marry a Mexican," 204, 206, 218, 221–22
"New Islands, The." *See* "Islas Nuevas, Las."
Night of Tlatelolco, See *Noche de Tlatelolco*
"Niña Perversa." *See* "Wicked Girl"
Nine Guardians, The. See *Balún Canán*
Noche de Tlatelolco, 229
"Nose, The." *See* "Nariz, La"
"Notas al margen: El lenguaje como instrumento de dominio," 92–93
"Notes on the Margin: Language as an Instrument of Domination." *See* "Notas al margen: El lenguaje como instrumento de dominio"
nouveau roman, 91
Novela negra con argentinos, 230
Nuestro silencio, 228

Ocampo, Victoria, 60
Oficio de tinieblas, 80
Of Love and Shadows, 33, 104, 105, 109, 110, 112, 118–22, 240 nn. 4 and 7
"One Holy Night," 222
Oreamuno, Yolanda, 228
Our Silence. See *Nuestro silencio*
Outer Door, The. See *Mámpara, La.*
overreading, 31, 35–38, 49, 55, 70

Pandora's Papers. See *Papeles de Pandora*
Papeles de Pandora, 34, 138, 139, 160, 164, 165, 226
paradigmatic indices, 30, 34, 139–43, 153, 155, 242 n. 2
paratextuality, 183, 246 n. 14
parentheses, 32, 33, 80, 92, 99–101
Parker, Gabrielle, 99
parody, 11, 30, 34–35, 44, 164, 171–72, 174, 181–90, 192–93, 200, 227, 232, 245 n. 1, 246 nn. 2 and 12
"Participación de la mujer mexicana en la educación formal, La," 94
"Participation of the Mexican Woman in Education, The." *See* "La participación de la mujer mexicana en la educación formal"
Paseo de la reforma, 229
Path of their Evasion, The. See *Ruta de su evasión, La*
patriarchy, 11, 17, 33, 37–42, 46–48, 50–54, 56, 61–63, 65, 67–68, 71–73, 77–78, 84, 87, 90–93, 97, 99–100, 102, 107–8, 111–21, 127, 134–35, 151, 155, 158, 160, 163–64, 167–69, 171, 173–75, 183, 185, 189, 218, 227–29, 233 n. 2, 239 n. 2, 240 n. 2, 241 n. 9, 245 n. 1, 246 n. 2, 247, n. 1
Paula, 104
Paz, Octavio, 229
Pearce, Lynne, 151
performance, 11, 220, 221, 224
Perón, Eva, 101
Perrein, Michèle, 99
Perricone, Catherine, 183, 241 nn. 10 and 13, 247 n. 17
"Piedra callada," 46–48, 54, 58
Pinochet, Augusto, 104–11, 117, 118, 120, 122, 240 nn. 3 and 5
Plan Infinito, El, 104
Poniatowska, Elena, 229
Portrait in Sepia. See *Retrato en sepia*
postmodernism, 9, 11, 217, 229–21, 223–24, 227, 231–32, 247–48
poststructuralism, 9–11, 230

INDEX

Pratt, Annis, 48, 52, 96, 117, 121, 134, 192, 223
Pratt, Mary Louise, 247 n. 2

quest novel, 183–84

Rachilde (Marguerite Vallette-Eymery), 43–44
Radner, Joan, 32, 81–82, 86, 98,100, 127, 234 n. 1
Radway, Janice, 34, 172–73, 185
Raíz de sueño, 37
"Raíz de sueño," 37, 40
rape, 48, 109, 110, 113, 118, 121, 126, 129, 142, 147, 154, 184, 200, 215, 217, 240 n. 4
reader-reception theory, 24–26, 29, 31, 35, 234 n. 6
Recollections of Things to Come. See *Recuerdos del porvenir*
Recuerdos del porvenir, 229
"Regalo, El." *See* "Gift, The"
Reino del dragón de oro, El, 104
Reloj del sol, 37
Retrato en sepia, 104
"Revenge," 129
Rito de iniciación, 81, 91–101
ritual, 18, 22, 29, 34, 45, 49, 51, 56, 58, 62, 65, 68, 96, 114, 115, 118–21, 128, 133, 140, 143, 155–57, 159, 161, 169–71, 176, 178–81, 226, 230, 246 n. 9
Rodríguez, Rubén, 229
romance novel, 30, 34, 44, 171–74, 176, 178, 181–89, 192, 193, 203, 227, 232, 246 n. 5
Ross, Stephen, 63, 183, 234 n. 7
rowan tree, 75–76, 237 n. 25
Rubio, Cecilia, 43
Rueda, Ana, 70
Ruta de la evasión, La, 228
"Ruth Werner," 43, 47, 48, 195

Sacred Memory. See *Sagrada memoria*
Sagrada memoria, 230
Saint-Phalle, Raphael, 60
Saldívar-Hull, Sonia, 195, 247 nn. 1 and 2

Salkjelsvik, Kari, 246 n. 11
Santiago, Esmeralda, 231
Saville-Troike, Muriel, 21–22, 34, 120, 175–78
Schild, Victoria, 240 n. 5
science fiction, 30, 34, 227, 246 n. 16
sculpture, 50, 115
"Secreto, Lo," 60
"Secret Thing, The." *See* "Secreto, Lo"
"Seed Necklace, The," 167–69
Sefchovich, Sara, 231–32
Señora de los sueños, La, 231–32
Shrauf, Robert, 35, 211
"Shrouded Woman, The," 32, 60–62, 68–73, 76, 78, 237 n. 16
Showalter, Elaine, 20, 22–24
Siege upon Eros: Thirteen Literary Essays. See *Sitio a Eros: Trece ensayos literarios*
"Silent Stone." *See* "Piedra callada"
"Si me tocaras el corazón." *See* "If You Touched My Heart"
"Simple María," 132, 133, 136
single woman plot, 52–53, 58–59, 91, 192
Sitio a Eros: Trece ensayos literarios, 138
"Sleeping Beauty," 146–48, 154, 157, 160, 165, 167–69, 244 n. 21
Smoke toward the South. See *Humo hacia el sur*
soap operas. See *telenovelas*
socialism, 117
social protest, 44, 115, 117, 122, 137, 208
"Soledad de la sangre," 44–48, 54, 58, 74, 133
Solita Alone. See *Solita sola*
Solita sola, 37
Sommer, Doris, 35, 211
Sonatinas, 138
Sorensen, Anne Scott, 221, 233 n. 1
South. See *Sur*
Spanos, Tony, 246 n. 10
speech, 18, 21, 24, 27, 93, 97, 134, 152, 176. *See also* language
Spencer, Laura Gutiérrez, 200
Spender, Dale, 20, 96

Steele, Cynthia, 238 n. 1
stereotypes, 19, 33, 42–44, 52, 93, 95–96, 101, 119, 122–28, 130, 131, 133, 134, 151–52, 158, 160, 187, 189–90, 192–93, 202, 206, 227, 242 n. 14
Stories of Eva Luna, The, 33, 105, 111, 122–37, 239–40 n. 2, 241–42 n. 14
Stories of Juan Bobo, The. See *Cuentos de Juan Bobo, Los*
"Story of María Griselda, The." See "Historia de María Griselda, La."
Stout, Janis, 27
Strange Things Happen Here. See *Aquí pasan cosas raras*
structuralism, 9–11
Suerte de la consorte, La, 231
suffrage, 54, 57, 58, 76, 101, 106, 227, 233 n. 1
Sundial. See *Reloj del sol*
Sur, El, 60
Swanson, Phillip, 115
Sweet Diamond Dust, 34, 138, 139, 148–52, 158, 160, 164–66, 168–69
Swift as Desire, 34, 170, 189–93
syntagmatic indices, 30, 34, 75, 143–49, 151, 153, 160, 158, 242 n. 6

Tannen, Deborah, 20–21
Tan veloz como el deseo. See *Swift as Desire*
telenovelas, 202, 208
Testimonies about Mariana. See *Testimonios sobre Mariana*.
Testimonios sobre Mariana, 229
textual voice. *See* voice
third-person narration, 32, 71, 72
Thousand and One Nights, 134
Tinísima, 229
Todorov, Tzvetan, 33, 75, 139–40, 153, 242 nn. 2, and 6, 243 n. 15, 244 n. 16
To Live Life. See *Vivir la vida*
Tonantzín, 207, 208, 222
Too Much Love. See *Demasiado Amor*
Torre, Guillermo de la, 60
Traba, Marta, 233 n. 1
transtextuality, 171
Treacherous Beast. See *Bestia dañina*

"Tree, The." See "Arbol, El"
"Trenzas," 60
Trigo, Benigno, 138
trivialization, 32, 81, 171.
Two Venecias, The. See *Dos Venecias, Las*
"Two Words," 124–25, 135, 240 n. 2

unreliable narration, 28, 151
Última niebla, La 32, 60–69, 76, 78, 232, 236
untranslatability, 210, 212
upper class, 44, 54, 78, 79, 107, 109, 118, 168, 188, 189
Ureña, Pedro Henríquez, 60

Valdivieso, Mercedes, 76
Valenzuela, Luisa, 230
"Valle alto," 228
Vallejos-Ramírez, Mayela, 70
"Venganza, La." *See* "Revenge"
"Viudo Román, El." *See* "Widower Román, The."
Vivir la vida, 231
voice, 58, 60, 62, 67, 70, 72, 73,77, 81, 82, 93, 98, 100, 107, 113, 116, 119, 132, 133, 151, 159, 190, 194, 196, 197, 201, 203, 215, 216, 219, 223, 231, 232, 243 n. 10; authorial, 32, 61, 70, 72, 150; communal, 61; double-voiced, 23–24, 86, 241 n. 9; personal, 32, 61, 70; textual, 27, 34, 63, 161–63, 183, 232, 234 n. 7
Vuelo del cine, 138

Walk of the Reform. See *Paseo de la reforma*
Warhol, Robyn, 97, 238 n. 9
Watkins, Beverly, 198
weaving, 31, 32, 45, 69, 70, 181. *See also* knitting
"Weeping Woman, The." *See* "Llorona, La"
When I Was Puerto Rican, 231
"Wicked Girl," 124, 128
"Widower Román, The," 83–83, 91
Williams, Robert Grant, 100

Wilson, Sharon, 244 n. 17
Within the Mountain. See *Montaña adentro.*
Woman Hollering Creek, 35, 195, 202–9, 218, 220, 247 n. 4
"Woman Hollering Creek," 204, 221
women writers, 9–11, 22, 24, 26–30, 32, 37, 60–61, 81, 151, 196, 217, 223, 226–28, 232, 233 n. 1, 242 n. 1
Woolf, Virginia, 27, 99

working class, 11–12, 31, 35, 47, 54, 102, 103, 107, 109, 110, 118, 122, 169, 188, 194–96, 213, 227, 231

"Youngest Doll, The" 139, 143–44, 153, 155, 165, 167, 168, 242 n.1, 243 n. 8

Zona de Carga y Descarga, 138
Zorro, 105